# A Theology of Migration

*The Bodies of Refugees
and the Body of Christ*

Daniel G. Groody

ORBIS BOOKS
Maryknoll, New York 10545

Founded in 1970, Orbis Books endeavors to publish works that enlighten the mind, nourish the spirit, and challenge the conscience. The publishing arm of the Maryknoll Fathers and Brothers, Orbis seeks to explore the global dimensions of the Christian faith and mission, to invite dialogue with diverse cultures and religious traditions, and to serve the cause of reconciliation and peace. The books published reflect the views of their authors and do not represent the official position of the Maryknoll Society. To learn more about Maryknoll and Orbis Books, please visit our website at www.orbisbooks.com.

Copyright © 2022 by Daniel G. Groody

Published by Orbis Books, Box 302, Maryknoll, NY 10545-0302.

All rights reserved.

Unless otherwise specified, Scripture texts in this work are taken from the *New American Bible, Revised Edition*, copyright © 2010, 1991, 1986, 1970 Confraternity of Christian Doctrine, Washington, D.C. and are used by permission of the copyright owner. All rights reserved. No part of the *New American Bible* may be reproduced in any form without permission in writing from the copyright owner.

*Cover Image*: During the sign of peace at a bi-national Mass along the US-Mexico border, a girl from Mexico and a person in the United States touch hands with each other through the border fence. "Mexico-U.S. Border Prayer," copyright © AFP 2022, by Herika Martinez.

All Vatican documents are available at www.vatican.va.

No part of this publication may be reproduced or transmitted in any form or by any means, electronic or mechanical, including photocopying, recording, or any information storage or retrieval system, without prior permission in writing from the publisher.

Queries regarding rights and permissions should be addressed to: Orbis Books, P.O. Box 302, Maryknoll, NY 10545-0302.

Manufactured in the United States of America

---

Library of Congress Cataloging-in-Publication Data

Names: Groody, Daniel G., 1964– author.
Title: A theology of migration : the bodies of refugees and the body of Christ / Daniel G. Groody.
Description: Maryknoll, New York : Orbis Books, [2022] | Includes bibliographical references and index.
Identifiers: LCCN 2022003234 (print) | LCCN 2022003235 (ebook) | ISBN 9781626984875 (trade paperback) | ISBN 9781608339495 (epub)
Subjects: LCSH: Emigration and immigration—Religious aspects—Christianity. | Catholic Church—Doctrines.
Classification: LCC BR115.E45 G76 2022 (print) | LCC BR115.E45 (ebook) | DDC 261.8/38—dc23/eng/20220215
LC record available at https://lccn.loc.gov/2022003234
LC ebook record available at https://lccn.loc.gov/2022003235

# Contents

*Foreword by Pope Francis* ........ ix

## Part One:
### The Gathering Narratives: The Human Face of Migration

**Introduction: A Theology of Migration** ........ 3
    The Life-Death-Birth Process of Migration ........ 3
    The Inner and Outer Journey of Migration ........ 6
    A Eucharistic Vision of Migration ........ 8
    Migration as a Personal Journey ........ 12
    Toward a Renewed Narrative on Migration ........ 14

**1. Migration and the Human Story** ........ 19
    Who Am I before God? ........ 19
    Migration and Family Genes ........ 20
    Migration and Biological Genes ........ 22
    Migration and Political Genes ........ 23
    Migration and Our Spiritual Genes ........ 24
    The Many Faces of Migration ........ 25
        *Economic Migrants* ........ 26
        *Forced Migrants or Refugees* ........ 29
        *Internally Displaced Persons* ........ 31
        *Human Trafficking Victims* ........ 33
    The Xenophobic Shadow ........ 36
        *A Deep Ambivalence and a Dark Shadow* ........ 37
        *The Sins of Imperialism: Native American Migration* ........ 39
        *The Sins of Racism: Forced African Migration and Slavery* ........ 40
        *The Sins of Nativism: Anti-Immigrant Nationalism* ........ 42
        *The Sins of Militarization: Death at the Border* ........ 45
        *The Sins of Money-Theism: The Idolization of Capital* ........ 46

|   |   |
|---|---|
| The Human Person Fully Alive | 49 |
| Biblical Narratives and Migration | 52 |

## Part Two:
## The Biblical Narratives: Migration and the Christian Scriptures

| | | |
|---|---|---|
| 2. | **The First Reading: The Old Testament and Migration** | **65** |
| | Adam, Eve, and the Fall: The Migration from Home | 66 |
| | Abraham and the Covenant: Migration and the Promise | 69 |
| | Jacob and Identity: Migration and Border Crossings | 74 |
| | Joseph and Slavery: Migration and Human Trafficking | 79 |
| | Moses and the Exodus: Migration and Liberation | 82 |
| | The Israelites and the Desert: Migration and Transformation | 86 |
| | The Prophets and Idolatry: Migration and the Deported Heart | 90 |
| | Ruth and the Alien: Migration and Human Solidarity | 95 |
| | Migration and the Journey from God, in God, and to God | 99 |
| 3. | **The Responsorial Psalm: The Inner Landscape of the Refugee Journey** | **101** |
| | The Syrian Refugee Story and the Psalms | 103 |
| | A Psychospiritual Framework for Refugee Healing | 106 |
| |    *The Need for Freedom and Self-Expression: God as Liberator and Companion* | 108 |
| |    *The Need for Safety and Protection: God as Fortress and Shield* | 114 |
| |    *The Need for Agency and Justice: God as King and Judge* | 117 |
| |    *The Need for Community and Belonging: God as Home and Dwelling Place* | 122 |
| | God as Refuge for the Refugee | 125 |
| 4. | **The Second Reading: The Early Church and Migration** | **128** |
| | The Early Christian Community: Four Marks of Its Migrant Identity | 128 |
| |    *The One Church: The Body of Christ and Many Cultures* | 131 |
| |    *The Holy Church: The Followers of the Way and the Law of Love* | 137 |
| |    *The Catholic Church: A Bridge to Eternity and a Heavenly Homeland* | 142 |
| |    *The Apostolic Church: Disciples to All Nations and a Global Mission* | 148 |
| | The Migrant Church as Pilgrim in the World | 153 |

| | |
|---|---|
| **5. The Gospel Reading: The Divine Migration** | **155** |
| The Migration of God to the Human Race and His Return Migration | 155 |
| The Virgin Mary and the Jewish Law: Migration and the Illegal Alien | 156 |
| The Holy Family and the Flight into Egypt: Forced Migration and Its Root Causes | 159 |
| John the Baptist and Conversion: Migrating to a New Way of Thinking | 164 |
| Jesus of Nazareth and the Incarnation: The Divine Migration and the Cosmic Border Crossing | 167 |
| The Good Samaritan and the New Law: Migration and Neighborliness | 175 |
| The Samaritan Woman and the Other: Migration and Transformative Encounters | 183 |
| Migration and the Christian Scriptures | 190 |
| **6. The Word in Movement: Transforming Migration Narratives** | **192** |
| Canterbury Tales and Refugee Tales | 193 |
| The Tradition of Pilgrimage and Creating a New Tale | 196 |
| Unlocking Human Dignity | 200 |
| An Immigrant Creed | 203 |

## Part Three:
### The Eucharistic Narratives: Migration and the Body of Christ

| | |
|---|---|
| **7. The Bodies of Refugees and the Body of Christ** | **207** |
| The Foundations of Migration and the Eucharist | 207 |
| *The Table: A Symbol of Universal Love* | 209 |
| *The Kingdom of God: The Key to Understanding Jesus' Message* | 211 |
| *The Passover: Israel's Migration Story and the Eucharist* | 212 |
| "This Is My Body": A Spiritual Vision of Human Solidarity | 214 |
| *Lampedusa: The Real Presence of the "No-Bodies"* | 214 |
| *The Global Indifference to the "No-Bodies"* | 216 |
| *The Desire to Become "Some-Body"* | 219 |
| *The Connection to "Every-Body"* | 222 |
| "This Is My Blood": A Mission of Reconciliation | 224 |
| *Passing Over from Migrant to Person* | 226 |
| *Passing Over from Injustice to Justice* | 228 |

| | |
|---|---|
| *Passing Over from Alien to Neighbor* | 233 |
| *Passing Over from Nationalism to the Kingdom of God* | 235 |
| "Do This in Memory of Me": Anamnestic Solidarity | 239 |

### Part Four:
### The Mission Narratives: Migration and Mercy

| | | |
|---|---|---|
| 8. | **The Body of Christ as Bread for the World** | **249** |
| | The Real Presence of Christ in the Eucharist and in the Poor | 250 |
| | Feeding the Hungry: The Kino Border Initiative | 254 |
| |    *A Faith-Based, Humanitarian Response to Hunger* | 255 |
| |    *The Mission of the Kino Border Initiative* | 257 |
| |    *Theological Foundations and Organization of the Kino Border Initiative* | 258 |
| | Giving Drink to the Thirsty: Humane Borders | 260 |
| |    *A Faith-Based, Humanitarian Response to Those Dying in the Deserts* | 262 |
| |    *The Mission of Humane Borders* | 265 |
| |    *Theological Foundations and Organization of Humane Borders* | 267 |
| | Sheltering the Homeless: Casa Juan Diego | 269 |
| |    *A Faith-Based, Humanitarian Response to Multilayered Homelessness* | 271 |
| |    *The Mission of Casa Juan Diego* | 272 |
| |    *Theological Foundations and Organization of Casa Juan Diego* | 275 |
| | Visiting the Imprisoned: The Interfaith Committee for Detained Immigrants | 278 |
| |    *A Faith-Based, Humanitarian Response to Immigrant Imprisonment* | 280 |
| |    *The Mission of the Interfaith Committee for Detained Immigrants* | 283 |
| |    *Theological Foundations and Organization of the Interfaith Committee for Detained Immigrants* | 286 |
| | Burying the Dead: Reuniting Families | 289 |
| |    *A Faith-Based, Humanitarian Response to the Nameless, Migrant Dead* | 290 |
| |    *The Mission of Reuniting Families* | 291 |
| |    *Theological Foundations and Organization of Reuniting Families* | 293 |
| | Living Out a Renewed Narrative of Migration | 296 |

| | |
|---|---|
| **Conclusion: "Go in Peace": A Sacramental Vision of Migration** | **297** |
|    The Liturgies of Society and the Search for Authentic Worship | 299 |
|    Toward a New Narrative about Migration | 302 |
| *Acknowledgments* | 305 |
| *Index* | 309 |

Padre Daniel Groody, csc
Universidad de Notre Dame
Indiana, Estados Unidos

Querido hermano:

Recibí el manuscrito de tu libro "A Theology of Migration", que me enviaste a través de un amigo común. Lo leí con detenimiento y me siento conmovido por la belleza, la ternura, el dolor y el compromiso que surge de cada una de sus páginas.

Veo el trabajo del pastor involucrado e inmerso en la sanación y restitución de derechos fundamentales de comunidades tan distantes pero cercanas entre si: Siria, Ruanda, México, Lampedusa; todas ellas son imágenes y voces de realidades que en tu narrativa expresan la necesidad del compromiso de la Iglesia para con los migrantes y refugiados. Una Iglesia llamada a tender la mano, abrazar y acoger a los débiles, invisibles y descartados de la Tierra.

Una teología de la migración es un desafío complejo que tu libro descubre y enseña. Es sobre todo una teología "situada" que no quiere ser indiferente al clamor concreto de hermanas y hermanos nuestros que nos interpela y moviliza (Ex. 3, 7-10). Tantas veces vimos los mares convertidos en cementerios de vidas e historias, de sueños y de anhelos por una vida digna que nos unimos en oración, trabajo y presencia para hacer frente a la indiferencia y crear puentes de fraternidad.

La migración, tan propia de la condición humana, es también expresión feroz de las desigualdades. Nuestro compromiso con los migrantes debe ser a su vez propiciatorio de una pedagogía del cuidado, del respeto al prójimo, en definitiva, de una propuesta creativa y creadora de una genuina cultura del encuentro donde aprendamos a reconocernos y tratarnos como hermanos.

Gracias por todo lo que haces y propones; que tu libro pueda movilizar y ayudar a volvernos más sensibles a esta realidad. Dios te bendiga y bendiga a todos los migrantes y a aquellos que se vuelven compañeros de su viaje; y, por favor, no te olvides de rezar por mi.

Fraternalmente

Ciudad del Vaticano, 12 de febrero de 2022

# Foreword

Father Daniel Groody, CSC
University of Notre Dame
Indiana, USA

Dear Brother:

I received the manuscript of your book *A Theology of Migration*, which you sent me through a mutual friend. I read it with great care, and I feel moved by the beauty, the tenderness, the pain and the commitment that come forth from each one of its pages.

I see the work of the shepherd involved and immersed in the healing and restoring of fundamental rights of communities so distant yet so close to each other: Syria, Rwanda, Mexico, Lampedusa. All of them are images and voices of realities that, in your narrative, express the need for the Church's commitment to migrants and refugees: a Church called to extend a hand, to embrace and to welcome the weak, the invisible, and the discarded of the world.

A theology of migration is a complex challenge that your book unveils and teaches. It is above all a "situated" theology that does not want to be indifferent to the concrete cry of our sisters and brothers, which challenges and mobilizes us (Ex. 3:7–10). So many times we have seen the seas turned into cemeteries of lives and stories, of dreams and yearnings for a dignified life that we unite in prayer, work, and presence to confront indifference and create bridges of fraternity.

Migration, so much a part of the human condition, is also a fierce expression of inequalities. Our commitment with migrants, in turn, must be propitiatory of a pedagogy of care, of respect of our neighbor, ultimately, of a creative and generative proposal of a genuine culture of encounter, where we learn to recognize and treat each other as brothers.

Thank you for everything you do and propose; may your book mobilize and help us become more sensitive to this reality. God bless you and bless all migrants and those who become companions on their journey; and please do not forget to pray for me.

Fraternally,

Francis
Vatican City
February 12, 2022

*Part One*

# The Gathering Narratives

*The Human Face of Migration*

# Introduction

## *A Theology of Migration*

**The Life-Death-Birth Process of Migration**

*When a woman is in labor, she has pain, because her hour has come. But when her child is born, she no longer remembers the anguish because of the joy of having brought a human being into the world.* (Jn. 16:21 NRSV)

Shortly after I was ordained and began working at my first parish, I received an unexpected call at 5 a.m. I was still learning the ropes of ministry in a Mexican-immigrant community, and the ringing phone jolted me out of bed. Thinking it was an emergency at the hospital, I quickly answered, and a woman named Margarita was on the other end of the line. She was the eldest of fourteen children, and a few months earlier Margarita's family had immigrated to the United States. They were one of the first families I had met at the parish.

Margarita was in a panic because her car would not start, and she feared losing her job if late for work. She asked for help, and I told her I would come over to do what I could. Before we finished talking, however, she asked if I could talk to her sister Cristina, who also had something she wanted to tell me. Seventeen years old and nine months pregnant, she gasped when she got on the phone and said, "I think I am going into labor."

With those words, I was suddenly wide awake, and taking a deep breath, I said, "Be right down!" I was about to cross over into a whole new frontier. I rushed to the family's house, and when I got to the door, Maria—the mother of the fourteen children—said to her daughter, "Just be calm and relax, Cristina. It may not be time yet. Keep walking back and forth, and the contractions may go away." Since Maria had done this fourteen times before, I trusted her judgment more than mine. In the meantime, I took Margarita to work and came back about a half-hour later.

When I got to the house, Maria looked at me and said, "Cristina is ready to go! But I have to stay here with the other kids. You have to take her!" With those words, my heart sank; my pulse spiked; and I began sweating profusely. For a moment I frantically searched my background for some insight into what I should do next, but I found nothing in my personal experience, formal studies, or seminary training that prepared me for what was about to unfold. As I got closer to the border of this foreign territory, I realized I did not have much of a choice and that nature would have its say. So I joined arms with Cristina and slowly walked her out to the car.

As I got behind the wheel, she started struggling and then looked over at me with this pained look on her face and said, "*Tres minutos, Padre*. Three minutes!" "Three minutes what, Cristina?" I asked. "My contractions are three minutes apart," she said. Then a flood of images started pouring over me: sacs breaking, fluid bursting, and a baby screaming. We were on the precipice of natal chaos—all on the front seat of my car!

So I hit the gas pedal, trying to reach the hospital as soon as I could. After arriving we got Cristina to a room, where she began to settle down. I sat beside her for a while, still at a loss for words. But then an idea came. I remembered something I had seen on a television show some time before, so I said, "Just breathe, Cristina. Just breathe." She took it all in, then deeply exhaled. Then I said, "Take my hand." She took my hand. When the nurse came in, she looked at me and asked, "Who are you?" I thought it might not be a good idea to begin with "father," so I just said, "I am a very close friend of the family." And I waited by Cristina's bedside, holding her hand for some time.

A few hours later, we were still waiting for the baby, and I became fidgety. In addition to being present to Cristina, I also had to prepare my first funeral homily for the next day. It was a tragic case of a thirteen-year-old Hispanic boy who took his own life. Having no idea where to begin my reflections—especially one with such emotional heaviness—I looked over at Cristina and said, "Do you have any idea how long this process usually takes?" Realizing we might be there for a while, I turned my attention to this other work I needed to address.

As I held Cristina's hand, I picked up the phone with my other hand and called a priest-friend who had preached at a funeral for a suicide the year before. We talked for a while about what to say in the homily, but he had no idea where I was. In the middle of the conversation, and without warning, Cristina started going through painful contractions again and began screaming in the background. On the other end of the line, my friend said, "Is everything okay over there?" "Things are fine," I said. "It's just another day at an immigrant parish, and I am helping a woman give birth to her baby."

A few hours later, Cristina gave birth to a little girl. They named her Crista. After a long time of waiting, struggling, and hoping, a "Christ-child" was born in our midst.

In many ways, this story is a window into the book that follows because it is an extended reflection on the experience of death and new life, especially in the context of the immigrant journey. On the one hand it speaks to the painful experience of death for many immigrants who leave from their homelands; on the other hand, it reflects on the experience of new life as they find their way in a new place. Through my own research and pastoral work, I have come to reflect not only on the outer migration of people but also on the inner migration of the soul. This work is an attempt to explore where the God of Jesus Christ is entering our midst, even amid the deadly challenges of immigration, and through it all is bringing new life to our world.

Twenty-five years after Crista was born, as I was writing this book, I presided over her wedding. I later celebrated with her family after their first child was born as well. My journey with her has reminded me that, when a woman gives birth, as they say in Spanish, she gives "light" (*dio luz*). While much of the narrative forged by politics and the media forges a dark narrative of immigrants seizing, stealing, and ruining all that is "native" to a culture and taking away all that we think is "ours," another narrative of new life and light is at work in the world that is bursting in our midst.

This book seeks to closely examine the current divisive, operative narratives about migrants, but it also offers alternative narratives that foster human development and spiritual communion. At its core, the book asks, what if the struggles surrounding migration are not something to fear but are in fact the beginning of a birth process leading to new relationships with God, others, and even our very selves? This work reflects on such a process. As it explores the search for God's presence amid the signs of our times, it offers a theological perspective on migration.

Approaching the issue of migration from a theological point of view opens a space to discern the light of God's presence amid the labor pains of the modern world. As the Vatican document *Erga Migrantes Caritas Christi* ("The Love of Christ Towards Migrants") so aptly puts it, "The suffering that goes with migration is neither more nor less than the birth-pangs of a new humanity, [and] . . . the inequalities and disparities behind this suffering reveal the deep wounds that sin causes in the human family. They are thus an urgent appeal for true fraternity" (13).

### The Inner and Outer Journey of Migration

While the outer journey of migrants has been central to my research for more than three decades, my interest in the subject emerged above all from an inner journey into the human heart. It began while I lived in Uruguay and Argentina as a foreign exchange student in 1981. Amid the displacement I felt in leaving my own homeland, it opened up an honest search for God amid the loneliness and searching of the human journey. It also took shape in the context of the human rights abuses and military repression these countries were going through in the 1970s and 1980s. The family I lived with then was profoundly affected by these events, and their struggles inspired me to explore the integral relationship between spirituality and justice.

The relationships I formed since then have shaped much of my own perspective about migration. My perspective has also been informed and motivated by an interest in Christian spirituality. The Spiritual Exercises of St. Ignatius of Loyola in particular have guided me in connecting the inner and outer journeys of life, and have shaped much of my core theological vision over the years. As they helped me explore the life of the soul, they also helped me discover a faith-based response to the challenges of the modern world. These journeys came together when I was ordained a priest in the Congregation of Holy Cross in 1993.

As a young priest I began working with Latin American immigrants in parish ministry, which taught me about not just their pain and suffering but also their faith and dignity. The beauty of their lives touched my heart, and the more I learned about their journey, the more my own journey became intertwined with their own. In response to a desire to understand more my own spirituality and theirs, I began doctoral studies in the field of Christian spirituality, and for several years I moved back and forth between the academic world of northern California and migrant camps in southern California.

Migrating between these two worlds, I learned quickly that most migrants do not care what I know, but want to know that I care. In the universities where I studied, however, I found that most academics do not care that I care, but only care that I know. Even though this dynamic encouraged me to put up a wall between my mind and heart, I knew it would not help me better understand how to think about God from the context of the migrant experience. As I went between the academic world and the grass roots, it often meant feeling not completely at home in either world. Eventually I came to feel most at home on the border.

As I embraced the tensions of the border, and rooted my theological reflection there, it became a privileged place of revelation.[1] In this sense, the border is more than a geographical place. It is a space where worlds come together and new creation emerges. In my case it has involved building a bridge that enables me to move back and forth between grass roots and academy, heart and head, Church and the world. This process has led me to an interest in contextual theology that emerges from the life and soul of a people.

While the subject of migration is studied from the perspective of many different disciplines, this book is a theological exploration of the subject. This theology is more than an academic exercise, arising instead from a desire to understand the spiritual journey. Borrowing from Thomas Aquinas and Bernard Lonergan, I define *theology* as faith seeking understanding that generates knowledge born of love. It is a way of thinking about God from ordinary places, events, experiences, and relationships. As I became more interested in doing theological reflection from the social, cultural, political, and religious context of migrants today—and from their spiritual journey— a theology of migration began to emerge.

I started writing about the inner and outer journey in my first book, *Border of Death, Valley of Life: An Immigrant Journey of Heart and Spirit* (2002). This work stimulated further conversations about this topic, which led me to organize conferences at the University of Notre Dame with the Scalabrinians (the Congregation of the Missionaries of Saint Charles

---

[1] In technical theological terms, the border became my *locus theologicus*. *Loci theologicus* refers to sources and context from which one does theological reflection. See James T. Bretzke, *Consecrated Phrases: A Latin Theological Dictionary,* 3rd ed. (Collegeville, MN: Liturgical Press, 2013), 79.

Borromeo) and others on theology and migration. Gioacchino Campese and I worked on these conferences together, and eventually we coedited *A Promised Land, A Perilous Journey: Theological Perspectives on Migration* (2007). This work prompted me to explore in more detail the theological foundations of this research, which resulted in *Globalization, Spirituality, and Justice: Navigating a Path to Peace* (2007, revised 2016).

Three of my closest thought partners in this research were Tim Matovina, Virgil Elizondo and Gustavo Gutierrez. We were working and teaching together at Notre Dame, and we collaborated on various research projects together. Tim, Virgil, and I explored themes related to Christology, devotion, and culture, and Gustavo Gutierrez and I collaborated on *The Option for the Poor in Christian Theology* (2007), *The Preferential Option for the Poor beyond Theology* (2014), and *Gustavo Gutierrez: Spiritual Writings* (2011). We also began producing films on related topics such as *Dying to Live: A Migrant's Journey* (2005) and *One Border, One Body: Immigration and the Eucharist* (2008). Together we sought to explore something of what it means to be Christian in the context of global poverty.

While Tim wrote on the history of US Latinos, Virgil wrote on a theology of US Latinos, and Gustavo wrote about a theology of liberation. I began writing on a theology of migration and refugees. Words cannot express the ways these three people shaped my own life and reflection, and they helped me discover that migration is not only a sign of our times but also at the very heart of salvation history and the work of the Church in our own times.

### A Eucharistic Vision of Migration

In its broad contours, the present work explores the relationship between faith and justice, theology and migration, and Christian spirituality and the challenges of the modern world. It is about the God who first migrated to our world in the Incarnation and the God who calls us through Christ to migrate back with him to our spiritual homeland. It explores the body of Christ as encountered inside of a Church building in the sacrament of the Eucharist and the body of Christ as encountered outside of it in the least and the last of our world today (Mt. 25:31–46).

The heart of this book revolves around the outer journey of migrants, the inner journey of faith, and the divine journey into our world. In the context of the global migration and refugee crisis, it examines various ways in which the divine and the human intermingle on our earthly pilgrimage.

In addition to exploring the topic of migration throughout biblical history, a central focus of this work will highlight God's initiative to "leave" his homeland, to enter into our human territory, to journey through the borderlands of our broken existence, to lay down his life on the cross, and to give himself for the salvation of all in order to reconcile those who had become aliens because of sin. It seeks to understand the significance of Jesus' death and resurrection, his "return migration" to the Father, the provision of the divine Advocate (Jn. 14:26), a pathway to "naturalization," and the gift of citizenship in his kingdom. Finally, it seeks to navigate the route of the return journey, to stand in solidarity with all on this earthly sojourn, to welcome the stranger, to guide the lost, and to strengthen especially the most vulnerable, until we arrive at last at our heavenly home.

In different ways this is also a book about stories. It looks at the stories we tell about ourselves, the stories we tell about others, and the stories we tell about God. Stories are critically important because they shape our imagination, which in turn shapes the development of our character. They influence our thoughts, identities, values, and decisions. They can either liberate or enslave us, connect or alienate us, draw us closer to God's image and likeness or move us away from it. As we tell narratives in this book, our purpose is not simply to offer more information about migration but to stimulate a new imagination that opens up the possibility of living out a different story.

The liturgy is one of the privileged places for telling these stories.[2] Originally, the term *liturgy* was used to refer to a public work in civil society directed toward the common good, but over time it became more commonly associated with religious worship. People from all the world's major religions

---

[2] The word *liturgy* comes from the Greek word *leitourgia*, which combines two other Greek words, *leitos* [public] and *ergon* [work]. Originally coined in civil society, liturgy referred to work on behalf of the people or "public service," but over time the early Church adopted the term to speak about liturgy as "service to God." Gradually, liturgy became known as the work of Christ on behalf of the people and the work of people in service to God. In its civil and ecclesial usage, however, liturgy, by nature, was understood as a social event directed toward the common good. When seen only as a place where one has a private connection with God without connection to the larger gathering of believers, all liturgy is diminished. For these reasons and many others, "the intrinsic relationship between liturgy and justice," as Anne Koester notes, "is critical to the ongoing renewal of Church life and the created world." See Maxwell E. Johnson, *Praying and Believing in Early Christianity: The Interplay between Christian Worship and Doctrine* (Collegeville, MN: Liturgical Press, 2013), xi; and Anne Y. Koester, *Liturgy and Justice: To Worship God in Spirit and Truth* (Collegeville, MN: Liturgical Press, 2002), ix.

participate in liturgies because these are ways of mediating our relationship with sacred realities. They put us in touch with stories of salvation history and offer ways of understanding who we are before God and who we are called to be in relationship with each other. For many Christian communities, one of the foremost liturgies is the Liturgy of the Eucharist.

The Liturgy of the Eucharist has been understood in various ways throughout history: as a meal that commemorates the Last Supper, a sacrifice that reflects Jesus' self-giving love for others, a memorial of Jesus' life and mission, a sacrament that unites others with Christ in communion, and a Mass that sends (Latin *missa*) people out to live the Gospel message. Common to all these interpretations is the belief that the Eucharist ritualizes the movement from alienation to communion with God and others.

In the Roman Catholic tradition, the Liturgy of the Eucharist is considered the Church's most important activity. Vatican II described it as "the summit toward which the activity of the Church is directed [and] ... the source from which all her power flows" (*Sacrosanctum Concilium* 10).[3] The Liturgy helps immerse us in the story of salvation history, and in the process gives us opportunities to understand, reframe, and transform our stories. Our focus here is to explore the ways the Liturgy of the Eucharist offers a privileged space to understand the story of God's migration to us, our return migration to God, and our response to those migrating today.

The flow of this work follows the flow of the Roman Rite of the Liturgy of the Eucharist. It draws upon various theological threads that are woven through the Introductory Rite, the Liturgy of the Word, the Liturgy of the Eucharist, and the Concluding Rite, which I refer to here as the *Gathering Narratives, Biblical Narratives, Eucharistic Narratives,* and *Mission Narratives*.[4] As we draw upon these narratives to reframe the operative narratives around migration, it is not intended to be a book for specialists in liturgy,

---

[3] The word *Eucharist* comes from the Greek *eucharistein*, which means "to give thanks." Through the Liturgy of the Eucharist the Church gives thanks for God's action in the world, especially through the life, death, and resurrection of Christ. As the summit, it is the vantage point from which to gain a panoramic vision of the rest of life. As the source, it is a living fountain through which God's transformative love flows out to the world.

[4] The Liturgy of the Word and the Liturgy of the Eucharist are the two central parts. These parts, as noted in the General Instruction for the Roman Missal, are "so closely interconnected that they form but one single act of worship." See *General Instruction of the Roman Missal* (Washington, DC: United States Conference of Catholic Bishops, 2011), 28.

scriptural exegesis, or sacramental theology. Instead, it draws upon these elements and explores ways they can contribute to the framing of a life-giving vision about migration.

Chapter 1 offers a global overview of migration and looks at the long journey of human life. Following the sequence of readings in the Sunday liturgical celebration, chapters 2 through 5 explore the subject of migration in the Old Testament, the Psalms, the early Church, and the Gospels. Chapter 6 functions integratively, structurally placed as a "homily" that connects the message of the Scriptures with our own times. It does this by narrating one migrant's journey and search for dignity and liberation against the larger background of the tradition of pilgrimage and the practice of storytelling. As these chapters highlight the hope for healing and brokenness of the human condition, chapter 7 offers a vision of solidarity and reconciliation. Looking more closely at the narrative of the Eucharist, the chapter explores various points of correlation between the bodies of refugees and the body of Christ. Chapter 8 then examines some examples of Christian mission that have emerged as faith-based responses to the challenges of migration today. The profiles of these organizations illumine some pathways toward communion as practiced through the works of mercy. Overall, this volume offers a Eucharistic hermeneutic of migration directed toward the redemption of the world. The central thesis is that, while the dominant political narratives have been moving the human community from oneness to "otherness," the central focus of the Eucharistic narrative is centered on the movement from otherness to oneness or human and divine communion.

Although the outer migration of peoples and the inner migration of the spiritual journey are central, this book is not primarily about policy, statistics, liturgy, or even doctrine, important as these may be. It draws from the wellspring of Catholic thought, teaching, and liturgy, but it is not addressed only to Catholics. My hope is that the universal message it contains also speaks to those working to create a new social order and integral human development. "Action on behalf of justice and participation in the transformation of the world," note the bishops in *Justice in the World*, "fully appear to us as a constitutive dimension of the preaching of the Gospel, or, in other words, of the Church's mission for the redemption of the human race and its liberation from every oppressive situation."[5] This involves more than physical

---

[5] World Synod of Catholic Bishops, *Justice in the World*, 1971, 6, https://www.cctwincities.org/wp-content/uploads/2015/10/Justicia-in-Mundo.pdf.

movement because it is above all about migrating more deeply into the heart of God and seeing the world and each other in a new way.

Because this book is primarily about Christian spirituality and migration, it seeks to understand the different ways the Eucharist draws us into a "spiritual borderlands" of its own kind: a liminal space where earth and heaven meet, where the human and divine intersect, and where this present life meets eternity. As it draws us into closer union with God, it transcends borders and transforms us more fully into God's own image and likeness so that we can also grow into communion with one another. Moreover, because it is a privileged place where one encounters the presence of Christ who offers Himself as a Sacrament of love, it also is the place from which God sends out his followers to become a living sacrament that reveals God's love for the world.

### Migration as a Personal Journey

I approach this topic as a human being, a Christian, a Catholic priest, a theologian, and a filmmaker. As a human being, migration speaks to me as the face of people on the move searching for more dignified lives. As a Christian, migration speaks to me as the gift and challenge of Christian faith and the claim that vulnerable and marginalized people make on the human conscience. As a priest, migration speaks to me as the path to reconciliation with God, neighbor, creation, and with our very selves. As a theologian, migration speaks to me as understanding how to think about God from the context of the challenges of the modern world. As a filmmaker, migration speaks to me as the need for a new imagination of who we are and who we are called to be to each other.

All of these dimensions play a role in the formulation of a theology of migration. My research draws predominantly on theology and the social sciences, but also emerges from reading the living texts of migrants around the world and the regional contexts in which they live. Rooted in my experience and pastoral work among immigrants, my research often emerges from the settings where they migrate, particularly the deserts, mountains, and canals along the Mexico-US border. It has been further enriched by my research and reflection with colleagues at the University of Notre Dame and others I work with in different parts of the world.

Over the years this research has led me into various countries in Central and South America, including El Salvador, Guatemala, Honduras, Peru,

Argentina, Chile, Bolivia, Uruguay, and Colombia. It draws on work in refugee camps and border territories in the regions of Spain–Morocco, Slovakia–Ukraine, Malta–Lampedusa–Libya, Haiti–Dominican Republic, South Korea–the Philippines–Australia, South Africa–Zimbabwe, Rwanda–Uganda, Ghana–Western Africa, and various countries in the Middle East, especially those surrounding the areas of conflict in Syria–Iraq–Afghanistan–Turkey–Lebanon, Bulgaria–Greece, Egypt–Israel–Palestine, and parts of Asia including Thailand–Burma.

    The people I have met in these contexts have grounded my reflection in the search for Christian hope amid the realities of acute human suffering. They have revealed to me the resiliency of the human person and gratuitous presence of the Holy Spirit, irrupting in places that most of the world has turned away from, except for God. My research continues to make clear to me that, as much as I have learned about this complex and controversial topic, I have blind spots of my own. I recognize that not every immigrant is noble or virtuous or spiritual or saintly. Some are crude and selfish, manipulative and merciless, criminal and cowardly, and even exploitative of their own. The places where migrants traverse are often profoundly marked by violence and the brutality of gangs, cartels, and criminals, who can bring out the worst in people. The challenges of global terrorism and religious extremism have only further complicated the conversation about migration, especially as it confronts us not only with issues surrounding national security but also human insecurity.

    At the same time, my work compels me to resist the increasing rhetoric that dehumanizes and even demonizes migrants. This negative and recurring trend, which arguably is older than the Scriptures, is both transhistorical and transnational. Xenophobic attitudes have existed in every generation. Throughout the world the migrant is frequently targeted and scapegoated for a society's social problems. Nonetheless, so many of the immigrants I have encountered—even amid insult, injury, and rejection—have been courageous and selfless, grateful and generous, honest and honorable. For these and many other reasons, I consider these people not just subjects to be studied but brothers, sisters, and friends whom I love and admire—human beings whom I am grateful to accompany on a common pilgrimage of faith and hope.

    These contexts have helped me understand the global scope of migration and the utter vulnerability of millions of economic migrants and refugees, internally displaced persons, victims of human trafficking, asylum seekers, and genocide survivors. From these places, I have tried to listen to ways that people believe in the midst of unbelievable circumstances: how they find hope amid some of the most hopeless of situations, how they find life in the midst of death, and how they trust in God within some of the most seemingly "godless" of experiences. These are the frontiers–and places of revelation–of Christian faith and human transformation.

So the words that follow flow from who I am as a human being and sojourner in this world. I see myself as a Christian, Catholic, contemplative, priestly, pastoral, and practical border theologian who seeks to reflect on the inner and outer journey of people in an age of migration. My experience of accompanying migrants throughout the world compels me to speak about this issue in light of the dignity of the human person, the exigencies of the Kingdom of God, the gift of the Eucharist, the mission of reconciliation, the search for justice, the building of right relationships, and the call to journey through this land in solidarity with others en route to our eternal homeland.

### Toward a Renewed Narrative on Migration

How is a Christian called to respond to this global challenge, this incendiary topic, and this pastoral need facing churches and communities around the globe?

Migration and the needs of migrants are pressing topics of discussion in our time.[6] They are challenging and changing cultures everywhere. By the first two decades in the third millennium, there were more than 281 million international migrants around the world.[7] This number could rise to as much as 405 million by 2050.[8] At the end of 2019, there were approxi-

---

[6] The terms *migrant, immigrant, refugee,* and *internally displaced persons* are often used interchangeably, although they carry different nuances. The United Nations uses *migrant* generally to refer to people living outside their homeland for a year or more, regardless of their reason or legal status and often includes international business people or diplomats who are on the move but not economically disadvantaged. Though some choose to make sharp distinctions among different types of migrants, here I use *migrant* as an umbrella term to refer to economic migrants, forced migrants or refugees, and internally displaced peoples. For more on this topic, see "Key Migration Terms," International Organization for Migration, January 17, 2020, www.iom.int.

[7] United Nations Department of Economic and Social Affairs, "International Migration 2020 Highlights," January 15, 2021, www.un.org.

[8] International Organization for Migration, *World Migration Report 2010* (Geneva: International Organization for Migration, 2010), 3.

mately 79.5 million forcibly displaced persons on our planet, including 26 million refugees, 45.7 million internally displaced persons (IDPs), and 4.2 million asylum-seekers.⁹ In 2019, as many as 40.3 million people around the world lived in "modern-day slavery" as forced laborers, bonded laborers, child soldiers, and sex-trafficking victims.¹⁰ My aim in this study is not only to highlight these numbers but to bring out the human faces behind them.

I also seek to offer a constructive theology of migration, for Christians to better understand their role and responsibilities. The theological exploration of migration interweaves three interrelated levels of action and contemplation: (1) the pastoral level (or the outer journey of migrants and the Church's response to them), (2) the spiritual level (the inner journey of migrants and their integral development), and (3) the theological level (the divine presence within the migrant reality and reflection upon it). All of these are part of the tapestry of a theology of migration, which is woven together through reflection on Scripture, systematic theology, and the stories of migrants.

*Migration and Theology: 3 levels of Engagement*

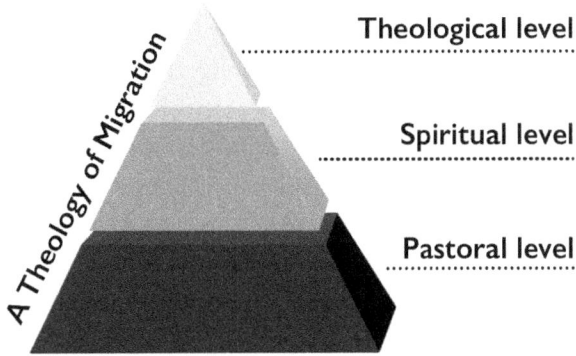

Despite the enormous human costs associated with the migration of peoples, there are ways to offer some help to people navigating the conflict and controversy surrounding these issues. I have tried to understand not only triggers surrounding migration but also the unjust targets of people's unrest. We have lost not only a sense of empathy but also of civil debate, intellectual dialogue,

---

⁹ United Nations High Commissioner for Refugees, *UNHCR Figures at a Glance*, www.unhcr.org.

¹⁰ Walk Free, Global Slavery Index, "2019 Findings: Highlights," www.globalslaveryindex.org.

and even humane discourse, and my hope is that we can find more constructive and life-giving approaches to the complex challenges migration poses.

The humanizing and demonizing rhetoric makes this work particularly necessary. Despite modest gains regarding undocumented childhood arrivals to the United States, Barack Obama's immigration policies still earned him the title of "Deporter in Chief." Donald Trump's toxic, anti-immigrant policies fanned the flames of xenophobia and brought anti-immigrant sentiment in the United States to the level of a cultural bonfire. President Joe Biden has prioritized this issue more than his predecessors, but little has changed under his leadership, and in many ways the problem has grown worse. The tasks of immigration reform are long and hard and demand more than policy changes. At present we have more than a migrant and refugee crisis: We have a leadership crisis. This work seeks to challenge the inadequate response of both the Democratic and Republican Parties in addressing the issue of immigration. It also challenges many foreign responses to the global crisis of migration. As Salil Shetty, secretary general of Amnesty International, put it, "With few exceptions, many world leaders failed to rise to the occasion, making commitments that still leave millions of refugees staring into the abyss."[11]

Regardless of one's political loyalties, and however one evaluates the issue, virtually everyone can agree that the current approach in the United States is not working. I hope that a theological perspective can contribute to reforming our dysfunctional policies and to reframing how we think, respond, and structure our responses. The world needs more creative and compassionate ways to work toward a just and humane society.

Precisely because of the human suffering involved, many faith-based communities have tried to respond to migration issues through direct service, legislative advocacy, and education. In the United States, many immigrants are Roman Catholic, although increasingly they come from other denominations and other religions as well. Still, unfortunately, most churches are poorly equipped to meet the challenge of pastoral care. As pastoral workers reach out to these newcomers, more and more requests have come to understand the spiritual and theological bases that undergird this ministry, especially in the face of public criticism of such work. May this book help bring out the migrant's human face as well as Christ's face in the migrant.

---

[11] Amnesty International, "Refugee Crisis: 'Leaders' Summit' Fails to Show Leadership on Refugees," September 21, 2016, www.amnesty.org.

In the public forum, however, much of our operative imagination about migration leaves us stifled and stuck in our entrenched positions. We are not only building bigger, wider, and higher political walls, but too often we find ourselves at a binary impasse, a linguistic barrier, and a cognitive wall as well. The categories that shape much of our contemporary discourse of citizen/foreigner, native/stranger, and legal/illegal do not help us foster the creation of right relationships. Consequently, we not only exclude and reject others in need, but, as Bill Ong Hing notes, we deport something of our souls in the process and become less human as a result.[12]

These issues point to the need for a new framework that helps us think about migration in more comprehensive, creative, and integrated ways—grounded not in political pragmatism, economic efficiencies, or cultural self-centeredness, but in the search for a just and interconnected social order. Christian faith can help in this process, not because it offers easy answers to migration's complex issues, but because it keeps us in touch with the bigger picture of who we are before God and who we are called to be to one another.

---

[12] Bill Ong Hing, *Deporting Our Souls: Values, Morality, and Immigration Policy* (New York: Cambridge University Press, 2006).

# 1

# MIGRATION AND THE HUMAN STORY

**Who Am I before God?**

Beginning April 7, 1994, Rwanda underwent a full-blown civil war. For the next one hundred days, the Interahamwe—who were Hutu extremists—carried out a genocide against the Tutsi minority group, Hutu moderates, and the Twa. One week after the violence irrupted, thousands of people fled to a local church in Bugesera, hoping to find refuge there. Anticipating this move, the Interahamwe hid at a distance until the frightened, huddled masses crammed into the church. Once inside, they threw hand grenades into this sacred space, then hailed bullets, and then took machetes and physically hacked to death any who survived. By the time it was over, more than five thousand people lost their lives. Within three months, more than a million people in the country suffered a similar fate.

Almost twenty years later I visited this church in Bugesera, which is now the Ntarama Genocide Memorial. When I entered, the horror of those days confronted me in graphic detail as I came upon the clothes, bones, and skulls of all who perished there. It was all the more troubling to consider that it happened in one of the most "Catholic" countries in Africa. Struggling to find some light amid this darkness and evil, I noticed a purple cloth draped over the altar. On it is inscribed a saying in the native language of Kinyarwanda that reads, "If you knew who you were, and you knew who I am, you would not have killed me."[1]

Stories like these reverberated in the background of my mind and heart as I began writing this book. While it is tempting to talk about what "they"

---

[1] The original inscription reads, "Iyo Umenya Nawe Ukimenya Ntubi Waranyishe."

did, a more challenging question is, how did "we" get to this point as a human community? This story happened in our own times, but it is sadly one that has repeated itself in various ways throughout all of human history, a history that each and every person continues to shape. Underneath it are different layers of sin and grace that make up the particular dimensions of my story, your story, their story, and our story.

We reflect on these stories under the light of the Liturgy of the Eucharist. This liturgy tells the Christian story and reminds us of our journey from God, in God, and to God. At its core, this journey is a mystery, but with the help of Spirit-inspired Scriptures, rituals, symbols, and sacred practices, we begin to find the light needed on our own migration through this world.

In contrast to a world that is quick to separate "me" from "them," the liturgy gives us a different place to start. It reminds us that my migration through this world is never a solo journey. It recalls that I am part of something bigger than myself and that I can never understand my own life independently of God or other people. In fact, the liturgy points out that I am in fact part of a common body and destined for a spiritual communion with it. In many different ways, the Eucharist helps me remember who I am before God, who I am called to be to my brothers and sisters, and where I am going in this life.

The entrance and recessional parts of the Eucharist ritualize the beginning and end of this journey. From birth and baptism to death and rebirth, it dares to speak about the One who migrated into our world so that we might in turn migrate back to our divine homeland.

**Migration and Family Genes**

From the beginning of time, migration has been a central part of human identity. It is connected to our origin and our destiny, our hopes and our struggles, and our dreams and our opportunities. In many different ways, migration is intimately intertwined with the long journey of the human story, and it is an essential dimension of understanding our movement through this world.

As we begin our reflection on this journey, I want to share something of my own family's story, where they have come from, and where they landed. While it is unique in its particular dimensions, it shares common themes with every other story. A number of years ago, I received word that my uncle Bill Groody had passed away. He was my baptismal godfather and a beloved member of our extended family. More than anyone else, he kept alive the memory and treasure of our Irish heritage. When it came time for his funeral, friends and relatives came to his hometown of Ashland, Pennsylvania, to remember him and pay their last respects. We celebrated the Mass of Christian Burial and then went to the cemetery to bring Bill Groody's body to its final resting place.

After the services I traveled back home, and shortly after I arrived, I opened my email for the first time since the funeral. I was particularly struck by one that said on the message line, "A note from Bill Groody." My first reaction was, "Wow! . . . He made it!" For a moment I thought, *He is "wireless," now, and just wanted to let us know he was okay.*

It turned out this Bill Groody was from northern California, and I had never met him. His wife had gone away for the weekend, and during her absence he decided to go on the internet and Google the name "Groody." When he found some web pages that detailed some of my work, he decided to contact me. He later invited me to visit him the next time I was in the area.

A few weeks later we met in San Francisco and started piecing together the oral narratives of our family history, and we eventually discovered that we were related to two brothers from Ireland—where there is a Groody River—who came over to the United States in the early 1800s. They migrated into Canada first and then settled in the New York area. It is probable that they had a common Irish name like Ryan, but because of the anti-Irish sentiment in the United States at the time, they changed their name to Groody, which sounded less Irish to the outside world.

Groody is a Gaelic name that means "winding," "meandering," and by some accounts, "crooked." As the story unfolded, it became clear that our family's history was anything but linear—and far from virtuous. After living together for a number of years, the two brothers got into a fight, we believe, because one decided to marry a woman from another culture. Enraged by his brother's decision to marry outside the clan, the other brother wanted to do something that would make the other as angry as possible. So he became Protestant! As events evolved, Bill's family went with the Protestant line and mine with the Catholic. And it took two hundred years to bring us back together again.

Reconnecting with Bill Groody felt like finding a long-lost brother. Over time we also began working on a number of projects together, including various film productions on migration and theology. As our work evolved, we discovered an even deeper connection to our stories.

## Migration and Biological Genes

The Human Genome Project is an international research initiative that has identified and mapped out the sequence of human DNA. This groundbreaking study provides insight into the elemental building blocks of human nature. If the code in this sequence were read at one letter per second, it would take thirty-one years to read. If printed out in a regular font, it would yield a stack of paper the size of the Washington Monument. With the help of advanced computing and sequence analysis in genomic studies, scientists presented a "rough draft" of this genome on June 26, 2000, at the White House. At this conference, President Bill Clinton remarked, "Without a doubt, this is the most important, most wondrous map ever produced by humankind.... Today we are learning the language in which God created life. We are gaining ever more awe for the complexity, the beauty, and the wonder of God's most divine and sacred gift."[2]

Five years later, the National Geographic Society and IBM built on this research and launched a genetic anthropology study that sought to understand the broad contours of human migration through the ages. The project relied on identifying certain genetic markers on the DNA sequence that are passed down from generation to generation. By collecting and analyzing specimens from over one million people and comparing these with samples from indigenous communities around the world, this study began to sketch out the ancient routes of human migration. With a microscopic sample from the inside of one's cheek, this project traced back the path of a person's migration history from as far back as eighty thousand years ago, when scholars estimate that Homo sapiens began migrating from the African continent. Such scientific discoveries have given us an entirely new way of discovering that migration is literally "in our genes."[3]

When Bill Groody and I independently participated in the genographic project study, the history of our DNA matched exactly. The map here shows the migration route of our paternal ancestors over the last eighty thousand years.

---

[2] National Institutes of Health, National Human Genome Research Institute, "June 2000 White House Event," June 26, 2000, www.genome.gov.

[3] For more, see National Geographic, "The Genographic Project," https ://help.nationalgeographic.com/s/article/Genographics-DNA-Ancestry.

## Groody Paternal Migration Map

## Migration and Political Genes

In addition to our biological and family origins, migration is written into the national DNA of countries throughout the world. From the beginning of time, people have migrated, but in recent centuries the frontier spirit of pioneering and adventurous migrants has profoundly shaped the national psyches of places like New Zealand, Canada, South Africa, Brazil, Argentina, Australia, the United States, and many other countries. Since the United States is the country I know best, I most frequently refer to the US-Mexico context, although I draw upon experiences from other parts of the world as well.

In *The Uprooted*, Oscar Handlin wrote, "I once thought to write a history of immigrants in America. Then I discovered that the immigrants were American history."[4] The first Paleo-Indian settlers migrated from Eurasia along the land bridge on the Bering Strait (Beringia) to the Americas. Much later the Pilgrims migrated from England to North America in search of religious freedom; Lewis and Clark migrated from established territories in search of new routes across the vast unknown of the American West; pioneers and trailblazers migrated along the Oregon Trail in search of a prosperous future. And throughout recent centuries, waves of immigrants

---

[4] Oscar Handlin, *The Uprooted: The Epic Story of the Great Migration that Made the American People* (Boston: Little Brown, 1951), 3.

have come from around the world to the United States seeking a better life. In the process, the country has become known as a "mixing bowl," a "melting pot," and a "stew pot" of different races, creeds, and cultures.

In the Declaration of Independence, the US Founding Fathers declared, "We hold these truths to be self-evident, that all men are created equal, that they are endowed by their Creator with certain unalienable Rights, that among these are Life, Liberty and the pursuit of Happiness." From these began the great American experiment, an experiment shaped by migrants from virtually every country around the globe.

People journeyed from foreign lands to America in search of new possibilities, iconically represented by the Statue of Liberty, at whose feet are inscribed these famous words of Emma Lazarus:

> *Mother of Exiles. From her beacon-hand*
> *Glows world-wide welcome; her mild eyes command*
> *The air-bridged harbor that twin cities frame.*
> *"Keep, ancient lands, your storied pomp!" cries she*
> *With silent lips. "Give me your tired, your poor,*
> *Your huddled masses yearning to breathe free,*
> *The wretched refuse of your teeming shore.*
> *Send these, the homeless, tempest-tost to me,*
> *I lift my lamp beside the golden door!"*[5]

These words have been emblazed on the American psyche, but in time a far more complex and ambivalent attitude toward immigrants would unfold on the US landscape, which we explore later in more detail.

## Migration and Our Spiritual Genes

Migration is woven not only into our biological and national genes but into our spiritual DNA as well. Throughout the Judeo-Christian Scriptures, migration is inextricably linked to God's covenant and our response. From the call of Abraham to the exodus, from exile to return, from the Incarnation to the resurrection, and from discipleship to mission, the theme of migration is interwoven into our spiritual consciousness, which we discuss at length in the following chapter.

---

[5] Emma Lazarus, "The New Colossus," www.poetryfoundation.org.

Migration and spirituality are related not only to our journey through this world but are central principles at work in the heart of creation. St. Thomas Aquinas' whole theological vision is framed by this notion that everything comes from God and is called to return to God (*Exitus et Reditus*). It acknowledges the movement from the Creator, movement through this world as a creature, and the return movement to God through Christ the mediator.[6] Our sojourn through this world, as the Second Vatican Council articulates it, makes us "pilgrims in a strange land" on our return journey to God (*Lumen Gentium* 6).

**The Many Faces of Migration**

The scope and scale of migration today are unprecedented, making it one of the most pressing signs of our times. Because approximately one out of every seven people around the world are migrating in one form or another, the issue touches every area of human life. Consequently, some have referred to our own generation as the "age of migration."[7]

But behind the numbers and statistics are human beings, each with a story to tell. People are central to theological reflection on migration because we are human beings created in God's image and likeness. Looking at migration from a theological perspective roots our reflection in the search to understand what it means to be human before God and what it means to move toward union with God and communion with one another.

Ideally, people would never need to leave their homelands.[8] For many people, however, staying home makes it difficult, if not impossible, to live dignified lives. Various push factors and pull factors cause people to migrate, including the violation of human rights, religious persecution, weak juridical systems, the breakdown of the rule of law, the collapse of governments, poor economic conditions, unemployment and underemployment, and many

---

[6] Marie-Dominique Chenu is credited with developing the notion of *Exitus et Reditus,* the centrality of the movement to and from God in the superstructure of Thomist thought. See Marie-Dominique Chenu, *Towards Understanding St. Thomas* (Chicago: Regnery, 1964).

[7] Stephen Castles and Mark J. Miller, *The Age of Migration: International Population Movements in the Modern World,* 5th ed. (New York: Guilford Press, 2013).

[8] Catholic Social Teaching affirms this belief as well. For more on this topic, see United States Conference of Catholic Bishops, "Strangers No Longer Together on the Journey of Hope," Issues and Action, January 22, 2003, sec. 34, www.usccb.org.

other issues. These multiple causes have given rise to different classifications of migrants.

I use the word *migrant* in a variety of ways. The United Nations uses *migrant* generally to refer to "any person who lives temporarily or permanently in a country where he or she was not born, and has acquired some significant social ties to this country."[9] Because my primary focus relates to people on the bottom rung of the socioeconomic ladder, I use *migrant* to refer primarily to those who are poor, vulnerable, and marginalized, especially economic migrants, forced migrants or refugees, internally displaced peoples, and victims of human trafficking.[10] As we examine this differentiated landscape of the migrant population in more detail, we also want to look underneath the labels and statistics in order to listen to their stories and shed more light on the human face of those on the move.[11]

*Economic Migrants*

Moises comes from a rural area near Jiquilpan, in the state of Michoacán, Mexico. He and his wife had just had their fifth child. Though it was an occasion of joy for them, it was also a time of increasing stress, tension, and responsibility.

For generations his family had made their living on the land, especially in sowing and selling corn, but the current trade policies in countries like the United States had undercut their ability to make any sustainable living off the land.[12] His mother-in-law also lives with them, and her health is

---

[9] United Nations Educational, Scientific and Cultural Organization, "Migrant/Migration," Glossary, https://wayback.archive-it.org.

[10] Although these classifications help determine what legal protections are available to certain migrants, many scholars today agree that at some point these categorizations blur and are not easily differentiated. Some people may flee their homelands because of political persecution and fall under the category of forced migrants or refugees, for example, but their motivations may also stem from economic considerations and therefore these people can be considered economic migrants as well. Most migrants are motivated by push factors that drive them away from their homelands and pull factors that draw them to better lives in another place.

[11] To protect some of the migrants who were interviewed, some details of these stories have been modified or aggregated with other accounts.

[12] For a thorough treatment of the impact of the North American Free Trade Agreement (NAFTA) on poverty and migration from and within Mexico, see David Bacon, "Displaced People: NAFTA's Most Important Product," North American Congress on Latin America, September 3, 2008, https://nacla.org.

failing, but they have no money for desperately needed medication. Occasionally, Moises can get small jobs in neighboring towns, but only for a day or two at a time; there is no steady income due to underemployment. The day before his daughter complained of hunger, and knowing he did not have enough food to give her, he felt he was failing as a parent. With more mouths to feed, deteriorating conditions at home, and only beans and tortillas for meals, he had to start thinking about other options if he and his family were to live in dignity and peace. The difficult choices ahead began to weigh on him.

To make matters worse, the week before, two men had come by his house demanding money to "protect" him from the very drug cartels for which these men were working. They also required access to his property, which was located on the strategic routes they used to smuggle drugs northward. If he refused, they would harm his family, which they had done to other people he knew. He suddenly found an economic gun at his back, a moral dilemma on his hands, and only three choices in his mind: steal, collude with the cartels, or migrate.

When Moises was younger, his father would migrate up north for a period of time and then return. But it is different now. Not only is it more difficult to cross the border without papers, but it is also unlikely that he would be able to return home with any regularity. He knows the trip would be dangerous and that many from his own village have died in their attempts to cross the deserts of the American Southwest. As border enforcement has increased, people have taken more clandestine and difficult routes to enter the country, causing thousands to perish along the way. Because he makes only fifteen hundred dollars a year, he cannot cross legally; smuggling fees would be thousands of dollars, which means he would have to take out a loan, or risk being sold and trafficked into bonded labor. He has no money to apply for a tourist visa and no skills that would enable him to obtain a work visa.

Wanting to live an honest life but needing to provide for his family, he saw no other option but to migrate without papers. Even though he would take this move to help his family, it could also break up his family, as it has many others' before him. Unlike those who went north during his father's generation, the increasing difficulties involved in crossing the border today meant that he would rarely, and possibly never, see his family again.

When Moises arrived at the border on the Mexican side near Tijuana, I asked him why he wanted to pass over to the United States. He said, "My family is in need of bread, and I need to provide for them." On the other side of the border near Coronado Island in San Diego, life is a little different. As a major resort area, people come from long distances to relax and to shop. Another woman there—only a few geographical miles from where I met Moises—said she came to the area because "There is a specialty bread I can buy in this area, and I can't find it anywhere else." Although both are searching for their daily bread and occupy the same geographical space on this planet, they live in two totally different worlds. In between the lives of these two people, the complex drama of economic migration unfolds.

The United Nations defines *undocumented* or *irregular migrants* like Moises as "people who enter a country usually in search of employment, without the necessary documents and permits." An economic migrant, or a migrant worker, is defined by the International Organization for Migration as "a person who is to be engaged, is engaged or has been engaged in a remunerated activity in a State of which he or she is not a national."[13] In our own times there are more than 22 million people like Moises who are irregular migrants, and millions cross borders without papers each year. Europe has as many as 4.8 million irregular migrants, and the United States has as many as 11.3 million.[14] By the first two decades of the twenty-first century, approximately 602,000 people were irregular migrants in the European Union.[15] These numbers have historically grown alongside increasing political, social, and economic instability, such as during the peak of the Syrian refugee crisis, which saw over 1 million migrations in 2015 alone.[16] Rates of irregular migration, however, have declined in recent years due to increased enforcement.[17]

---

[13] International Organization for Migration, "Key Migration Terms," www.iom.int.

[14] Migration Policy Institute, "Frequently Requested Statistics on Immigrants and Immigration in the United States," February 14, 2020, www.migrationpolicy.org; Phillip Connor and Jeffrey S. Passel, "5 Facts about Unauthorized Immigration in Europe," Pew Research Center, November 14, 2019, www.pewresearch.org.

[15] Eurostat, "Enforcement of Immigration Legislation Statistics," https://ec.europa.eu.

[16] Migration Data Portal, "Irregular Migration," March 22, 2020, https://migrationdataportal.org. International Organization for Migration, *Mixed Migration Flows in the Mediterranean and Beyond: Compilation of Available Data and Information* (Geneva: International Organization for Migration, 2015).

[17] The number of irregular migrants declined significantly after 2015, from over one million to less than four hundred thousand, and then in 2017 this number declined to less than two hundred thousand. Eighty-eight thousand irregular migrants

## Forced Migrants or Refugees

In June 1985, *National Geographic* photographer Steve McCurry captured the human face of the refugee crisis in a photo that has become one of the most recognizable pictures in the world.[18] While covering the war in Afghanistan in the 1980s, when the Mujahideen were fighting the Soviet army, he found his way into a refugee camp along the Afghan-Pakistan border. McCurry wanted to capture the feminine face of this global crisis, but it was difficult for foreign men not only to talk to women but especially to photograph them. Eventually, he found his way into the Nasir Bagh refugee camp, which had an elementary school for fifteen to twenty students.

When he got there, he snapped a quick picture of a frightened girl who was about twelve years old, but then she disappeared. A glimpse of her traumatized eyes left behind an imprint of human vulnerability that became an icon of refugee suffering around the world. Yet even as her photo became known globally, no one in the larger public knew her name or her particular story, not even McCurry.

Seventeen years later, McCurry tracked her down in a remote village of Pakistan and found out her name is Sharbat Gula (sweetwater flower girl). Her identity was confirmed through a sophisticated form of biometric identification known as iris recognition. She had been photographed only twice in her life—both times by McCurry—but the second time the world found out more of the story, the struggle, and the soul of this person.

She lived in a country that had witnessed twenty-three years of war. The Soviets constantly leveled Sharbat's village with bombs, and more than 1.5 million people had died in the fighting, including Sharbat's parents, who were killed when she was six years old. With Russians everywhere, Sharbat, her grandmother, her brother, and four sisters eventually fled from their village to Pakistan, as did 3.5 million others. Kashar Khan, her brother, said, "We left Afghanistan because of the fighting." Traveling by foot through

---

had entered Europe during 2019 by October of the same year, on track to finish the year with about half 2017's number of irregular migrations. Similarly, the total number of deportation orders have risen, and there are 3 percent fewer non-EU citizens found to be "illegally present" in the European Union in 2018 than 2017. See Eurostat, "Enforcement of Immigration Legislation Statistics."

[18] Debra Denker, "Afghan Girl," *National Geographic*, June 1985.

mountains in the thick of snow, they hid in caves and begged for blankets to stay warm. Eventually, they ended up in a refugee camp in Pakistan, living with strangers and depending on the mercy of others.[19]

Grateful to find her again, McCurry observed, "Such knife-thin odds. That she would be alive. That she could be found. That she could endure such loss. Surely, in the face of such bitterness the spirit could atrophy. How, she was asked, had she survived?" McCurry notes, "The answer came wrapped in unshakable certitude." She said, "It was the will of God."[20]

Although Sharbat's displacement as a refugee happened decades ago, Afghanistan continues to be one of the largest refugee-sending countries in the world.[21] Afghan refugees are joined by tens of millions of refugees around the world who are fleeing situations of war, persecution, and human rights violations.[22] These include countries like Sudan, Syria, the Democratic Republic of the Congo, Venezuela, Ukraine, and many others.

The United Nations defines *a refugee* as a person who, "owing to well-founded fear of being persecuted for reasons of race, religion, nationality, membership of a particular social group or political opinion, is outside the country of his nationality and is unable or, owing to such fear, is unwilling to avail himself of the protection of that country."[23]

Unlike economic migrants, refugees face the prospect of being killed or tortured if sent back to their homelands. International law distinguishes the economic migrant from the refugee through various legal instruments, one of which is the principle of non-refoulment, under which no state can expel, return, or "refoul" (French: *refouler*) a person back to a homeland where their lives or freedoms are threatened.[24] This notion emerged in the wake

---

[19] Cathy Newman, "Afghan Girl, A Life Revealed," *National Geographic*, April 2002.
[20] Ibid.
[21] United Nations High Commissioner for Refugees, *UNHCR Global Trends: Forced Displacement in 2014* (Geneva: UNHCR, 2015), 49.
[22] For up-to-date statistics on refugees, see the United Nations High Commissioner for Refugees, "Figures at a Glance," United Nations High Commissioner for Refugees, www.unhcr.org.
[23] United Nations High Commissioner for Refugees, *Convention and Protocol Relating to the Status of Refugees* (Geneva: United Nations High Commissioner for Refugees, 2010), 3.
[24] In contrast, an *asylum seeker*, as briefly explained by Amnesty International, "is an individual who is seeking international protection. In countries with individualized procedures, an asylum seeker is someone whose claim has not yet been finally decided on by the country in which he or she has submitted it. Not every asylum seeker will

of World War II when the international community came to recognize the failure of nations to provide a safe haven to refugees fleeing the genocide in Nazi Germany. Since then it has been a means through which refugees can find asylum in countries that have signed on to the 1951 Refugee Convention relating to the Status of Refugees and the 1967 Protocol.[25]

John Paul II called the refugee situation "the festering of a wound which typifies and reveals the imbalances and conflicts of the modern world: the millions of refugees whom war, natural calamities, persecution and discrimination of every kind have deprived of home, employment, family and homeland. The tragedy of these multitudes is reflected in the hopeless faces of men, women and children who can no longer find a home in a divided and inhospitable world" (*Sollicitudo Rei Socialis* 24). As their numbers continue to rise, they remain some of the most vulnerable people on the planet.

*Internally Displaced Persons*

After a civil war overtook Syria following the Arab Spring in 2011, Ayyoush, a mother of two girls and two boys, fled her home in eastern Aleppo in search of safety. She was never able to cross an international border for protection but found temporary refuge in a different neighborhood in her same city. After one of her sons tragically died in the conflict, she and her remaining family were displaced again to a different part of the country. At the age of seventy-two, she now stays in a collective shelter without much hope of returning to her home village.

Suffering from cardiovascular disease, high blood pressure, and malnutrition, Ayyoush survives daily under hot and harsh conditions. Though she lives in her home country, she is surrounded by people and places that are unfamiliar. Her living conditions are crowded, and there are no job opportunities anywhere in the area. Ayyoush relies completely on assistance from the United Nations High Commissioner for Refugees (UNHCR) to survive, hoping for better times ahead. "No one likes to leave home or lose property,"

---

ultimately be recognised as a refugee, but every refugee is initially an asylum seeker." Amnesty International, "What's the Difference between a Refugee and an Asylum Seeker?" January 24, 2019, www.amnesty.org.au.

[25] The list of countries can be found at United Nations High Commissioner for Refugees, "States Parties to the 1951 Convention Relating to the Status of Refugees and the 1967 Protocol," www.unhcr.org.

Ayyoush said, "but I hope that time can go back and I can live in my house again with my family."²⁶

In Syria alone, as of 2016, more than 6.5 million people are internally displaced like Ayyoush, the largest population of internally displaced persons in the world.²⁷ Approximately 4.3 million of them need shelter.²⁸ While Ayyoush fled because of violence, others are displaced because of natural disasters, economic collapse, and political instability. Broadly, *internally displaced persons* are those "who have been forced or obliged to flee or to leave their homes . . . in order to avoid the effects of armed conflict, situations of generalized violence, violations of human rights or natural or human-made disasters, and who have not crossed an internationally recognized State border."²⁹

At the end of 2018, there were approximately 41.3 million internally displaced persons in the world. Countries that have large populations of internally displaced persons include Colombia, the Democratic Republic of the Congo, Pakistan, Afghanistan, Iraq, and Somalia.³⁰ They are especially vulnerable because they often stay underneath the jurisdiction of their own government, which itself may have been the cause of their displacement.³¹ These same governments may turn away aid organizations at the border, putting refugees in remote locations far from foreign assistance. For the internally displaced, migration is not simply a matter of changing locations but of losing a home, lifestyle, family, and traditional support systems.

---

²⁶ Vivian Tou'meh, "Displaced by War, Syrians Endure Poor Living Conditions in Shelters," United Nations High Commissioner for Refugees, May 12, 2017, www.unhcr.org.

²⁷ United Nations High Commissioner for Refugees, "Internally Displaced People," July 7, 2016, www.unhcr.org.

²⁸ Tou'meh, "Displaced by War."

²⁹ United Nations High Commissioner for Refugees, *Guiding Principles on Internal Displacement* (Geneva: UNHCR, 2004), 1.

³⁰ Another country with a large population per capita of internally displaced persons is Israel/Palestine. These IDPs as well as refugees writ large from this area constitute the longest-lasting protracted refugee situation in the world. As such, they are under the jurisdiction of a special UN protocol. For more information about this refugee situation, see United Nations Relief and Works Agency for Palestine Refugees in the Near East, UNRWA.org. For updated and detailed statistics about IDPs, see Internal Displacement Monitoring Centre, www.internal-displacement.org/.

³¹ United Nations High Commissioner for Refugees, "Internally Displaced People."

*Human Trafficking Victims*

Though the numbers are uncertain, some estimates conclude that human trafficking ensnares as many as forty million people around the world. Whether victims of sexual, labor, or other forms of exploitation, trafficking degrades both perpetrators and victims. It is a new and widespread form of slavery, although arguably worse now than in previous generations.[32] In 1850, the cost for an average slave in the southern United States would be the contemporary equivalent of forty thousand dollars. Today, a person can be bought and enslaved for one hundred dollars on average.

As noted in the *Global Slavery Index*,

> Whether it is called human trafficking, forced labour, slavery or slavery-like practices (a category that includes debt bondage, forced or servile marriage, sale or exploitation of children including in armed conflict) victims of modern slavery have their freedom denied, and are used and controlled and exploited by another person for profit, sex, or the thrill of domination. This means that more people are enslaved today than at any other point in history. Such trafficking may or may not involve crossing an international border, and both men and women are its victims and its perpetrators.[33]

According to a recent estimate, 71.1 percent of all human trafficking victims are women, and 28 percent are minors.[34] Each year, approximately six hundred thousand to eight hundred thousand are trafficked across international borders.[35] While labor trafficking occurs primarily within national

---

[32] Global Slavery Index, "Highlights," 2018, www.globalslaveryindex.org.

[33] Global Slavery Index, *The Global Slavery Index 2018* (Nedlands: Global Slavery Index, 2018).

[34] United Nations Office on Drugs and Crime, "Global Report on Trafficking in Persons 2020," www.unodc.org.

[35] Current estimates are that 77 percent of victims are trafficked within their countries of residence. In recent years, according to the International Labor Organization, it was found that in terms of total human trafficking victims (not merely international victims and not including those in forced marriages), 71.1 percent are female victims and 24.7 percent are minors. This information is from International Labor Organization and Walk Free Foundation, *Global Estimates of Modern Slavery: Forced Labor and Forced Marriage* (Geneva: International Labor Organization and Walk Free Foundation, 2017), 23–24.

borders, sex trafficking remains mostly international. Sex trafficking may include prostitution, pornography production, strip clubs and exotic clubs, sex tourism, mail-order brides, and other activities.

Maya is one such victim of sex trafficking. At nineteen, she had already spent four years as a sex slave in each of Mumbai's two main red-light districts, Kamathipura and Falkland Road. Born in a poor part of Nepal, where the annual per capita income was $180 (50 cents per day), her family struggled to survive. With the assurance that her daughter would get a job at a carpet factory and then send home up to $10 per month, her parents sold her to an agent for $55. The night Maya left home, this agent resold her to a *dalal* (trafficker), who then smuggled her over the border into India. Then, in Maya's words,

> Once I came to Mumbai, the *dalal* sold me to a malik [brothel boss] in Kamathipura. The malik told me I owed him thirty-five thousand rupees [$780], and I must have sex with any man who chooses me until this debt is repaid. I refused, and this man raped me and did not feed me. When I agreed to do sex, they gave me medicines because I had a urine infection. I was in that bungalow two years and made sex to twenty men each day. There were hundreds of girls in this bungalow, many from Nepal. One time I tried to escape. I complained to the police, but they did nothing. A few days later the malik's men found me on the streets and took me back to the brothel. The malik put chili paste on a broomstick and pushed it inside me. Then he broke my ribs with his fist. The *gharwali* [house manager, madam] tended my wounds for a short time, and after this time I went with clients again, even though my ribs pained very badly. The *gharwali* gave me opium to make the pain less. After two years, the malik sold me to another malik on Falkland Road. During this time I lived in a *pinjara* [cage] with one other woman. It was very small and it was on the street, so it was very noisy at night. I was pregnant two times, and the *gharwali* gave me pills to kill the baby. The second time I became very ill. When I was strong I ran away. I went to a shelter near Falkland Road. They told me I have HIV. They helped me contact my father, but he told me not to come home. He said I can never be married and because I have HIV, I can only bring shame.[36]

---

[36] Siddharth Kara, *Sex Trafficking: Inside the Business of Modern Slavery* (New York: Columbia University Press, 2009), 2–3.

In addition to sexual exploitation of people like Maya, human trafficking also involves people who are subjected to forced labor, debt bondage, prison labor, begging rings, and child soldiering. Labor trafficking is widespread in agriculture, construction, food processing, contract cleaning, sweatshops, restaurants, domestic work, and elsewhere. It happens in factories, fields, offices, eateries, homes, mines, and war zones worldwide. In all of these situations, children are the most vulnerable and subject to the worst labor abuses.

Traffickers make in excess of $150.2 billion a year, which is more than the profits of Nike, Facebook, and Starbucks combined. It has become the fastest-growing criminal industry in the world, second only to the illegal drug trade and on par with the illegal arms industry.[37] Globalization has made it possible for human traffickers to expand into new markets, lure the vulnerable through new technologies, and target the weak and desperate, especially migrants who have few employment options.

Overall, what distinguishes victims of trafficking from other types of migrants is the use of force, fraud, or coercion. The United Nations clarified this distinction when it defined *trafficking in persons* as

> the recruitment, transportation, transfer, harbouring or receipt of persons, by means of the threat or use of force or other forms of coercion, of abduction, of fraud, of deception, of the abuse of power or of a position of vulnerability or of the giving or receiving of payments or benefits to achieve the consent of a person having control over another person, for the purpose of exploitation. Exploitation shall include, at a minimum, the exploitation of the prostitution of others or other forms of sexual exploitation, forced labour or services, slavery or practices similar to slavery, servitude or the removal of organs.[38]

Although economic migrants, forced migrants, internally displaced people, and victims of human trafficking differ in various ways, they share much in common with each other. Their experiences of poverty, oppression,

---

[37] International Labour Office, *Profits and Poverty: The Economics of Forced Labor* (Geneva: International Labour Office, 2014), 13.

[38] United Nations High Commissioner for Refugees, *Protocol to Prevent, Suppress, and Punish Trafficking in Persons, Especially Women and Children, Supplementing the United Nations Convention against Transnational Organised Crime* (Geneva: United Nations, 2000), 2.

and marginality leave them vulnerable to manipulation, domination, and exploitation. They suffer the effects of family breakdown, the disorders of structural systems, and the effects of poverty on multiple levels. But how are we to interpret the acts of human cruelty at work in human trafficking and the ways they assault the dignity of the human person? Here the language of theology, and the rituals of the liturgy, begin to give us a language to speak about the breakdown of human relationships and its impact on the dignity of people.

**The Xenophobic Shadow**

While migration is frequently seen as a problem in and of itself, it is also fundamentally connected to original, personal, and social sin. Sin involves more than breaking established laws; it is rather about rupturing our connection with our brothers and sisters and severing the bonds of communion with God and one another that unite us as a human family. The penitential rite of the Eucharistic liturgy offers an opportunity to step back from our destructive spirals, to take responsibility for the ways our action and inaction contribute to unraveling our relationships, and to move us toward right relationship with ourselves, with others, with the created world, and ultimately with God.

The inclusion of the *Kyrie Eleison* in the Eucharistic liturgy underscores the importance of acknowledging our personal and collective histories, especially the destructive dimensions, in order to name, heal, and transform them. Not only does this process offer us some hope that we can avoid repeating these mistakes in the future, but it also gives us hope of not being in bondage to it. It also orients our lives toward a future that is positive and constructive. Without doing so, we become "aliens" not only to others but even ourselves. The more we become disconnected from each other, the more we find ourselves lost on a road that leads us nowhere.

The Eucharistic liturgy reminds us that the long arc of human history is a story of blessing and a story of sin, and that our world needs to take a turn in a new direction. In theological terms, this means repentance (Greek: *metanoia*, which means "changing one's mind") personally and collectively. Sin is part of our personal story, and it has been part of our collective story. The United States gives us one context to see how this phenomenon has taken shape over time.

## A Deep Ambivalence and a Dark Shadow

Despite its persona as a land of opportunity and a promised land for the poor and oppressed, the United States and its citizens have had a deep ambivalence about migration, and the history of immigration has always offered a mixture of light and darkness. In 1630, Puritan refugees like John Winthrop described America as a shining "city upon a hill" and a model of Christian charity. But to others the light reflected against this hill would cast a very long, xenophobic shadow. Not a few of the immigrants who came seeking to realize the American dream discovered instead a virtual nightmare. Alongside migrant "success" stories are stories of internal displacement, forced migration, and sins of many kinds, including imperialism, colonialism, slavery, nativism, militarism, and many others.

Even though eight signers of the Declaration of Independence were born abroad, negative sentiments about immigration emerged in America from the early days of its founding.[39] As one man described the challenges,

> Why should Pennsylvania, founded by the English, become a colony of aliens, who will shortly be so numerous as to Germanize us instead of our Anglifying them, and will never adopt our language or customs, any more than they can acquire our complexion.... The number of purely white people in the world is proportionally very small. All Africa is black or tawny. Asia chiefly tawny. America (exclusive of the new comers) wholly so. And in Europe, the Spaniards, Italians, French, Russians and Swedes, are generally of what we call a swarthy complexion; as are the Germans also, the Saxons only excepted, who with the English, make the principal body of white people on the face of the Earth. I could wish their numbers were increased. And while we are, as I may call it, scouring our planet, by clearing America of woods, and so making this side of our globe reflect a brighter light to the eyes of inhabitants in Mars or Venus, why should we in the sight of superior beings, darken its people? Why increase the Sons of Africa, by planting them in America, where we have so fair an opportunity, by excluding all Blacks and

---

[39] Richard D. Brown, "The Founding Fathers of 1776 and 1787: A Collective View," *William and Mary Quarterly* 33, no. 3 (1976): 474–76, quoted in Peter Schrag, *Not Fit for Our Society: Immigration and Nativism in America* (Berkeley: University of California Press, 2010), 23.

Tawneys, of increasing the lovely White and Red? But perhaps I am partial to the complexion of my country, for such kind of partiality is natural to Mankind.[40]

These are the words of Benjamin Franklin, whom some consider "the first American."[41]

In 1851, the US government internally displaced Native Americans and began putting them on reservations. In 1882, Congress passed a Chinese Exclusion Act and made it illegal for any Chinese person to enter or work in the United States. In 1942, Congress relocated more than one hundred thousand Japanese Americans and Japanese natives into internment camps. And as it held a door open to the Germans, Indians, Italians, Irish, and other groups, it also tolerated, if not endorsed, discrimination against them at the same time. The door to citizenship would not be open to blacks until after the Civil War and Asians until the middle of the twentieth century.[42]

As the United States began forging a new identity, it faced new challenges in determining whom to let in to America, under what criteria, and according to which laws. In the early years of the country, Congress passed a law that would allow a person to become a resident of the United States within two years. In 1795, it was extended to five. As fears about immigrants began to rise, the Naturalization Act of 1798—part of the Alien and Sedition Acts—extended the period required for citizenship to fourteen years. But by this point the dye of the country had set; citizenship was primarily intended for "free white persons" of "good moral character," and the shadow side of federal legislation would unjustly marginalize and exclude many groups that did not fit these criteria in the years that followed.

As America became increasingly shaped by Anglo-Protestant values, the white race, and the English language, a new vision of "native America" emerged. Both in what that vision did and failed to do, sins against immigrants became a permanent part of the American landscape. This xenophobic legacy has continued up to the present day and has scarred the inner landscape of the national psyche.

---

[40] Kathleen R. Arnold, *Anti-Immigration in the United States: A Historical Encyclopedia* (Santa Barbara, CA: Greenwood Press, 2011), 1:523.

[41] H. W. Brands, *The First American: The Life and Times of Benjamin Franklin*, 1st Anchor Books ed. (New York: Anchor Books, 2002).

[42] Schrag, *Not Fit*, 23.

*The Sins of Imperialism: Native American Migration*

This new vision of America would redefine who belonged in this new country and who would be categorized as an outsider. This clash of civilizations has continued into our own time. According to a story from the American Southwest, a woman at a store in Santa Fe, New Mexico, decided to make a call on her cell phone while waiting in line to check out. The man in line behind her noticed she was speaking in a different language. After she hung up, he said to her, "I didn't want to say anything while you were on the phone, but you're in America now. You need to speak English." She said, "Excuse me?" In a condescendingly, slow tone of voice, he furthered his point, saying, "If you want to speak Mexican, go back to Mexico. In America, we speak English." She replied, "Sir, I was speaking Navajo. If you want to speak English, go back to England."[43]

It is believed that the first migrants to what is now the United States set foot in Alaska between twelve thousand and fourteen thousand years ago and then moved southward. Traveling via a land bridge across what is now called the Bering Strait, they inhabited the American territory for so long that they became known as the Native American people, who differentiated into hundreds of distinct nations and tribes.

Despite inhabiting American territory for hundreds of generations, they became the first internally displaced people in the United States. On May 28, 1830, President Andrew Jackson signed into law the Indian Removal Act. Though in theory it was supposed to be voluntary, in practice it forcibly compelled five Native American nations from the southeastern part of the United States to relocate elsewhere. These included many members of the Cherokee, Muscogee, Seminole, Chickasaw, and Choctaw Nations. Many suffered disease and starvation during this migration, and countless numbers died in the process of this forced displacement. The journey of these internally displaced peoples, and their compulsory relocation to designated lands, is commonly known as the Trail of Tears.

With their political and territorial ambitions, European immigrants to America moved westward, seeking to remove any who stood in the way of their expansionism. The rhetoric around the nation's democratic ideals of equality masked a larger agenda at work. As the sins of imperialism were unleashed, a legally sanctioned, ethnic cleansing began on American soil.

---

[43] Not Always Right, "The First and True Language Of America," September 23, 2013, https://notalwaysright.com.

## The Sins of Racism: Forced African Migration and Slavery

Once the settlers from Europe began to colonize the land, a new kind of migration emerged: psychological territoriality. It would launch the beginning of what Peter Schrag has called "the great awhitening."[44] It not only marginalized and excluded many groups of people, but it also created the conditions that gave rise to African slave migration; slaves were the first forced migrants and trafficked persons to the United States.

In 1619, African slaves started coming to Colonial America after being forcibly uprooted from their homelands. By 1670, with the increasing demand for cheap labor to tend to agricultural needs, black slavery became an institution. As the plantation system bloomed in South Carolina, Virginia, Maryland, and later Georgia, the demand for slaves and trade in them continued to increase.

Between the sixteenth and nineteenth centuries, an estimated 12 million African slaves were forcibly brought to the Americas, about half a million of whom would end up on North American soil. Captured and bound in their homelands, they were crammed into ships, subjected to merciless journeys across the ocean, and forced into cruel servitude. Moreover, more than half of all European immigrants who came to the United States in Colonial America arrived as indentured servants.[45]

Men, women, and children were captured and forced from their homes in West and Central Africa and trafficked to other countries. They were bound, chained, and loaded onto ships built in England, and then transported through horrible journeys lasting months at a times through what was known as the Middle Passage of the Atlantic Ocean. The conditions were so horrible that many died en route. Those who survived were later imported and exported in American cities. Although the slave trade would form the backbone of western European and American economies, it would also leave in its wake a legacy of prejudice, discrimination, and racism.[46]

When slaves were unloaded from ships in places like Richmond, they were paraded in chains to jails and then commodified on auction blocks along the James River.[47] Such experiences left deep impressions on those who

---

[44] Schrag, *Not Fit*, 139.
[45] Deanna Barker, "Indentured Servitude in Colonial America," National Association for Interpretation, March 10, 2004, http://mertsahinoglu.com.
[46] http://media.maps.com/magellan/images/USAH003-H.gif.
[47] Turner and White, "Richmond Slave Trail Tour."

suffered these misfortunes, and some others who witnessed the ordeals of their journey. As one naval officer observed at the time,

> I had noticed the bad condition of this gang several times on the road, the poor wretches being travel-worn and half-starved, and having large sores caused by their loads and the blows and cuts they received. The ropes that confined them were also, in some instances, eating into their flesh. And I saw one woman still carrying the infant that had died in her arms of starvation.[48]

## *The Forced Migration Routes of African Slaves*

But this journey was never done in broad daylight, because guilt and shame—as well as the need to preserve outward appearances of decency and civility—kept this process literally in the dark. It also started a long process that began legitimating and legalizing the injustice of slavery.

---

[48] Veney Lovett Cameron, "Across Africa," 1877. From a marker on the Richmond Slave Trail.

Even after the laws changed, still other levels of emancipation were needed. In addition to physical bondage, there was a "psychological conquest" that resulted in social slavery as well. This meant not only the rights to occupy the land but also the right to tell a story, related from the perspective of the victors. Woven within this story was the "othering" of the conquered and the dominated, which gave expression to various forms of discrimination. It gave rise to Jim Crow laws in the late 1800s that legalized racial segregation.

Social classifications and social structures created systems of relationships that defined the white race as superior over every other, especially the black race. It set forth exclusionary social patterns and political policies that would reverberate for the centuries to follow. Tragically, this forced migration would leave scars on American society for generations to come, and it planted the seeds of a social violence that would wound the soul of a nation that continues to bleed today. It plays out still in the stories of racial discrimination and unjust brutality against people like Eric Garner, Michael Brown, Freddie Grey, Breonna Taylor, and George Floyd.

*The Sins of Nativism: Anti-Immigrant Nationalism*

Although sins against immigrants have manifested themselves in different ways, the common thread is distinguished by different variations of nativism. Nativism seeks to protect the interests of those born in the country over and against newcomers. It stresses the return to traditional (i.e., Anglo/white) customs in opposition to outside or foreign influences, and it resurfaces with distressing regularity.

Over time, nativists have argued that immigrants threaten the health of "American culture" with "viruses" like Catholicism, monarchism, anarchism, Islam, criminal tendencies, defective genes, "mongrel" bloodlines, or some other such alien infections.[49] Through such mentalities and the policies that emerged from them, immigrants are systematically marginalized, alienated, or excluded entirely.

By the middle of the nineteenth century, nativist organizations such as the Know-Nothings sought to curb the cultural influence of immigrants and to keep them from holding political office. By the 1870s, nativists targeted Irish, Italian, Chinese, and Japanese immigrants, who were met with signs

---

[49] Schrag, *Not Fit*, 4.

like, "No Irish Need Apply" and "No Wops Need Apply," and slogans such as "Rum, Romanism, and Rebellion," "The Chinese Must Go," and, after Pearl Harbor, "Japs Keep Moving."[50]

Roger Daniels identifies three waves of anti-immigrant activity that led to "the triumph of nativism": the anti-Catholic phase, the anti-Asian phase, and the anti-all-immigrant phase. The anti-Catholic phase was aimed at Irish and, to some extent, German Catholics during the 1830s–1850s period. The anti-Asian phase was directed at Chinese immigrants in the 1870–1880s, Japanese immigration in the early twentieth century, and later Filipino immigration in the 1920s–1930s. The anti-all-immigrant phase began in the mid-1880s and triumphed in the Immigration Act of 1924, which has shaped American immigration policy until now. As Roger Daniels summarizes it, "There was never a time when nativist attitudes were not present in American society,"[51] and to some extent the anti-Catholic, anti-Asian, and anti-all-immigrant phases have never completely died out.[52]

These attitudes continue to irrupt in society as migration brings different races, cultures, and religions into closer contact with each other. According to a 2012 report by the Pew Research Center, Christians comprise nearly 49 percent of the world's international migrants. Muslims make up the second-largest group at 27 percent. The remaining quarter are a mix of Hindus, Buddhists, Jews, adherents of other faiths, and the religiously unaffiliated.[53] In this pluralized, multicultural, and multireligious landscape, anti-immigrant sentiment has arguably become stronger than ever, bringing the issue of identity to the forefront on the sociopolitical and cultural stages.

Especially in times of social unrest and economic downturn, nativist mentalities frequently target immigrant groups and make them scapegoats of the country's collective anxiety. The attitudes typical of such a mindset are reflected in people like Samuel Huntington, who, like Benjamin Franklin in earlier times, has argued that the Anglo-Saxon ideal is now under threat by

---

[50] Ibid., *Not Fit*, 3–4.
[51] Roger Daniels, *Coming to America: A History of Immigration and Ethnicity in American Life*, 2nd ed (New York: Perennial, 2002), 265.
[52] Ibid., 267.
[53] Joseph Liu, "Faith on the Move—The Religious Affiliation of International Migrants," Pew Research Center, March 8, 2012, www.pewforum.org.

a new wave of "aliens." This time they are not Germans but Latinos, Syrians, Muslims, or other such newcomers. Observers like Huntington believe that these groups' failure to assimilate Anglo-Saxon values is putting the whole American identity at risk.[54] Contemporary politicians continue to exploit this sentiment for their own political ambitions, and not only do they rewrite American history in the process, they also undermine the prodigious efforts of countless immigrants who have contributed to the making of America.

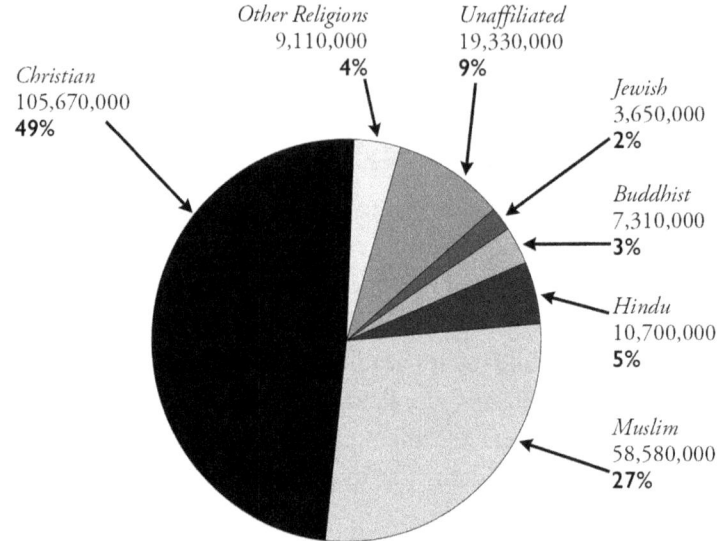

*Religious Composition of International Migrants*

*Percentage and estimated number of all migrants who belong to each religious group*

Other Religions
9,110,000
4%

Unaffiliated
19,330,000
9%

Christian
105,670,000
49%

Jewish
3,650,000
2%

Buddhist
7,310,000
3%

Hindu
10,700,000
5%

Muslim
58,580,000
27%

Throughout the report, the "other religions" category includes Sikhs, Jains, Taoists, Chinese folk religions, African traditional religions and many smaller groups.

Population estimates are rounded to ten thousands. Percentages are calculated from unrounded numbers and may not add to 100 due to rounding.

**Pew Research Center's Forum on Religion & Public Life**
**Global Religion and Migration Database 2010**

---

[54] Samuel Huntington, *Who Are We? The Challenges to America's National Identity* (New York: Simon & Schuster, 2004).

## *The Sins of Militarization: Death at the Border*

In more recent times, the nativistic shadow of the American psyche is expressing itself through the militarization of the border. As of early 2020, the United States has 5,525 miles of border with Canada, 1,933.4 miles with Mexico, and there are 95,000 miles of shoreline that make up the maritime border.[55] Although sovereign nations have a right and duty to protect their borders—something that Catholic Social Teaching also recognizes—the current militarization of the border symbolizes the triumph of the nativist mentality and the effect it has had on our political system.

The sins of militarization are not about legitimate efforts to address the problems of terrorism, drugs, or violence at the border. These sins have to do with mixing these problems with those of economic migrants, whose only "crime" has to do with crossing a border without official permission in order to find a life of dignity and often provide for their families in need. No matter how one parses the statistics, the vast majority of immigrants crossing the border—and the ones against whom so much of our military effort is being used—are hardworking people looking for work, not criminals, terrorists, and drug dealers.

Although the United States dispatched mounted watchmen along its border as early as 1904, it significantly increased the number of agents during President Ronald Reagan's war on drugs in the 1980s. In the 1990s, this militaristic approach intensified in an attempt to deter and prevent waves of immigrants from crossing into the United States. As nativist fears triggered Proposition 187 in California in 1993, which sought to deny health care, education, and social service benefits to undocumented immigrants, Border Patrol sectors began to address the problems through military-styled enforcement initiatives. In 1993, it started a program called Operation Hold the Line in El Paso, Texas, and in subsequent years, it launched similar programs such as Operation Gatekeeper in San Diego (1994), Operation Rio Grande in southeastern Texas (1997), and Operation Desert Safeguard in Tucson (2003).

These deterrent strategies relied on two types of barriers: natural barriers, or the forbidding natural terrain, particularly deserts and mountains, of the American Southwest; and enforcement barriers, 700 miles of

---

[55] Federation of American Scientists, "U.S. International Borders: Brief Facts," https://fas.org.

fence built along the southern border.⁵⁶ These barriers were supplemented by various surveillance mechanisms, including Border Patrol agents, unmanned aerial drones, ground sensors with seismic imaging and infrared technology, mobile surveillance systems, and night vision technology. In order to avoid detection, migrants began relying on coyote-guides to take them through more clandestine routes, which made the trip not only more costly but also more dangerous. Cartels profited from such syndicates (which charge thousands if not tens of thousands of dollars) as did defense contractors such as Raytheon, Lockheed Martin, and General Dynamics, charged with finding new mechanisms to reinforce the border.

In addition to the enormous financial costs, these policies have exacted tremendous human costs. Since these policies were initiated in the early 1990s, thousands of migrants have died in the treacherous terrain along the US-Mexico border, although numbers on the Mexico side are estimated to be much higher. Policies toward immigrants in the United States have escalated this trend, but migrant death tolls have increased exponentially in other parts of the globe as well. Since 2000, more than forty-six thousand migrants have died along migratory routes around the world, a phenomenon that the International Organization of Migration has described as "an epidemic of crime and victimization."⁵⁷

*The Sins of Money-Theism: The Idolization of Capital*

To the above litany of sins, we must also add our disordered relationship to capital, which has been so central to creating our current social disorders. Money has become the foremost criteria for assessing a person's value. Whatever arguments can be made about the strengths of the free market, they must be assessed also with regard to the weaknesses of human nature.

One of the most fundamental challenges human beings have faced throughout history is not atheism per se but idolatry. Idolatry is not just about whether one believes in God or not, but in what god one ultimately believes. One's god in this sense is revealed by what one devotes one's heart to, what one most values, and even what one sacrifices for.

---

⁵⁶ Michael John Garcia, *Barriers along the U.S. Borders: Key Authorities and Requirements* (Washington, DC: Congressional Research Service, 2016).

⁵⁷ For updated statistics on migrant deaths throughout the world, see UN Dispatch, "Missing Migrants Project, Latest Global Figures," www.undispatch.com.

As Abraham Joshua Heschel asks, "What is an idol? Any god who is mine, not yours, any god concerned with me but not with you, is an idol."[58] Anytime we become concerned about national security but not human insecurity, when we are more preoccupied with civil law than natural law, when we emphasize sovereign rights but not human rights, and when we look at citizenship but not discipleship, we are worshipping idols.

In large part, the root cause of global injustice is anchored in a fundamental theological and anthropological error that we can call *money-theism*.[59] Money-theism deals with the idolization of capital, expressed as the worship of the gods of the marketplace, and is often practiced through the rituals of the stock market and the liturgies of global capitalism. In this system, people are measured in terms of their net worth, accumulated possessions, and incomes, rather than their human worth, the quality of their character, and their spiritual depth. The value of human beings has become more and more reduced to a "market fundamentalism," where the market alone defines what it means to be human.[60]

The asymmetries of wealth offer further clarification as to why people leave their homelands and seek opportunities elsewhere. And our current economic structure raises many questions in view of the designs of a loving Creator and the human choices that have created our current social order. At present, 17 percent of the world lives on $1.25 a day, 31 percent struggle to live on $2 a day, and 70 percent survive on $10 a day. According to the World Bank, two-thirds of the world population lives in poverty. The world's 2,153 billionaires collectively have as much wealth as the assets of the poorest 4.6 billion people, or 60 percent of the world's population.[61] Overall, the richest 1 percent of the world has as much as the rest of the world combined.[62]

---

[58] Susannah Heschel, ed., *Abraham Joshua Heschel: Essential Writings* (Maryknoll, NY: Orbis Books, 2011), 66.

[59] I am grateful to David R. Loy, who first gave me this insight into the concept of "money-theism." See David R. Loy, "The West against the Rest? A Buddhist Response to 'The Clash of Civilizations,'" in *The Twenty-First Century Confronts Its Gods: Globalization, Technology, and War*, ed. David J. Hawkin (Albany: State University of New York Press, 2004). See also Daniel G. Groody, *Globalization, Spirituality and Justice: Navigating the Path to Peace* (Maryknoll, NY: Orbis Books, 2017), 23–25.

[60] Richard Falk, "The Monotheistic Religions in the Era of Globalization," *Global Dialogue* 1, no. 1 (1999): 148.

[61] Oxfam International, "World's Billionaires Have More Wealth Than 4.6 Billion People," January 20, 2020, www.oxfam.org.

[62] Some of the most significant studies on global poverty and global inequali-

The asymmetries of wealth diverge along gender lines as well. Every day, women and girls contribute literally billions of hours of unpaid labor in care sectors, such as childcare, education and health. Meanwhile, the twenty-two richest men in the world have more wealth than all the women in Africa.[63]

These disorders are rooted in unjust structures, but as the Second Vatican Council said, they are also rooted in the disorders of the human heart (*Gaudium et Spes* 10). Without attending to the original, personal, and social sins that cause these disorders, we mistakenly see migration as the problem in itself rather than a symptom of much deeper imbalances. These imbalances are woven into the light and darkness of humanity's immigration story.

While the United States has traditionally been perceived as a country that has virtuously opened its door to immigrants, its sins are also part of its own narratives. America has been a country of imperialism, racism, nativism, militarism, and other sins. While many of these are hardly unique to the United States, as Peter Schrag notes, "What makes them significant in America is that they run almost directly counter to the nation's founding ideals. At least since the enshrinement of Enlightenment ideas of equality and inclusiveness in the founding documents of the new

---

ties come from the United Nations and the World Bank. In particular see the annual human development and world development reports: *Human Development Report 2005: International Cooperation at a Crossroads* (New York: United Nations, 2005); *Inequality Predicament: Report on the World Social Situation 2005* (New York: United Nations, 2005); and *World Development Report 2006: Equity and Development* (New York: Oxford University Press, 2005). See also Jeffrey Sachs, *The End of Poverty: Economic Possibilities for Our Time* (East Rutherford, NJ: Penguin Press, 2005); Branko Milanovic, *Worlds Apart: Measuring International and Global Inequality* (Princeton, NJ: Princeton University Press, 2005); and Bob Sutcliffe, *100 Ways of Seeing an Unequal World* (London: Zed Books, 2001). The World Bank describes three degrees of poverty: extreme or absolute poverty, moderate poverty, and relative poverty. *Extreme poverty* means living on less than $1.25 per day. People in this category do not have enough to survive and lack the basic necessities of life; extreme poverty is "poverty that kills." More than eight million people worldwide die each year—twenty-two thousand die each day—because they are too poor to survive. *Moderate poverty* is defined as living on $1.25 to $2 per day. People in this category have just barely the basic needs of life. *Relative poverty*, defined as a household income below the national average, means a living standard below the common middle class. See www.worldbank.org and Sachs, *The End of Poverty*. See also Groody, *Globalization, Spirituality, and Justice: Navigating a Path to Peace*, 1–32.

[63] Oxfam International, "World's Billionaires Have More."

nation, to be a nativist in this country was to be in conflict with its fundamental tenets."[64]

Such attitudes have resulted in blatant exclusionary policies, and many other forms of discrimination have embedded themselves in social structures in more subtle and pernicious ways. Not only have anti-immigrant mentalities continued, but in times of social and economic challenges, immigrants have become easy targets and frequent scapegoats for the country's anxiety and unrest. All these sins are rooted in a common issue, namely, the fear of "otherness," which we discuss more later.

Nonetheless, no matter how one frames the American story, immigration is an integral part of the historical landscape. As Robert Guest puts it, "Thanks to immigration, America enjoys intimate ties with every other culture. America is 'polygamously' married to every other nation."[65] And alongside its sins are its success stories. Immigration has also enabled God's glory to shine forth as human begins begin to flourish and discover all that it means to be created in God's image and likeness.

**The Human Person Fully Alive**

Even with its long history of nativism, racism, and xenophobia, the United States has offered opportunities to generations of immigrants who have sought to find on its shores a space where they can become fully human and fully alive. For those marginalized and excluded in their homelands, the United States has often symbolized a place of hope and possibility. For those persecuted and violated, it has represented a land of refuge and protection under the law. For those pressed down and oppressed, it has been a country of freedom of worship and social equality. Over time this vision has been born of struggle, fostered in the furnace of creativity, forged on the frontier, fired through hard work, and often inspired by religious faith and the enduring belief in the dignity of the human person. And although its achievements in the areas of economics, culture, and science have given expression to the glory revealed in the human person, its life-giving spirit at the service of the common good has also revealed the glory of God in the care of others.

The founding mythology of the United States offers a set of ideals that has shaped American consciousness and that is inseparable from the immi-

---

[64] Schrag, *Not Fit*, 2.
[65] Robert Guest, *Borderless Economics: Chinese Sea Turtles, Indian Fridges, and the New Fruits of Global Capitalism* (New York: Palgrave Macmillan, 2011), 181.

grant story. According to the mainstream narrative of the nation's founding, the rugged conditions of an unsettled land have given rise to an enterprising and adventurous spirit. As migrants ventured into new territory in the West, they also left behind some of the psychological territory of the old world of Europe, forging a new social territory that has become a testing ground for the ideals of democracy and self-determination, justice and equality, peace and prosperity, liberty and opportunity.

Since its founding, the United States hast been host to the largest population of immigrants in the world. Over 44.7 million people living in the United States are first-generation immigrants.[66] Some of the better known include naturalist John Muir, who immigrated in 1849 and is known today as the father of our National Park System. Joseph Pulitzer immigrated to Boston in 1853 and built a legacy in journalism and the arts. Nobel Prize–winner Albert Einstein immigrated to the United States in 1933 and became one of the greatest physicists of the twentieth century. David Ho emigrated from Taiwan in the 1960s and was named *Time* magazine's "Man of the Year" for his pioneering work in AIDS research. In 2016, all six Nobel Prize winners in the United States in economics and the science fields were immigrants.[67]

And the list goes on. Athletes like Patrick Ewing and Martina Navratilova, entertainers like Gloria Estefan and Neil Young, actors like Sydney Poitier and Audrey Hepburn, political figures like Madeleine Albright and Henry Kissinger, and businesspeople like Andrew Carnegie and Sergey Brin all came to the United States as immigrants and left behind legacies in the arts and sciences, sports and entertainment, politics and business. Immigrants have been at the heart of making America great; they have brought with them a spirit of hard work, hospitality, sacrifice, innovation, self-determination, creativity, and entrepreneurship.[68]

In the first part of the twenty-first century, immigrants in America started 25 percent of all public companies backed by venture capital; they have also founded some of the most robust companies in our current economy, like Intel, Sun Microsystems, eBay, Yahoo!, and Google.[69] These

---

[66] Jeanne Batalova, Brittany Blizzard, and Jessica Bolter, "Frequently Requested Statistics on Immigrants and Immigration in the United States," Migration Policy Institute, February 14, 2020, www.migrationpolicy.org.

[67] Stuart Anderson, "Immigrants Flooding America with Nobel Prizes," *Forbes*, October 16, 2016.

[68] Richard Kluger, "The Old Frontiers," *The New Republic*, May 7, 2008.

[69] Report of the University of Denver Strategic Issues Panel on Immigration,

companies employ thousands of US workers, many in specialized industries such as biotechnology and computer science.

But it would be too reductive to see the glory of the human person only in light of financial success or cultural recognition. That glory is also revealed in a generosity of spirit, especially toward society's most vulnerable members, and in order to make life better for the good of all. Immigrants have constructed our roads, taught in our schools, and built our hospitals. They have created our families, healed our wounds, taught our children, and nurtured our spirits. St. Frances Cabrini, in 1889, to cite one example, emigrated to the United States to found orphanages and assist poor and vulnerable immigrants. She made real the paraphrased words of the second-century church father Irenaeus, who said, "The Glory of God is the person fully alive, and the life of a person is the vision of God."[70]

The glory of a nation has been revealed in the flourishing of its peoples, the empowering of the poor, and the inclusion of the marginalized. As it has welcomed those from other lands, it often has seen a mirror of its own story in the story of migrants and refugees. While some political currents have sought to counter this same spirit throughout history, the American story is inextricably intertwined with the immigrant story, and it has resettled more refugees than any other country in the world.

The Catholic Church within the United States has animated much of the spirit toward refugees, especially because so many Catholics themselves have ancestral connections to other countries. Catholics continue to resettle approximately 30 percent of all refugees arriving in America; if it were a country of its own, it would be the second-largest resettler of refugees on the planet. In the pages that follow we explore the integral connection between the Christian story and the immigrant story in much greater detail.[71] But for now, it is time to step back, pause, and listen to a deeper spirit at work underneath the movement of peoples.

---

*Architecture for Immigration Reform: Fitting the Pieces of Public Policy* (November 2009), 36.

[70] Paraphrased from Irenaeus, *Against Heresies* 4.20.7, in Iustinus Martyr and Irenaeus Lugdunensis, *The Ante-Nicene Fathers: Justin Martyr, Irenaeus,* ed. Alexander Roberts, James Donaldson, and Arthur Cleveland Coxe (Edinburgh: T&T Clark, 1989), 490. The actual quote from this source is, "For the glory of God is a living man; and the life of man consists in beholding God."

[71] United States Conference of Catholic Bishops, "Resettlement Services," www.usccb.org.

## Biblical Narratives and Migration

Throughout this chapter we have explored how the story of migration is as old as the human story. It is an ancient theme with a new face. As we have laid out some foundational dimensions of the global phenomenon of migration, we have seen how migration is connected to our past and our present. We have explored how it is intertwined with our biological and familial stories as well as our national and spiritual identities. We observed that migration has brought out the best and the worst in us. And we have considered how it is both a sign of the times and a challenge to the human conscience. With nearly a billion people migrating around the world, including 272 million international migrants, our own day is appropriately deemed the "age of migration."[72]

Because the problems of migration today are complex and challenging, we need more than arguments of political pragmatism, economic efficiency, or utilitarian logic if we are to find an immigration reform that is comprehensive, just, and durable. More than even more information, we need a new vision and imagination for who we are before God and who we are called to be to each other. For that to happen, we need a deeper spirit of contemplation, or the ability to step back, listen, and look within and from above to rewire the unhealthy mindsets that alienate us from God and one another. Only with transformed minds and hearts can we faithfully discern God's presence amid such issues and our response to them. Only then can we make a stronger connection between what is happening inside of churches with what is happening outside them.

In the context of speaking to Jesuits in Thailand during the global refugee crisis, Fr. Pedro Arrupe said, "Pray. Pray much. Problems such as these are not solved by human efforts.... We have to be enlightened by the Holy Spirit.... There has to be a basic unity of minds for this new type of apostolate just about to be born."[73] This perspective begins with looking for wisdom beyond our own opinions and cultivating an ability to listen to the undercurrents of human experience that are operative underneath the debates and controversies surrounding migration. Given the busyness of our

---

[72] Stephen Castles and Mark J. Miller, *The Age of Migration: International Population Movements in the Modern World*, 4th ed. (New York: Guilford Press, 2009).

[73] Kevin Burke, ed., *Pedro Arrupe: Essential Writings* (Maryknoll, NY: Orbis Books, 2004), 168–71.

lives and the hurried pace of our world, this work of discernment is particularly difficult—and is impossible unless there is a willingness to change and migrate beyond our own mindsets.

It also entails listening to the stories from the past that put us in touch with enduring truths that transcend the vicissitudes of cultural debates, self-centered politics, and partisan concerns. One of the places where we can search for such wisdom is the Sacred Scriptures. Because migration has been going on since the beginning of human history, and because it figures prominently in the Bible, how can the Scriptures give us new insight in understanding the contemporary issues of migration, and how can migration give us a new vantage point from which to read the Scriptures?

The Bible has much to say about migration and the challenges we face in our own times.[74] But before examining a biblical understanding of migration in more detail, I want to say a few words about migration studies and theology, a biblical spirituality of migration, and the critical correlation between biblical narratives and our own personal narratives. Our aim is not to offer proof-texted responses to predetermined positions about migration but rather to search for wisdom and discern a faith-based response to this difficult issue.

Because of the complex problems and opportunities at work within the global phenomenon of migration, scholars from virtually every discipline have taken up this subject and studied it in different ways.[75] Much of the literature is dominated by the social sciences, and by and large the discipline of theology has been left on the margins of the conversation until very recently. While the social sciences have added much to our understanding of migration issues, their own methodological approaches and

---

[74] For this reason in this section of the book, I use what biblical scholars call the *historical present tense*, which is a way of reading the Scriptures not just as something that happened in the past and is over but also as a living word that speaks to us in our own times.

[75] The field is vast, and only a brief sampling of some of the literature is possible here. Some of the most common approaches are in the social sciences and humanities. Political theorist Joseph Carens, for instance, has tried to overcome the operative dualism by rooting his analysis in the importance of "social membership." He argues that human dignity offers an important starting point for sifting through the issues and agendas in the arguments and is indispensable for reaching just resolutions to the debate. See Joseph Carens, *The Ethics of Immigration* (New York: Oxford University Press, 2013).

disciplinary commitments limit the scope of the questions they explore.⁷⁶ Since migration raises central questions related to who we are before God and to each other, theology can make important contributions to the existing literature.

Exploring the connection between the Bible and migration is not an easy task, especially because the Bible can be used to legitimate underlying political biases, distorted perceptions, and ideological agendas. Throughout history it has been invoked to justify all kinds of abuses including war (Ecclus. 3:1, 8), slavery (Gn. 9:25–27; Lv. 25:44), murder (Gn. 10:5; 11:9), genocide (Ex. 34:11–14), racism (1 Tm. 6:1), anti-Semitism (1 Thes. 2:14–15), and sexism (1 Tm. 2:11–15), among other injustices. It can also be used to affirm narrow positions and predetermined conclusions for or against migration, which I hope to avoid here.

When done in a spirit of humility—and as seen as a first word about God rather than a final one—theology can help us reflect on important issues related to creation, community, meaning, compassion, healing, connection, and many others. It asks who God is, who we are, why we are here, how we are called to live together, and where we are going. In addition to reflecting more consciously about divine realities, theology offers us the opportunity to ask what it means to live authentically before God.

Christian theology starts from the premise that our lives are ultimately interconnected and interdependent with each other, and therefore the fundamental task of life is to work out the healing, just ordering, and integration of our relationships. In the context of the world's disorders, theology speaks first and foremost about the need for reordering these relationships through conversion, repentance, grace, ethics, solidarity, and redemption—all of which are directed toward finding our true selves in God and building a more humane society.

---

⁷⁶ Philosopher Martha Nussbaum highlights how emotions (more specifically "political emotions") shape our deliberations. These emotions influence the way we understand social values like equality, respect, and compassion, which give rise to the primacy of love. She argues that without prioritizing love, a society will eventually unravel because justice itself cannot prevail. For Nussbaum, justice involves more than legal adjudication, democratic principles, or human dignity, as Carens puts it; justice, she argues, is about making possible human flourishing and inspiring people to sacrifice for the common good, not just their personal self-interests. See Martha Nussbaum, *Political Emotions: Why Love Matters for Justice* (Cambridge, MA: Harvard University Press, 2013).

In addition to exploring the connection between migration and theology, this section focuses on migration and biblical spirituality. Theology and spirituality have a close, integral relationship with each other, but they are not synonymous. Whereas theology traditionally is about faith seeking understanding, spirituality is about the lived experience of that faith and how it transforms us into becoming loving, generous, and wise.

In the most general terms, spirituality has to do with how one lives out what one most values. Christian spirituality, as a very specific expression of spirituality, has to do with what Jesus most valued. At the heart of what Jesus valued was the Kingdom of God. Vatican II describes this as "a kingdom eternal and universal, a kingdom of truth and life, of holiness and grace, of justice, love and peace" (*Gaudium et Spes* 39). Biblical spirituality has to do with what happens when our values meet Jesus' values, or when his Kingdom meets our kingdoms, especially through the scriptural text. This process either moves us toward the reign of likeness to God through obedience, or it drives us further away from it into an existential exile.

In recent decades, spirituality has also emerged as a field of study. Spirituality as an academic discipline investigates experience as such and seeks to understand its multidimensionality. It engages theology but draws upon other disciplines in order to understand the complex experience of human beings in relationship to God. In other words, spirituality is a bridge discipline. While this book has a strong theological focus, it also draws upon history, sociology, psychology, anthropology, economics, and political science. The disciplinary sinew that holds the body of this particular work together is spirituality.

As Sandra Schneiders puts it, biblical spirituality is "a transformative process of personal and communal engagement with the biblical text. The scholar, the non-specialist, and perhaps especially the minister called to mediate the Word to others can approach the text not merely as an historical record or even as a literary mediation of religious meaning but as the Word of God."[77] The process of transformation is about what happens when our personal narratives meet the narratives of the Scriptures in the context of what is happening in the world.

---

[77] See Sandra M. Schneiders, "Biblical Spirituality," *Interpretation* 56, no. 2 (2002): 136. See also Sandra Schneiders, *The Revelatory Text: Interpreting the New Testament as Sacred Scripture,* 2nd ed. (Collegeville, MN: Liturgical Press, 1999), 27–63.

Our disposition before God is an important foundation to biblical interpretation. Openness to the gift of God's love through grace helps heal the wounds of our inner nature that distort our reading of reality caused by sin.[78] Without a healing of our disordered inner nature, our perceptions of what we see—including how we understand issues like migration—will be skewed; we end up looking at the world as if through the prism of a circus mirror.

For biblical spirituality to have this transformative effect, more is required than cognitive data about the text or mastering specific techniques of interpretation. Rather, it involves an inner "migration" of its own, in the sense that it means moving from our fallen selves and toward our redeemed selves in God in order to become "another Christ," who embodies the authentic image and likeness of God. One of the foremost Christian theologians on this subject is St. Augustine.

In his work *De doctrina Christiana*, which is one of the most influential texts on biblical interpretation in Western history, Augustine notes that reading the Bible fruitfully begins with humble prayer and contemplation. In his words, "Whoever, then, thinks that he understands the Holy Scriptures, or any part of them, but puts such an interpretation upon them as does not tend to build up this twofold love of God and our neighbor, does not yet understand them as he ought."[79] Moreover, Augustine draws on this notion

---

[78] See Augustine, *De doctrina Christiana* 1.36.40.

[79] Ibid. The "hermeneutical principle of charity" is also presented in other sections of *De doctrina* as well as in the *Confessions*. In the case of the former, see, for instance, Augustine, *De doctrina Christiana* 3.10.14 ("Whatever there is in the word of God that cannot, when taken literally, be referred either to purity of life or soundness of doctrine, you may set down as figurative. Purity of life has reference to the love of God and one's neighbor; soundness of doctrine to the knowledge of God and one's neighbor"); Augustine, *De doctrina Christiana* 3.10.15–16 ("Now Scripture enjoins nothing except charity, and condemns nothing except lust, and in that way fashions the lives of men.... I mean by charity that affection of the mind which aims at the enjoyment of God for His own sake, and the enjoyment of one's self and one's neighbor in subordination to God; by lust I mean that affection of the mind which aims at enjoying one's self and one's neighbor, and other corporeal things, without reference to God"). In the *Confessions,* see, for example, 12.25.35 ("Let us not, then, be puffed up for one against the other, above that which is written; let us love the Lord our God with all our heart, with all our soul, and with all our mind, and our neighbor as ourself. As to which two precepts of charity, unless we believe that Moses meant whatever in these books he did mean, we shall make God a liar when we think otherwise concerning our fellow-servants' mind than He has taught us").

of migration when he writes, "We have wandered far from God," and we must reorient our lives "if we wish to return to our Father's home."[80] Augustine maintains that love is essential to our return migration to God, and the person who makes love most evident in human form is Jesus Christ.[81]

God's self-revelation in Christ reveals God's heart and thereby how God loves and how we in turn are called to love. In the end, love is the key that opens the meaning of the Scriptures and leads us into understanding the whole meaning of human existence. As the Scriptures lead us through a process of the transformation of the heart, they call us to build a better world through a conversion to love and justice. We explore this story—and its connection to our own—in more detail in the following pages. We discover the ways that this love is made known to us through God's migration to the human race, and how it helps us not only find our way home but how to live, to love, and to become authentically human in this world.

As we read the Scriptures, we encounter a range of narratives. Our reading also brings us face-to-face with ourselves. What is the relationship between the narratives in the scriptural texts and the narratives formed over time in the text of our own lives? To explore this question, we need to become more aware of the narratives that shape our consciousness through our culture, conditioning, and personal and collective choices. The Scriptures can affirm the ways these inner stories are in sync with the Spirit of God, but they can also challenge them, especially in those spaces where we are most out of alignment with divine designs. When the Scriptures disrupt the stories that have been scripted in us over time, they have the potential to transform our hearts and offer us a new way of living and being in the world.[82]

Because the Scriptures do not offer a clear immigration policy that can be easily applied to our current challenges, no single narrative or theology of migration appears in them. The Bible has a range of narratives about migration, and the diversity of their historical contexts—and the complexity of

---

[80] Augustine, *De doctrina Christiana* 1.4.4.
[81] See Augustine, *Confessions* 13.9.10.
[82] In Ricoeur's words, "Religious language—at least this religious language—uses limit-expressions only to open up our very experience, to make it explode in the direction of experiences that themselves are limit-experiences. . . . But it does not redescribe it in the fashion of one more poetic language among others, but according to its intending of the extreme." By "extreme," Ricoeur is referring to the impact that religious experience can have on people's lives. See Paul Ricoeur, *Figuring the Sacred: Religion, Narrative, and Imagination* (Minneapolis: Fortress Press, 1995), 43–44, 61.

issues surrounding these texts—brings out tensions within the text, just as we deal with tensions in our own times. Our goal is not to eliminate these tensions but through them to discern the ways in which the Bible discloses a transgenerational message that can transform the narratives within us that shape our contemporary consciousness about migrants and migration.[83]

I draw primarily from the Scriptures in their historical and literary contexts, as well as from the context of migration today. Nonetheless, I do not pretend to offer an in-depth work in historical criticism or literary analysis. Others are more skilled than I at this task, and I would be the first to admit that more detailed exegetical work is needed beyond what I do here. My intent, rather, is to offer some of the broad outlines of a theology of migration rooted in biblical spirituality. In much the same way that a builder would take string and stakes to delimit a construction site before a future building project, I offer an outline on this subject with the hopes that other scholars down the road will dig into this topic and build it out in more detail.

Instead of doing a literal reading of the text and applying it to the issue of migration, my focus is to do a literary reading of the text to see how this approach can liberate us and help us discover more life-giving narratives. One way to begin this is by attending to biblical archetypes, central characters, and root metaphors that shape the central story lines of the Scriptures. As Diane Bergant puts it,

> Biblical language is basically metaphorical in character. Imaginative and paradoxical, it opens us to possibilities of expression and insight that precise philosophical or descriptive discourse cannot provide. It generates impressions rather than propositions. It seeks to capture the power and emotion of the event of God and to draw the hearer (only secondarily the reader) into an experience that transcends both the past and the present, and opens to the future. It is impor-

---

[83] In broad terms, three major paradigms of biblical studies have bearing on our discussion. The first is the premodern approach, which is largely an uncritical faith-based reading of the text that often involves proof-texting to uphold one's respective position. The second is the modern approach, characterized largely by a historical-critical reading of the text. The third is more of a postmodern approach, which takes seriously the reader's response to these texts. My approach draws on the second and third approaches with an eye toward understanding how the literary text itself can offer a liberating approach to our subject under study.

tant to understand this dimension of religious language, not only for the sake of a method of interpretation that will reveal original meanings (theological reconstruction), but also for the sake of one that will provide new understandings (constructive theology).[84]

I make the case here that migration is not only one of the central root metaphors in the Scriptures but is also key to understanding the meaning of human existence. What makes this process more complicated today, as David Tracy rightly points out, is that faith-based claims assumed as self-evident in previous generations can no longer be taken for granted. Consequently, in our pluralistic and postmodern society, theologians have the moral and intellectual responsibility to make these claims accessible, intelligible, and compelling to the wider public—not just to one's religious "tribe."[85] One way to speak to a broader community is through what he calls a method of critical correlation.[86]

---

[84] Diane Bergant, "Ruth: The Migrant Who Saved the People," in *Migration, Religious Experience, and Globalization,* eds. Gioacchino Campese and Pietro Ciallella (New York: Center for Migration Studies, 2003), 49.

[85] Tracy recognizes the importance of Christian doctrines and the relevance of the church's interpretation of them, but also invites people to assess their internal coherence and intrinsic truth claims. In order for this to happen, both the Church and the modern world need a spirit of humility. While the issues related to the modern world are a subject of their own, Tracy's point is that, as the church enters into dialogue with the modern world, it must do so not just as teacher but as listener. A different kind of wall is created when it does not enter into a space of mutuality through honest and open dialogue with human experience and language. Only if there is this *fusion of horizons*, as hermeneutical theory refers to it, can insight and wisdom emerge. See David Tracy, *Blessed Rage for Order: The New Pluralism in Theology* (Chicago: University of Chicago Press, 1996), 10–14, where the author presents his critical remarks regarding the secular mind.

[86] See ibid., 43–46, and esp. chapter 3 for a summary of the argument. Later Tracy refers to the method of critical correlation as the analogical imagination. The analogical imagination is rooted in two principal sources for Christian theological reflection: (1) Christian texts and doctrines, and (2) human experience and language. The former involves the Sacred Scriptures and their tradition of interpretation; the latter, everyday life and the diverse language games at play in human experience, which also include the scientific description of experience, the arts, and other means. In Tracy's method, both sources must be in permanent and critical conversation with each other if religious claims are to speak to the wider public. He maintains that Christian beliefs offer an important lens through which to interpret human experience, but he also maintains that human experience and language should have a mutual role in

Tracy claims that, for such correlation to happen, a "classic" text is needed.[87] He makes the claim that the Bible is a classic text because it narrates "the classic event for the Christian, [i.e.,] the religious event of God's self-manifestation in the person of Jesus the Christ: an event that happened, happens, and will happen."[88] This truth must be rediscovered, rearticulated, and reappropriated in every generation. The value of the classic rests not in popular vote nor rigid, linear logic but in the truth that they "artistically" center on the person of Jesus in the Gospels, the doctrines of Christian faith, the lives of the saints, and the lived experience of believers.

With Tracy's framework in mind, we can make the case that the Scriptures offer more to us than stories about migrants and migration.[89] They offer instead "classic events" that can disclose enduring truths about the meaning of life itself. As they speak to the spirit of sacrifice, the capacity of resilience, the gift of empathy, and the challenge of human solidarity, they

---

reshaping our understanding of Christian beliefs. See David Tracy, *The Analogical Imagination: Christian Theology and the Culture of Pluralism* (New York: Crossroad, 1981), esp. chapter 10 and the epilogue for a summary of the argument. For some of the differences between the method of critical correlation of *Blessed Rage for Order* and the approach of *The Analogical Imagination* and Tracy's later work, see the preface to the 1996 edition of the first book. Also, *The Analogical Imagination* provides a great number of clarifications about the differences in its footnotes. In my view the differences are not substantial, but instead represent an effort of refining the previous version of the method, particularly being more aware of the plurality and ambiguity in the methodological steps themselves.

[87] "What we mean in naming certain texts, events, images, rituals, symbols and persons 'classics,'" Tracy notes, "is that here we recognize nothing less than the disclosure of a reality we cannot but name truth." He goes on to say, "When a text is a classic, I am also recognizing that its 'excess of meaning' both demands constant interpretation and bears certain kind of timelessness.... That is, the classical text is not in some timeless moment which needs mere repetition. Rather its kind of timelessness as permanent timelessness is the only one proper to any expression of the finite, temporal, historical beings we are. The classic text's real disclosure is its claim to attention on the ground that an event of understanding proper to finite human beings has here found expression." Tracy, *The Analogical Imagination*, 102, 108.

[88] Ibid., 249.

[89] David Tracy, "The Catholic Imagination: The Example of Michaelangelo," in A. Bolton et al., *Heavenly Bodies: Fashion and the Catholic Imagination* (New York: Metropolitan Museum of Art, 2018), 15.

can liberate us from psychosocial patterns that enslave us and help us find the path to personal and communal flourishing.

In summary, here we explore how the Scriptures give us insight into the issue of migration and how migration can give us a new way of understanding the Scriptures. We do not just want to interpret the Bible; we want to explore how the Bible interprets us and helps us see our own life in light of migration. As it illuminates the mystery of God's migration to us, it also helps us understand our collective migration through this world and ultimately our return migration to God.

Because theology is done at the border between the past and the future, our task is to correlate the truths of faith with the challenges of our time. Through this *border-correlation method*, as I call it, we seek to better make the integral connection between migration in biblical times and the stories of migrants, refugees, and victims of human trafficking in our own time. By doing so, we hope to discover how the phenomenon of migration itself has the potential to disclose truth not only for the liberation of others but for ourselves.[90] Ultimately what is at stake is our humanity, our journey through this world, or—in a word—our salvation.

---

[90] Biblical scholars and theologians from the Global South have also contributed to this discussion by calling for more responsible and ethical scholarship that recognizes the ways in which Scripture functions to determine and prescribe norms for how people live (see, e.g., Musa Dube, Madiponae Masenya, Dora Mbuwayesango, and Sarojini Nadar). They have argued that it is not enough for the biblical scholar to provide pathways to understanding what the text meant in its own context, but more importantly to understand how the text functions in our current context. While many scholars within the liberation tradition have sought to show how the text functions to genuinely free people, I am interested in searching the Scriptures for resources that enable us to see the manifold opportunities that migration presents for Christians to demonstrate the love of God.

# Part Two

# The Biblical Narratives

*Migration and the Christian Scriptures*

# 2

# The First Reading:
# The Old Testament and Migration

*You know the heart of an alien, for you were aliens in the land of Egypt.* (Ex. 23:9)

As the drama of immigration plays out at the US-Mexico border and in other parts of the world, a biblical archetype is unfolding. In our own times, as in the days of the Old Testament, there are famine and the slave trade; family betrayal and human trafficking; new pharaohs that oppress and newly oppressed people; taskmasters and harsh labor; brickmaking and empire building. There are cries to heaven and the hope for deliverance, rivers to cross and mountains to ascend, leaders to guide and deserts to traverse. There are new armies and new chariots. There are wilderness and wandering; exile and displacement; scouts and spies; tent cities and cities of refuge; there are deportees and returnees; the hope for freedom and the vision of a Promised Land. And, in the midst of this epic journey—as humanity's fragmented and broken condition unfurls before us—the mercy of God breaks forth in new and surprising ways.[1]

---

[1] In the second part of the Eucharistic celebration, the Church proclaims the Scriptures in the Liturgy of the Word. On Sundays, four readings are read, and each comes from a different part of the Bible. The first usually comes from a section of the Old Testament. The second, the Responsorial Psalms, comes, as its name indicates, from the book of Psalms. The third, depending on the liturgical season, comes either from the Acts of the Apostles, an Epistle (the majority of which were written by Paul), or the book of Revelation. And the fourth comes from the Gospels. These readings give expression to the continuity of the work of salvation in both Testaments, in which the central focus is Jesus Christ, who calls us to holiness through our participation in the paschal mystery. As the Introduction to the Lectionary notes, "Throughout the liturgical year, but above all during the seasons of Easter, Lent, and Advent, the choice and

Migration runs through all these stories like a golden thread of revelation. It stitches together a tapestry of human experiences—and like today, sometimes this migration is voluntary, and sometimes it is involuntary. It is linked to disaster and destiny, to curse and blessing, and to human crisis and divine providence. In many ways, migration is inextricably connected to the journey of faith and often functions as a root metaphor for the search for a deeper knowledge of God, the hope for a better life, and the path of salvation. The biblical narratives, filled with persons and nations that experienced many of the same things we are undergoing now, transform our journey into a spiritual adventure.

Because the human person often gets lost amid the conflict and controversies of migration, we first look at migration in the Scriptures through the lens of the biblical figures who themselves were migrants. They include Adam and Eve; Abraham, Sarah, and Hagar; Moses and the Israelites; Ruth and the Prophets; and the Jewish people in the Diaspora. We also explore how their migrations are integrally related to important theological themes like the fall, vocation, covenant, the exodus, the desert, the foreigner, the land, and human solidarity. Intertwined with the core theological themes of the Scriptures, these migrants shaped Israel's character as a people, their relationship with God, and their responsibility to people on the move.

### Adam, Eve, and the Fall: The Migration from Home

> The LORD God sent him forth from the garden of Eden.
> (Gn. 3:23 NRSV)

Genesis is commonly referred to as the book of "beginnings." It introduces theological prototypes, spiritual archetypes, and foundational themes for the rest of the Scriptures. Migration is one of these. It emerges so frequently

---

sequence of readings are aimed at giving the faithful an ever-deepening perception of the faith they profess and of the history of salvation." Thus, "the Order of Readings for Mass aptly presents from Scripture the principal deeds and words belonging to the history of salvation. As its many phases and events are recalled in the Liturgy of the Word, the faithful will come to see that the history of salvation is contained here and now in the representation of Christ's paschal mystery celebrated through the Eucharist." See the Catholic Church in England and Wales, Liturgy Office, England and Wales, *General Introduction to the Lectionary*, 61, www.liturgyoffice.org.uk.

that Andrew Walls rightly suggests that the book of Genesis might well have been named the book of "migrations."[2]

We meet the first migrants of the Bible in the Garden of Eden. They are the first to set up residence in a "homeland," and they are the first to leave it as forced migrants. This initial migration is involuntary and punitive; it follows from the first couple's misguided decisions and results not only in a movement from home but a movement into a foreign land (Gn. 3:24).

Although the text makes note of a geographical dislocation from Eden, the story speaks to something more fundamental: a movement from being at home with our true selves to living in a state of alienation. We cannot adequately read the human drama of migration today without first viewing it through the lens of this primordial migration. With the breaking of God's commands, the "illegal alien," or the "disconnected self," breaks into human history.

Before the fall, human beings live in harmony with their Creator, other creatures, and all of creation. They dwell in paradise and live in ordered relationships expressed through mutual care and concern. But with the fall, human beings begin moving away from God's image and likeness, from their true home, and from their integral connection to others. This original sin so distorts our inner nature that it warps how we see the world and those around us. We lose a sense of who we are before God and who we are in relationship to others.

The fall offers us an important vantage point from which to read contemporary challenges. Pope Francis has drawn upon this text in his own reflection on the global refugee crisis. Shortly after he began his pontificate, a tragic shipwreck happened off the coast of Lampedusa, Italy, and hundreds of refugees perished. Moved by this tragedy, Francis traveled to Lampedusa a few days later, and he began his remarks reflecting on the refugee crisis in light of the book of Genesis:

> "Adam, where are you?" This is the first question which God asks man after his sin. "Adam, where are you?" Adam lost his bearings, his place in creation, because he thought he could be powerful, able to control everything, to be God. Harmony was lost; man erred and this error occurs over and over again also in relationships with

---

[2] Andrew F. Walls, "Mission and Migration: The Diaspora Factor in Christian History," *Journal of African Christian Thought* 5 (December 2002): 3–11.

others. "The other" is no longer a brother or sister to be loved, but simply someone who disturbs my life and my comfort. ("Homily of Holy Father Francis," July 8, 2013)

As a consequence of the fall, we humans begin to lose touch with our own humanity. Pope Francis poignantly asks,

> Has any one of us wept because of this situation [of migrants who have drowned in the Mediterranean] and others like it? Has any one of us grieved for the death of these brothers and sisters? Has any one of us wept for these persons who were on the [refugee] boat? For the young mothers carrying their babies? For these men who were looking for a means of supporting their families? We are a society which has forgotten how to weep, how to experience compassion–"suffering with" others: the globalization of indifference has taken from us the ability to weep! ("Homily of Holy Father Francis," July 8, 2013)

As the book of Genesis continues, the bonds of human interconnectedness unravel even further. After Cain murders his brother Abel, the Lord asks Cain about Abel's whereabouts, and he answers, "I do not know. Am I my brother's keeper?" (Gn. 4:9). Reading this story in light of the plight of migrants today, Francis continues, "The illusion of being powerful, of being as great as God, even of being God himself, leads to a whole series of errors, a chain of death, even to the spilling of a brother's blood!" ("Homily of Holy Father Francis," July 8, 2013).

Though lured into this state to protect something for himself, he begins to realize that his sin comes with a great price. His desire for independence has disconnected himself from his brother and left him isolated and restless. As punishment for murdering his brother, Cain is driven even further away from his homeland, from his God-given likeness, from his God-given family, from his God-given connection to others. Cain laments this alienation and confesses, "My punishment is greater than I can bear! Today you have driven me away from the soil, and I shall be hidden from your face; I shall be a fugitive and a wanderer on the earth" (Gn. 4:13–14).

With the breaking of God's command, then, the first forced migrants and "illegal aliens" enter the biblical stage. To become an illegal alien in this sense means becoming alienated from one's intimate connection with God, with other people, and one's authentic self. Although Adam and Eve were sent into exile, the story does not end there. We learn that Yahweh does not want human beings to remain in their alienation, nor does he desire to permanently seal off the borders of paradise to them and their descendants. In response, Yahweh sets in motion a series of merciful initiatives aimed at restoring them to their original, created natures. This movement back to the "home country" is another way of speaking about the journey of redemption.

This story of the fall provides us with an important prism through which to view the reality of migration today. Although some may connect it with an element of sin on behalf of the migrant, the more fundamental rooting of this story is in the problem of alienation, the rupturing of our relationships, and the warping of our perceptions. And as the story of sin and redemption continues to unfold, the return journey to God takes shape on the borderlands between the land of exile from the original garden (Gn. 2–3) and the land of promise in the new Jerusalem (Rv. 21).

**Abraham and the Covenant: Migration and the Promise**

> Yahweh said to Abram, "Leave your country, your kindred and your father's house for a country which I shall show you." (Gn. 12:1 NJB)

Unlike Adam and Eve, most migrants set out on the road because they dream of a better future. These dreams are a seed of promise, no matter how small. Nowhere in the Scriptures is the theme of migration and promise more intertwined than in the narrative of Abraham and his wife Sarah. Their story begins on a note of migration, but their lives reveal more than an account of their physical movements; they also speak to the journey from a state of alienation to one of connectedness, which takes place through the healing blessings of the covenant. The covenant is the central unifying theme of the Bible, and it lays the foundation for grace and redemption in the rest of the Scriptures. As E. A. Speiser puts it, "Abraham's journey to the Promised Land was thus no routine expedition of several hundred miles. Instead, it was the start of an epic voyage in search of spiritual truths, a quest that was to constitute the central theme of all biblical history."[3]

---

[3] E. A. Speiser, *Genesis: Introduction, Translation, and Notes* (New Haven, CT: Yale University Press, 2008), 1:88.

After the first eleven chapters of the Bible, the book of Genesis takes a decidedly different literary turn. The spotlight is put on Abraham and his family in the geographical area known today as the Middle East. This territory is one of the oldest continually inhabited regions of the world. With the Tigris and Euphrates Rivers running through its core, agriculture has flourished here, civilizations have prospered, and kingdoms have reigned for thousands of years.

Abraham and Sarah migrated through this land more than four thousand years ago.[4] Their journeys would have taken them across the borders of what we know today as Iraq, Turkey, Syria, Lebanon, Israel, Palestine, Egypt, and Jordan. They would have traveled seven hundred miles to the borders of present-day Iraq, then another seven hundred miles into Syria, then another eight hundred miles down to Egypt, and then back into Canaan, which is now Israel and Palestine. Ironically, this same geographical territory is still a major epicenter of the global refugee crisis today.

*The Migration of Abraham*

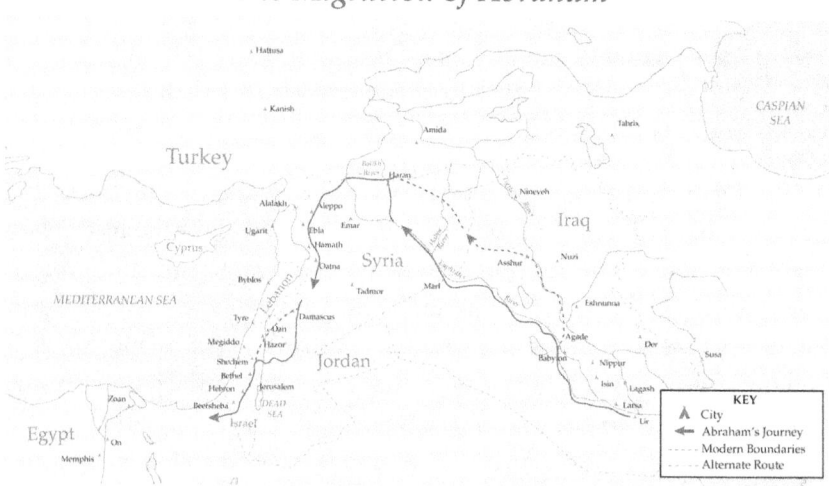

---

[4] Abraham's concubine Hagar also undergoes an arguably unjust, forced migration (Gn. 16:1–16; 21:8–21). By reading "with" Abraham and Sarah, I recognize that I am making, in some sense, a reading from the perspective of the "powerful." Several scholars within the liberation tradition have taken the time to show how narratives of this migration—and in particular of the exodus (Kirk-Duggan, Allen Warrior, Randall Bailey)—are not liberating for the *Am ha'aretz* (the people of the land), whose lands are colonized in the name of a God they do not worship or a promise they do not understand. I accept that this is a concern, even though I do not develop it at length here.

To understand this migration better, we need to delve more into Abraham's story. He was born in the city of Ur in the land of the Chaldeans, which is about 120 miles from the Persian Gulf and about 220 miles from contemporary Baghdad. Ur at the time had about one hundred thousand people, and it was a flourishing center of the neo-Babylonian/Chaldean Empire.[5]

The notion of empire in the Scriptures has complex connotations. More often than not it is negatively associated with abusive power, control, and self-sufficiency. In Ur—where more than five hundred gods and goddesses were worshipped—an idol-governed empire, egocentric nationalism, and self-interested tribalism were theologically reinforced. It drove its leaders to subjugate others to its imperial designs and disordered desires and to arrogate to themselves the power that belongs to God alone.[6]

While Yahweh commands Abram—which is his name at the beginning of the story, before it is changed to Abraham—to move to a different physical location, the substance of the calling involves more than a change of address: Yahweh ultimately calls Abram and his descendants to live and move in the world in a different way. We read in Genesis 12, "Yahweh said to Abram, 'Leave your country, your kindred and your father's house for a country which I shall show you; and I shall make you a great nation, I shall bless you and make your name famous; you are to be a blessing!'" (vv. 12:1–2 NJB). Accepting this call and setting out on the road entail not only leaving behind a specific geographical part of the world but also moving into an entirely different lifestyle, social system, and way of thinking.

In Abram's case, migration means letting go of all prior mindsets, conventional politics, and spiritual practices.[7] It demands surrendering any

---

[5] Shaped by the legendary King Hammurabi, Ur became a legendary commercial, cultural, and political center that had beautiful towers, palaces, gardens, monuments, temples, and shrines. Ur's proximity to seaports and the Indian Ocean made possible lucrative commercial connections to present-day Africa, India, Malaysia, and the Arabian Peninsula. Abram probably came from a wealthy merchant family, who bought and sold in Ur's prosperous marketplace.

[6] For more on empire, see R. S. Sugirtharajah, *The Bible and Empire: Postcolonial Explorations* (Cambridge: Cambridge University Press, 2005); Daniel G. Groody, *Globalization, Spirituality, and Justice: Navigating a Path to Peace* (Maryknoll, NY: Orbis Books, 2015), 36–39; Walter Brueggemann, "At the Mercy of Babylon: A Subversive Reading of the Empire," *Journal of Biblical Literature* 110, no. 1 (1991): 3.

[7] J. H. Walton, *Zondervan Illustrated Bible Backgrounds Commentary (Old Testament): Genesis, Exodus, Leviticus, Numbers, Deuteronomy* (Grand Rapids: Zondervan, 2009), 1:68.

fixed and settled notions of independence and self-sufficiency, and letting himself be powerless so that he could be subject to God and God alone. The call also entails leaving his kin and possibly his inheritance provided by his father's house. Because Ur was also a center of moon worship (along with other gods), he is called away from that religious world by a totally different God to a land he does not know.

Abram's experience highlights how migration from one's homeland inevitably involves various levels of physical, psychological, social, and emotional vulnerability. But his experience also highlights how an authentic calling can help people grow and develop in new ways when willing to migrate from familiar territory and into unknown spaces. In Abram (Abraham)'s case, moving from a place of control to a place of absolute risk and vulnerability inevitably demands unlearning and a re-forming an established mindset. Because this calling takes shape within the larger narratives of the covenant, it becomes a promising ground for development and transformation; although it involves leaving one world behind, it is also what makes a new world possible.

In Genesis 17, Yahweh renames Abram (Hebrew, "exalted father") as Abraham (Hebrew, "father of a multitude"). This renaming leaves room for interpretation, but for our purposes, might it bring out the ways in which Abraham was called to move beyond his tribal mindset to a more universal consciousness? However one reads it, Abraham's name change speaks to the way he experiences a new and expanded way of understanding of who he becomes in relationship to God and to others.

Because their migration is grounded in a journey of faith, however, the path that Abraham and Sarah travel is neither perfectly clear nor perfectly lived. It will demand trust without certainty, assurance without omniscience, and sometimes decisions without surety. Their journey presents many challenging ethical dilemmas along the way, like many migrants in our own times. When Abraham and Sarah cross the Egyptian border, Abraham lies about his relationship with Sarah and says she is his sister when confronted by Pharaoh's border patrol (Gn. 12:11–20). Such subterfuge may make contemporary readers bristle, but his use of essentially false documentation at border checkpoints is noteworthy. While he does not physically present papers, he hides the details of his identity from local authorities to keep them from taking advantage of them, like many migrants do in our own times.[8] Sarah's willing-

---

[8] V. H. Matthews, M. W. Chavalas, and J. H. Walton, *The IVP Bible Background*

ness to go to extraordinary lengths for the couple's survival has many parallels with those migrants today who subject themselves even to sexual exploitation to preserve themselves or their families (Gn. 12:15).

Did the kindnesses extended to Abraham and his family along the way shape and sensitize him later to the plight of others who were on the road? We do not know for sure, but the Scriptures make note of Abraham's hospitality to strangers. One day while looking outside his tent, Abraham sees three strangers and offers them water, shade, and food (Gn. 18:1–22). Such hospitality was expected in these times; indeed the Romans considered it a sacred obligation, the Greeks a virtue, and the Egyptians a pathway to a favorable afterlife.[9] For Abraham, however, hospitality was set against the horizon of the covenant; above all, it was a gracious response to the God who first called, guided, and provided for him on his journey.

In Abraham's case, the story of his hospitality also comes with a twist. We learn that while he provides gifts for these migrants, they paradoxically offer him a gift in return; they share the news of a blessing for him and his wife Sarah, who will bear a son, Isaac.[10] This theme of hospitality will become a defining characteristic of Israelite faith.[11] Like the migrant Abraham, Israel will come to understand in time their own moral duty to extend hospitality to the stranger, the sojourner, the alien, the foreigner, and the migrant (Dt. 26:5). The letter to the Hebrews will pick up on this story later when it says, "Do not neglect hospitality, for through it some have unknowingly entertained angels" (13:2).[12]

As Abraham's story unfolds, we learn that his migration involves a series of steps in trust, which deepen as he progresses on the journey. When Yahweh calls Abraham to bind Isaac and sacrifice him, Abraham is about to risk his whole family's future. As with his earlier migrations, he has to leave his secu-

---

*Commentary: Old Testament*, electronic ed. (Downers Grove, IL: InterVarsity Press, 2000).

[9] Leland Ryken, James C. Wilhoit, and Tremper Longman III, eds., *Dictionary of Biblical Imagery* (Downers Grove, IL: InterVarsity Press, 2000), 402.

[10] V. Matthews, "Hospitality and Hostility in Genesis 19 and Judges 19," *Biblical Theology Bulletin* 22 (1992): 3–11; W. Fields, *Sodom and Gomorrah* (Sheffield, UK: Sheffield Academic Press, 1997), 54–64.

[11] Ryken et al., 403.

[12] This subject of the divine presence under the guise of the migrant is also powerfully expressed in contemporary art, most notably in the work of Timothy Schmalz. Timothy P. Schmalz, *Angels Unawares*, September 5, 2019 (St. Peter's Square), https://angelsunawares.org.

rity behind and trust in a promise of a future he cannot see. Although this bond with Isaac is inseparable from his own bond with God, the summons to sacrifice his son tests his own priorities and shapes the person he becomes (Gn. 22:1–19). It is, in Jon Levenson's words, "a test of which is stronger, Abraham's fear of God or his love of Isaac."[13] We discover that this binding will only be released by an even more radical surrender to God en route to a new and uncharted land. Such faithfulness does not go without its reward.

The migration of Abraham and Sarah "etched a crescent of hope and faith so indelibly," says Malachi Martin, "that it determined the motive and course of events for centuries down to this day."[14] Their story will lay the foundation for the three monotheistic faiths. New Testament writers in time will look back to Abraham as a model of faith for future generations and a prototype for all who trust in God's promise in their migration through this world (Acts 7:2–50; Rom. 4:1–25; Gal. 3:1–29; Heb. 7:1–10; 6:13–14; 11). As the author of the letter to the Hebrews writes, "By faith Abraham obeyed when he was called to go out to a place that he was to receive as an inheritance; he went out, not knowing where he was to go" (Heb. 11:8). Like other migrants, he and his family will have to take each step forward with the hope and trust in a more promising future, which will be made clearer to them—not at the outset—but only with each successive step on the road of faith.

### Jacob and Identity: Migration and Border Crossings

> After he had taken them across the stream . . . Jacob was left there alone. Then some man wrestled with him until daybreak. (Gn. 32:23–24 NJB)

After the story of Abraham and Isaac, we meet Jacob. Genesis recounts three times when Jacob becomes a migrant: first he flees four hundred miles from his home to Haran because he fears death at the hand of his brother Esau (Gn. 27:42–44). The second time he seeks to escape exploitation and return to his homeland in Canaan (Gn. 31:1–22; 37:1). And the third time he leaves this homeland because of famine and migrates to Egypt (Gn. 41:53–

---

[13] Jon Levenson, *The Death and Resurrection of the Beloved Son: The Transformation of Child Sacrifice in Judaism and Christianity* (New Haven, CT: Yale University Press, 1993), 137.

[14] Malachi Martin, "Footsteps of Abraham," *New York Times*, March 13, 1983.

57; 42:1–2; 43:1; 45:6; 47:4).[15] How did these experiences of migration shape Jacob's identity? While the text gives us only a few clues, his experience of fear of death, abuse, fraudulent wages, exploitation, and poverty inevitably affected his life and his future (Gn. 29:15–27).

*The Migration of Jacob*

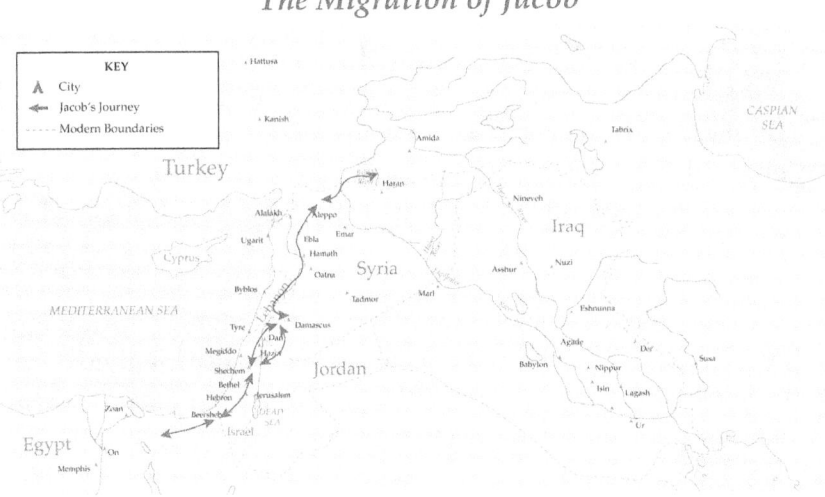

Although he faced many trials as a migrant, Jacob cannot be seen as just a victim of his circumstances. Like Adam and Eve, he was forced at times to migrate because of his own destructive choices. Other times he became an economic migrant because of poverty and oppression. Lest we romanticize biblical migrants—or those in our own day—Jacob could be stubborn, ruthless, deceitful, cunning, and manipulative (Gn. 25:19–34). It is not clear why Genesis dedicates half of its pages to his journey, but the contrast between divine grace and human sinfulness is striking. In between the story lines we see a merciful force at work that is greater than the character flaws of this divinely blessed migrant.[16] In fact, Jacob's experience as a migrant directly contributes to his conversion and transformation.

Jacob's border crossing at the Jabbok River reveals a particularly compelling and revelatory figure as we explore further a biblical theology of migration. In Genesis 32 we read,

---

[15] Doris Garcia Rivers, "Jacob the Threefold Migrant—Puerto Rico," Global Ministries, www.globalministries.org.

[16] Ryken et al., 432.

> In the course of that night, however, Jacob arose, took his two wives, with the two maidservants and his eleven children, and crossed the ford of the Jabbok. After he had taken them across the stream and had brought over all his possessions, Jacob was left there alone. Then some man wrestled with him until the break of dawn. When the man saw that he could not prevail over him, he struck Jacob's hip at its socket, so that the hip socket was wrenched as they wrestled. The man then said, "Let me go, for it is daybreak." But Jacob said, "I will not let you go until you bless me." "What is your name?" the man asked. He answered, "Jacob." Then the man said, "You shall no longer be spoken of as Jacob, but as Israel, because you have contended with divine and human beings and have prevailed." (vv. 22–28)

This story is about Jacob's journey back home and his return migration to Canaan, "where his father had lived as an alien" (Gn. 31:1–22; 37:1). In biblical times the Jabbok River was a natural border that separated Sihon's kingdom from Og's kingdom (Nm. 21:24; Jo. 12:2; and Jgs. 11:13, 22).[17] This border—like other borders—is not just a political border; it also circumscribes aspects of people's tribal, cultural, and spiritual identity.

According to Greco-Roman accounts and anthropological folklore, the borders at river crossings were often guarded by different river demons, and passing over them meant engaging and combating these deities.[18] These forces are powerful, and because Jacob crosses at night, we do not know whether they come from God, a human being, or something else within him. To be sure, the encounter involves dealing with internal matters, but the account is presented as something external to himself that leaves him with a limp for the rest of his life. However symbolic the account might be, it presents the event as a real encounter in some way with God—something reflected in the name change.

---

[17] R. W. Younker, "Jabbok (Place)," in D. N. Freedman, ed., *The Anchor Yale Bible Dictionary* (New York: Doubleday, 1992), 3:593.

[18] An older version of the story suggests that the adversary was a demon who guarded the river. See ibid; D. Bergant and R. J. Karris, *The Collegeville Bible Commentary: Based on the New American Bible with Revised New Testament* (Collegeville, MN: Liturgical Press, 1989), 69.

Jacob's confrontation with these forces is intertwined with the discovery of his own calling. These forces will demand in particular that he work out three questions on this journey that are connected to understanding his true identity: Who am I? Who is God? What is my relationship to others? These questions will thrust him into wrestling with a mix of psychological, spiritual, and social forces at the border; and as he engages this conflict, his identity and destiny will never be the same.

We get more insight into Jacob's transformation when we learn that, after crossing the border and wrestling with human and divine forces, his name changes. In the ancient world, names capture something of a person's identity, and a new name is always the sign of a new beginning, a new life.[19] When Jacob comes through the other side of the struggle, the divine emissary announces that he is no longer to be called "Jacob" (which means "grabby" or "he grabs the heel") but "Israel" (which means "he struggles with God," "God rules," and "God heals").[20] While grabbing after his own needs and agendas shaped the first part of his life, he must now surrender to a larger vocation beyond himself if he is to live up to his name as Israel.

Therefore, we see that more is at work in this narrative than a historical chronicle of his physical journey. Because his story is read against the backdrop of the covenant, Jacob's journey is inseparable from the quest to leave this fallen world behind, to find the road of redemption, and to become authentically human in God. Only as he takes up this journey and leaves his former ways behind him will he discover his destiny, his calling, and his true identity. This transformation will not happen without a struggle, as the events at the Jabbok River make known.

Because identity issues are at work in contentious debates surrounding migration, the figure of Jacob offers much material for reflection. Like Jacob, migrants often have to deal with the arduous physical terrain of border crossings and wrestle with emotional and spiritual trials related to deep inner forces including doubt, fear, and despair. Receiving communities likewise have to deal with the fears surrounding newcomers from foreign places and the different creeds, values, and mindsets they bring with them. Crossing over into the world of otherness involves more than

---

[19] Ryken et al., 432.

[20] C. Brand et al., eds., "Israel," in *Holman Illustrated Bible Dictionary* (Nashville: Holman Bible, 2003), 844.

crossing geopolitical borders; it also means crossing psychosocial and cultural-spiritual borders that move us often into unknown and unfamiliar territory. Those willing to struggle with the forces involved in crossing over are those who have the most potential to grow into more expansive identities. By contrast, "grabbing" onto personal agendas limits our capacity to grow in relationship to others and to follow God into a new and promising future. Jacob emerges not only with a new understanding of himself and his place but also of God.

Jacob's struggle made possible a new life, but crossing the border also comes with a cost. Although he successfully triumphs over the forces that threaten to overtake him, he was maimed at the hip during his wrestling match (Gn. 32:25, 31–32) and suffers injuries on the journey that will stay with him for the rest of his life (Gn. 32:24, 25; cf. Hos. 12:5). So, too, many migrants incur life-altering scars that serve as constant reminders of their struggles searching for better lives. Some of the deepest and most enduring wounds migrants suffer, however, are those in the depths of the heart—scars that come from leaving family and home behind, only to be alone and unwanted in a new country, wondering if their lives mean anything to anybody.[21] Jacob's "return migration" also presents him with new challenges as he comes to understand where he came from, where he traveled to, and who he has become.

While many migrants identify first with their homeland, the process of movement also changes and transforms people. Jacob gives us a window into the dynamic and evolving process of identity formation. When he crosses over into a new land and when he returns to a familiar place, he must renegotiate his identity, for he is no longer the same person he was when he left. Migration has changed his perspective because life on the road has changed his character. As the crucible of the journey refines, redirects, and matures him, he is no longer the same deceitful and devious person of his earlier years (Gn. 25:19–34; 27:1–41), and he must enter into a new psychological and spiritual territory. Having wandered far from home in his earlier years, he is now beginning to find his way back to God's image and likeness, even as he and his descendants like Joseph will encounter new struggles down the road.

---

[21] For more on this topic, see Daniel G. Groody, *Border of Death, Valley of Life: An Immigrant Journey of Heart and Spirit* (Lanham, MD: Rowman and Littlefield, 2001).

### Joseph and Slavery: Migration and Human Trafficking

> When some Midianite traders passed by, they drew Joseph up, lifting him out of the pit, and sold him to the Ishmaelites for twenty pieces of silver. And they took Joseph to Egypt. (Gn. 37:28 NRSV)

In the twists and turns of Joseph's story, we read one of the most painful yet enigmatic tales of forced migration and human trafficking in the Bible. While it is the story of one particular migrant, the narrative contains many universal themes that have parallels in every generation. The tales of sibling rivalry, personal jealousy, and human cruelty have archetypal plots of their own, but we also see a migrant's particular struggle to overcome misfortune, fulfill dreams, and use gifts in the realization of one's destiny.

*The Migration of Joseph*

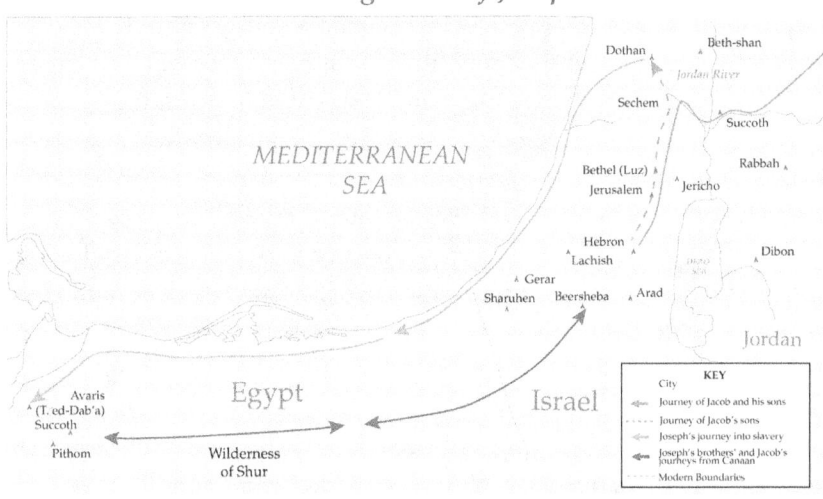

Joseph was the eleventh and most beloved son of Jacob, which triggers envy and resentment within his family. When some of his brothers come up with plans to dispense with him, they instigate a series of events that set him up to become a forced migrant and a trafficked person:

> When Joseph came to his brothers, they stripped him of his robe . . . and they took him and threw him into a pit. The pit was empty; there was no water in it. Then they sat down to eat; and looking up they

saw a caravan of Ishmaelites coming from Gilead, with their camels carrying gum, balm, and resin, on their way to carry it down to Egypt. Then Judah said to his brothers.... Come, let us sell him to the Ishmaelites.... And his brothers agreed... And they took Joseph to Egypt.... Meanwhile the Midianites had sold him in Egypt to Potiphar, one of Pharaoh's officials, the captain of the guard. (Gn. 37:23–28, 36)

There is more at play in this story than Joseph's trials as a migrant and his movement into another country. On another level, it reveals the unfolding narrative of the fall. As his brothers betray Joseph, they migrate further from the relational harmony of the Garden of Eden and move more and more into a space of family disintegration and away from their likeness to God. We come to see that Joseph's brothers not only strip him of his robe, but also of all that defined him: his homeland, his father's favor, and his connection to his family. While suffering from hunger, thirst, and nakedness in the pit, Joseph finds himself in more than just an empty and dry cistern. He experiences the degrading and humiliating confinement that will characterize his life as a trafficked person, like many enslaved in our own time. And by depriving him of his own God-given dignity, Joseph's brothers lose a sense of their own as well. As Joseph descends into the darkness of the pit, they descend even deeper into the darkness of human cruelty.

It is hard to imagine falling into a deeper or darker pit than Joseph's brothers did, but some contemporary forms of human trafficking outdo even the nefarious deeds in this story. While I was doing research in the same geographical area where this narrative took shape, some migrants shared with me their story of being kidnapped and trafficked through the Sinai Peninsula in Egypt. After being sold into slavery to Bedouin traffickers, their captors extorted relatives from abroad for a forty-thousand-dollar ransom. When their families refused, their captors melted plastic water bottles, dripping the hot plastic on their backs as they screamed for help to their relatives on the phone. Their captors said if they did not pay, they would kill the victims and sell their organs on the black market for the same amount.

The connections between Joseph's story and trafficked persons today are striking. In Joseph's story, his own family members, not villainous strangers, sell him into human trafficking. They were not the first to sell family members into slavery for profit, nor the last. Indeed, relatives are involved in nearly half of the child trafficking cases in the world today.[22]

---

[22] International Organization of Migration, "Family Members Linked to Nearly

Joseph was sold for twenty shekels, or about ten ounces of silver, which in today's economy is approximately $220. As little as this seems, today people can be sold into human trafficking for as little as $90.[23] When the love of money starts mastering decisions and profit takes center stage, financial gains become more important than people, and the ones who pay the greatest price are those trafficked and sold.

After the transaction between the brothers and the Midianites is complete, Joseph would have had to walk, bound and chained, for probably thirty days through the desert.[24] Like many refugees today who cross the Sahara Desert in Africa, the seas of the Mediterranean, or the arid landscapes of the American Southwest, the weak and injured are particularly vulnerable, and many die en route.[25] Even if they make it to their destination, another kind of bondage awaits them on the other side. We see this illuminated in Joseph's experience. After he is trafficked over the border into Egypt, he is sold to Potiphar and forced to work as a bonded laborer. Joseph will be abused, exploited, and subjected to domestic servitude, and he will be the victim of unjust treatment and sexual abuse, eventually thrown into prison for bringing his abuse to light after attempting to defend himself.

Even though Joseph suffers injustice and misfortune at every turn, we learn in time that God is at work through this migrant in ways that human eyes cannot see. Through divine providence he finds his way out of prison and helps Pharaoh interpret his dreams. Pharaoh recognizes his wisdom, entrusts him with a senior administrative role in his kingdom, and calls upon him to guide the nation through the crisis of famine (Gn. 40–41).

As the tables turn in this story, Joseph's brothers now are forced to leave Canaan and to beg for food in Egypt (Gn. 37:28). The ones who sold their brother into bondage now find themselves in a bondage of their own. As they cross the Egyptian border, they are scrutinized extensively by authorities and questioned at every turn. What is revealed is one of the great dramas of justice, conversion, and forgiveness in the Bible. Ironically, the one who was powerless is now the one in power; the ones who feasted are now the

---

Half of Child Trafficking: New TOM, Polaris Data," https://www.iom.int/news/family-members-linked-nearly-ha1f-child-trafficking-new-iom-polaris-data.

[23] Free the Slaves, "Slavery Today," www.freetheslaves.net.

[24] *NIV Life Application Study Bible* (Wheaton, IL: Tyndale House, 2019), 71.

[25] For global statistics on those who die on migratory routes, see UN Dispatch, "Missing Migrants Project, Latest Global Figures," www.undispatch.com.

ones starving; the ones who trafficked are now economic migrants (Gn. 42–44:3).

As this story of repentance and reconciliation unfolds, this family—with all its dysfunctions—is reunited once again. In contrast to the treatment he received, Joseph does not descend to a pit of revenge, jealousy, and greed, but he rises above his pain and betrayal and exercises his position of authority with dignity and justice. We get a glimpse of what can happen when empathy trumps empire, solidarity defeats selfishness, and God's sovereignty reigns over narrow nationalism. In gratitude for the contribution of this immigrant to the security and development of the nation, Pharaoh establishes more humane border policies, opens the country of Egypt to Joseph's family, and gives them a place to multiply, flourish, and prosper (Gn. 47).

Although Joseph's story shares many similarities with those trafficked today, the parallels can only be taken so far. Joseph overcomes his imprisonment, ascends to positions of social and political prominence, and acquires a costly freedom. Others today are not so fortunate. Today more than forty million people are living in a modern form of slavery.[26] Unlike Joseph, many victims of human trafficking never leave the dark cisterns of brothels, prisons of forced servitude, or chains of unjust treatment of human torture.

Yet many of these same victims can see something of their own story in Joseph. Some Christian refugees in the Middle East expressed to me how the Joseph story gives them a way of reading their own. "The person of Joseph is a model of hope for us," said one Iraqi refugee who fled the ISIS violence in Mosul and escaped to Jordan. "Our lives are full of pain and suffering now, like we are in a bondage of sorts. But like Joseph, some day we hope to be free from these chains, even though our liberation may only be realized by our children."[27]

## Moses and the Exodus: Migration and Liberation

> But Moses said to God, "Who am I that I should go to Pharaoh and lead the Israelites out of Egypt?" (Ex. 3:11)

The book of Exodus is about the migration of the Israelites from Egypt to the land of Canaan. Moses plays a key role in this process, and more than

---

[26] Walk Free Foundation, The Global Slavery Index 2018, https://downloads.globalslaveryindex.org.

[27] Iraqi refugee, interview by author, March 7, 2015, Amman, Jordan.

any other figure in the Bible, he occupies multiple migration identities in the storyline: an asylum-seeking boat person (Ex. 2:3), an unaccompanied migrant child (Ex. 2:4–6), an exiled and criminal alien (Ex. 2:15), and the coyote-guide of a stateless people who leads people through the desert to the Promised Land (Ex. 3:10).[28] The book deals with push factors of oppression, slavery, and poverty, but it also names enduring pull factors such as liberation, freedom, and the hope of a better life.

As the story begins, Joseph has been forgotten and there is a new Pharaoh in Egypt. Pharaoh's ambitions for empire come at a human cost. As the growing number of Israelites triggers a xenophobic alarm, fear of the other begins to dominate Egypt's political agenda:

> [Pharaoh] said to his people, "Look, the Israelite people are more numerous and more powerful than we. Come, let us deal shrewdly with them, or they will increase and, in the event of war, join our enemies and fight against us and escape from the land." Pharaoh instructed that they set taskmasters over the Israelites to oppress them with forced labor, making their lives bitter with hard service in mortar and brick and in every kind of field labor. (Ex. 1:8–14 NRSV)

The more they are oppressed, however, the more they multiply and spread, so that the Egyptians come to dread the Israelites. As this fear takes over, Pharaoh institutes an infanticide policy to limit their numbers (Ex. 1:15–22).

When the infant Moses enters the biblical stage, his mother puts him in a papyrus basket and hides him among the reeds on the bank of a river to keep him from being killed (Ex. 2:3). On this rickety boat, Moses begins his journey in this world as an internally displaced person and an asylum seeker. The fate of this child will become inextricably intertwined with the liberation of the Israelite people, but the hopes of the entire nation are at risk as this vulnerable child rests on this fragile life raft in the reeds of the Nile. What is so ironic is that he is taken in by Pharaoh's daughter into the very heart of the empire that is oppressing his people!

As their bondage worsens, the cries of the Hebrews reach to the high heavens. "It is a cry that evokes God's care," says Walter Brueggemann.[29] We

---

[28] A coyote is a colloquial Mexican-Spanish term that refers to the guides who help guide immigrants across the US-Mexico border.

[29] Walter Brueggemann, "Exodus 2," in *The New Interpreter's Bible: A Commentary*

read in Exodus 3, "Then the LORD said, 'I have observed the misery of my people who are in Egypt; I have heard their cry on account of their taskmasters. Indeed, I know their sufferings, and I have come down to deliver them from the Egyptians, and to bring them up out of that land to a good and broad land, a land flowing with milk and honey'" (Ex. 3:7–8 NRSV).

After being rescued from the river by the royal household, Moses grows up in Pharaoh's court as a foster child. As he gets older, he too will hear the cries of the oppressed. In seeing how his own people need liberation, he sees that Pharaoh's own house does as well.[30] Moses will discover the need for liberation in both the oppressed and the oppressors, in whom God's image is obscured and his likeness is diminished. This is because one can never be free when it comes at the cost of another person's freedom.[31] God will call both to freedom, but not all will listen (Ex. 9:12). Some will obstinately choose to see the other as distinct from themselves, but as Moses' eyes open, he will see in the oppressed and oppressors brothers, sisters, and people who share a similar destiny.

As his divine calling unfolds, Moses realizes he must migrate from the comfort of Pharaoh's house to the vulnerable periphery of the city where his people live. On the margins he has to redefine what authentic power looks like: He learns the power of relationship, empathy, and compassion. He will discover that it is not the love of power that will lead him to his destiny but the power of love. Opening himself to that love will entail emptying himself of his previous life, which will bring a profound liberation for both himself and his people. As Noah once built an ark (Hebrew: *tabah*, Gn. 8:1) to save humanity from destruction, and Moses' own mother helped save him from death with a boat (Hebrew: *tabah*, Ex. 2:3), so now Moses will stand at the helm to guide his people through the Red Sea, to migrate across the desert, and to journey to a new land of freedom (Ex. 13:18).[32]

---

*in Twelve Volumes* (Nashville: Abingdon Press, 1994), 1:707.

[30] For more on this topic of liberation of the powerful and the oppressed, see John J. Markey, *Moses in Pharaoh's House: A Liberation Spirituality for North America* (Winona, IN: Anselm Academic, 2014).

[31] As Nelson Mandela put it, "I am not truly free if I am taking away someone else's freedom, just as surely as I am not free when my freedom is taken from me. The oppressed and the oppressor alike are robbed of their humanity." Nelson Mandela, *Long Walk to Freedom: The Autobiography of Nelson Mandela* (Boston: Little, Brown, 1994), 544.

[32] Umberto Cassuto, *A Commentary on the Book of Genesis* (Jerusalem: Hebrew University Magnes Press, 1992), 2:59.

# The Biblical Narratives

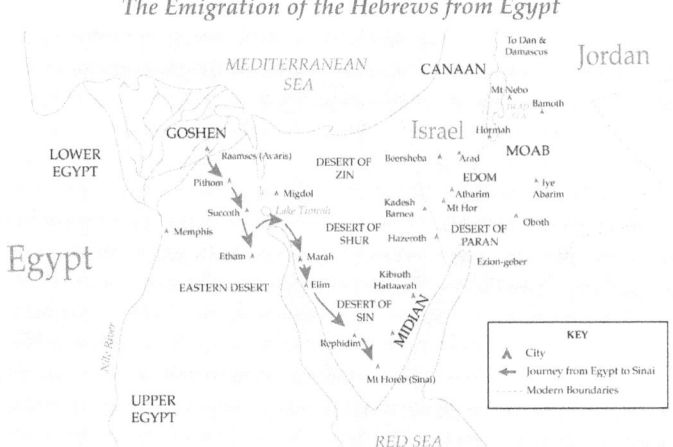

*The Emigration of the Hebrews from Egypt*

This path to freedom, however, is not straightforward; it begins painfully. Seeing the abuse and raw pain of his people, Moses kills an Egyptian in the heat of the moment. When his crimes force him into exile, he has to migrate through the desert in order to purify his vision of life, which we explore more in the next section. He flees from Egypt to escape punishment but has to learn how to fight for righteousness in ways that do not create new injustices. As Dr. Martin Luther King Jr. put it, "Darkness cannot drive out darkness; only light can do that. Hate cannot drive out hate; only love can do that."[33] In the arid wilderness, Moses has to learn a new way of living and being in the world.

As his social location changes, so too must his self-understanding. His experience as a migrant so profoundly reshapes his identity that he names his firstborn son "Gershom," which means "sojourner there" (Ex. 2:22). It is an etymological reminder of Moses' migration into Midian.[34]

This identity is further reshaped after a divine encounter in the burning bush: "Moses said to God, 'If I come to the Israelites and say to them, "The God of your ancestors has sent me to you," and they ask me, "What is his name?" what shall I say to them?' God said to Moses, 'I AM WHO I AM.' He said further, 'Thus you shall say to the Israelites, "I AM has sent me to you"'"

---

[33] Martin Luther King Jr., *Strength to Love* (New York: Harper & Row, 1963), 37.

[34] Paul J. Achtemeier and Society of Biblical Literature, "Gershom," in *Harper's Bible Dictionary* (San Francisco: Harper & Row, 1985), 341, and J. W. Wright, "Gershom (Person)," in *The Anchor Yale Bible Dictionary*, ed. D. N. Freedman (New York: Doubleday, 1992), 2:993.

(Ex. 3:13–14 NRSV). As Yahweh identifies himself as "I AM," he calls Moses to be who he is and to liberate people to be free to be themselves.

In many ways this means that at the heart of migration is the search for just this: to be human. In our own day we hear echoes of similar cries. While on the border of Morocco, in the small Spanish city of Ceuta on the north coast of Africa, one refugee from Somalia put it this way: "I am not trying to get rich. Nor am I looking for handouts. I just can't take living like a dog anymore. All I really want to be is just a human being."[35]

Although the parallels between Moses' migration and those in our own day can only be taken so far, the similarities are striking. Like Moses the unaccompanied minor, many children today are at risk as they cross rivers like the Rio Grande. Like Moses the refugee, many people board unseaworthy vessels in the Mediterranean.[36] Like Moses the asylum seeker, many flee life-threatening dangers at home. As in biblical times, unsafe living environments, harsh labor, and persecution have not diminished, nor have people's desperate attempts to seek freedom in new lands.

In the end, the exodus is a human story about the search for dignity, freedom, and life. It would become so etched into the heart and soul of the Jewish people that they would gather every year in Jerusalem to remember their oppression in Egypt, God's liberating action on their behalf, and their sojourn through the desert to the Promised Land as immigrants. Recalling this Passover would become more than just an exercise in historical recall; it would also serve to challenge them to live a holy life in the present: "You shall not oppress an alien, for you know the heart of an alien, since you were aliens in Egypt" (Ex. 23:9). It is a refrain they frequently recalled and one they annually recited. But ironically it is one they all too often forgot.

### The Israelites and the Desert: Migration and Transformation

> They said to Moses, "Was it because there were no graves in Egypt that you have taken us away to die in the wilderness? What have you done to us, bringing us out of Egypt?" (Ex. 14:11 NRSV)

---

[35] Somali immigrant, interview by author, Ceuta, Spain, July 5, 2008.
[36] See United Nations Office for the Coordination of Humanitarian Affairs, "The Boat Is Safe and Other Lies: Why Syrian Families Are Risking Everything to Reach Europe," https://reliefweb.int; "Eighty More Drown in Latest Boat Tragedy," Yahoo News, July 2, 2014, https://au.news.yahoo.com/.

The journey of the Hebrews to the Promised Land after liberation from Egypt is one of the most important and foundational migration stories in the Old Testament. It involves not only a geographical movement but also a social, psychological, and spiritual climb over many years. This journey is difficult. It takes them through the outer terrain of the desert and transforms their inner landscape as well. This desert brings them face-to-face with temptation, punishment, and death, and in the process purifies and heals them to become more faithful witnesses to God's holiness and justice (Ex. 13:17–18).

*The Immigration of the Hebrews to the Promised Land*

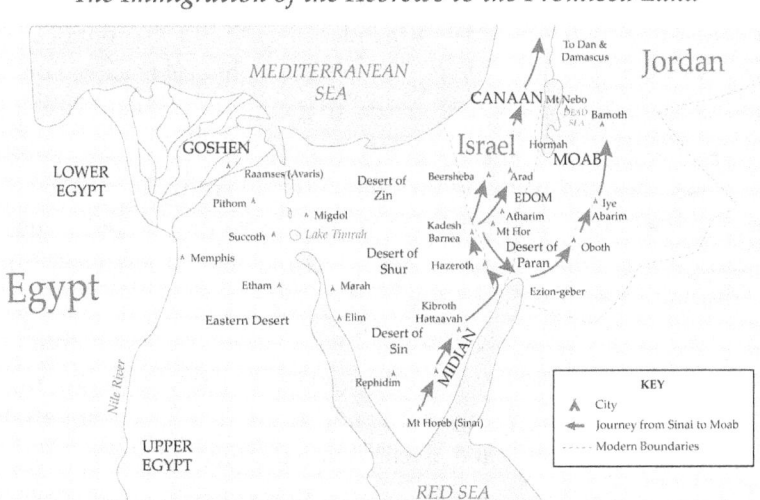

Although it would take the Hebrews only one day to leave their bondage in Egypt, it would take much longer to find the path to authentic freedom. The physical journey from the edge of Pharaoh's empire to the Promised Land is a relatively short distance.[37] Scholars calculate that their route was anywhere between 250 and 400 miles, although there were a lot of twists and turns in the actual journey they undertook. Estimating they could travel about ten miles a day, it should have taken about forty days to complete the trek. Instead, it took them forty years. Why did it take so long?

---

[37] For an alternative reading of how the Canaanites might read the narrative of the Promised Land, see Robert Allen Warrior, "Canaanites, Cowboys, and Indians: Deliverance, Conquest, and Liberation Theology Today," *Christianity and Crisis* 49, no. 12 (1989): 261.

Deliverance from oppression was one level of the Israelites' liberation, but aligning their lives with their liberator and becoming transformed into his image and likeness was a much longer road. Israel would learn that freedom from Egypt involved more than changing laws, structures, and social locations. In fact, the word *Egypt* (Hebrew, *mitsrayim*) has multiple connotations. On the one hand it literally means "double straits," referring to the territory formed by the upper and lower straits through which the Nile flows. On another level, Egypt can also mean "narrow places" or "narrow confinement."[38]

The figurative interpretations are particularly significant for our study here. At Sinai they discover that liberation means more than simply taking off the shackles of Egypt (Ex. 19–40). In leading the Israelites out of Egypt, the Lord not only intends to deliver them from a physical place of bondage but also a state of psychological slavery that comes from narrow ways of thinking. It requires leaving the fallen world behind, deconstructing an empire mentality, and being transformed into something anew into God's image and likeness. It also means taking on a new mindset and living out a different story in one's personal and communal life. Ultimately freedom means learning to love as God loves.

In other words, authentic freedom involves more than correcting a few grammatical errors in the Israelite storyline; they have to script an entirely different narrative. Passing over political borders is hard enough, but passing over social, cultural, and psychological borders will prove even more demanding. This is true not only in biblical times but in our day. Nowhere is this more evident than in the debate about migration. Many refuse to pass over from narrow, tribal, and territorial ways of thinking and move into more liberating narratives rooted in truth, life, freedom, community, gratuity, grace, justice, love, and peace.

The implications of living out of this new narrative are made clear in Leviticus 11:45: "Since I, the LORD, brought you up from the land of Egypt

---

[38] The Hebrew letters for "Egypt" are those found in Ps. 116:3: "the snare [literally "the oppressive confinement" or "narrow straits"] of Sheol" and Ps. 118:5 "out of my distress" [literally "strait," "narrow confinement," "tight place"] I called on the LORD." There is an exact match between the unvocalized Hebrew "Egypt" and "narrow straits" as it is spelled in Lamentations 1:3: "All her persecutors come upon her where she is narrowly confined." The author of Lamentations is clearly using a play on words here between "narrow confinements" and Egypt. See also Laurel A. Dykstra, *Set Them Free: The Other Side of Exodus* (Maryknoll, NY: Orbis Books, 2002), 58.

that I might be your God, you shall be holy, because I am holy." Holiness demands a way of thinking and living that is different from that of the empire. Otherwise, when the roles are reversed and the oppressed come into power, they run the risk of instituting the same abusive practices as their oppressors. As Israel lives into the gift of their liberation, they are called to respond by becoming agents of the same liberating God. Having been refugees, they must now help others seeking refuge. Because historical amnesia can short-circuit the transformative process, rabbinic wisdom has taught that it was far easier to take Israel out of Egypt than to take Egypt—and its empire narrative—out of Israel. For Israel to live in God's image and likeness, they must undergo a repatterning of their inner lives. They must be set free both from being "victims" of oppressors and oppressing others when they come into power. Yahweh will call them to find their true power through love, which begins with empowering the lowly and needy.

This transformation takes place for Israel in the desert, a place as mysterious as it is dangerous. It is where snakes bite and serpents heal (Nm. 21:4–9); where people hunger and where manna comes from heaven (Ex. 16:4–5, 14–15, 31); where they wrestle with evil spirits and encounter the consolation of angels (Gn. 16:7–11; 1 Kgs. 19:3–8); where they experience solitude and finitude; where they realize their human vulnerability and God's glory (Ex. 13:20–22); where everything is stripped away and where they discover that God is all that matters. When one undergoes a journey through the desert and lives to reflect upon it, a new person emerges. The desert reeducates Israel about the sovereignty of God, the order of nature and creation, the interconnectedness of the human family, and the primacy of love. Such repatterning is a difficult and lengthy physical, emotional, psychological, and spiritual process. Israel will wander, complain, and stumble as they migrate in the desert for forty years—a process that is not meant to afflict them but to heal them from all that keeps them from right relationship with the Creator, creation, and other creatures (Dt. 8:15–16).

In the third century, the Christian theologian Origen preached a homily where he correlated the places along Israel's sojourn in the desert with progress in the spiritual life:[39] "When the soul sets out from the Egypt of this life to go to the Promised Land," he said, "it necessarily goes by certain roads and . . . observes certain stages that were made ready with the Father from the

---

[39] Rowan A. Greer, ed., *Origen* (New York: Paulist Press, 1979), 245–69.

beginning."⁴⁰ He goes on to illustrate how Israel's physical migration is an archetypical elaboration of a people's return journey to God.

Like the Israelites, many migrants today have to travel through the desert in search of their own Promised Lands. None, as far as I know, undergo the perils of the desert for the sake of their own spiritual growth, but it can and often does change those who have to migrate through. When researching along the US-Mexico border, I met a man named Manuel just after he had walked more than forty miles in the desert. He was already worn down by the long journey. He began walking with friends, but he could not keep up, so they left him behind and he got lost. He wandered everywhere and wondered if he would ever make it out alive. When we met along the road, where he was asking for help, I asked what he learned in the desert. He said, "All I could do was pray to God because I had nothing left and no one else to turn to. I came to realize that God was the one friend who would never abandon me, and God is the One who stayed with me even after my friends left me to die alone in the desert."⁴¹

The exodus from Egypt and the Israelites' wanderings in the desert reveal important dimensions of the journey of human transformation. Through these experiences the Israelites will rediscover the fundamentals of God's graciousness and compassion. This love is an unmerited gift, but it comes with a hook: as God cares for Israel in their need and vulnerability and guides them on their migration to the Promised Land, they now are called to love as they have been loved. Their moral and spiritual progress will be gauged by how they respond to the most vulnerable and insignificant in society, namely, how they treat the widow, the orphan, and the immigrant (Dt. 10:14–19; 24:17–22; 27:19). It will take years to live into this call. And when they forget where they have come from, what they have experienced and how God has cared for them, God sends the prophets to call them back to reform and reorient their lives.

### The Prophets and Idolatry: Migration and the Deported Heart

> You have been told, O mortal, what is good, and what the LORD requires of you: Only to do justice and to love goodness, and to walk humbly with your God. (Mic. 6:8 NABRE)

---

[40] Ibid., 250.
[41] Manuel, personal communication with author.

As difficult as it was to leave Egypt, and as dangerous as it was to migrate through the desert, Israel's greatest challenges come not only from the journey but also from their false sense of security as they settle into the new land.[42] Settlement has its advantages, but also creates new problems. The new land gives the Israelites a place to call home and set down roots, but the more they become domesticated, the more they try to domesticate God. The more powerful they become, the more they lose touch with the powerless. The more affluent they become, the more they forget the poor. As they fail to remember their migrant identity and their call to mirror God's goodness, they lose sight of their vision of the Promised Land and deport their hearts to alien territory.

As historical amnesia sets in with Israel, the prophets enter the biblical stage. When Israel forgets their slavery in Egypt, their debt to Yahweh for liberation, and their call to be God's holy people, the prophets remind them where they come from, who they belong to, and what they are called to be as a chosen people. The message of the prophets is not an easy one to understand nor a comfortable one to hear. They speak on behalf of God in history and play a critical role in keeping Israel from—or at least warning them of—new forms of enslavement so that they can free their hearts for Yahweh and be free to serve others.

The Hebrew Scriptures identify fifty-five prophets of Israel, forty-eight of whom are men and seven of whom are women. They are people like Amos, Hosea, Isaiah, and Micah who warn of a time of exile and speak to captive refugees when Assyria rises to power after 750 BC; Jeremiah, Ezekiel, and Daniel, who offer hope to exiles during the time of the Babylonian powers after 597 BC; and Malachi, Zechariah, and Haggai, who speak to the challenges of the return journey to the homeland at the time of Persian Empire after 538 BC. All the prophets are touched, directly or indirectly, by the experience of migration, and write from various contexts, including social marginalization, internal displacement, and exile.

To understand their teachings better, it is important to see the prophets as more than political protesters, social activists, or predictors of the future. They live over a span of more than three centuries and their audience, historical context, and content vary, but their central task is to call the people of God back to covenant faith and the demands it places upon them. What

---

[42] Jehu J. Hanciles, *Beyond Christendom: Globalization, African Migration, and the West* (Maryknoll, NY: Orbis Books, 2008), 139–40.

does this message have to say to our reflection on migration in our own times? While many themes have a connection to our study, my central focus here is to explore the ways in which the prophets' intimate connection to the heart of God helps transform the heart of Israel.

The heart is one of the most significant anthropological and spiritual words in the Scriptures (mentioned 814 times).[43] It is a physical organ with a mystical quality that is paradoxically always moving yet also always looking for a home. In the Bible, the heart is more than the sentimental and emotional center of a person; it is the symbol of one's whole being.[44] It includes reason, but also transcends and transforms reason, integrating and informing all aspects of a person. It is always searching, always migrating, and always looking for a resting place. In biblical theology, the heart is the place of our deepest desires, but it is also the place of our deepest conflicts and divisions.

In many ways the prophets are spiritual cardiologists charged with bringing the hearts of God's people back into tune with the heart of God (Jl. 2:13; Jer. 24:7). Israel's indifference to suffering, deafness to the cries of the poor, and neglect of the vulnerable reveal that they have become the oppressors, a fundamental illness (Is. 1:9–17), rooted in idolatry. With the passing of time, the memory of Yahweh's mighty deeds begins to recede into the background. As Israel becomes more comfortable, their attention begins to shift from the God they cannot see to the gods they can see. When neighboring nations present other theological options that are more in line with their self-interests, worshipping idols becomes more attractive. They start giving their hearts to gods that are easier to fashion, easier to manage, and easier to control. Instead of changing their hearts and ordering their lives to the heart of Yahweh, they make God into their own disordered image and likeness and move into the world of false gods or idols.

The more they move into the territory of idols, however, the less God rules and directs Israel's heart. As Israel loses sight of God's image and likeness, they try to reshape God into their own disordered image and likeness. Yahweh, however, does not cooperate with their plans, and the prophets challenge Israel's attempt to manipulate reality. When they go astray from

---

[43] Paul J. Achtemeier and Society of Biblical Literature, "Heart," in *Harper's Bible Dictionary* (San Francisco: Harper & Row, 1985), 377.

[44] Jean de Fraine and Albert Vanhoye, "Heart," in *Dictionary of Biblical Theology*, ed. Xavier Léon-Dufour (Paris: Desclée, 1967), 200–202.

the path of Yahweh, they make themselves captive again to a foreign influence and deport their hearts in a figurative way back to Egypt. This time, however, they are the oppressors—not the oppressed.

Ezekiel sounds the alarm and calls Israel to turn from its evil ways and return to Yahweh, the divine physician (Ez. 14). His diagnosis is that the Israelites' heartbeat has become so arrhythmic with self-centeredness, their spiritual arteries so stagnant with indifference, and their moral veins so clogged with injustice that heart failure is imminent: as God's holy people, they no longer live and love with a heart that feels and cares; Israel's heart has turned to stone. The prophets realize that if they are going to find their way back to spiritual health, they need emergency surgery.

Ezekiel makes the case that Israel needs more than a coronary bypass; in order to love as God loves, Israel will need a heart transplant. In Ezekiel 11, we read God's promise of healing to the dispersed migrants of Israel and Judah:

> Thus says the LORD God: Though I removed them far away among the nations, and though I scattered them among the countries. . . . I will gather you from the peoples, and assemble you out of the countries where you have been scattered, and I will give you the land of Israel. . . . I will give them one heart, and put a new spirit within them; I will remove the heart of stone from their flesh and give them a heart of flesh, so that they may follow my statutes and keep my ordinances and obey them. Then they shall be my people, and I will be their God. (vv. 11:16–17, 19–20 NRSV)

When Israel refuses to listen, the Lord admonishes Ezekiel to "pack a bag for exile, and . . . go into exile from your place to another place" (Ez. 12:3).

Why was Israel deported from the land promised to their ancestors to a foreign territory? This problem poses one of the greatest theological challenges for Israel, and the prophets point to some of the central reasons behind it. In the Mosaic covenant, Yahweh gives Israel land as a gift, and it is given in trust (Ex. 19–24). If Israel is unfaithful to this covenant, however, they will lose the land (Lv. 18:24–28).[45] While Israel is quick to remember the promise and gift of this new homeland (Dt. 1:8), they agree

---

[45] Diane Bergant, "Ruth: The Migrant Who Saved the People," in *Migration, Religious Experience, and Globalization*, eds. Gioacchino Campese and Pietro Ciallella (New York: Center for Migration Studies, 2003), 55–56.

much more slowly to live out the demands and responsibilities that come with it, namely, loving others as they were loved: listening to the cries of the suffering, freeing them from their burdens, and liberating them from their idols.

The prophets rebuke Israel for their worship of the Baals and Ashteroths in biblical times, but what would they say about the idols we worship in our own day? What prognosis would they give about the state of our own hearts? What would they say about migration? While making direct parallels from biblical days to contemporary times has its risks, it is important to take those risks if we are to understand the ways idols are at work in the immigration debate and if we are to engage the transformative potential of the Scriptures.

If the prophets lived today, would they chastise our worship of the self-absorbing god of Narcissus, who seduces us to worry more about our own image than the image of God in the poor and needy (Am. 2:6–8; 5:21–24; 6:4–7; 8:4–6)? Would they rebuke the insatiable deity of consumerism, who leads us to focus more on what we have than who we are (Heb. 2:6–9)? Would they challenge the elitist gods of racism, who dupe us into policies that marginalize rather than reconcile (Zec. 7:9–12)? Would they denounce the idols of legalism, who advocate for shallow certitudes over the divine requirements of justice and mercy (Mi. 6:6–8; Is. 58:3–7; Am. 5:24)? Would they denounce the gods of nationalism, who lull us into erecting walls rather than building bridges (Mi. 4:2–5)? Would they rebuke the empty gods of imperialism, who hail state sovereignty but evade international solidarity (Am. 2:6a–8)? Would they take aim at the deities of militarism, who promote national security at one's borders but ignore human insecurity beyond them (Ez. 13:10–12; Jer. 9:23–24)? And would they denounce the gods of money-theism, the unquestioned liturgies of the marketplace and the creeds of global capitalism, which prioritize financial costs over human costs (Mi. 3:9–11)?

We simply cannot understand the deeper issues at work in the debate over migration without serious reflection on how these gods of narcissism, consumerism, racism, legalism, nationalism, imperialism, militarism, and money-theism influence our personal and collective narratives, shape our values, and sway our decision making. Some of these idols work their way into contemporary worship in churches and synagogues, and they are not infrequently preached from pulpits in our own times! Without discernment and the critical evaluation of our own beliefs, these idols lead us astray, take us off the path of the God of life, and derail the mission of building a civilization of love.[46] They are at work, for instance, when governments create policies that result in migrant deaths, when organizations slash water jugs in deserts to keep "illegals" from the search for more dignified lives, and when vigilantes threaten unaccompanied minors at gunpoint after fleeing violence in their home countries. Worshipping these idols turns our hearts into stone and makes us alien even to ourselves.

Denouncing the worship of many of these same idols, Pope Francis highlighted the "human face" of the global community and rebuked "the dictatorship of an impersonal economy lacking a truly human purpose."[47] He urged communities toward an "ever watchful scrutiny of the signs of the times" that calls people to say "no to an economy of exclusion," "no to the new idolatry of money," "no to a financial system which rules rather than serves," and "no to an inequality which spawns violence" (*Evangelii Gaudium* 51, 53–59). Like the prophets of biblical times, Pope Francis reminded us to see our lives within the bigger picture of the covenant, the larger meaning of our lives, and the greater call to communion with each other. Prophets help us become conscious of the idols that enslave us and keep us from right relationships—and remind us of who we are, whose we are, and who we are called to be to each other. Above all they help us become more human and more capable of loving as God loves.

**Ruth and the Alien: Migration and Human Solidarity**

> "Where you go, I will go; where you lodge, I will lodge;
> your people shall be my people, and your God my God."
> (Ru. 1:16 NRSV)

The story of Ruth takes shape in the period of the Judges, between the exodus from Egypt and the rise of the monarchy in Jerusalem.[48] It is the story of two resident aliens, their experience of living in one another's

---

[46] For more on this topic, see Daniel G. Groody, *Globalization, Spirituality and Justice: Navigating the Path to Peace* (Maryknoll, NY: Orbis Books, 2015), 92–122.

[47] "Pope Francis' South America Tour Slammed the 'Idolatry of Money,'" Religion News Service, July 13, 2015, http://religionnews.com.

[48] The period of Judges is a subject of scholarly debate but it likely occurred between 1200 BC and 1020 BC. There is more debate regarding the date the book of Ruth was written. See P. Trible, "Book of Ruth," in *The Anchor Yale Bible Dictionary*, ed. D. N. Freedman (New York: Doubleday, 1992), 5:843.

country, and ultimately their ancestral connection to King David.[49] In it we see how one foreigner became naturalized into the Israelite community and how one immigrant became a key link in the destiny of a nation and the salvation of a people.

## The Migration of Ruth

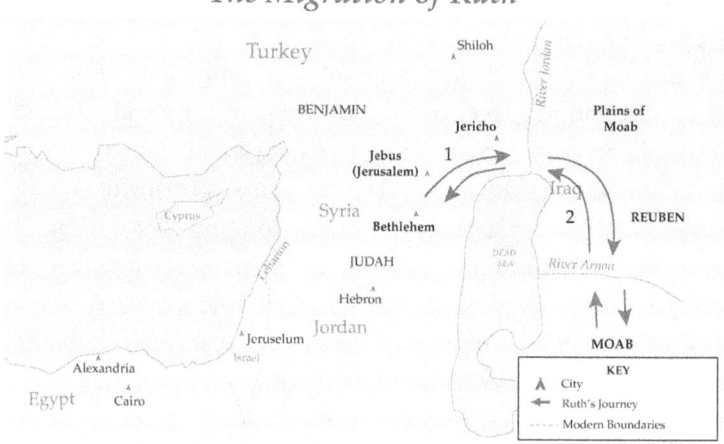

In the book of Ruth, the narrative begins with a man named Elimelech, who is forced to migrate because of famine in his hometown of Bethlehem. In Hebrew, the name Bethlehem (*Beth lehem*) means "house of bread." In Arabic, Bethlehem (*Beit lahm*) means "house of meat."[50] It is striking that the land that would someday be known as the city of David and birthplace of the Savior is so closely associated with such basic human needs as food. These needs are at the heart of the story of Ruth and of many migrants today.

The Bible likewise mentions numerous times when food was scarce, especially in times of famine, such as in the days of Abraham (Gn. 12:10), Isaac (Gn. 26:1), Joseph (Gn. 41:53–57; Acts 7:11), David (2 Sam. 21:1), Elijah (1 Kgs. 17:1; 18:1–5; Lk. 4:25), Elisha (1 Kgs. 8:1; 2 Kgs. 4:38; 6:25), and the prophets (Is. 51:19; Jer. 44:13; Ez. 7:15; Jl. 1:10–12). Famines were caused by unstable agricultural conditions stemming from crop failure (Lv. 26:20; Heb. 3:17), drought (Dt. 28:22; 1 Kgs. 17:1; 18:1–2; Jer. 14:1–6),

---

[49] Joseph A. Mindling, "Chosen People in Foreign Lands: Scriptural Reflections on Immigration and the Uprooted," *New Theology Review* 12, no. 1 (1999): 9.

[50] Paul J. Achtemeier and Society of Biblical Literature, "Bethlehem," in *Harper's Bible Dictionary* (San Francisco: Harper & Row, 1985).

locusts (Jl. 1:4), war (2 Kgs. 6:24–25), and foreign invasion (2 Kgs. 25:1–3; Jer. 32:24; 52:6; Ez. 5:12, 16–17). At times, food shortages were so severe, and people so desperate, they resorted to eating donkey heads and even their own children (2 Kgs. 6:24–29).[51]

Because they had no social security or government welfare programs in biblical times, assistance had to come from outside the community or from the inside through extended family. Gleaning laws, tithes, and other covenant regulations offered some measurable relief for the needy in Israelite society, but when these were not enough, people would migrate across borders in order to provide for their families (Gn. 12:10; 41:57; Ru. 1:1; 2 Kgs. 8:1–2). Such displacement caused other challenges, like the trials of being a foreigner in a new land.

This theme of being a foreigner figures prominently in the Old Testament in general and the story of Ruth in particular. Various terms are used to describe the foreigner in the Old Testament, such as *gēr, zār, ben nēkār, nokrî*. Sometimes these are translated as *stranger, sojourner, immigrant*, and *alien*, but underneath their different shades of meaning, they describe people who are estranged and totally outside of, or "other to," the community of Israel.[52] All of these terms refer to people within Israel's borders, but what they represent are different labels communicating the degree of integration into national life (with the *ger* as the most integrated and, therefore, the one to whom most of the immigrant laws are directed). The *nokrî* (and the various related terms) were not perceived favorably.

Israel generally categorized such outsiders in two fundamental ways: (1) those foreigners who lived outside of Israel's borders, such as "the nations" or "the Gentiles," and (2) those foreigners who lived within its borders— what we call today "permanent residents"—who had some privileges under covenant stipulations. The latter might have left their homelands for political or economic reasons and sought refuge in another community, such as Abraham in Hebron (Gn. 23:4), Moses in Midian (Ex. 2:15, 22), the Israelites in Egypt (Ex. 22:21), and Elimelech and his family in Moab (Ru. 1:1).[53]

---

[51] This scene is one during a siege. One of the strategies in a siege was to starve a city into submission.

[52] C. T. Begg, "Foreigner," in *The Anchor Yale Bible Dictionary*, ed. D. N. Freedman (New York: Doubleday, 1992).

[53] A. H. Konkel, "Gwr," in *New International Dictionary of Old Testament Theology & Exegesis*, ed. Willem VanGemeren (Grand Rapids: Zondervan, 1997), 837.

As highlighted in previous sections, because the Israelites were aliens in Egypt, they are commanded not to oppress aliens (Ex. 22:21–23; 23:9) but to have rather "the heart of an alien" (Ex. 23:9). This means they are not to strip their fields and vineyards bare so the poor and alien can glean and eat (Lv. 19:9–10). This is critical to understanding the story of Ruth.

When the husbands of Naomi, Ruth, and Orpah die in Moab, the women have to fend for themselves. Naomi is particularly vulnerable because she is both a widow and a foreigner. When Naomi learns that the famine in her homeland is over, she decides to return to Bethlehem. As she says good-bye, Naomi discourages her widowed, Moabite daughters-in-law from migrating with her because then they would be foreigners in Israel, and their vulnerability would likewise be doubled. Orpah finally agrees to return to her father's home, but Ruth takes another route and says to Naomi, "Do not press me to leave you or to turn back from following you! Where you go, I will go; where you lodge, I will lodge; your people shall be my people, and your God my God. Where you die, I will die—there will I be buried. May the LORD do thus and so to me, and more as well, if even death parts me from you!" (Ru. 1:16–17 NRSV)

In this case, Ruth makes a decision not only to undergo a geographical and cultural migration but also a religious one. This point should not be glossed over: Ruth even agrees to commit herself to Israel's God and Israel's ways. As she prioritizes her relationships over her homeland, her region, and even her religion, she enters into this space of otherness and becomes one of the foremost biblical prototypes of human solidarity. She must wait for a new identity to emerge, but for now she knows this new identity can only be built on love expressed through the care of another and the other.

As the narrative unfolds, however, we learn that God is not outdone in generosity. In the pages that follow we find out God's provision for Ruth as she and Naomi arrive in Judah. Boaz figures prominently in the progressive revelation of God's providential care for them. Seeing Ruth's plight, Boaz is moved by her need. With a heart attuned to the cry of the poor and heeding the call to compassion, Boaz makes it possible for Ruth to glean in his fields for needed provisions. Ruth learns in time that Boaz is her husband's next of kin or kinsman-redeemer (*gō'ēl*). According to the Mosaic law, when a family had fallen on hard times, the kinsman-redeemer could reacquire the property of the poverty-stricken or deceased relative (Lv. 25:25; Jer. 32:6–8). In addition, if someone was sold into slavery because of their poverty, the kinsman redeemer could play a critical role in their legal status in the land

(Lv. 25:47–55). As such, Boaz was able to help facilitate Ruth's permanent residency.

As the drama surrounding Ruth's living situation unfolds (Ru. 4:1–6), Boaz seeks to fulfill all the legal requirements necessary to marry her. Recognizing that the higher purpose of the law is not to enrich the settled but to safeguard the marginalized such as Ruth and Naomi, Boaz prioritizes people over property. With the heart of a true Israelite, he puts the needs of the poor and vulnerable over the ambitions of the rich and privileged.

The story of Ruth is a microcosm of the enduring biblical drama of widows and aliens, famine and migration, family ties and transnational friendship. It deals with crossing borders and overcoming barriers, transcending differences and journeying in solidarity, and moving into new territory and finding one's way home. Not only is the story about how the community of Israel saves one migrant from despair, but also paradoxically how that same migrant saves a people. In the end Ruth becomes a key link between the royal lineage of David (Ru. 4:13–17) and Jesus (Mt. 1:5–6).[54] In many ways, Ruth foreshadows the God who aligns himself with this same family, migrates to this same village in a "foreign" land, and proclaims the good news of reconciliation to an alien people.

### Migration and the Journey from God, in God, and to God

In this chapter we have done a first reading of migration by looking at some of the most prominent migrants in the Old Testament, including Adam and Eve, Abraham and Sarah, Jacob, Joseph, Moses, the Israelites, the Prophets, and Ruth and Naomi. The record of their stories of migration, internal displacement, and exile—and their place in the memory of Israel—is a point of revelatory significance. We also have examined how the stories of these migrants are connected to central spiritual and theological themes like creation, sin, the covenant, memory, justice, liberation, transformation, idolatry, and hospitality. Because these are so central to salvation history, we come to see how the concept of migration is inextricably intertwined with understanding our journey from God, in God, and to God.

As we have examined these biblical migrants and corresponding theological themes, we have discovered critical corollaries to issues of migration in our own time. The biblical narratives we have studied have something

---

[54] Bergant, "Ruth," 49–61.

important to say about the search for God amid the challenges of leaving home, taking risks, crossing borders, suffering misfortune, enduring trials, losing the way, receiving hospitality, and finding liberation. As these people, themes, and topics bring out the rich interrelationship between migration in biblical times and our own, they also have the potential to transform our personal narratives into new, life-giving stories. All of these are foundational to a theology of migration that is further developed later in this text.

The memory of Israel's own migration shapes significantly how they understand their identity as a people and the God they follow on the way. It becomes so intertwined with Israel's identity that it shapes its earliest confession of faith.[55] In Deuteronomy we read, "Then you shall declare before the Lord, your God, 'My father was a wandering Aramean who went down to Egypt with a small household and lived there as an alien. But there he became a nation great, strong, and numerous'" (Dt. 26:5). Walter Brueggemann points out that at the heart of Israel's faith is the experience of the God who is (1) merciful (in Hebrew, *rhm*), (2) compassionate (*hnn*), (3) steadfast in love (*hsd*), (4) tenaciously faithful (*'emeth*), and (5) forgiving (*ns'*).[56] This credo also profoundly shapes Israel's ethics and understanding of those migrating in their midst. At the end of the Old Testament, the Israelites still are depicted as wanderers, captives, and exiles looking for a home, which is one of the core longings of the human heart and a theme addressed in more detail in the New Testament.

Before looking at migration in the New Testament, we want to give more attention now to the inner migration into the human heart. In particular, we look at the way the Scriptures give us insight into an emotional map of the migrant experience. To do this we turn our attention to the Psalms, where we hope to understand not only something of the inner terrain of migrants in biblical times, but also the more universal experience at work in the inward, outward, and upward journey to God.

---

[55] See also Dt. 6:20–25. First published in German but now available in English in Gerhard von Rad, *The Problem of the Hexateuch and Other Essays* (Norwich, UK: Hymns Ancient & Modern, 1966), 1–78. See also Gerhard von Rad, *Deuteronomy: A Commentary* (London: Westminster Press, 1966), 155ff., and J. A. Thompson, *Deuteronomy: An Introduction and Commentary,* vol. 5 (Downers Grove, IL: InterVarsity Press, 1974).

[56] Walter Brueggemann, *Theology of the Old Testament: Testimony, Dispute, Advocacy* (Minneapolis: Fortress Press, 1997), 216.

# 3

# THE RESPONSORIAL PSALM

## *The Inner Landscape of the Refugee Journey*

> *Say to the Lord, "My refuge and fortress, my God in whom I trust." (Ps. 91:2)*

When visiting the Syrian-Turkish border a few years ago, I met a large Syrian family who lived near the border town of Urfa. In memory of Abraham a shrine is erected there that is circumscribed by the waters of a moat-shaped pool. After fleeing the violence in their home country, many displaced Syrians have come to this place to worship and rest after enduring the stress in their war-torn homeland. During our conversation I asked one of them, "What is the most challenging aspect of being a refugee?" Although two of the men had been physically paralyzed during the fighting, one spoke of another pain inside of him: "To lose one's country is the most difficult," he answered, "because it is to lose something very precious."

His sorrow echoes the words of a forced migrant-psalmist who was exiled from his home to Babylon more than twenty-five hundred years ago:

> By the rivers of Babylon we sat and wept when we remembered Zion. There on the poplars we hung our harps, for there our captors asked us for songs, our tormentors demanded songs of joy; they said, "Sing us one of the songs of Zion!" How can we sing the songs of the LORD while in a foreign land? If I forget you, Jerusalem, may my right hand forget its skill. May my tongue cling to the roof of my mouth if I do not remember you, if I do not consider Jerusalem my highest joy. (Ps. 137:4–6)

No matter where one goes, one never loses the need to belong and for a place to call home. In any generation, the experience of exile traumatizes and dehumanizes people on multiple levels.

Although they expressed their sorrow thousands of years apart from each other, the psalmist's and this Syrian family's lament were both uttered in the same part of the world. Geographically and historically, this area is often referred to as Greater Syria, which is one of the globe's oldest continually inhabited areas.[1] It is a territory that refers to the land of modern-day countries including Iraq, Syria, Lebanon, Cyprus, Jordan, Israel, Palestine, and Egypt, where agriculture has flourished, civilizations have prospered, and kingdoms have reigned for thousands of years. It is also the territorial stage on which much of the migration drama unfolded in biblical times as well as in our own.

The recent civil war in the modern state of Syria, and the ensuing conflict with the Islamic State (ISIS), have triggered waves of seismic violence that have shaken the region, displaced millions of people, and created the "worst humanitarian disaster of our time."[2] As these forces have destabilized the region, a tsunami of refugees has flooded into neighboring countries, attempting to escape the brutal violence.[3] Like those in biblical exile who once lamented their plight beside the rivers of Babylon, so now do refugees weep of their own experience of exile, hoping one day to return to the land of their birth.

This chapter is about the Psalms and human experience, especially as read through the life of Syrian refugees. Having looked at the outer journey of migrants, we now turn our attention to the inner journey of refugees to under-

---

[1] Before being divided by Western colonial powers in the twentieth century, Greater Syria (or Shaam as the conquering Arabs in the sixth century called it) included most of the western Mediterranean coast and Mesopotamia, a land much vaster than modern-day Syria. From the Taurus Mountains in the north to the Arabian Desert in the south, the land of Greater Syria extended between the Mediterranean Sea and the Euphrates River, covering the modern-day states of Syria, Lebanon, Palestine/Israel, Jordan, Iraq, and parts of southern Turkey. It gave the world its first alphabet, its first civilization, and its three greatest religions. See John McHugo, *Syria: A Recent History* (London: Saqi Books, 2015), 35.

[2] Amnesty International, "Syria: The Worst Humanitarian Crisis of Our Time," www.amnesty.org.nz.

[3] The United Nations estimates that over 5.4 million people have fled Syria to neighboring countries. The bulk of those, 3.4 million, reside in camps and cities across southern Turkey. Lebanon hosts roughly a million Syrian refugees, and Jordan over seven hundred thousand (United Nations High Commissioner for Refugees, "Syria Regional Refugee Response," https://data2.unhcr.org).

stand better the emotional and spiritual terrain of their lives. As we listen to the experience of Syrian refugees today—many of whom are from the same region where these biblical texts were written—we also look at some of the ways they echo the experience of those who gave utterance to the Psalms thousands of years ago. We examine how these same texts give expression to some of the central images of God that are at the heart of Judeo-Christian faith. As we explore the graced-human interplay between the lived experiences of Syrian refugees and the Psalms, we seek to open a sacramental window into the refugee heart, the spiritual journey, and the migrant God.

**The Syrian Refugee Story and the Psalms**

The events that have unfolded in Syria since March 2011 have led to a complex crisis that stems from various social, historical, religious, economic, and political issues. Many of the grievances of the Syrian people are rooted in the totalitarian rule of the Assad regime, which has controlled the country since forcefully taking power in 1970. The roots of this violence reach much deeper into the country's history.[4]

Greater Syria's five-thousand-year history tells a recurring story of war, conquest, and occupation. From the third millennium BC, Sumerians, Eblaites, Akkadians, Assyrians, Egyptians, Hittites, Hurrians, Mitanni, Amorites, Persians, and Babylonians successively took over Sumeria.[5] The Romans annexed Syria to their empire for six centuries before the Arab Muslims conquered it and made Damascus the capital of their Umayyad Empire in 661. A succession of Islamic empires lasted until the end of the Ottoman Empire. After collapsing following World War I, the region was delivered into the hands of Britain and France. The colonial powers, operating under a UN mandate, arbitrarily divided Greater Syria into modern-day Syria, Lebanon, Palestine, Jordan, Iraq, and Turkey.[6]

---

[4] Totalitarian authoritarianism continues to result in the direst living conditions for humans, simply because this system of government prioritizes the interests of the state (in reality the ruling class) over the needs of the people. As such, not only are human needs violated in every imaginable way, but that violation is justified as long as the ruling class claims it within the public or national interest. For a more detailed expose of authoritarianism, see Hannah Arendt, *Totalitarianism: Part Three of the Origins of Totalitarianism* (New York: Harvest Books, 1976).

[5] Richard F. Nyrop, *Syria: A Country Study* (Washington, DC: American University, 1979).

[6] McHugo, *Syria*, 35–69.

Eventually the Syrians would fight a war of independence from the French, but unfortunately it did not end the suffering of the Syrian people, and the fragile-yet-promising democracy of the country was short-lived. In 1970, after a series of military coups, Syria fell under the grip of Hafez al-Assad and his Baathist pan-Arabian regime. Hafez, ostensibly driven by the Israeli threat to the south, ruled the country with an unprecedented iron fist.[7] He suspended the constitution, assumed absolute power over the military and intelligence, and initiated a reign of terror. The Assad regime instilled fear in the Syrian people. By the time Bashar al-Assad came to the throne, the grievances had reached a boiling point, and in 2011 the nation finally had enough of the repression.[8]

After decades of authoritarian rule in Syria—and inspired by the wave of protests unfolding in the Middle East in early 2011—the Syrian people finally decided to speak out. It started when a group of children painted four Syrian words of graffiti on their school wall that translates, "Your turn has come, doctor," it said, referring to their ophthalmologist-turned-regime-president, Bashar al-Assad. These four Syrian words would ignite a spark that set the country ablaze.[9] When massive peaceful demonstrations calling for political and civil rights were met with military force, the people took up arms, and a bloody civil war began.

As the regime bombed entire neighborhoods with its brutal arsenal, employed chemical weapons against its people, and tortured those who resisted, insurgency and religious extremist groups like the Islamic State of

---

[7] Ibid., 155–79.

[8] It is difficult to describe life in Syria under the rule of Assad without conjuring images of dystopia. The Assad family has ruled Syria since the military coup in 1970. When Hafez al-Assad died in 2000, his son, Bashar, inherited the country's carefully engineered apparatus of repression. In Assad's Syria—the colloquial name used by the state's propaganda to refer to the country—the ruling class comprising Alawites, a Shia'-derived religious sect generally, and Assad's family specifically, hold absolute power. In that world, one can conceive of very little that can be said or done outside the authority of the regime. The fifteen branches of Mukhabarat, the state's unofficial intelligence force, are ruthless. Torture and executions are common practice on those citizens who dare challenge the supreme authority of the state. When someone is taken prisoner by the Mukhabarat, the Syrians say they have been "taken beyond the sun." They say this because they do not return. Knowing fully well the horrific torture that awaits any opposition, most never dare think even about the prospect of protest. For more, see ibid., 179–203.

[9] Ibid., 203–37.

Iraq and Sham (ISIS) and the Jabhat al-Nusra Front (JNF) emerged in the region. Initially, these Islamist fundamentalist groups exploited the regime-inflicted grievances of the people, but eventually they began abusing people in their own way as they sought to gain power and establish their extremist ideology. To further their objectives and subjugate people to their control, they initiated their own reign of terror. Islamist extremists like ISIS and JNF assumed totalitarian control, massacring non-Sunna minority groups and even insubordinate Sunna. They established slave and concubine trades, enforced child-marriages, subjugated women, mandated the Niqab,[10] banned secular education, threatened critics, and decapitated "infidels," sometimes rolling their heads down the streets.[11]

Caught in the crossfire between the oppression of the regime and the oppression of secular and Islamist revolutionary forces, most residents had few—if any—good choices in front of them. By joining these revolutionary groups, they could be killed or tortured. By resisting, they could be assassinated. By leaving home, they would be setting out on a precarious boat and cast upon a merciless sea with a tempestuous social, political, and cultural horizon in front of them.

For years the war has decimated the country of Syria and its people. In addition to destroying much of the country's infrastructure and cultural heritage, tens of thousands have been tortured, hundreds of thousands have died, and millions more have become forcibly uprooted.[12] It has also wreaked havoc on the hearts and souls of countless people who live there, causing an inner wreckage that is difficult to see with the human eye but is arguably the most devastating part of the war over the long term. Healing the inner wounds of this trauma is critical to the future of the country and the land. Without conscious efforts to do so, it will remain a world of unresolved conflict littered with social, emotional, and psychological debris of every kind.

---

[10] A niqab is a garment of clothing that covers a woman's entire face and hair down to the shoulders, leaving only the eyes. The niqab is worn by some Muslim women as part of a particular interpretation of hijab [modesty].

[11] Joby Warrick, *Black Flags: The Rise of ISIS* (New York: Anchor Books, 2015).

[12] United Nations High Commissioner for Refugees, "Syria Regional Refugee Response."

## A Psychospiritual Framework for Refugee Healing

During a visit to the Turkish-Syrian border, I met Jude Ash, who at the time was working on a project aimed to provide trauma therapy for Syrian refugee children. Jude is a Syrian human rights activist who has been a part of the Syrian nonviolent movement of 2011, and he has paid the price for his commitment to his country's liberation. He was arrested by the Assad regime, tortured for his involvement in the peaceful demonstrations, and threatened with death by Islamist militants. He knows firsthand the challenges of being a Syrian and a refugee.

Subsequently, Jude came to study with me at the University of Notre Dame. He started as a master's student in peace studies and later he became a doctoral student in clinical psychology and peace studies. He worked with me as a research assistant, and his insights have been invaluable while I was writing this book, especially this chapter. As we researched the Psalms and the refugee experience, we talked about how the disciplines of psychology and spirituality can reveal more of the emotional and traumatic dimensions of the Syrian refugee experience.

Understanding better this inner terrain among those who are uprooted and forced to flee, however, is difficult. Especially because it is problematic to overly generalize about refugees' experience, it requires special tools from multiple disciplines to grasp some of its complex dimensions. I readily acknowledge my own limitations and experience in undertaking a topic of such depth, which is why I rely not only on my own research but on the insights and experience of Jude and other scholars.

Drawing a portrait of the inner life of a Syrian refugee requires some kind of framework of human psychological needs. Over the years, scholars have proposed various theoretical constructs to account for human needs and their role in the overall process of human growth and development.[13] Such theories offer important elements that help us formulate a conceptual map for this research. Having a cognitive map assists us in navigating

---

[13] Among the various schemas offered in scholarly literature, the framework of fundamental human needs proposed by Manfred Max-Neef and Maslow's hierarchy of human needs appear to have the closest resonance to our research among refugees. See especially Manfred A. Max-Neef, Antonio Elizalde, and Martín Hopenhayn, *Human Scale Development: Conception, Application and Further Reflections* (New York: Apex Press, 1991), and Abraham H. Maslow and Robert Frager, *Motivation and Personality*. 3rd ed. (New York: Harper and Row, 1987).

the complex terrain of human emotions and the inner journey of human beings. Traditional frameworks of psychological development are useful and can also be refined to our particular interests. Thus, we focus on four basic human needs that are critically important for refugees, namely, freedom and self-expression, safety and protection, agency and justice, and community and belonging. This framework, while by no means exhaustive of the refugee experience, offers a valuable starting point as we enter into the emotional landscape of Syrian refugees.

In addition to this psychological framework, a closer study of the Psalms is important here. The Psalms offer vivid imagery that has nourished the hearts and minds of believers for centuries, especially because they capture a range of human emotions, from suffering and pain to joy and wonder, in one's journey with God through life. The Eucharistic liturgy is one of the privileged places where these Psalms are read, which the Church calls the Responsorial Psalm.[14]

In the Bible, the Psalms have traditionally been divided into five "books" (Pss. 1–41; 42–72; 73–89; 90–106; 107–50) and categorized according to genres that relate to a range of emotional responses before God, such as lament, gratitude, trust, and praise.[15] Others have categorized them according to the life setting and events (*Sitz im Leben*) in which they were used and from which they developed. These include moments of thanksgiving, enthronement, wisdom, and pilgrimage.[16]

---

[14] The other major Catholic use of the Psalms is in the Liturgy of Hours, which is the daily prayer of the Church. The Psalms form the bulk of this prayer, and they are arranged in a regular order, so that within one to four weeks the whole Psalter is prayed.

[15] Nowell conceptualized the Psalms as general genres of (1) lament (e.g., Pss. 22; 51), which reflect the cry for help to God and the complaint to a God who allows catastrophes to strike; (2) thanksgiving (e.g., Pss. 18; 107), which express heartwarming gratitude to a God who has fulfilled His promise; (3) confidence (e.g., Pss. 23; 27), which echo the authors' trust in a God who has consistently delivered; and (4) praise (e.g., Pss. 100–146), which are oriented toward God alone, Whom all creation is invited to join in praising (Irene Nowell, *Pleading, Cursing, Praising: Conversing with God through the Psalms* [Collegeville, MN: Liturgical Press, 2013]).

[16] For more on Psalms and genres, see Hermann Gunkel, and Joachim Begrich, *Introduction to Psalms: The Genres of the Religious Lyric of Israel* (Macon, GA: Mercer University Press, 1998), and Bernard W. Anderson and Steven Bishop, *Out of the Depths: The Psalms Speak for Us Today*. 3rd ed. (Louisville, KY: Westminster John Knox Press, 2000).

Reading these texts from the context of refugees gives us insight not only into times of oppression, fear, helplessness, and estrangement but also into the God who is present on the journey of life as a friend who liberates the oppressed, a shield who protects the fearful, a king who provides justice for the helpless, and a secure dwelling place for the estranged. Because refugees are often pushed to the edges of human vulnerability, they also can give us a unique insight into biblical revelation and the God who is present on the journey and ultimately reveals himself as a refuge for the refugee (Ps. 144:2). On the following pages we will explore these themes in more detail.

*The Need for Freedom and Self-Expression: God as Liberator and Companion*

> Hear my cry, O God, listen to my prayer! From the ends of
> the earth I call; my heart grows faint. (Ps. 61:2–3)

At the core of every human heart is the desire to be known and understood. Nowhere is this need felt more acutely than in times of calamity and distress, a state that is especially familiar to the uprooted and marginalized. After basic physiological needs have been met, many refugees say that one of their most vital needs is a strong desire to express one's self and reveal one's story, to speak out and feel heard.

In order to share one's story, however, a certain measure of safety and security is necessary. Without it, no trusting disclosure is possible. It must also take place where there is a significant degree of political, social, and cultural freedom that allow one to speak honestly and authentically, without fear of recrimination. Both freedom and security are needed for genuine self-expression to happen.

For over forty years the Assad regime sought to limit—and when necessary repress—the need for self-expression among its people, especially in the political arena. When Hafez al-Assad took power in 1970, his first priority was to transform the military into an institution loyal only to him, his family, and officers belonging to the Alawi sect, to which the Assad family belonged. His firm grip on the military prevented counterinsurgency groups from regaining any control in the period that followed the coup d'état that enthroned him and his family as the de facto dictatorial leaders of Syria. Because Hafez al-Assad wanted to leave nothing to chance, he clamped down on social resistance movements and established Syria's infamous intelligence apparatus, which included fifteen intelligence agencies that maintained totalitarian vigilance over the population.[17]

While most Syrian citizens enjoyed a certain measure of religious and social freedom, this freedom ended at political lines. Willing to squash any threats to the operative power structures of the state, Assad's intelligence agencies prohibited any public expression of political dissent. To speak of politics meant risking horrendous torture, suffering, and death. In this system, only the dictator's voice mattered, and all others were expected to conform to his will with unquestioning obedience. Over time this form of state-sponsored terror fostered a culture of fear and self-sanctioning that severely limited Syrians' ability to speak freely and openly.[18]

When Jude first returned to Syria for college after being raised in the United Arab Emirates, his family warned him against engaging in any form of political dissent. "The walls have ears," his uncle told him, a phrase eerily evocative of George Orwell's ever watchful Big Brother, who exercises totalitarian control of people through propaganda, secrecy, surveillance, and brutal punishment.[19] Most people accustomed to Western democracies have difficulty imagining a world where external authorities monitor their every word and thought, but in Syria such free speech was risky and costly.

Even if states like Syria succeed in their quest to intimidate those who desire to speak out, the need for self-expression—and the emotions connected to it—never fully disappear, even when pressed down and buried. Instead, these pent-up emotions boil under the surface until they eventually explode. This irrepressible desire for freedom was at work when the events of the Arab Spring irrupted in 2011.[20]

The word for "freedom" in Syrian (*hureyye*) captured the people's deeply felt need for self-expression. While this word would soon become

---

[17] McHugo, *Syria*, 179–203.
[18] Ibid.
[19] George Orwell, *Nineteen Eighty-Four* (New York: Knopf, 1992).
[20] Not all those involved in protests in the Middle East in the spring of 2011—like many Syrians—were Arabs. In fact, a pan-Arabian identity to Greater Syria is arguably the product of pan-Arabian movements in the twentieth century like that of King Hussain and Ba'thism, with detrimental results to other Syrian ethnic identities such as Kurds and Assyrians. Syria is home to a diverse array of ethnic groups, such as Arabs, Syriacs, and Kurds. In recent years, movements calling for a Syrian pluralistic identity that offers a sense of belonging for all Syrian components (including non-Arabs) have emerged and gained considerable support.

the rallying cry for the peaceful demonstrations that swept the country in 2011, it would also trigger alarms within the Syrian regime. When the people demanded their right of self-expression, the regime made painfully clear that such freedom would come at a terrible cost.

In areas controlled by the Syrian army, security forces painted on walls and houses the slogan, "Assad or we burn the country." The regime was aware that Syrians wanted liberation, but they sought to diffuse it by pitting the desire for freedom against the need for safety. They propagated the message, "If you want freedom, then the price you will pay will be your safety." Many Syrians heeded these threats and accommodated the regime, but others only became more resolute in their determination, even in the face of violence and intimidation; thousands were willing to lay down their lives for the sake of that freedom.

As the violent crackdown ignited the fires of the revolution, Jude and his friends began mobilizing in the southern city of As-Sweida. They joined the millions of Syrians who dreamed of liberation from the political tyranny of the Assads, even with all the risks and costs involved. As Jude recalls, at times during the uprisings the need for self-expression surpassed even the need for safety and protection:

> On a calm April night in 2011, seven of us planned to meet at a predetermined place, but only three of us arrived. The rest had changed their minds, which—given the possible consequences of what we were about to do—was not surprising. Protesting was not only illegal, but unthinkable. To the regime it was treason, a blasphemous assault on the authority of the supreme leader. As I thought about what I was about to do, fear overwhelmed me at times, but eventually the moment came. As we met with other groups in a dark alley, with only dim yellow lights before us, a young man in our group lifted up a banner that called for the freedom of one of our detained brothers, and chanted, "Freedom . . . forever . . . Like it or not, Assad!" As we burst forth onto the street, we began chanting for the liberation of our country.

In no time, however, the regime unleashed its mercenaries (known in Syria as the Shabbiha[21]) to crush Jude and his companions. Within minutes, the

---

[21] *Shabbiha* is a Syrian word that roughly translates to "ghosts." The Shabbiha are criminals who were organized and paid by the secret police to repress protesters

Shabbiha inflicted unimaginable suffering upon them. Even in the face of his own anxieties, however, Jude discovered that once he had a taste of authentic self-expression, it could no longer be suppressed:

> As the events unfolded around me, I felt paralyzed with fear and couldn't even chant with my friends, nor absorb what was happening. But as we marched through the neighborhood and called for freedom, people showered us with rice and encouraged us onwards. Although they did not feel at liberty to chant with us, their hearts were jumping at the sight of a group of young men chanting for our country's liberation. Then it happened to me: a sudden burst of energy flowed through me, breaking down the wall that had barricaded every suppressed thought and emotion in me. What exploded in my mouth was one word: "FREEDOM!" That feeling felt more important than life itself and was stronger than the fear of dying. From that moment, I became a different man, a free man, a new man. It was like I was born again. Soon after I had the phrase, "The one who is fearful shall not truly live," tattooed on my wrist, and fear never held me back again.

Other Syrian refugees, like Jude, have a need to share their story, but the political and cultural context have made it difficult to safely do so. Many find themselves in a state of psychological bondage that cripples the emotional life.[22] The violence has particularly affected children and produced a deeply wounded and traumatized generation, which has put at risk the country's hope for a peaceful future.

When Jude and I first met, he was conducting trauma therapy projects for refugee children in Turkey at the Syrian border. The children had physically survived the horrors of war but were devastated on the inside. To address this need, Jude and his team eventually developed a trauma therapy program that helped these children experience, name, and express their emotions. This process allowed them to speak about their pain

---

during the Syrian uprising from 2011 onward. The word itself reflects the brutality and ruthlessness of these thugs who are blindly loyal to the regime and willing to commit the most horrific atrocities.

[22] For more on this topic, see Richard F. Mollica, *Healing Invisible Wounds: Paths to Hope and Recovery in a Violent World* (Nashville: Vanderbilt University Press, 2009).

and reveal their story in a safe and secure environment to staff who were trained for empathic listening. The team began discovering that the children started to heal when they could share their story in this supportive and affirming context.

When given the chance, these children would talk for hours. Amal, for example, spoke about how she watched her mother die under the rubble; Ahmad about how both his brothers were killed by a sniper; Safa about her fear of airplanes and the sounds of gunshots in the night.[23] Over time the team developed multiple activities to facilitate the healing process, such as creating interactive theater productions and painting exercises that facilitated self-expression. "As we saw the transformation in these children and the impact it had on their thoughts, actions, and behavior," Jude said, "it was as if we were witnessing a miracle happen in our midst."

When they first joined the program, for example, some children were extremely violent, in large part because of the traumatic violence they had experienced themselves. They did not know how to express their emotions except in hostile ways. As the children were coached on more constructive and creative approaches, violent behaviors dramatically decreased. Some metrics documented as much as a 90 percent decrease in swearing and antisocial behaviors after they participated in this program. Finding safe spaces for emotional expression opened a way to healing, growth, and personal development.

The Psalms give voice to the basic human need for self-expression. These texts were, in fact, first written and recited in Greater Syria, and although written thousands of years ago, they give expression to a range of emotions and prayers that have resonance for every generation. Some emerge from similar social locations as that of migrants, refugees, and displaced persons today (Pss. 91; 107; 121; 126; 137), offering us insight into the complex interplay between the outer journey of migration and the inner journey with God.

In the context of captivity, war, and exile, they give voice to experiences of loneliness, fear, insecurity, and vulnerability. The Psalmist is not afraid to speak to God about sadness, doubt, abandonment, anger, hatred, and even revenge. What is striking, however, is not only the way they name the inner terrain but also the Psalms' movement from places of pain to places of faith,

---

[23] The actual names of these children have been changed.

joy, gratitude, trust, confidence, and love. They cover a wide range of psycho-spiritual territory; their passionate pleas to their God are, as N. T. Wright puts it, "full of power and passion, horrendous misery and unrestrained jubilation, tender sensitivity and powerful hope."[24]

As they give voice to some of the deepest soul searching of the human heart, the Psalms testify to this fundamental need for self-expression. Finding no consolation in this world, the Psalmist turned to God and cried, "Hear me and answer me. My thoughts trouble me and I am distraught. . . . My heart is in anguish within me; the terrors of death have fallen on me. Fear and trembling have beset me; horror has overwhelmed me" (Ps. 55:2–5). In addition to giving expression to emotional terrain, these texts also offer some of the richest images of God in the scriptural canon. These images have much to say about the God who meets people in the context of their migration through this world.

"During the most difficult times," said Jude, "prayer helped me express my pain to a God who listened to me and who at times seemed as present as a close friend who suffers with me in my own pain. I see my own experience reflected in the words of the Psalmist who prayed, 'Give ear to my words, O LORD; understand my sighing. Attend to the sound of my cry'" (Ps. 5:1–3 NABRE). "When I could depend on no one else, I discovered a depth in my soul where I too prayed: 'Answer me when I call, my saving God. When troubles hem me in, set me free; take pity on me, hear my prayer'" (Ps. 4:2 NABRE).

One of the central images of God that emerges in the midst of Israel's own migration is that of a God who knows how to listen to and accompany his people. As Creator, he knows the needs and designs of his creatures: "You have searched me and known me. You know when I sit down and when I rise up; you discern my thoughts from far away. You search out my path and my lying down, and are acquainted with all my ways" (Ps. 139:1–3 NRSV). Rich in mercy, abounding in kindness, and steadfast in his love, he is able to respond to the deepest and most personal of emotions in order to meet, accept, and love his people where they are in their journey through this world.

---

[24] N. T. Wright, *The Case for the Psalms: Why They Are Essential* (New York: HarperOne, 2013), 2.

*The Need for Safety and Protection: God as Fortress and Shield*

> "I will now arise," says the Lord; "I will grant safety to whoever longs for it." (Ps. 12:6 NABRE)

On the night of August 22, 2012, amid all the risks and dangers, Jude and his friends staged a nonviolent protest in the southern Syrian village of Qurayya. This town was the home of the legendary figure Basha Sultan, who led the 1912 Syrian revolution against the French occupation. The territory's rich symbolism held much promise for the group's goals for mobilization, but it was also a heavily militarized region. If successful, they could electrify a nonviolent movement around the country. If unsuccessful, they would suffer greatly.

When Jude and his friends arrived at a designated place, about forty-five young men and women were there, starting that night with high ideals. They did their best to conceal their plan, inviting only a small group of experienced activists. The Syrian intelligence, however, eventually ferreted out their strategy and prepared accordingly.

By the time Jude's group got to the scene, they found an army of three hundred Shabbiha ready to trounce them. "We saw what we were up against, and then we looked at each other and exchanged fearful glances," Jude said. "At that moment we felt that all our preparations had been in vain. If we started chanting, they had the power to crush us within seconds." They were about to flee and merge with the crowd, but then a young man named Jubran jumped on someone's shoulder and shouted, "Syria is free. . . . Bashar must go out!"

"I was stunned by his courage," Jude said. "It was practically suicide! The Shabbiha were notorious for stomping people to death or tearing them to pieces under torture." Even though they were outnumbered by Assad's forces, the young man had dared to speak out. His words galvanized the group and inspired them to march forward to demand their rights and their dignity. "As our voices multiplied and others joined us," Jude remembered, "it felt like our chants were shaking the ground beneath us; it seemed like we were a crowd of thousands!"

At first the Shabbiha were shocked and did not know what to do. They were accustomed to Syrians bowing to their intimidating presence. Before long, however, they mobilized quickly and brutally retaliated. Chaos ensued. Jude managed to escape by blending into the crowd, but after attempting to save a friend who was being beaten to death, the Shabbiha started pummeling Jude. Then they threw him in a crammed truck and took him and the others to a prison.

Bruised and battered when they arrived, they began torturing them physically and psychologically. "After beating us, they herded us like sheep into a large room, locked the gates behind us, and made us face the wall." The prison guards then started using taser guns on their backs, legs, and heads. "I can never forget," Jude recalled, "the first time I felt that sharp, burning burst of pain penetrating through my waist. It was unlike anything I had ever felt before."

Then the torture of sleep deprivation began. "The officers would barge in our crowded cell every couple of minutes, select people from their group and start beating them. One of the hardest moments," he said, "was when this menacing guard came in and demanded to know who carried the sign that said, 'Freedom!' A fifteen-year-old boy named Shihab—who was detained with his father—reluctantly raised his hand. The guard then came over to him and punched his face, tossed him to the ground, and kicked him in the stomach. 'He is but a child!' the father screamed. The guards were heartless, however, and deaf to their cries."

To break them down they began the systematic torture of each individual. They would call each prisoner by name and take them away, and Jude would never see the majority of them again. "We wondered what kind of abuse awaited us. For hours on end, I sat with fear and anxiety, hoping it would soon be over. Nothing described my feelings better than the words of the Psalmist: 'I lie surrounded by lions, greedy for human prey, their teeth are spears and arrows, their tongue a sharp sword'" (Ps. 57:4 NJB).

When guards came to interrogate Jude, they wanted him to confess that he had planned an armed rebellion, even though they were always unarmed and nonviolent. And when they did not get the answer they wanted, they beat him. "That is how interrogation works in Assad's prisons. Because I was under the threat of violence, it was hard to decide if I should tell the truth, knowing I would be tortured if I did. But I spoke truthfully anyways, even though I knew it would cost me." In sadistic ways, the Assad regime twisted the basic human need for safety and used it as a weapon against people; they used state-sponsored terror as their main tool to subjugate the people.

During their arrest, Jude and his friends were taken to the "Underground." Formally known as the state's "political intelligence" branch, these stations existed in every Syrian town, village, and city. These torture chambers are typically located several stories beneath the ground, with cells painted with blood. They are unspeakable places of suffering where people are taken but never return. As Jude remembers,

> One of the most difficult parts of my experience was my solitary confinement. Having no one to talk to and no one to listen to my thoughts and feelings was more difficult than the torture itself. I know of people who even befriended cockroaches and ants in solitary confinement in order to feel some sense of connection. Nowhere was my humanity more violated than in this isolation. I would bang on the door and yell to the guard. I knew he would come in and beat me, but at least then I felt like my humanity was acknowledged. While in solitude, I felt like an inanimate object in a dead cell.

Reflecting on those times of crippling fear, Jude saw something of his own desolation echoed in the words of the Psalmist: "How many are my foes, LORD! How many rise up against me!" (Ps. 3:1 NABRE); "More in number than the hairs of my head are those who hate me without cause; many are those who would destroy me, my enemies who accuse me falsely" (Ps. 69:4 NRSV); "For I am treated harshly; attackers press me all the day" (Ps. 56:2); "They hold fast to their evil purpose; they talk of laying snares secretly, thinking, 'Who can see us? Who can search out our crimes? We have thought out a cunningly conceived plot'" (Ps. 64:5–6 NRSV); "Insults have broken my heart, so that I am in despair. I looked for pity, but there was none; and for comforters, but I found none" (Ps. 69:20 NRSV). Like a lone sparrow on a roof (Ps. 102:8), Jude was left struggling with immeasurable fear, abandoned, with no consolation from anybody.

During this time when he felt such violations of safety, however, Jude discovered a surprising strength that kept him going: "Although I feared the torture that awaited me," Jude said, "something happened at that time that I find difficult to put into words. I felt I could die at any moment, but surprisingly felt very safe. For the first time I can remember, I felt God intervening in my life, protecting me, revealing himself and letting me know he was there and that I could trust him, whatever was about to happen." "The Psalmist puts into words," Jude noted, "what I could only faintly articulate: 'But you, LORD, are a shield around me; my glory, you keep my head high.

With my own voice I will call out to the Lord, and he will answer me from his holy mountain. I lie down and I fall asleep, [and] I will wake up, for the Lord sustains me. I do not fear, then, thousands of people arrayed against me on every side'" (Ps. 3:4–7).

Jude hoped to avoid the torture that awaited him but knew that having God with him was no guarantee. "I knew that they could torture me physically," he said, "I just prayed that they would not reach into my soul and break me down." Turning to God like the Psalmist, Jude cried out, "Guard me from the trap they have set for me . . . from the snares of evildoers" (141:9). Finding his safety in God alone, he trusted in God as "my rock and my fortress, my stronghold and my deliverer" (Ps. 144:2 NRSV).

*The Need for Agency and Justice: God as King and Judge*

> How long must your servant endure? When will you judge those who persecute me? (Ps. 119:84 NRSV)

> Listen to the sound of my cry, my King and my God, for to you I pray. (Ps. 5:2 NRSV)

"When I was released from prison," Jude recalls, "my whole life was torn asunder. My friends and companions either disappeared in prison under torture or were killed. My family was dispersed into three different countries, and I was forced to say good-bye to my home country forever. It was hard to make sense of what was happening."

Amid the degrading oppression, Syrians came up with a slogan that expressed the sentiment of many: I am a human being, not an animal. "All we wanted were some basic rights," Jude recalled, "some freedom of expression and the right to be treated with respect and dignity." While he felt God's presence at critical moments, it was hard still to make sense of why God would allow all this to happen or why he did not do more to stop it. The conflict and unjust suffering raised a number of challenging theological and spiritual questions. "If our intentions were indeed noble," Jude asked, "where was God? How could he let all this violence happen? If he truly loved us, why did our oppressor seem to have the upper hand? These questions and others afflicted me beyond the physical suffering, and they compounded my external displacement with a great deal of internal emotional upheaval as well."

When refugees are forced to flee situations of violence, they seek protection anywhere they can find it. The first recourse for most is to seek shelter somewhere within their own country. When this fails, they cross international borders, hoping that a neighboring country will offer some measure of protection. Then they are often funneled into refugee camps run by the host country, an international nonprofit organization (such as the Red Cross) or the United Nations High Commissioner for Refugees (UNHCR).

Refugee camps offer a thin line of protection, but they are not ideal. They are meant to function as temporary shelter, not as a permanent dwelling. Ranging in size from ten thousand to one hundred thousand people,[25] they are built to meet basic human needs, not the full services of an urban setting. Many prefer not to live in the camps because, even if people gain a modicum of security, they often lose a significant say over their lives. For these reasons and others, more than 67 percent of the world's refugees live outside camps.[26] If people decide to stay inside the camp, however, many of the decisions about their lives and future are in the hands of others.

One of the most challenging aspects of living in a refugee camp, for example, is the diminished sense of personal agency. *Agency* refers to the capacity to act with reasonable autonomy and to make free choices about one's life and future. While no human being has total control over one's future, all of us have a need to make choices that shape the direction of our lives. The chaos created by the Syrian war created a crisis where millions were detained and deprived of a basic sense of appropriate control over important decisions in their lives and where they were going.

Camp-based refugees have little control even over their access to food and water supplies. While life-saving measures offer immediate response to a disaster, they can have detrimental effects over the long term. Even if such measures help stop the immediate bleeding in a refugee crisis, they do not create the conditions necessary to ensure human flourishing over the long haul. Without creating spaces where people have some say over their lives, they wither through a disempowering dependency. This setup can often erode people's inner dignity and make them feel powerless and helpless, as if they are children. Such a scenario is further complicated when life demands

---

[25] United Nations High Commissioner for Refugees, "Displacement: The New 21st-Century Challenge," https://fas.org.

[26] United Nations High Commissioner for Refugees, "Global Trends in Forced Displacement," 58, www.unhcr.org.

adult responsibilities such as providing for families. In such circumstances, people do not develop a healthy sense of their own abilities, nor are they able to mature into psychosocial patterns of healthy personal independence and relational interdependence.

These feelings of powerlessness take on added intensity in a world where there have been egregious human rights violations. When those in power carry out their crimes with impunity, victims often have few if any resources to come to their defense. People frequently cry to heaven for redress, especially when there is no end in sight and no justice for the oppressed. In these times the emotional terrain of one's life can become a war zone of its own. After everything has been taken away, Syrians can still be heard in the streets chanting, "Oh Lord, we have only You!"

Even for those who believe, such conditions can bring up feelings of God's agonizing absence. Millennia ago, the Psalmist cried out to God when all hope for justice seemed lost. "How long, LORD, will the wicked be jubilant?" (Ps. 94:3). "How long must I bear pain in my soul, and have sorrow in my heart all day long? How long shall my enemy be exalted over me?" (Ps. 13:2 NRSV). "How long will you judge unjustly and show partiality to the wicked?" (Ps. 82:2 NRSV). "How long must your servant endure? When will you judge those who persecute me?" (Ps. 119:84 NRSV). The Psalmist penetrates deep into the soul's experience of desolation and baldly names what it feels like to migrate into places of trust in God without fully knowing, to surrender without understanding, and to persevere even when no end is in sight.

Amid feelings of desperation, people understandably take the cause of justice into their own hands. Armed conflict, however, has never been a viable option for Jude, who knew that violence only creates more violence. When he and his friends mobilized, they were committed to achieving peace only through nonviolent means. When snipers from the regime started assassinating people in cold blood, protesters all around the country called for peaceful responses—not violent reactions. Even as people faced the regime's ruthless brutality, they chanted, "*Selmeyyeh*," which means "peaceful." This decision for nonviolence was made not because they felt peaceful inside. To the contrary, they chose the path of nonviolence even while they were struggling with difficult and violent feelings that arose within them.

Jude recalls how confused he felt when explosive emotions erupted inside him during detention. "After we were subjected to the most horrific forms of torture, I cried to God to punish the oppressor. I was ashamed of myself for all these violent wishes, but could not help it. Like the Psalmist, I prayed, 'Vindicate me, O LORD, my God, according to your righteousness, and do not let them rejoice over me' (Ps. 35:24 NRSV); 'Defend my cause against an ungodly people; from those who are deceitful and unjust deliver me!'" (Ps. 43:1 NRSV).

The Psalms give expression to feelings that are difficult to name like sadness, doubt, abandonment, loneliness, fear, insecurity, hatred, even revenge. These emotions are strong and intense, but frequently they are not expressed because of the perception that they go beyond the bounds of what is socially accepted.

Not only are difficult emotions challenging to accept personally, but they are difficult to accept within religious contexts, perhaps for fear that God will reject one who dares to speak so freely and honestly. Even if God is not offended by such brutal honesty, the institutional Church appears less receptive to them. Although these disturbing emotions are preserved in the biblical text, surprisingly they are not included in the Common Lectionary used at Mass; the texts used in liturgy omit those Psalms that deal with such violent emotions, such as 58, 83, and 109. Irene Nowell argues that our difficulty including such Psalms is due to a contemporary distaste for lament and a cultural aversion to vulnerability, anger, and violence.[27]

The book of Psalms records some thirty-three "cursing" or "imprecatory" ones, but as Sheila Carney points out, "[a] significant number of Psalms have been deemed unacceptable for use in worship."[28] However, their inclusion in the biblical record is an invitation to rediscover the wisdom that comes with expressing difficult emotions on the journey of life, something that recent studies in psychology have affirmed as well. Emotions provide information, not conclusions, and the nonjudgmental expression of emotion is, by itself, a therapeutic process.[29] Under this light, the imprecatory Psalms

---

[27] Nowell, *Pleading, Cursing, Praising*.

[28] According to various authors thirty-three Psalms, either entirely or in part, are considered imprecatory: Pss. 5, 7, 9, 10, 13, 16, 21, 23, 28, 31, 35, 36, 40, 41, 44, 52, 54, 55, 58, 59, 63, 68, 69, 70, 71, 73, 83, 94, 104, 109, 137, 139, and 140. For more on this topic, see Sheila Carney, "God Damn God: A Reflection on Expressing Anger in Prayer," *Biblical Theology Bulletin* 13 (1983): 116.

[29] One example of a school of psychotherapy that utilizes the experiencing and expression of emotion is emotion-focused therapy (EFT). EFT is predicated on the theory that genuine and nonjudgmental expression of emotion is, in itself, a healing process. In EFT, "a person needs to experience emotion to be informed and moved by

are not prescriptions for violence but genuine expressions of a believer's inner life and emotional experience.

After undergoing unjust persecution, the Psalmists are transparent about their emotional state and unafraid to express explosive emotions, even asking God to make their enemies' children into orphans and their wives into widows (Ps. 109:9–10). They are honest enough to ask God to "Break the teeth in their mouths . . . [and to] tear out the fangs of the young lions!" (Ps. 58:6 NRSV). And perhaps most jolting of all, amid the agony of exile and the unrelenting treatment of his persecutors, one Psalmist cries out, "Blessed the one who pays you back what you have done us! Blessed the one who seizes your children and smashes them against the rock" (Ps. 137:8–9 NABRE). These words are enough to make anyone shudder, but their inclusion in the biblical canon validates important emotional territory, even if not intended to give literal license to destructive behavior. But they give voice to the sometimes agonizing landscape of the soul.

Even though such words are an affront to contemporary religious sensibilities, they can be seen as healthy expressions of anger from a psychological perspective. From the agony of conflicting feelings, the Psalmist dares to speak. From the context of powerlessness, the Psalms confess God's kingship (5:2; 10:16; 20:9; 47:2; 47:8; 63:11; 89:18; 99:4; 145:1). From the context of injustice, they affirm God as judge (Ps. 7:8, 11; 50:4; 67:4; 72:2; 82:2, 8; 94:2; 96:10, 13; 98:9; 119:84). And while honest with these feelings of anger, resentment, revenge and hatred, they do not arrogate the task of justice to themselves but confess, rather, the larger frame in which one reads the journey of life: God's sovereign rule over all creation and human affairs, even when this was not readily apparent. As king and judge, God alone has power to mete out justice, to deliver those who suffer and ultimately to restore creation. "God is a just judge," the Psalmist proclaims, "powerful and patient" (Ps. 7:12). Acknowledging God's sovereignty, the Psalmist trusts the One who alone has power to control the universe and restore order to a chaotic and unjust world. From the midst of relentless injustice,

---

it and to make it accessible to change. People do not change their emotions simply by talking about them, by understanding their origins, or by changing beliefs. Instead, people change emotions by accepting and experiencing them, by juxtaposing them with different emotions to transform them, and by reflecting on them to create new narrative meaning." Leslie Greenberg, *Emotion-Focused Therapy: Coaching Clients to Work through Their Feelings* (Washington, DC: American Psychological Association, 2015), Kindle location 93.

the Psalmist cries to the heavens, "Rise up, LORD, in your anger; be aroused against the outrages of my oppressors. Stir up the justice, my God, you have commanded" (7:6).

Jude's first exposure to the Psalms occurred after his traumatizing experience:

> I did not expect to find such emotional authenticity in a religious text. . . . It was liberating. I never really identified with any religious tradition. What really mattered to me were the images of the God in whom I believed and with whom I was in relationship at an emotional level. Going into those times of upheaval, I had known a very different God than the one I came to know during my most vulnerable moments.

Through the process of self-expression, the Psalms give us an archetypal window into the timeless human experience. Such a process is therapeutic, but these texts are more than mere venting. In revealing this pain, the Psalmist gives utterance to the God who hears the cries of his people, accompanies them in their pain, and offers a sense of justice when all meaning seems lost.

*The Need for Community and Belonging: God as Home and Dwelling Place*

> He who dwells in the secret place of the Most High Shall abide under the shadow of the Almighty. (Ps. 91:1)

Although physical homelessness creates enormous stresses in the life of refugees, some of the most difficult displacements are related to the loss of relationships and a place to call one's own. The reasons that millions of Syrians cannot return to their homes are many. Some, like Jude, fear persecution and death for having protested for democracy and human rights. Others fear mandatory conscription in the army that would require them to kill innocent women and children in order to keep the regime in power. Still others are threatened because they fear the wrath of Jihadists. All these factors uproot people and force them to leave their homes and homelands. In the process they become disconnected from families, communities, home cultures, and native countries.

"The first thing they did when they arrested us," Jude remembers, "was search us and confiscate our belongings. I came to the protest with only one thing in my pocket: the key to my house. When the guards took it, I felt that they were taking away from me more than a piece of metal: I realized I might never see my home again. Never did I expect the physical, psychological, and spiritual homelessness that was to define my life in the months and years that followed."

The Syriac word for home (*beit*), which was incorporated into both the Arabic language and the Syrian dialect, means more than a physical dwelling. It also connotes the psychological sense of belonging. One's *beit* is a symbol of safety and protection, the soil in which one's life grows and one's relationships develop; it is what makes human flourishing possible. Taking away one's home means taking away emotional refuge and the context where one first learns how to be human. More importantly, it involves taking away a sense of identity. "Leaving one's home behind," as a local Syrian proverb puts it, "means losing one's dignity." For people like Jude and many others, the Syrian crisis has not only destroyed homes but destroyed communities.

Refugees forced to flee Aleppo, for example, are often no longer able to go back home. Their *beit* becomes unwelcoming and unsafe, and for many, their homes and entire neighborhoods have been obliterated by mass bombardment. As refugees flee to other countries, they not only face the challenge of building a new identity but also of finding a new network of life-giving relationships. Xenophobic labels and other negative social and exclusionary undercurrents make creating a new *beit* in a new land a challenge: physically, economically, socially, culturally, and emotionally. Defining their lives as migrants, refugees, and more generally the unwelcome "others"—a message they are constantly reminded of—degrades and diminishes their sense of well-being and leaves them with a feeling of estrangement.

Jude's family once lived together on Syrian soil, but they are now scattered all over the world. His mother and father are in the United Arab Emirates, his brother is in Germany, and his sister remains in Damascus. Jude was fortunate enough to be released from prison, but his freedom came at a price. Those who tortured and interrogated him told him he had to leave Syria and never return again. "The next time we take you down there," the political intelligence officer told him, "you'll never see daylight again." Seeing many of his friends meet that dreadful fate, Jude knew that they meant it. Because Jude is now "marked" by those in authority, he cannot return to the home where he was born and raised.

Reflecting on his experience of rootlessness, Jude writes,

> What is an exile? It is the abrupt undoing of everything you've built in a place you once called home; a square-one restart, toiling in a new land because your own won't (or can't) have you anymore. Exile is when your mother's gentle kiss and your father's warm embrace become fleeting fantasies, lingering oceans away in a fierce struggle against the forgetfulness of time. It is when pictures sent from overseas remind you of new wrinkles on your aunt's face, testifying to your absence; when you wonder if you'll ever see your loving aging grandma once again before she dies. Exile is your friends, their warm love strangled by the distance, and the faces you spent a lifetime knowing all too well, now slated for forgetfulness. Exile is the death of you, as you've always known yourself, and the forceful rebirth of someone else, brought to speed on life in this fancy new tent you are now to call home.

This need for belonging is so central to his own heart that today Jude carries the Syriac word for "home" tattooed on his wrist.

The Psalmist also knew times of being displaced to a foreign land, and knew very well the pain of homelessness and nonbelonging. Various tribes of Israel were forced to live away from their birthplace, and many were exiled or held captive in Greater Syria and later Babylon. These experiences critically shaped the consciousness of the Jewish people, linking their identity inextricably with the land, which was home to them.

Jerusalem, in particular, occupied a central place in that identity, and it became known as the house of God. It was the Jewish *beit*, always in the forefront of the Psalmist's mind and heart: "Let us go to the house of the LORD. Our feet are standing in your gates, Jerusalem" (Ps. 122:1–2). Amid their rootlessness, the Psalmist lamented that "Even the sparrow has found a home, and the swallow a nest for herself, where she may have her young" (84:3) ... "they are ever praising you" (84:4). In the most beautiful of words the Psalmist tells of a God that provides the spiritual and psychological at-home-ness to those who believe in him.

For those who are refugees today, the words of the Psalmist not only name many of their emotions but also anchor their hope. Jude recalls that after three days in the civil prison, the guards barged into his cell and told him and his companions that they were finally going to be released. They were so overcome with joy that they even asked for supplies to clean their cell. But within a short time, they realized they were only torturing them in a different way. "When we left the prison, it dawned on us that they were just playing another psychological game with us." Shortly after reaching the open air, they stuffed them into a prisoner transport vehicle and threw them back into darkness. Except for a few small holes that penetrated the truck's steel-cased shell, they had no windows to the outside world. They worried about what was about to transpire and feared the worst. One detainee recounted a story about a person who, after his initial interrogation, was taken to an intelligence branch, where they tortured and killed him. "That only fueled our anxieties," Jude recalled. "The agonizing uncertainty tormented me, and all I could think was, *Who can deliver us from our impending fate?* Feeling powerless at the hands of our captors, to whom could we turn to for help?"

As the truck passed through the town, Jude and the others tried to peer through the small holes in order to see where they were going. He recognized a familiar intersection and knew that, if the truck went straight, they would take them to the town of Salkhad, where they might be released. If it turned left, however, they would be heading for the political intelligence branch, where they worried that they would never see daylight again. "Left! It went left!" a boy screamed. "We're doomed!"

"The five days that followed," Jude said, "were the most difficult days of my life." They cut them off from all ties to the outside world, locked them in an underground cell, and then tortured them physically and psychologically. "I found myself," as the Psalmist put it, "'in the midst of lions hungry for human prey'" (57:4). Everywhere I looked, I saw only suffering. "Never have I ever experienced such levels of pain, fear, and terror," Jude remembers. "Their aim was not just to inflict physical injury. Above all they wanted to take away our hope and lead us to utter despair. It often felt like 'my only friend is darkness'" (Ps. 88:19).

### God as Refuge for the Refugee

> Because you have the LORD for your refuge and have made the Most High your stronghold, No evil shall befall you, no affliction come near your tent. For he commands his angels with regard to you, to guard you wherever you go. (Ps. 91:9–11)

In 1951, the United Nations defined a *refugee* as someone who has been forced to flee his or her country because of a "well-founded fear of persecution for reasons of race, religion, nationality, political opinion, or membership in a particular social group."[30] We have looked at the experience of one such person in the efforts to understand better both his outer and inner journey. At the same time, we have tried to explore the connection between the inner terrain of refugees like Jude Ash with the words of the Psalmist, who lived thousands of years ago. Both speak of the search for God amid the emotional upheaval of displacement and the hope for a place to call home in the context of exile.

Although Jude's experience is very personal, we see reflected in his life universal themes that resonate with other refugees and are an integral part of every human journey. They are themes pertaining to freedom and self-expression, safety and protection, agency and justice, and community and belonging. These issues tap into some of the deepest longings of the human heart. They are intrinsic to every person, yet they become particularly manifest in times of vulnerability, crisis, and distress. From this perspective the experience of migrants and refugees exposes something at our inner core that can be difficult to speak about, even to ourselves.

The Psalmist risks total transparency with God and does not hold back from expressing anything, even the most difficult of feelings, like anger, hatred, doubt, and violence. Contemporary psychological studies likewise affirm that expressing and processing these feelings, however difficult, is an important step toward healing and integral human development. The God in whom Israel trusts is capable of receiving the entire range of emotional experience—not just those we currently find acceptable. "As I look back at this whole ordeal, and I read my experience in light of the Scriptures," Jude recalls, "I realize how the Psalms put into words what I had so much trouble articulating. For me it was not just reading about some experiences of people in the past. The words of the past revealed something important about my present and my journey into the future."[31]

These feelings, however, are not the last word for the Psalmist. In addition to trusting their inner experience, the Psalmist does not make gods out of emotions by giving them all their attention. Ultimately, the Psalmist

---

[30] United Nations High Commissioner for Refugees, "What Is a Refugee?," www.unrefugees.org.

[31] These images of God presented in the Psalms are never complete or exhaustive; Israel was reluctant to even speak the inexpressible name of God. They are but a first word on a God whom we know only in part, yet who speaks nonetheless in human experience.

comes to see their place within the larger horizon of who he is before God. While learning to deal honestly with struggles, the Psalmist also learns to affirm that God alone is sovereign, and all life is ultimately in God's hands. For this reason, the Psalmist does not arrogate to himself the task of justice, instead learning that the only path to wholeness and healing rests in surrendering trust to the One from whom all life has come. As Jude says.

> I have trouble putting this experience into words, but oddly enough, the more threatening and painful the outside world became, the more I turned inside, to my relationship with God. I realized that my torturers had power over my body but they could never control other things—especially my soul. I imagine that frustrated them. In a strange way I felt a sense of peace because I had this deep inner sense that I could trust a power that was bigger than me and greater than those who threatened my life.

While struggling to discern God's presence amid the trials of the journey, the Psalmist gave expression to different images of God which we have explored, such as God as Liberator and Companion, Listener and Friend, King and Judge, and Home and Dwelling Place. All of these might best be summarized under a more comprehensive image of God that appears more than fifty times in the Psalter: The refugee-psalmists of yesterday and refugees like Jude in our own time often look to God alone as the central refuge of the human heart.

For many on the move today, this image of God as refuge is inseparable from the experience of being a refugee, even and especially when the world treats them as refuse. "My relationship with God was more real for me than the lashes of the torturers' whip or the pain of their punches and kicks," Jude said. "He gave me the space to speak when I was isolated, to feel safe when I felt afraid, to find strength when I felt helpless, and to feel connected when I felt estranged. I know very personally now," Jude said, "what it means when the Psalmist declared, 'Happy are all who take refuge in him!'" (Ps. 2:12 NRSV).

"The words of the Psalmist not only give voice to my pain and suffering," Jude said, "but also my hope and my gratitude. For this reason, I can unite my own words with the Psalmist, who says, 'I love you, LORD, my strength, LORD, my rock, my fortress, my deliverer, My God, my rock of refuge, my shield, my saving horn, my stronghold! Praised be the LORD, I exclaim! I have been delivered from my enemies'" (Ps. 18:2–4).

# 4

# The Second Reading

## *The Early Church and Migration*

*You are no longer strangers and aliens, but you are citizens with the saints and also members of the household of God.* (Eph. 2:19)

### The Early Christian Community: Four Marks of Its Migrant Identity

In the previous chapters we looked at various Old Testament migrants, refugees, and trafficked persons and explored their connection to central theological themes and issues of migration in our time. We also examined the topic of exile, the language of the Psalms, and their correlation to the emotional landscape of today's refugees. Now we turn our attention to the New Testament.[1] This chapter will focus primarily on readings from the Acts of the Apostles, the Epistles of Paul and others, and the book of Revelation.[2] The next chapter will look more closely at the Gospels and migration.

---

[1] In the Sunday liturgy, the texts for the Second Reading are ordinarily drawn from the Acts of the Apostles, the Epistles, and the book of Revelation. These texts were written in the first and possibly the second century AD and cover the life, growth, and development of the early church. After the Holy Spirit descended on the apostles at Pentecost (Acts 2:1–31), the Christian community was sent around the world to proclaim the Gospel.

[2] Because Christians see the Scriptures as a "living word," even as it recounts something that happened in the past, I use what scholars refer to as the *historical present tense*. Because it contains a message not just for the original hearers but for all generations, this present tense seeks to discern how this message speaks to our own times.

Because of the extensive connection between New Testament literature and migration, we limit our focus to the connection between these texts and what became known in time as the four key "marks" of the church—namely, that the church is one, holy, catholic, and apostolic. These attributes were initially articulated at the First Council of Constantinople in AD 381, and they help unite the church amid its increasing diversity. They are drawn in part from four key images from the New Testament and play important roles in shaping the Church's self-understanding of who it is before God and how it is called to live in the world.[3] They are (1) the body of Christ, (2) the followers of the Way, (3) the disciples to all nations, and (4) a pilgrim people. These images shape not only the church's emerging migrant identity but also inspire it to be in closer solidarity with others migrating around the globe.

A number of years ago I was giving a talk in New Hampshire to a group of leaders from Catholic Charities on migration and theology. As I began to lay out the foundation for the topic, I described a number of global calamities that gave rise to refugee crises in recent decades. One of them was the Rwandan genocide of 1994, when, in the course of one hundred days, Hutu extremists—armed mostly with machetes—killed almost a million people, the majority of whom were Tutsis.[4]

After the talk a woman named Christine came forward and introduced herself. She was a Tutsi from Rwanda and lived through the events of 1994. During the killing sprees, she and her husband Jean Bosco took refuge in the Hotel Mille Collines, popularly known from the Academy Award–winning film as *Hotel Rwanda*. After narrowly escaping death, they came to the United States as refugees.

A few weeks after we met, they invited me to write a book with them on the search for God amid the genocide.[5] I knew from the start this would be a

---

[3] Vernon Robbins draws on the notion of "rhetography" as a way of analyzing how the visual imagery or pictorial narrative and scene construction shapes rhetorical arguments. Vernon Robbins, *The Invention of Christian Discourse*, Rhetoric of Religious Antiquity (Blandford Forum, UK: Deo Publishing, 2009), 6, 16.

[4] Among the many books on the Rwandan genocide, see in particular Romeo Dallaire and Brent Beardsley, *Shake Hands with the Devil: The Failure of Humanity in Rwanda,* 1st Carroll & Graf ed. (New York: Carroll & Graf, 2004), and Emmanuel Katongole, *Mirror to the Church: Resurrecting Faith after Genocide in Rwanda* (Grand Rapids: Zondervan, 2009).

[5] See Daniel Groody and Jean Bosco Rutagengwa, *Love Prevails: One Couple's*

difficult project, not only because of the theodicy problems it presented, but because this genocide happened in a nation that was known at the time as one of the most Catholic countries in Africa. How could a good God allow such evil to happen, especially in a country where most of the people called themselves Catholic? Exploring insight into this question was a challenge I could not decline.

As we began probing the multidimensional questions related to the Rwandan genocide, we continually asked what prompted Hutu extremists to systematically plan the extermination of their Tutsi counterparts and fellow Rwandan citizens. We eventually went back to Rwanda and visited the places where many of their friends and relatives were killed and the villages where community members were murdered.[6] As we accompanied them in the agony they experienced, we remembered the dead and often celebrated the Eucharist over the burial sites where many of their family members died.

In the course of our research, we kept coming up against the issue of identity. We found that much of the genocide revolved around establishing who "I am" and who "the other" is. The genocide memorials around the country constantly presented this vexing issue to us. Though I originally thought the acrimony between Tutsis and Hutus was the consequence of centuries of unresolved tribal tension, I realized the issue is more complicated. The distinction between Tutsis and Hutus is in fact less than a hundred years old and the byproduct of Belgian colonization and perverted social ideologies. When this forced distinction began after World War I, the difference between a Hutu and a Tutsi was determined by how many cows one had. One could switch between groups as their livestock count changed. But at some point, this administrative marker evolved into an economic divider, then a social classification, and then an ethnic identity.

Whereas once they understood each other in fraternal terms, now they typecast their social relationships into a Hutu-Tutsi dualism, with clear markers between "me" and "them." As this distinction created walls, the gap worsened and the alienation deepened. The neighbor who at one time was a brother or sister then became viewed not only as other but also as an enemy, one who must be controlled, marginalized, and even eliminated.

---

*Story of Faith and Survival in the Rwandan Genocide* (Maryknoll, NY: Orbis Books, 2019).

[6] See also a film from this project, *Return to Rwanda*, https://vimeo.com.

In many ways, Rwanda fleshes out in our own time some of the biblical typologies introduced earlier in the Old Testament: the migration from the land of likeness to God in Adam and Eve, the disintegration of fraternal relationships in Cain and Abel, the othering of the Hebrews in Egypt, the lure of idols in Israel, and many others. Through its varied texts, the Scriptures reveal this deeper, fallen substrata at work in the world; as we let these Scriptures interpret us (rather than think we interpret them), we can unmask some of the hidden agendas in identity politics that are frequently at work in debates over migration.

Migration brings the issues of identity to the front burner. This does not mean identity is always something negative; as social creatures, the task of identity construction, and consequently identity politics, is unavoidable. Identity formation is a necessary part of psychological growth, cultural development, social relationships, and nation building. But identity can also become a weapon that justifies social exclusion, party politics, collective narcissism, and even unimaginable violence. The genocide in Rwanda is a tragic example but also a reminder of how identity shapes and influences how we see each other.

As we explore these questions in the New Testament literature, we look at some of the ways the early church understands itself and some of the beliefs that shape its identity and its mission. Because every generation is tempted to domesticate the Scriptures to fit preexisting tribal mindsets and provincial ways of thinking, we also explore the ways in which these texts challenge existing Christian communities to conversion, renewal, and transformation—in brief, to a new way of living and being in the world. Because the conviction of a citizenship beyond this world transforms everything—even the "territoriality" of political, social, and religious worlds—we examine how the encounter with the risen Christ calls people from otherness to oneness and from alienation to communion.

*The One Church: The Body of Christ and Many Cultures*

> For in one Spirit we were all baptized into one body, whether Jews or Greeks, slaves or free persons, and we were all given to drink of one Spirit. (2 Cor. 12:13)

After the first believers experience God's boundless mercy through the risen Christ, they begin crossing borders of every sort to share this good news with all peoples. This activity makes them migrants in many different ways. As their missionary work brings them into contact with diverse languages, cultures, and customs, however, they have to wrestle with new and deeper understandings of who they are before God and in relationship to others. The more that people of other identities are added to their ranks, the more they have to work out together the complex task of discerning a common identity (Acts 2:5–13).

As it faces challenges related to unity in diversity, the New Testament presents a number of images that shape the early church's evolving self-understanding. One of the most important is the image of the body of Christ.[7] This image reveals much about the divine desire to bring wholeness and unity to a fragmented and divided human family (Jn. 17:21). The more its members realize a universal connection in Christ, they begin to break down the walls between us and them (1 Cor. 12:12–14). As they start transcending their local and tribal identities, they realize a fundamental interconnection beyond the sociopolitical boundaries that circumscribe their daily lives.

As the identity of first Christian communities evolves, they speak of the body of Christ in three overlapping ways: the physical body in the person of Jesus of Nazareth; the social body of Christ in the community of believers, especially in relationship to the poor; and the sacramental body of Christ in the Eucharist. All three dimensions name the radically interconnected nature of human existence and possibilities for spiritual communion in the Kingdom of God.

One reason the New Testament draws upon the image of the body is that God took on a human body in Jesus (Jn. 1:14). As such, God takes the body seriously, and the body itself is an important source of revelation about God. Jesus understood the experience of living in the flesh, and he responded to people's bodily needs with attentiveness, compassion, and care (Mt. 15:29–32). He also knew that religion can play an important role in healing, protecting, and uniting people.

As a Jew, Jesus knew that the laws of religion can play an important role in ordering life toward its ultimate end. But as the divine physician, he also knew that, in and of itself, religion and its laws are not the main goal (Mk. 2:17). When some Pharisees appeal to the laws of religion to create social border policies that are alienating, isolating, and excessively self-serving,

---

[7] Others include images such as the temple of God (1 Cor. 3:16–17), the building (1 Pt. 2:5), the chosen people (1 Pt. 2:9), and the family of God (Eph. 3:14–15).

Jesus challenges and even transgresses the borders created by them for the sake of the bigger picture of healing and salvation (Mt. 9:13; 23:24).

After the resurrection, the body of Christ takes on another layer of meaning for the Christian community. The church now comes to understand its relationship to Christ through baptism, which incorporates (Latin: *in-corporare*, to form into a body) that community into his mystical body. As they become integrated into the life of the risen Lord, the community becomes, as John Haughey puts it, the "social flesh of Christ."[8]

When Paul uses the term "body of Christ," he is speaking about the disciples' connection to Christ in his risen body (1 Cor. 12:27; Eph. 1:22–23) and to one another in this social flesh (Eph. 5:30). Transcending all borders, this body binds all people together through love (Col. 1:18–22; 3:15; 2:19; Eph. 1:22–23; 4:4, 12–16).[9] This love also calls them to re-member especially those who have been dis-membered from the body of society like the poor, the vulnerable, and forgotten (Mt. 25:31–46). This process of re-membering is an important part of justice making and the building of a humane community.

The Epistle of James makes frequent reference to the integral connection between faith and justice, such as when Paul reminds the church at Galatia of the need and duty to remember the poor (Gal. 2:19). In our own time, Martin Luther King Jr. spoke to this connection between the body of Christ and real, corporeal needs when he said,

> As Christians we must think not only about "mansions in the sky," but also about the slums and ghettos that cripple the human soul, not merely about the streets in heaven "flowing with milk and

---

[8] See Michael Downey, *The New Dictionary of Catholic Spirituality* (Collegeville, MN: Liturgical Press, 2000), 100–105, and John Haughey, "Eucharist at Corinth: You Are the Christ," in *Above Every Name: The Lordship of Christ and Social Systems* (New York: Paulist, 1980), 126.

[9] See Leland Ryken, James C. Wilhoit, and Tremper Longman III, eds., *Dictionary of Biblical Imagery* (Downers Grove, IL: InterVarsity Press, 2000), 109. Boyd Luter Jr., "Christ, Body of," in David N. Freedman ed., *The Anchor Yale Bible Dictionary* (New York: Doubleday, 1992), 1:921–23; Dale B. Martin, *Slavery as Salvation: The Metaphor of Slavery in Pauline Christianity* (New Haven, CT: Yale University Press, 1990); Margaret M. Mitchell, *Paul and the Rhetoric of Reconciliation: An Exegetical Investigation of the Language and Composition of 1 Corinthians* (Louisville, KY: Westminster/John Knox Press, 1991); Ben Witherington, *Women and the Genesis of Christianity* (New York: Cambridge University Press, 1992).

honey" [Ex. 3:8], but also about the millions of people in this world who go to bed hungry at night. Any religion that professes concern regarding the souls of men and fails to be concerned by the social conditions that corrupt and economic conditions that cripple the soul is a do-nothing religion, in need of new blood.[10]

Because all human beings share in this inescapable network of mutuality, whatever one does or fails to do to another affects the whole body (Mt. 25:31–46).

Similarly, Paul's letter to the Ephesians speaks to the human predicament of living on the other side of the wall created by sin. In many ways the outer walls we build in our communities reveal something of the inner walls we construct within us. Because sin divides us from God and one another, he came to see that the answer to our existential alienation is not resolved by building bigger walls but by breaking down these walls altogether. In Ephesians, Paul writes, "In Christ Jesus you who once were far off have been brought near by the blood of Christ. For he is our peace; in his flesh he has made both groups into one and has broken down the dividing wall, that is, the hostility between us" (2:13–14 NRSV). In place of a fragmented body, Christ's death promises a reconciliation that brings all people into unity in his body, transforming strangers into friends.

This mystical understanding of Christ's body has very practical implications for the way we relate to each other in this age of migration and can challenge much of the way we think about this topic. Some oppose immigration out of ignorance, fear of change, or perceiving it as a disruption to culture or economy. In such cases it is important to move beyond perceived fears and to critically evaluate some of the dominant narratives about migration. More and more evidence-based research highlights the positive contribution of immigrants, challenging some of contemporary society's prevailing myths.[11]

For others, the response to immigrants is more extreme. When deteriorating socio-economic and security conditions in Central America sent waves of unaccompanied minors coming across the US-Mexico border in

---

[10] Wolfgang Mieder, *Making a Way out of No Way: Martin Luther King's Sermonic Proverbial Rhetoric* (New York: Peter Lang, 2010), 242.

[11] See, for example, the work of the George W. Bush Presidential Center at www.bushcenter.org.

2014, one American citizen said, "If we can't turn them back, I think if we pop a couple of them off and leave the corpses laying on the border, maybe they'll see that we're serious about stopping immigration."[12] Such hardheartedness not only deprives immigrants of their God-given dignity but also demeans one's own God-imaged nature. In addition to threatening unaccompanied minors, this mindset injures the whole body as a people.

If we do not make a connection between my body and my neighbor's body, then worship itself becomes empty and meaningless. We explore the relationship of the sacramental dimensions of the body of Christ to migration in subsequent chapters, but for now we note how the New Testament writings came to incorporate the notion of the body of Christ into the liturgy.

In Galatians Paul brings out this radical unity when he says, "There is neither Jew nor Greek, there is neither slave nor free person, there is not male and female; for you are all one in Christ Jesus" (Gal. 3:28). After the Last Supper, Christ says to his disciples, "This is my body broken for you.... This is my blood ... poured out for many" (Mt. 26:26; Mk. 14:22; Lk. 22:19; 1 Cor. 11:24). These powerful, generative words disclose Christ's self-giving love offered for the mending of broken relationships and for the healing of the broken bodies of the human condition (Mt. 8:17; 1 Pt. 2:24; see Is. 53:4–5). Ultimately, at work here is the universal language of love expressed through ritual that mediates grace and redemption.

This multidimensionality of the body of Christ in its physical, social, and sacramental dimensions is a two-edged sword that critiques narratives of excessive privatization and individualization and promotes a vision of social concern and responsibility. As it challenges the world's exclusive, alienating frameworks, it highlights the inclusive framework of salvation history that reconciles. As Don Senior puts it,

> God's embrace reaches to the ends of the earth and all its peoples. Here is the ultimate bond that ties the human family together. Before God all are one. Here is the bulwark against an ideology of racial superiority, here is the challenge to the absolute claims of national or cultural boundaries, here is the basis for all human dignity, including the dignity of the stranger in the land—the right

---

[12] Keegan Hankes, "KKK Joins Immigration Debate with Calls for 'Corpses' on the Border," Southern Poverty Law Center, July 31, 2014, www.splcenter.org.

of the migrant to cross borders, whether in fleeing danger or seeking opportunity; the obligation to welcome the stranger and to provide refuge and respect. For the Christian all of these commitments flow ultimately from the biblical vision of the human family as one before God.[13]

How can this image of the body of Christ offer us insight into a theology of migration?

One important area for reflection comes from the physical body. Because the human body has its own natural laws and "border policies" that manage its inner life and relationship to the outside world, the body can offer some helpful perspective on this topic. The skin, for example—the body's largest border area—plays a critical role in healthy thermoregulation. If this border of the skin were either completely permeable or sealed off to become an impenetrable barrier, the whole body would suffer, even to the point of death.

In the same way that the human body needs borders, the body of a nation also functions more effectively when it has borders. Catholic Social Teaching recognizes the right and duty of a nation to create and protect its borders for the protection of its members and for the regulation of its life and society.[14] For this reason and many others, it does not promulgate a teaching requiring completely open border policies.

Catholic Social Teaching does not, however, grant that nations have an absolute right to control borders. It insists that the body of any particular nation cannot be understood independently of its relationship to the larger body of the human community. In the same way that any one body cannot understand itself apart from its relationship to a larger social network, the body of any one country cannot understand itself as isolated from the world outside its borders. Its rights to national sovereignty can never be argued only from its self-interest and need for security: It must also take into account other duties to the poor and the international common good, without which no just and sustainable peace—or social homeostasis—is possible.

---

[13] Donald Senior, "Beloved Aliens and Exiles: New Testament Perspectives on Migration," in *A Promised Land, A Perilous Journey: Theological Perspectives on Migration*, ed. Daniel G. Groody and Gioacchino Campese (Notre Dame, IN: University of Notre Dame Press, 2008), 20–34.

[14] For more on this subject, see United States Conference of Catholic Bishops, "Catholic Social Teaching on Immigration and the Movement of Peoples," www.usccb.org.

The image of the body of Christ, at its core, is a constant reminder that we are social creatures—and that, flowing from our connection to God, we are interconnected as a human community. Our present fallen state makes this communion difficult, but it also highlights how much our relationships need healing and redemption, which only God can accomplish. The vision of Christ's body reminds us of another way to live and be in the world. It inspires people to welcome instead of marginalize and to unite instead of divide. To receive his body is a decision to move toward connection and communion over isolation and alienation.[15] Even if this goal is never fully accomplished in this world, the New Testament gives expression to the beginning of this reign in Christ and its promise of cosmic and universal fulfillment in the end of time.[16]

*The Holy Church: The Followers of the Way and the Law of Love*

The one who loves another has fulfilled the law. (Rom. 13:8)

One of the foremost ambassadors of Christ's body in the New Testament is the apostle Paul. He was an itinerant theologian, energetic missionary, and author of more than one-fourth of the New Testament. We know more about his outer migrations than any other person in the Bible, but his reflections on his inner migration into the human heart and his return journey to God also present some of the richest spiritual accounts in Scripture.

Paul's road, however, is not an easy one nor a straight path; it has more twists and turns than for any other individual in the Bible. His religious zeal is well documented from his early years, but his misguided attempts at holiness cause serious harm and injustice to the first Christians (Acts 8:3; 9:1–2; 22:3–4; 26:9–11; 1 Cor. 15:9). Still, his encounter with the risen Lord changes him and awakens him to a bigger understanding of God, religion, and holiness.

At its core, holiness is about becoming whole again and growing into an integrated and generative human being. In other words, it is the process of becoming another Christ who reveals truths about both God and being human. This entails the constant work of turning, changing, and rediscovering the way back home to our true image and likeness. Look at the way of the first believers, the way Paul persecutes them, and the way beyond the law to holiness.

---

[15] Downey, *The New Dictionary of Catholic Spirituality*, 100–105.
[16] Ryken et al., 109.

The first ones sent out to proclaim the Gospel message after Jesus' death and resurrection were not known specifically as "Christians" but as the people of "the way" (Acts 9:2–4; 18:25–26; 19:9, 23; 22:4; 24:14, 22). To follow the way means to follow Jesus, who describes himself as "the Way" (Jn. 14:6). It has less to do with physically falling in step with Jesus and more with following his attitudes, attributes, and actions.

As the first disciples follow this way, it calls into question the conventional "way" of society and often put them in conflict with its established norms. In the process the first disciples confront the disordered ways on which much of society is built: the economic systems structured around inordinate self-interest, the political policies aimed at protecting the powerful, the social disorders that result in marginalizing the poor, and the religious patterns constructed around elitism and clericalism. The way of Jesus, in contrast, challenges the idols of money and pleasure, the ways of empire and greed, the gods of self-interest and privatization, and the corrupt and misguided ways of the religious establishment.

The story of Paul, ironically, begins with his persecution of the followers of the way. Originally known as Saul of Tarsus, Paul was by all accounts a zealous Jew, and he presides intensely over the killing of the first followers of the way (Phil. 3:6). He went to great lengths "to destroy the church; entering house after house and dragging out men and women, he handed them over for imprisonment" (Acts 8:3). Such is his practice until an experience on the road to Damascus changes his life, when "a light from the sky suddenly flashed around him. He falls to the ground and hears a voice saying to him, 'Saul, Saul, why are you persecuting me?'" (Acts 9:3–4).

After this experience, Paul goes through a long period of disorientation. How could someone who so tenaciously defended his religion, and so vigorously adhered to the law, so completely miss the mark of genuine holiness? To find the right road again, Paul has to undergo a more fundamental migration from his religious ideals to his spiritual experience, and from his head to his heart, which will lead him from focusing on the law to relationships. In other words, he has to undergo a conversion, one that leads him to ripen as a human being in ways that produce the fruit of the spirit of God (Gal. 5:22–23). And in time he discovers that the road to holiness requires much more than adherence to religion and legal certitudes.[17]

---

[17] The literature on conversion is immense. I draw on the work of Bernard Lonergan and Donald Gelpi, who defined *conversion* as moving from irresponsi-

From a Christian perspective, religion is not God; it is at best a road to the Kingdom of God. Ongoing conversion is a way of finding and making progress on that road that leads to union with God and communion with others in his kingdom. The Church proclaims that kingdom, witnesses to it, and seeks to embody it—but can never be equated to it. As Pope Paul VI notes, "The Kingdom of God announced by Christ can be entered only by a "change of heart" . . . that is to say through that intimate and total change and renewal of the entire [person]—of all his opinions, judgments and decisions" (*Apostolic Constitution Paenitemini of the Supreme Pontiff Paul VI on Fast and Abstinence*).

The Kingdom of God, however, stands in direct conflict to the kingdoms of the world and its designs of empire, idolatry, and self-centeredness. The kingdom that Jesus proclaims, in contrast, is a kingdom of truth, life, grace, justice, peace, self-giving love, and holiness (*Gaudium et Spes* 39). When one turns from the values of the kingdoms of this world and centers one's life on the Kingdom of God, one sets out on a road to think, feel, act, and relate to others in a different way.

Paul's experience on the road to Damascus causes him to reorient his relationship with God and with religion. It raises questions about his operative understanding of holiness and consequently challenges his approach to the law. Whereas previously he believed that obedience to the law is the road to holiness, God's merciful intervention changes his vision altogether.

Underneath Paul's zealous defense of the law is a deep unrest. Paul's central existential angst is that all human beings are in a very real sense illegal aliens. Our illegal status comes from the fact that each and every one of us has broken God's law in one form or another and therefore no one is fully justified in God's sight (Rom. 3:9–20). Paul spends a good part of his life working out the strife around how such aliens can be put in right relationship with God (i.e., justified) and become citizens again in God's Kingdom.

In time, he discovers that human beings are powerless to overcome our existential alienation and cannot become naturalized citizens in God's Kingdom again by our own efforts. He will learn that only One person has entirely fulfilled the law, and only One is "justified" in God's eyes, and only

---

bility to responsibility in various areas of life. Gelpi differentiated the conversion process into five areas: affective, social, intellectual, moral, and religious. Bernard J. F. Lonergan, *Method in Theology* (Minneapolis: Winston/Seabury, 1972), and Donald L. Gelpi, *Committed Worship: A Sacramental Theology for Converting Christians,* vols. 1 and 2 (Collegeville, MN: Liturgical Press, 1993).

One is holy. Only by participating in Christ's life through faith and charity can anyone find the way back home to holiness. This leads Paul to the realization that justification—and justice—require more than getting the law right: above all it involves getting his relationships right, first with God, then with others, and only after with the law. Until he understands the primacy of the law of love, he cannot understand the role of every other law.

The divine irony in God's plan of salvation is that the One who redeems us from this condition of alienation became himself illegal for our sake. As Paul writes, "Christ redeemed us from the curse of the law by becoming a curse for us—for it is written, 'Cursed is everyone who hangs on a tree'" (Gal. 3:13). In the paradoxical designs of God's mercy, the righteous One of God became an illegal alien according to the laws of this world in order to save those who actually are illegal aliens! In this way God thwarts the way of this world and opens up a path to hope for all.

As Paul begins to read the law in light of Christ's law of love, he realizes that the law is something that is needed, but it cannot save us. It has its role but is not the remedy. The law can be a guide, but it can also blind us. In the end the law can give information but cannot bring transformation (Rom. 3:20; 7:7–13).[18] The only way of overcoming our alienation and finding true holiness is not through a rigid adherence to the law but through reconciliation to God through faith in Jesus Christ. Only Christ can accomplish this end through this self-giving sacrifice on the cross. As he begins to see the world through the eyes of the One who was crucified, Paul begins to find the way toward a more lasting spiritual liberation.

The experience of the risen Lord led to a faith beyond fear, a spirituality beyond religion, and a holiness beyond legalism. The life of Paul illumines that Christian holiness is about living in the world with the mind and heart of Christ and living out his supreme law of love and interpreting every other law in light of it. Now, how does this *imitatio Christi* affect how we think about issues like migration?

Our reflection around Paul's misguided take on the law, his spiritual experience of God's mercy, and his perspectives on alienation and justification should challenge any simplistic notions that dismiss immigrants as "illegal aliens." Could our inability to accept our own illegal-alien status before God contribute to our unwillingness to welcome other illegal aliens

---

[18] Richard Rohr, "Grace and Law, Part I," Daily Meditations, April 12, 2015, https://cac.org.

in our midst? While I would not want to risk overpsychologizing or over-spiritualizing the many reasons for such exclusionary mindsets, Paul's struggles reveal not only the human temptation to take refuge in legal certitudes but also the call to heed the weightier demands of the law of love in the search for authentic holiness. Our alien status in this life, and Christ's illegal status by the laws of this world, should challenge and relativize all notions of excluding people by virtue of their political documentation.

Paul's struggle over obedience to religious law in the search for genuine holiness also has bearing on what we would call *civil law* or *positive law* today. This topic is important for our discussion because few areas in the migration debate are more contested than migration and the law. Many Christians today even defend their positions on migration issues in light of Romans 13, where Paul says that "every person be subject to the governing authorities; for there is no authority except from God, and those authorities that exist have been instituted by God" (v. 1). This passage is often cited to legitimate current border policies and to justify legal exclusion of any immigrants who transgress the laws of a nation-state.

The problem, as Danny Carroll perceptively notes, is that we cannot read Romans 13 without first reading Romans 12. As he puts it,

> Romans 12 sets the stage for Paul's words concerning human government in chapter 13. It contrasts the mind-set and life of Christians with what they encounter in society. Romans 12 exhorts believers not to be molded by the "pattern of this world" (12:1–2). This includes being shaped by political ideologies—in this case, going along with what one's political party says about immigration and the treatment of immigrants. Instead, Christians should have their minds renewed through the Scripture so that they might know the will of God.[19]

Paul's testimony reveals another way of understanding our humanity, religion, the law, and ultimately life. He reminds us that finding the road to God's Kingdom demands the hard work of changing one's direction and discovering a different way, a different narrative, and a different road until it aligns with God's mind, heart, and ways.

---

[19] M. Daniel Carroll R., *The Bible and Borders: Hearing God's Word on Immigration* (Grand Rapids: Brazos Press, 2020), 111–12.

*The Catholic Church: A Bridge to Eternity and a Heavenly Homeland*

> Our citizenship is in heaven, and from it we also await a savior, the Lord Jesus Christ. (Phil. 3:20)

The third mark of the church is its catholic character. The word "catholic" (Greek *katolikos*) comes from two words *kata* (according to) and *holos* (the whole). While many commonly limit the meaning of this term to a religious denomination, its biblical meaning is more universal. The term *catholic* seeks to convey to the entire world the promise of human wholeness according to the creative, saving, and sanctifying designs of God's love. At its core, this involves the central mission of bringing a lost and broken human community back home to a place of wholeness, holiness, and oneness. The Scriptures, rituals, prayers, devotions, practices, and social teachings of Roman Catholicism seek to bring forth the truth that we are created by love, for love, and to love.

In the context of a world alienated by sin, being Catholic involves more than building a physical space we call the church; being Catholic means creating a relational space where people can form community by connecting to God, each other, and themselves. In Protestant circles, the notion of the "catholic" church refers to the global body of the Christian community. In the Roman Catholic Church, the pope is a symbol of unity and is called to be a bridge builder among nations. His title as pontiff (Latin: *Pons* [bridge] + *facere* [to make]) has much to say about his role as a mediator between God and human beings and his mission to unite all people together under the love of God.

But if the message of the Gospel that Catholicism proclaims is good news for humanity, why then have so many people been persecuted because of it? We first read about Christians being killed in the Acts of the Apostles, which uproots the early church and forces the community to become refugees. After Stephen's martyrdom, the early followers flee to Judea and Samaria (Acts 8:1–8). Later, Jewish Christians escape to Phoenicia and Cyprus (Acts 11:19–21). Then Greek-speaking Jewish Christians seek refuge in Antioch and other parts of the Mediterranean world. In the wake of imprisonment, torture, and harassment, many of the first Christians become forced migrants and are sent out to foreign lands around the globe.

While there are many reasons for this persecution, including their personal devotion to Christ, it was primarily because this devotion also makes a very subversive political statement. In many ways it challenges the established practices of power and disrupts the operative social, religious, and political order. Confessing "Jesus as Lord" means that Caesar is not. Such confessions violate the Roman state policies that require a pledge of such allegiance. To live according to the universal kingdom that Jesus announces means that the kingdoms of this world, its values, and its leaders do not hold primacy over their lives. Nor can they expect total obedience from Christ's followers. As they follow Jesus as Lord and seek to be obedient to him, Christians challenge the deification of money, the idolatry of the state, and the glorification of power.

In Jesus' own life and ministry, he disrupts established norms and exclusionary social patterns. Some scholars suggest that Jesus' table fellowship with sinners, in particular, is most likely what leads his critics to persecute him. Although his embrace of sinners and the outcast brings good news to the poor, it also offends those who profit and benefit from the existing system.[20] In this sense, Jesus is crucified, as Robert J. Karris put it, "because of how he ate."[21] How he ate challenges those who construct walls surrounding their self-interest and tribal concerns. Jesus instead wants a wider door to a bigger banquet hall with a larger table that includes the excluded. In other words, Jesus wants his followers to build a catholic community that proclaims God's universal love for all people, not just the privileged few.

When the first Christians continue these inclusive practices and threaten the established order, they too are persecuted. Peter is one of them. He is one of the most important leaders of the early church. He knew Jesus in the flesh, accompanied him in his earthly ministry, and—after Jesus rose from the dead—became one of the foremost apostles who migrates around the world preaching the Gospel message. As the rock upon which Christ promises to build his church, Peter will play a key role in shaping the emerging catholic community of believers (Mt. 16:18). Before he is martyred in Rome somewhere between 64 and 68 CE, he is forced to migrate because of threats to his own life. He, members of his community, or both, write letters to strengthen those who are displaced and on the move because of their preaching of the Gospel message.

---

[20] See Norman Perrin, *Rediscovering the Teaching of Jesus* (San Francisco: Harper & Row, 1976), 102.

[21] Robert J. Karris, *Luke: Artist and Theologian* (New York: Paulist Press, 1985), 47.

The New Testament, in fact, uses many terms to speak about those who are migrating. The Greek words that appear most often are *xenos*, *paroikos*, and *parepidemos*. Like economic migrants, foreigners, internally displaced people, permanent residents, and refugees today, those in the New Testament are frequently crossing borders, entering different lands, and taking up temporary or permanent residence in new places. They are not only geographically displaced but, like migrants today, are often politically, legally, socially, and even religiously marginalized.[22]

*Xenos* most commonly refers to a stranger. It is the root of terms like *xenophobia*, and often describes a fear or intense dislike of those who are different, such as foreigners or aliens (Acts 17:20; Heb. 13:9). In biblical times, *xenos* are frequently regarded with suspicion, if not hatred.[23]

The *paroikos* are sojourners who come from other places and stay for a time in another land.[24] These are more likely resident aliens. Although they are not naturalized citizens, *paroikos* pay taxes in order to occupy the land.[25] No matter how long they live on the land, however, they do not see themselves as belonging to it. Because they long for their country of origin, the new land never feels like home to them, and they always dream of returning to it (Heb. 11:9–10).

The *parepidemos* also stay for a time, but they have a permanent home somewhere else.[26] They are more like "visiting strangers."[27] And because they stay in a place for less time than the *paroikos*, the connection of the *parepidemos* to the life of the community is often limited.

These terms come into view especially in the First Letter of Peter, which is addressed to a community of persecuted Christians who are seeking refuge in the province of Asia Minor in the areas of Pontius, Galatia, Cappadocia,

---

[22] John Hall Elliot, *A Home for the Homeless: A Sociological Exegesis of 1 Peter, Its Situation and Strategy* (London: SCM, 1982), 48–49.

[23] W. Barclay, *The Letter to the Hebrews* (Louisville, KY: Westminster John Knox Press, 2002), 175.

[24] The word *paroikia* is the root word for the English word *parish*, which gives expression to how Christians are always looking toward the homeward journey and whose citizenship ultimately is beyond this world.

[25] W. Barclay, *The Letters to the Galatians and Ephesians* (Louisville, KY: Westminster John Knox Press, 2002), 131.

[26] Barclay, *Letter to the Hebrews*, 176.

[27] S. R. Garrett, "Sociology: Sociology of Early Christianity," in D. N. Freedman, ed., *The Anchor Yale Bible Dictionary* (New York: Doubleday, 1992), 6:95.

Asia, and Bithynia.[28] In the text, the words *paroikos* and *parepidemos* are used together when addressing the Christian community. The author also refers to them as the *eklektoi parepidēmoi* (1 Pt. 1:1). Modern versions translate this phrase in various ways, such as the "chosen sojourners of the dispersion" (NABRE), "those living as aliens in the Dispersion" (NJB), "elect exiles" (ESV), "God's elect, strangers in the world" (NIV), and "exiles scattered to the four winds" (MSG). Underlying these translations are three interrelated themes: Christians are chosen by God, they are migrants in this world, and their homeland is beyond this world.

Some commentators, including John H. Elliott, argue against the idea that *eklektoi parepidēmoi* is a spiritual metaphor for those journeying to the next world. Elliott makes the case instead that it refers to the social location of the early Christian community, which consists of socially marginalized migrant workers who experience social alienation because of their Christian identity. He believes many in this community are immigrant artisans, craftspeople, traders, and merchants residing permanently in, or temporarily traveling through, the towns and villages. Whether the terms are meant literally or figuratively,[29] the experience of displacement for the first Christians significantly shapes how they understand themselves as "passing strangers" in this world.[30]

Because the community of 1 Peter feels multiple levels of dissonance between the divine power they believe in and the earthly powers that rule over them, their way of life puts them at odds with temporal authorities. This forces them to reevaluate their political identities as well. They realize that even if these identities have a proximate value in the world, they are not big enough to contain their deepest beliefs. But if their ethnic, tribal, and political identities do not define them, what does?

Christians with Jewish roots frequently draw upon Scriptures that resonate with their own experience of displacement, such as bondage in Egypt, exile in Babylon, and dispersion to the ends of the earth. Those with gentile

---

[28] Scholars debate whether Peter himself was the author of this letter. Our central concern in this section, however, is more the audience of 1 Peter and its message.

[29] Elliott rejects the traditional "heaven-is-my-home" reading of 1 Peter, arguing that the terms *paroikos* [resident alien; 1 Pt 2:11] and *parepidēmos* [visiting stranger; 1 Pt. 1:1; 2:11] describe the political and social condition of the people addressed in the letter. See Elliott, *A Home for the Homeless*, 48–49.

[30] Christopher Naseri, "The 'Elect' as 'Resident Aliens' and 'Sojourners' in 1 Peter 2:11," *Caban* 8 (2016): 285–302.

roots, however, need a different way of making sense of their spiritual identity in the face of persecution. They too realize that the closer they come to living in union with Jesus, the more other identities become relativized. The more the vision of the Kingdom of God shapes their worldview, the more a heavenly homeland comes into focus. As they come to realize they are not permanent residents of this world, they begin to understand themselves, at best, as temporary residents in it.[31] Moreover, as they realize the nation and even the world do not foster their catholic connections to those living in other lands, they begin to redefine citizenship and homeland.

This theme of heavenly citizenship runs through the early church from its inception. It speaks to the belief that this world has never been, never is, and never can be a final destination or a lasting home, which means that migration is at the core of Christian identity. In Ephesians, Paul says, "You are no longer strangers and aliens, but you are citizens with the saints and also members of the household of God, built upon the foundation of the apostles and prophets, with Christ Jesus himself as the cornerstone" (2:19). In the Letter to the Hebrews we read, "For here we have no lasting city, but we are looking for the city that is to come" (13:12–14). Augustine adds, "This heavenly city, then, while it sojourns on earth, calls citizens out of all nations, and gathers together a society of pilgrims of all languages, not scrupling about diversities in the manners, laws, and institutions whereby earthly peace is secured and maintained, but recognizing that, however various these are, they all tend to one and the same end of earthly peace."[32]

Although the first Christians never see themselves fully of this world, they do not dispense themselves from civic duties and other obligations of human solidarity. Being naturalized as citizens of God's Kingdom does not mean ignoring their citizenship; it means rooting their citizenship on a higher plane. In other words, faith calls them not just to be against the world but to be in the world and for the world.[33]

Because the first Christians know what it feels like to be rejected, they have an acute appreciation for those who have welcomed them through the practice and virtue of hospitality (Greek: *philoxenos*, "lover of

---

[31] G. Kittel, G. W. Bromiley, and G. Friedrich, eds., *Theological Dictionary of the New Testament* (Grand Rapids: William B. Eerdmans, 1964), 2:64–65.

[32] Augustine, *The City of God* 19.17.

[33] Edward L. Cleary, "A New Ideology: The Theology of Liberation" in *Crisis and Change: The Church in Latin America Today,* 62 (Maryknoll, NY: Orbis Books, 1985).

strangers").³⁴ The disciples depend on hospitality, and they choose leaders who foster it (*episkopos*; see Acts 10:6, 18, 32, 48; 16:15; 18:7; 21:4, 8, 16; 28:7; 1 Tm. 3:2).³⁵ In 1 Peter, Christians are urged "to be hospitable to one another without complaining" (4:9),³⁶ because welcoming the migrant stranger is also a way of welcoming the hidden, divine presence in our midst: "Do not neglect to show hospitality to strangers, for by doing that some have entertained angels without knowing it" (Heb. 13:2). This call to hospitality has never lost its centrality in Christian life and is arguably more important now than ever, especially because of today's heightened religious persecution.

When visiting a refugee camp in Bulgaria, a man came up to me and said, "I am a Christian." I was surprised he began his conversation that way, so I asked, "Why are you a Christian?" He replied, "They [ISIS] came up to me [in Syria] and said, 'Are you a Christian?' And I said, 'Yes.' And when they asked why, I said, 'I am tired of the war, violence and bloodshed. I want peace. And Christ alone gives me peace.' I went away, but later that evening I came back and discovered they had killed my mother, my father, and my whole family."

In one form or another, more than three-quarters of the world's people today live in nations that have religious restrictions of some kind.³⁷ The US Department of State estimates that Christians in more than sixty countries are persecuted because of their faith.³⁸ This occurs in countries including North Korea, Somalia, Syria, Iraq, Afghanistan, Saudi Arabia, Maldives, Pakistan, Iran, and Yemen.³⁹

By some estimates, more Christians are persecuted in contemporary society than at any point today in human history. Although there is considerable debate on the precise number, more than 260 million people live in countries of high persecution: one in eight Christians worldwide.⁴⁰ Somewhere between seven thousand and one hundred thousand Christians

---

[34] It is also translated as "foreign peoples" and "resident aliens" (Rom. 12:13).
[35] Senior, "Beloved Aliens and Exiles," 20–34.
[36] Ibid.
[37] Peter Henne, "5 Key Findings about Global Restrictions on Religion," Pew Research Center, February 26, 2015, www.pewresearch.org.
[38] US Department of State, International Religious Freedom Report for 2013, www.state.gov.
[39] Open Doors USA, "World Watch List," www.opendoorsusa.org.
[40] For updated statistics on Christian persecution, see ibid.

are killed each year because of their faith, and many more are forcibly displaced.⁴¹ According to the organization, each month 322 Christians are killed for their faith; 214 churches and Christian properties are destroyed; and 772 forms of violence are committed against Christians, such as beatings, abductions, rapes, arrests, and forced marriages.⁴² Religious persecution, be it of Christians or adherents of other religions, is a major reason people still migrate around the world today.

While many people remain forced to migrate because of religious persecution, many others continue to migrate across borders because they have a message to share—a message that transcends borders and builds bridges, uniting all people in a common fraternal bond under the God who created every human being and seeks the redemption and deliverance of all. As the first Christians embraced the call to turn from ways that alienate and exclude, and to embrace ways that reconcile and connect, they migrated to all nations as apostles on a global mission.

*The Apostolic Church: Disciples to All Nations and a Global Mission*

> "You will be my witnesses, in all Judea and Samaria, and to the ends of the earth." (Acts 1:8)

The fourth mark of the Church is its apostolic nature. This means that the church is always migrating. Originally, the word apostle was a title used for a naval commander or Greek colonizers, and it later described a ship or fleet of ships sent overseas. Ironically, the first apostles were people who worked the seas as fishermen as well. Jesus met them where they worked and transformed them from being fishermen to being fishers of men and women in the work of salvation (Mt. 4:19).

The word *apostle* (Greek: *apostolos*) appears eighty-one times in the New Testament and refers to someone sent with a message. Jesus is the foremost apostle because he is the One sent by the Father (Heb. 3:1), then the twelve men sent by Jesus (Acts 1:24–25), then those sent to preach to Israel (Lk.

---

[41] See Ruth Alexander, "Are There Really 100,000 New Christian Martyrs Every Year?," BBC News, November 12, 2013, www.bbc.co.uk; Center for the Study of Global Christianity, "Status of Global Christianity 2020," Gordon Conwell Theological Seminary, www.gordonconwell.edu.

[42] Open Doors USA, "Christian Persecution," www.opendoorsusa.org.

11:49). In time, the word "apostle" became synonymous with all those who are sent across borders as migrants to proclaim the Gospel message to the whole world.

By far, the most visible migrant in the New Testament is the apostle Paul, whom we briefly examined earlier. His ministry lasted from 33 CE (when he was about thirty-one years old) to his martyrdom in Rome in 68 CE (at age sixty-six). The Acts of the Apostles details his migration routes, as do fourteen other books attributed to Paul: 1 and 2 Corinthians, 1 and 2 Thessalonians, 1 and 2 Timothy, Colossians, Ephesians, Galatians, Hebrews, Philemon, Philippians, Romans, and Titus. In his concern for the churches, he was constantly on the move, on the road or at sea.

*The Migration of Paul on His Missionary Journeys*

Scholars debate the specific number of missionary journeys Paul undertook after his conversion. His letters speak of only three migrations (Gal. 1:18; 2:1; Rom. 15:25), while the Acts of the Apostles speaks of five just to Jerusalem after his conversion (9:26; 11:30; 15:4; 18:22; 21:15).[43] All in all we have a record of approximately fifty cities that Paul visited in his various journeys.

The table on the next page names some of the cities Paul visited on his missionary travels.[44] According to the Stanford Geospatial Network Model

---

[43] Paul J. Achtemeier and Society of Biblical Literature, *Harper's Bible Dictionary* (San Francisco: Harper & Row, 1985), 760.

[44] Bible Study, "All Cities Visited by the Apostle Paul Map," www.biblestudy.org.

| | | | |
|---|---|---|---|
| **Amphipolis** (Acts 17:1) | **Caesarea** (Acts 9:30; 18:22; 21:8; 23:23) | **Miletus** (Acts 20:15; 2 Timothy 1:17) | **Rome** (Acts 28:16) |
| **Antioch (Pisidia)** (Acts 13:14) | **Cenchrea** (Acts 18:18) | **Mitylene** (Acts 20:14) | **Salamis (Cyprus)** (Acts 13:5) |
| **Antioch (Syria)** (Acts 11:26; 13:1; 15:22; 18:22–23) | **Corinth** (Acts 18:1) | **Myra** (Acts 27:5) | **Seleucia** (Acts 13:4) |
| **Antipatris** (Acts 23:31) | **Cyprus** (Acts 13:4) | **Neapolis** (Acts 16:11) | **Sidon** (Acts 27:3) |
| **Apollonia** (Acts 17:1) | **Damascus** (Acts 9:19) | **Nicopolis** (Titus 3:12, 15) | **Spain** (Romans 15:22–25, 28) |
| **Appian Way** (Acts 28:13–15) | **Derbe** (Acts 14:6; 16:1) | **Paphos (Cyprus)** (Acts 13:6) | **Syracuse (Sicily)** (Acts 28:12) |
| **Appii Forum** (Acts 28:15) | **Ephesus** (Acts 18:19) | **Patara** (Acts 21:1) | **Tarsus** (Acts 9:30) |
| **Arabia** (Galatians 1:17) | **Fair Havens (Crete)** (Acts 27:8) | **Perga** (Acts 13:13) | **Thessalonica** (Acts 17:1) |
| **Assos** (Acts 20:13) | **Iconium** (Acts 13:51) | **Philippi** (Acts 16:12; 20:6) | **Three Taverns** (Acts 28:15) |
| **Athens** (Acts 17:16) | **Jerusalem** (Acts 9:26; 18:21; 21:11–17; 23:11) | **Ptolemais** (Acts 21:7) | **Troas** (Acts 16:8; 20:6) |
| **Attalia** (Acts 14:25) | **Lystra** (Acts 14:6; 16:1) | **Puteoli** (Acts 28:13) | **Trogyllium** (Acts 20:15) |
| **Berea** (Acts 17:10) | **Malta** (Acts 28:1) | **Rhegium** (Acts 28:13) | **Tyre** (Acts 21:3) |

of the Roman World, Paul would have traveled 7,938 miles on his first three journeys through much of Asia Minor and Greece between 46 and 57 CE. In 60 CE he was taken to Rome, another 2,334 miles of travel. In total, the scriptural record reveals Paul logging at least 10,282 miles.[45] Assuming he made other journeys as well, his actual migrations were presumably even more extensive.

These distances are all the more impressive when we consider the difficulties of travel in the ancient world, even when journeying along established routes. Paul knew intimately the trials, sufferings, and vulnerabilities of the migrant journey. In his Second Letter to the Corinthians, he speaks of some of the perils he experienced on land and in the open waters:

> Three times I was shipwrecked; for a night and a day I was adrift at sea; on frequent journeys, in danger from rivers, danger from bandits, danger from my own people, danger from Gentiles, danger in the city, danger in the wilderness, danger at sea, danger from false brothers and sisters; in toil and hardship, through many a sleepless night, hungry and thirsty, often without food, cold and naked. And, besides other things, I am under daily pressure because of my anxiety for all the churches. (11:25–28 NRSV)

In the same Mediterranean waters where Paul was shipwrecked, near Malta and Italy today, thousands of migrants continue to drown each year.

The story of Rokaya Satar is just one contemporary example of perilous journeys and migrant shipwrecks. After fleeing Iraq, she hoped to seek refuge in Australia. She initially found her way to Indonesia, where she boarded a smuggler's boat called the *SIEV X*, and—along with 400 people (including 150 children)—was crammed into the ship's cabin. Many became seasick during the journey, but after about nine hours the engine stopped, the vessel split, and the boat began to sink. Because only about a hundred life jackets were available, people began to panic, and within no time all were thrown into the ocean. Rokaya recalls,

> I saw my small daughter Alya floating, eyes open, dead. A little later, we saw the body of my elder daughter. My husband looked

---

[45] See Stanford University, "Orbis: The Stanford Geospatial Network Model of the Roman World," http://orbis.stanford.edu, and Open Bible, "Calculating the Time and Cost of Paul's Missionary Journeys," www.openbible.info.

quite strong until he saw his daughters and he started choking. He said, "I have lost my family, I have brought you to this, I do not deserve to live." He said, "I cannot stay, I do not want to see you die in front of me." As he was talking, he was looking very tired, he was crying, his grip became loose because of his exhaustion. Then a wave came and washed him away from the timber. I felt alone until the middle of the night. I heard cries from others from time to time, but I could not see the other survivors. Later I saw two people. I yelled out to them, "Take me with you! I am alone!" They pulled my plank toward theirs where there was another woman holding on. The other woman became tired and sank under the water twice and died. . . . We remained until the boats came and rescued us.[46]

When night came, many more died in the water of exhaustion, hunger, thirst, and the consumption of fuel-polluted seawater. Some without life jackets died of the cold. The next morning, an Indonesian boat rescued forty-five survivors, but Rokaya had lost her husband and her two daughters in this tragedy at sea. Today hundreds of thousands of migrants like Rokaya hop onto rickety boats, hoping to find a new life in neighboring countries.

The apostolic mission of the Church includes welcoming people like Rokaya. It involves not only sending apostles to other places but also welcoming those from other places. In this sense an integral dimension of the saving mission of the Church is to help people like Rokaya find safety and protection. In many diverse ways, apostles are sent into the world today to address shipwrecks of many different kinds.

In addition to the vulnerabilities associated with the migrant journey, many people today are still drowning in the undercurrent of war, oppression, poverty, greed, abuse, drugs, fear, racism, meaninglessness, materialism, and many other problems. The mission of the Church is integrally related to liberating people from every oppression, protecting their lives, and developing their gifts and their flourishing as human beings. In this context, the

---

[46] International Organization for Migration, Missing Migrants: Tracking Deaths along Migratory Routes, "Families of Missing Migrants Speak," August 23, 2021, https://missingmigrants.iom.int. This story is an adaptation of an original transcript of the videotaped interview with the survivors in the week following the shipwreck. It was published on sievx.com, which gained access to the document via Tony Kevin, who presented the document to the CMI Inquiry as an attachment to his first submission.

apostles—like those of the early church—are likewise called to reach out to people who are shipwrecked in any way, to proclaim the God of life, and to build a civilization of love.[47]

## The Migrant Church as Pilgrim in the World

In this chapter we have explored the proclamation of the God of life in this second reading of the New Testament. As we have looked at writings in Acts, Paul's Epistles, and other texts, we have examined some of the external and internal factors that sent the early church around the world to share the Gospel message. We have seen how the images of the body of Christ, the followers of the Way, a heavenly homeland, and disciples to all nations give rise to four marks of its identity, namely that it is one, holy, catholic, and apostolic. These marks shape its mission of reconciliation and the call to bring people from a place of otherness to a vision of oneness. These marks also have deep resonance with central theological themes of communion, love, eschatology, mission, and many others.

To these four marks we add one final attribute that is particularly suited to the challenges of our own times. Peter Phan argues that "migrantness" is also a fundamental mark of the Church and, more importantly, of Christianity itself.[48]

As Phan reads the Church's mission through the lens of migration, he claims that (1) outside of migration there is no American Church (*extra migrationem nulla ecclesia America*); (2) outside of migration there is no Church (*extra migrationem nulla ecclesia*); and (3) because outside of the Church there is no salvation (*extra ecclesiam nulla salus*), he argues that outside of migration there is no salvation (*extra migrationem nulla salus*). This means that, as the Church imitates the life of Jesus, this migration entails moving from division to unity, from fragmentation to wholeness, and from tribal sectarianism to universality.

The New Testament writings we have considered here, along with many others, teach us that not only is there a history of migrants in the church, but in the words of *Erga Migrantes Caritas Christi* (17–18) migrants "can

---

[47] For more on this topic, see Daniel G. Groody, *Globalization, Spirituality, and Justice: Navigating a Path to Peace* (Maryknoll, NY: Orbis Books, 2017).
[48] Peter C. Phan, "Deus Migrator—God the Migrant: Migration of Theology and Theology of Migration," *Theological Studies* 77, no. 4 (2016): 845.

be seen as a call and prefiguration of the final meeting of all humanity with God and in God. Migrants' journeying can thus become a living sign of an eternal vocation, a constant stimulus to that hope which points to a future beyond this present world, inspiring the transformation of the world in love and eschatological victory." This message is at the heart of the book of Revelation as well, reminding us that we are pilgrims in the world on the way to an eternal homeland. Driven by a love that cannot be walled in, and inspired to a mission that does not let anyone be walled out, the church continues to transcend borders, build bridges, and create communities that are a sign of God's presence among us. In the next chapter, we turn our attention to the coming of the eternal migrant who pitched his tent in our human neighborhood in order to lead us back home.

# 5

# The Gospel Reading

## *The Divine Migration*

*The Word became flesh and blood, and moved into the neighborhood.* (Jn. 1:14 MSG)

### The Migration of God to the Human Race and His Return Migration

For Christians, the life, death, resurrection, and ascension of Jesus Christ are at the heart of biblical revelation. Because this paschal mystery deals with God's movement to earth—and as a consequence our return journey back to our heavenly home—they are especially important for our reflection on migration from a theological perspective. The central focus of this chapter is Jesus, the migrant Son of God. His journey is so significant to humanity, and so central to our return journey home, that I refer to it here as "the Great Migration." As the definitive event in salvation history, the Incarnation initiates a migration story that redefines and transvalues every other migration.

Before examining the Divine Migration in more detail, it is important to say something about the way Jesus teaches people as he moves throughout Israel, Judah, and the surrounding region. Though he embodies the wisdom of the unseen God, he does not come just to transmit doctrinal information to others, unlike many other religious leaders across time. He first draws people instead into a deeper relationship with himself and then calls them to a deeper journey into themselves and into community.

In the process, Jesus calls people to reflect on their lives, their choices, and their development (or lack thereof) as human beings. More often than not he does this by asking probing questions rather than by giving specific answers. Of the 183 questions Jesus is asked in the Gospels, he only directly answers three of them. In turn, however, Jesus asks 307 questions. For every question Jesus answers, he asks over 100. Though people commonly think of Jesus as "the answer man," he is "more like the Great Questioner," as Martin Copenhaver puts it.[1]

So why did Jesus migrate to our planet? Our aim is not just to unearth information about the Gospels but to explore how the questions presented in these texts can lead us to personal formation and social transformation. From this perspective, what questions would Jesus pose to us about the migration and refugee crisis today? How would he challenge the operative narratives of our life and times? What questions would he ask about where we are going in our own journey and who we are becoming? How would he challenge us to rethink everything in light of the primacy of God's Kingdom?

As we examine these questions, we take a closer look at the migration of Jesus, the people who accompanied him, the places he traveled, and the messages he taught. By taking a deeper journey with the Virgin Mary, the Holy Family, John the Baptist, the Good Samaritan, and the Samaritan woman, we explore more of what it means for our journey into ourselves, to God, and with one another.

## The Virgin Mary and the Jewish Law: Migration and the Illegal Alien

> Mary had been engaged to Joseph, but before they lived together, she was found to be with child from the Holy Spirit. (Mt. 1:18 NRSV)

In the mystery of the Divine Migration, God enters our human condition in the person of Jesus Christ. This is a striking starting point for the New Testament. It is a message that brings much to console us, but it raises questions that should confuse us as well, because it disrupts so many conventional understandings of law, religion, and morality. What led God, in Jesus, to cross the wall that separated the human from the divine? What made him

---

[1] I am grateful to Michael Galligan Stierle for first giving me this insight. See especially Martin B. Copenhaver, *Jesus Is the Question: The 307 Questions Jesus Asked and the 3 He Answered* (Nashville: Abingdon Press, 2014).

visit a people in the bondage of what effectively is the detention center of a sinful world? Above all, why would God initiate a plan to save the world through what was, in effect, an illegal border crossing?

At the center of this drama is the person of Mary of Nazareth. At the time of the Divine Migration, she is betrothed to Joseph. Betrothal in biblical times is a yearlong interim period between courtship and marriage, and while it is not exactly the same as a marriage today, it still has legal stipulations. The penalty under the Law of Moses for breaking this agreement by adultery, rape, incest, or fornication is death by stoning (Nm. 5:11–31; Dt. 22:23–30).[2] Sexual relations during betrothal are considered the equivalent to adultery, so to be found pregnant at that time—let alone by someone other than one's partner—put Mary's life at risk. If Mary stays home in Nazareth, she likely will be subjected to a trial and the death penalty.

When she finds out she is with child, Mary trusts God's promises not to be afraid, but the news of receiving the Divine Migrant into "her home" troubles her at the same time (Lk. 1:29–45). She knows others will gossip about her, judge and marginalize her, and even criminalize her. Yet she trusts God and accepts the risks associated with welcoming the migrant Son of God. She comes to understand that the path forward cannot be worked out through black-and-white certainties but only by love found through faith.

Although the law guides Mary's life, her spiritual experience asks more of her than adherence to the rules of organized religion; her life now demands a deeper vision of what God requires. Mary's life, calling, and destiny now must be fulfilled principally by God's grace, which goes far beyond a strict and narrow interpretation of Jewish law and human perception. Because many around her cannot perceive the deeper mystery at work in her, she moves in haste from Nazareth and migrates to Ein Karem to see her cousin Elizabeth (Lk. 1:39).

In addition to Mary, the Divine Migration disrupts Joseph's world and calls him to a level of trust beyond conventional securities. The few texts about him in the Gospels give us insight into the struggle between obedience to religious law and the law of mercy. This is not an easy or clean distinction, neither in biblical times nor in our own day, especially since the law—in its best light—is connected to mercy. Because Joseph is a religious man and a faithful Jew, he takes the prescriptions of the Jewish law seriously.

---

[2] Lawson G. Hatfield, "Betrothal," in Chad Brand et al., eds., *Holman Illustrated Bible Dictionary* (Nashville: Holman Bible Publishers, 2003), 199.

But at some point, his own spiritual experience brings his reading of the law to a crisis point.

Joseph's dilemma is that, if he does what the law requires, he exposes Mary to shame and assuredly gives her up to public disgrace and even capital punishment. But if he only heeds his personal affection for Mary, he compromises his religious integrity. Unable to work this conflict out in his mind, he tries to thread the needle between religious observance and mercy by attempting to divorce Mary quietly (Mt. 1:19).

In the midst of this crisis he has a dream that gives him another approach to thinking through this ethical dilemma. He begins to see that the requirements of his religious faith—and indeed an obedience to the heart of the law—demand more than simply keeping the rules. The dream offers him the possibility of forging a new narrative, taking moral integrity to a higher spiritual plane. Calling him beyond the shallow certitudes of legalism, an angel appears in a dream to assure him that more is at work than eyes can see. He then submits in faith to God's power, even though he has no clear blueprint of how it will ultimately unfold. He and Mary must undertake a migration with only the assurance that God's providential care is at work in their precarity.

The Divine Migration—as with migration in our own times—takes shape amid a drama of political documentation (Lk. 2:1–5), and it is an illegal act by the rules of this world. No matter how we may read the text, *Jesus himself became an illegal alien*: He is illegal in view of his lawbreaking conception, and he is an alien because he really does come from another world. If this does not confuse us, then we are probably not reading the text as closely as we need to.

Why would God choose this way to migrate into our world? Could God not have chosen a less scandalous and more palatable way to become human—or at least, from a legal perspective, a less complicated way to migrate into our world, one that many of the law-abiding religious people of his day probably would have found much more acceptable? These questions leave much room for reflection as we consider that God becomes illegal for the sake of all who have become alien to him because of their breaking the law (Rom. 1:18–20; 3:21–24; 13:9–10). While this reading does not disregard the need for the law, it does challenge any temptations to absolutize it. It also necessitates a more thorough contemplation of the law that goes deeper than our rational and reductive misappropriations.

Ironically, the entrance of the divine illegal alien into our world is the beginning of the good news. As we look underneath the surface of the narrative, much is there to facilitate human transformation. Much in this story can help rescript our operative narratives about legality, justice, and righteousness, especially regarding those deemed as undocumented, illegal, alien, and criminal. While the Incarnation scandalizes some people, we can only imagine how outcasts, criminals, and all rejected from society receive it. In revealing that no one is walled off from God's mercy, the God of Jesus Christ opens up a pathway to hope for all, beginning with those marginalized from society and deemed illegal by the social, political, and even religious powers of the world.

### The Holy Family and the Flight into Egypt: Forced Migration and Its Root Causes

> An angel of the Lord appeared to Joseph in a dream and said, "Get up, take the child and his mother, and flee to Egypt, and remain there until I tell you; for Herod is about to search for the child, to destroy him." (Mt. 2:13 NRSV)

Although God's migration to the human race brings good news, it also disorients people in different ways. The shepherds are amazed (Lk. 2:8–20); the Magi are enlightened (Mt. 2:1–12); but King Herod is paranoid (Mt. 2:3). This newborn migrant child brings out various reactions from people, and depending on where their hearts are, their response determines who they become. They will either walk further down the road of communion or fall deeper into the abyss of alienation.

This child comes to liberate people from bondage but also triggers a reaction of fear in people like King Herod. It is not the first time Herod's anxiety takes him captive and rules his life. In 7 BC he executes his sons Alexander and Aristobulus when they threaten his power.[3] Now the stakes are even higher. When the wise men deliver the message that a newborn king has crossed his country's borders and seeks to dethrone him, he sets forth a series of destructive policies aimed at eliminating this immigrant threat (Mt. 2:1–8).

---

[3] Benedict XVI and Philip Whitmore, *Jesus of Nazareth: The Infancy Narratives* (New York: Image Books, 2012), 108.

In the early days of the migrant Jesus, then, we are introduced to two kings and two kingdoms. It is a face-off between the king who takes the lives of others in order to save power and the king who gives up power in order to save lives. This biblical stage is more than a historical footnote: it is a microcosm of the human struggle, revealing an inescapable calculus within the soul where each person must determine where one looks for salvation and redemption: either through the love of power or the power of love.

But Herod is not an isolated historical figure. In different ways he is an iconic representation of the political and economic forces that directly contribute to the displacement of others. In our own times, leaders in countries like Syria seek to preserve their own power at any cost, even when it means uprooting more than 8 million people within the country and sending more than 6.6 million out of the country as refugees.[4] Amid the human wreckage, they leave us with enduring questions about sovereignty, authority, and the legitimate use of power.

When Herod puts a target on the backs of the Holy Family, they flee to Egypt. Herod then unleashes his plans to slaughter all the infant children under two years old in the Bethlehem region (Mt. 2:16–18).[5] What does the Holy Family experience after they leave Bethlehem? Does anyone help guide them? How do they experience divine assistance along the way? We know very little about the Holy Family's flight into Egypt, but what we have is recorded in the Gospel of Matthew. In ten brief verses, we learn about some of the root causes of their forced migration and how Joseph, Mary, and the child Jesus become refugees because of what the United Nations today describes as "a well-founded fear of persecution" (Mt. 2:13–23).[6]

As the Holy Family leaves Bethlehem in the dark of night, they flee toward the Egyptian border, approximately eighty miles away. Egypt is outside of Herod's jurisdiction, and during various points of biblical

---

[4] For more detailed information, see United Nations High Commissioner for Refugees, "About the Crisis in Syria," www.unrefugees.org.

[5] For more on this topic, see Paul Perry, *Jesus in Egypt: Discovering the Secrets of Christ's Childhood Years* (New York: Ballantine Books, 2003).

[6] In 1951, the Refugee Convention of the United Nations defined a *refugee* as one who, "owing to a well-founded fear of being persecuted for reasons of race, religion, nationality, membership of a particular social group or political opinion, is outside the country of his nationality, and is unable to, or owing to such fear, is unwilling to avail himself of the protection of that country." United Nations High Commissioner for Refugees, "Refugees," www.unhcr.org.

history, it is a place of refuge for Israelites during times of political upheaval (1 Kgs. 11:40; 2 Kgs. 25:26).[7] The Holy Family likely takes the route south to Hebron, then west to the coast of Gaza, along a road called the Way of the Sea, which is not the easiest to travel but is relatively safe. Likely they have to pass by certain Roman forts as well, which function as checkpoints at the Egyptian border. We do not know if the Holy Family passes through this border checkpoint legally or not, but if they were to undergo a similar journey across the US-Mexico border today and were apprehended, they would be divided and separated into different detention centers and required to secure their own legal help or make their own case for asylum.[8]

In addition to Matthew's brief biblical account, the story of the Holy Family's migration into Egypt appears in New Testament apocryphal literature and other extrabiblical accounts, particularly Christian midrash from the Coptic tradition, which recount the miracles that accompany them on their perilous journey. These texts speak of dragons protecting them, lions and leopards bowing down to them, and palm trees paying them homage.[9] The flight into Egypt is also a popular subject in art throughout the centuries, highlighting the Holy Family's escape from persecution, their vulnerability, and divine assistance along the way.

According to some of these extrabiblical sources, the Holy Family always has provisions on their journey because of the generosity of people in the towns and villages who receive them. We know that Alexandria had a community of Jewish refugees in the towns and villages of the Nile Delta who might have helped them.[10] Nonetheless, not everybody welcomes them in Egypt. One tradition holds that when the family enters the city of Cusae (today the village of al-Quisa), there is a temple of idols that has seven veils. When Jesus enters the gates of the town, the seven veils are torn asunder and the idols fall and are destroyed. Fearing a threat to their livelihood, hundreds

---

[7] Bruce B. Barton, *Matthew* (Wheaton, IL: Tyndale House, 1996), 31.

[8] There are a few family shelters in the country, but many families are separated on arrival. Joan M. Maruskin, "The Bible: The Ultimate Migration Handbook," *Church and Society* 95, no. 6 (2005): 87.

[9] See *Gospel of Pseudo-Matthew* 18–20 and Raymond E. Brown, *The Birth of the Messiah: A Commentary on the Infancy Narratives in the Gospels of Matthew and Luke* (New Haven, CT: Yale University Press, 1993), 203–4.

[10] Otto Friedrich August Meinardus, *The Holy Family in Egypt* (Cairo: American University in Cairo Press, 1986), 12.

of priests chase after the Holy Family with rods and axes, forcing them to flee to another area.[11]

Some sources calculate that the Holy Family migrates more than one thousand miles within Egypt, and they live there for anywhere from a few months to a few years.[12] Although the exact route is uncertain, Coptic Christians have identified about twenty-five places where they believe that Mary, Joseph, and Jesus stayed or passed through during their migration to Egypt, as shown in the map.

*The Migration of the Holy Family in Egypt*

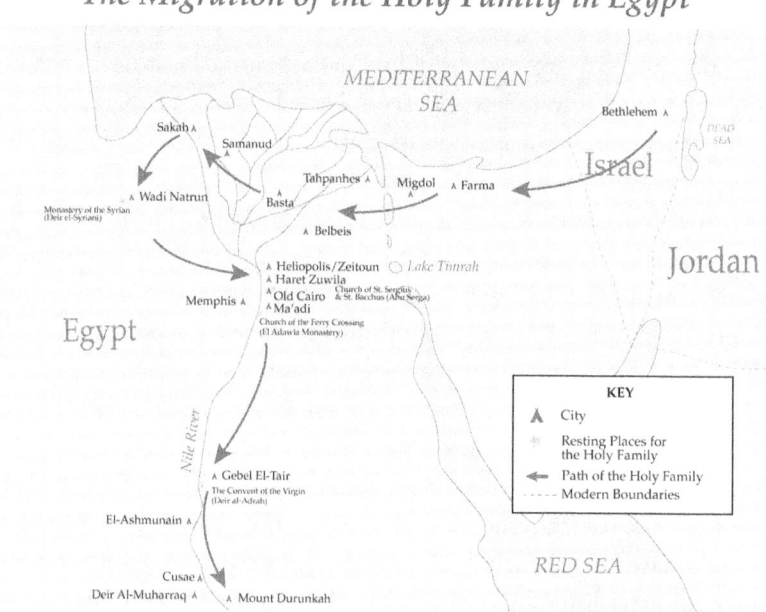

Some groups mark the place where they find rest on their journey (the Church of St. Sergius and St. Bacchus in Old Cairo or Abu Serga), some where the Virgin nursed the infant Jesus (the Monastery of the Syrian at Wadi Natrun or Deir el-Syriani), some where they embark on a wooden boat and sail up the Nile (the Church of the Ferry Crossing in Maadi or the El Adawia Monastery), and some where they shelter in a large cave (the Convent of the Virgin in Minya the Deir al-Adrah).[13]

---

[11] Ibid., 52.

[12] See Clinton E. Arnold, *Zondervan Illustrated Bible Backgrounds Commentary: Matthew, Mark, Luke* (Grand Rapids: Zondervan, 2002), 1:19–20, and Meinardus, *The Holy Family in Egypt*, 16.

[13] Bible Journey, "The Holy Family Flee to Egypt," www.thebiblejourney.org.

In a tale that resonates with many migrants who are robbed on their travels, one ancient account chronicles how bandits fleece the Holy Family along the road. After seeking refuge in a mountain west of Meir, two thieves—one Jewish and the other Egyptian—accost them with knives and swords. Ripping the child from his mother, they strip the couple of their garments. But one of the robbers, at the sight of the Virgin Mary's tears, laments his deeds and has a change of heart. When he sees a divine light in their faces, he implores his Jewish counterpart to return their garments. When his companion refuses, he asks for his portion. Legend recounts that upon receiving the garments, Jesus makes the sign of the cross over the robber and says, "The Jews will crucify me in Jerusalem. And these two brigands . . . will be crucified on my right hand, and on my left hand. The Egyptian will be crucified on my right, and the Jew on my left, and the brigand who hath returned our garments will confess Me and believe in me on the Cross, and he will be the first to enter Paradise, even before Adam and his descendants."[14]

From a theological perspective, Jesus' own migration into Egypt corresponds analogically with Israel's history.[15] Matthew portrays Jesus in his Gospel as the new Moses, and his own story aligns with the migration of the Hebrew people. Because in the Jewish mind Egypt conjures up images of migration that are inseparable from themes of oppression and liberation explored in previous chapters, Jesus' journey out of Egypt evokes a larger journey from slavery to freedom and the beginning of a new reign (Ex. 9–14). As Pope Benedict puts it,

> With the flight into Egypt and the return to the Promised Land, Jesus grants the definitive Exodus. He is truly the Son. . . . He returns home, and he leads others home. He is always on the path toward God and thus he leads the way back from exile to the homeland, back to all that is authentic and true. Jesus, the true Son, himself went into "exile" in a very deep sense in order to lead all of us home from exile.[16]

---

[14] See *The First Gospel of the Infancy of Jesus Christ*, www.pseudepigrapha.com, and Meinardus, *The Holy Family in Egypt*, 54.

[15] Arnold, *Zondervan Illustrated Bible Backgrounds Commentary: Matthew, Mark, Luke*, 1:17–19.

[16] Benedict XVI and Whitmore, *Jesus of Nazareth*, 111–12.

In different ways, the Holy Family comes to typify the vulnerability of so many mothers, fathers, and children throughout history who are uprooted from their homelands and seek refuge in other places. During the refugee crisis following World War II, Pope Pius XII penned an apostolic constitution titled *Exsul Familia*, in which he observed,

> The émigré Holy Family of Nazareth, fleeing into Egypt, is the archetype of every refugee family. Jesus, Mary and Joseph, living in exile in Egypt to escape the fury of an evil king, are, for all times and all places, the models and protectors of every migrant, alien and refugee of whatever kind who, whether compelled by fear of persecution or by want, is forced to leave his native land, his beloved parents and relatives, his close friends, and to seek a foreign soil. (Pope Pius XII, "Exsul Familia Nazarethana")

Since its publication in 1952, this document has been foundational to the Church's pastoral care of migrants and refugees, which is rooted in the belief that God not only came as a migrant to this world but entered deeply into the vulnerability of the human condition by becoming a refugee as well.

The Holy Family's flight into Egypt—their experiences of vulnerability, persecution, and uncertainty—would have made them intimately familiar with the trials and tribulations of the migrant trail. At the same time the gestures of solidarity, hospitality, and humanity would most certainly have lived long in their memory. In all these experiences the Church has seen important connections between the flight of the Holy Family into Egypt, its own story, and the story of refugees today. In the process it has upheld Mary as the mother to refugees and a mother of refuge for all struggling on their earthly sojourn.

### John the Baptist and Conversion: Migrating to a New Way of Thinking

> "Repent, for the kingdom of heaven has come near." (Mt. 3:1–3 NRSV)

John the Baptist is one of the most challenging and provocative figures in the New Testament. We know only a few things about his life, but the Scriptures speak of him as a righteous and holy man, a Jewish prophet, and forerunner to the Messiah. We are introduced to him prior to his birth in the visitation narrative (Lk. 1:39–55), but he comes to center stage in the desert, where he announces the Kingdom of God and its demands (Mt. 3:1–6; Mk. 1:2–6; Lk. 3:3–6; Jn. 1:6–8). How does the message he preached speak to our reflection on migration?

The Gospels do not identify John the Baptist specifically as a migrant, but in some ways he is one of the most intriguing internally displaced persons of the Bible. He comes from a small village called Ein Karem on the western edge of Jerusalem, and later is uprooted from the land of his birth and moves to a small cave a few miles north of the Dead Sea, where he takes up ministry as an itinerant preacher.[17] Like many migrants, the narrative of John the Baptist's journey takes shape in the desert, at the border, alongside a river, and in view of a Promised Land. These geographical markers add revelatory depth to our study because of their close association with central theological themes like purification, conversion, baptism, and freedom. He challenges his hearers to prepare the way for the Lord, who will make possible a way to return to the Father. For this to happen, John preaches that people need a requisite course correction in their life's journey in order to find the path to the Kingdom of God.

John the Baptist comes on the scriptural scene at the Jordan River (Mk. 1; Mt. 3; Lk. 3; Jn. 1; 3:22–30), which has deep spiritual resonances in biblical history. Abram and Lot divide up the land at the Jordan Valley (Gn. 13:11); Jacob undergoes a tumultuous border crossing at a tributary of the river (Gn. 32:22–26); Moses gazes on the Promised Land from the border of the Jordan (Dt. 34; cf. Nm. 20:10–13; Dt. 32:48–52); the Israelites cross over the river to inherit it (Jo. 3:14–17); Elijah migrates to heaven in a whirlwind from the water's edges (2 Kgs. 2:6–12); and Naaman the Syrian is cured of leprosy by its healing waters (2 Kgs. 5:8–14). Throughout the Old and New Testaments, the Jordan River is a liminal space of transcendence and transformation (Gn. 13:10–11; Jo. 3:15–17; 2 Kgs. 2:1–14; Heb. 49:19; Mt. 4:25; Mt. 19:1; Mk. 10:1).

The rich associations with the Jordan extend the scriptural message beyond mere geographical anecdotes to the human struggle with bondage and the promise of passing over to new spiritual and psychological territoriality.

---

[17] Richard R. Losch, *All the People in the Bible: An A–Z Guide to the Saints, Scoundrels, and Other Characters in Scripture* (Grand Rapids: William B. Eerdmans, 2008), 223.

"In the Deuteronomistic texts as well as in the Gospels," Rachel Havrelock states, "the Jordan is a threshold of redemption. The distinction between acts of crossing and immersing in the Jordan comes to define such redemption as either a Jewish return or a Christian rebirth."[18] How do this growth and transformation happen?

John's preaching speaks to two integral dimensions of passing over to new spaces: repentance and conversion. In the Old Testament, the word for repentance (Hebrew: *shub*) means to turn.[19] To repent means to turn from sinful acts, attitudes, and thoughts and to think about life in a different way. To turn also means journeying or walking with God in a new way that is different from its neighbors, different from the ways of Canaan, different from the ways of evildoers—in brief—different from the ways of the world (Ps. 1:1; Dt. 26:5–11).[20]

In the New Testament the most common verb used for repentance is *metanoein*. It is derived from two Greek words: *meta*, meaning "after" (suggesting some type of change), and *nous*, meaning "mind." It includes the Old Testament notion of turning to the Lord, but it also includes the idea of changing one's mind and thinking about things in a new way. This process of conversion involves turning from the dispositions of one's former self in favor of living, walking, and acting in a restored way in the world.

This transformation of the heart and mind begins with honoring the primacy of God's Kingdom above all other values, above all other possessions, and above all other kingdoms. To pray, "Thy kingdom come," entails that "my kingdom must go," which is one of the most difficult of all human relinquishments. John the Baptist challenges people to decide what ultimately rules and governs their hearts. When he calls people to repent on the edge of the Jordan River, he calls them to reformat the programming of the world, to reset their lives according the ways of the Kingdom, and to allow the Father's love alone to rule their hearts.

On May 24, 2014, Pope Francis visited the banks of the Jordan River and gathered Syrian and Iraqi refugees to share their stories at the water's edge. He spoke of John the Baptist as a model for Christians and highlighted

---

[18] Rachel S. Havrelock, *River Jordan: The Mythology of a Dividing Line* (Chicago: University of Chicago Press, 2011), 174.

[19] Paul J. Achtemeier and Society of Biblical Literature, "Repentance," in *Harper's Bible Dictionary* (San Francisco: Harper & Row, 1985), 861.

[20] Joseph P. Healey, "Repentance," in David N. Freedman ed., *The Anchor Yale Bible Dictionary* (New York: Doubleday, 1992), 5:671.

three verbs at work in his message: "prepare," "discern," and "diminish."[21] Addressing the need to pass over from tribal and territorial mindsets to the expansive terrain of the Kingdom of God, Pope Francis thanked the country of Jordan for its generous welcome of those displaced and addressed the challenges posed by a global refugee crisis.

When Fouad Twal, the former Latin patriarch of Jerusalem, met Pope Francis at the banks of the Jordan, he said that for many the river is a border that divides, but for us, "it is more a bridge that unites, a call to communion and unity."[22] Alluding to the pontiff's role in bringing nations together, Jordan's King Abdullah II said, "Jordanians, too, are building bridges. Our work includes concrete and tangible actions, over many years."[23] Collectively they addressed the need to move beyond excessively individual, personal, and even national interests to the plight of the poor and the international common good.

In the story of salvation, John opens up a new way. He points above and beyond himself so that people trust the One who is the Way (Jn. 14:6). John the Baptist's words were aimed at deprogramming from the way of the world in order to be made anew according to the heart of God. As he calls people into the gift and challenge of baptism, he reveals to the world an ever-present call to unite people rather than divide them and to cross over into a new territory rather than hide behind walls that isolate and alienate.

### Jesus of Nazareth and the Incarnation: The Divine Migration and the Cosmic Border Crossing

> As evening drew on, he said to them, "Let us cross to the other side." (Mk. 4:34)

At the center of the mystery of God's migration to our world is the person of Jesus of Nazareth. He is the Word made flesh, the Incarnate Son, the Divine Migrant who has come from heaven to dwell among us. As he enters into the sinful and broken territory of our human existence, he reveals, in Pope Francis' words, "the face of the Father's mercy" ("Misericordiae Vultus: Bull

---

[21] Philippa Hitchen, "Pope Francis Calls John the Baptist a Model for Christians Today," Vatican Radio, June 24, 2014, http://en.radiovaticana.va.

[22] Joe Thoma, "Pope Visits Bethany-Beyond-the-Jordan," Associated Church Press, February 28, 2016, www.theacp.org.

[23] Ibid.

of Indiction of the Extraordinary Jubilee of Mercy"). Through the Paschal Mystery, he makes it possible for men and women—lost in their earthly existence—to navigate their way through this life, to cross the borders of this world, and to find their way back home again to God.

Here we want to explore the way Jesus crosses over the borders of the cosmos, crosses into the borders of human skin, and ultimately crosses beyond the borders of life and death. It is significant for our discussion because it makes possible humanity's movement away from the land of unlikeness to God (which tradition calls the *regio dissimilitudinis*) and toward the land of likeness to God (*regio similitudinis*).[24] This mystery makes possible a redemptive journey, which is a way of speaking about becoming "permanent residents" of our country of origin and "naturalized" citizens of God's Kingdom (Eph. 2:19).

Each of the four Gospels begins its account of the Divine Migration from different starting points. The later the Gospel is written, the earlier the evangelist traces back Jesus' journey. Mark begins with John the Baptist in the desert at the start of his mission, some thirty years into Jesus' earthly sojourn (Mk. 1:1–8). Matthew and Luke begin with his divine-human border crossing at his birth in Bethlehem (Mt. 1:18–25; Lk. 2:1–7). John starts with Jesus' residence in his celestial homeland and his cosmic movement to the human race (Jn. 1:1–5). Matthew, especially, highlights in unique ways how the Incarnation brings earth and heaven together. He makes note of the fact that when God descends to the human race, a star arises in the cosmos, a signal that something powerful is happening in the universe (Mt. 2:2).

The first to behold its message are not the scholars, the powerful, nor even the Jewish religious leaders. The initial witnesses are migrant Gentiles from the East, who come from afar to pay homage to the infant king of the Jews. Traveling from Babylon, Persia, or perhaps the Arabian desert, they testify to the advent of a boundless love that reaches across all borders, to all people, in all lands, and for all generations (Mt. 8:11–12; 28:18–20).[25]

---

[24] The concept of *regio dissimilitudinis* has its origin in Platonic thought but has parallels in the Scriptures. Mystics like Bernard of Clarivaux, and others in the Middle Ages, also used the concept when speaking about the movement of people away from the divine image and likeness toward a state of alienation. For more on this topic, see Etienne Gilson, "*Regio dissimilitudinis* de Platon à Saint Bernard de Clarivaux," *Medieval Studies* 9 (1947): 109–17.

[25] Dianne Bergant and Robert J. Karris, *The Collegeville Bible Commentary:*

The Magi travel from the East to Jerusalem (Mt. 2:1–2) and then from Jerusalem to Bethlehem (Mt. 2:9). If they were to make this journey today, they would have run into a number of modern barriers along the way. Bethlehem is now part of Palestinian-controlled territory, and after the Second Intifada in 2000, the modern state of Israel began constructing a twenty-six-foot-high wall that separates the West Bank territories from Israeli-controlled land. While Israeli leaders today consider these barriers as a necessary security measure to prevent terrorism, Palestinians see it as a racial segregation policy that divides the people of the Holy Land on multiple levels.

Reading these biblical texts in light of the current political geography sets up a striking contrast between the God who migrates to the human race to break down walls that divide and the present climate that erects them to separate one people from another (Eph. 2:14). If Jesus were born in Bethlehem today, he would have been born outside the walls of contemporary Israel, at the border, on the margins, in divisive territory, and in the shadow of an imposing barricade. Some local Palestinian merchants in Bethlehem have picked up on this theme by creating Nativity sets that include a separation wall that keeps the migrant Magi from paying homage to the Christ child.

Unlike these imposing barriers, the traditional site of Jesus' birth at the Church of the Nativity in Bethlehem offers another perspective. To enter the church, one has to pass through what is called the "Door of Humility." It is a small door, only about four feet tall and two feet wide. Some historians argue it was built to prevent horse and camel-riding looters from pillaging the church at the time of the Crusades, but its figurative renderings offer much material for spiritual reflection. In what is regarded as one of the earliest Christological hymns, St. Paul writes,

> Have among yourselves the same attitude that is also yours in Christ Jesus, Who, though he was in the form of God, did not regard equality with God something to be grasped. Rather, he emptied himself, taking the form of a slave, coming in human likeness; and found human in appearance, he humbled himself, becoming obedient to death, even death on a cross. Because of this, God

---

*Based on the New American Bible with Revised New Testament* (Collegeville, MN: Liturgical Press, 1989), 865.

greatly exalted him and bestowed on him the name that is above every name, that at the name of Jesus every knee should bend, of those in heaven and on earth and under the earth, and every tongue confess that Jesus Christ is Lord, to the glory of God the Father. (Phil. 2:5–11)

The Church of the Nativity reminds us that, in imitation of the God of the Universe who lowers himself when he migrates to the human race, one has to bow down to enter its mystery. The Magi are some of the first to grasp the arrival of the One who came for the salvation of the human race— and among the first to cross the borders of their own worlds to greet him. As they open themselves in vulnerability and receive the One who became vulnerable for their sake, they share in response their own treasure with him, because they have discovered something in him greater than any other possession in the world.

Yet as these wise men open themselves to this divine epiphany, the powerful like Herod close their hearts to the coming of the Divine Migrant. Choosing to worship the gifts of creation rather than the God who created them, they mistakenly center their lives around the love of power rather than the power of love. In the process they lose their souls. Building walls they think protect them, they erect instead a prison within themselves that encloses them in fortresses of disordered desires. Refusing to bow, Herod takes refuge behind palaces like Herodium, seeking to protect his possessions, property, and power. Christ's humble entrance in human estate, in contrast, signals the beginning of a new reign and the end of all human kingdoms, including Herod's own.

When God enters our world as the Divine Migrant, he moves into the vulnerability of our flesh, takes on the absolute otherness of our human condition, and allows himself to be circumscribed by human skin. To return to a metaphor used earlier, the skin is the largest border of the human body, and it is essential in regulating the inner life of the person and the outside world. To some degree the Incarnation validates the value of borders and reveals that it plays a role in our survival. Removing the border of the skin from a human being, for example, would expose a person to external aggressors such as bacteria, viruses, and pollution that can be harmful and even fatal. Sealing the border completely and turning the skin into a barrier, however, would cause overheating, toxicity, and eventual death. The porous nature of human skin allows the body's temperature to adjust through sweating, shivering, vasodilatation, and vasoconstriction. As a protective and permeable border, the skin manages a necessary and complex process that helps the human body maintain an internal balance or homeostasis.

In a similar way, borders can play a positive role in the body of society. They are especially important as the human community struggles to attain a global homeostasis, another way of speaking about the state of justice and peace. But achieving such a state is dependent upon what St. Augustine referred to as "*tranquillitas ordinis*," or "the tranquility of order."[26] While a detailed discussion of this subject is beyond the scope of this section, it illuminates how borders must be understood in light of the well-being of the whole body, not just an isolated part of it. In the plan of salvation, Jesus becomes bordered by the human body, not to exclude people but to reconcile people to himself and to make them a part of his own body.

In a similar way, the right to construct borders must be viewed not simply in light of the desire to protect a privileged few but in view of the need to provide for the neglected many. This involves recognizing a larger responsibility to the whole body and its well-being. This analysis is particularly important in light of the socioeconomic disorders of our present age, without which a global homeostasis can never be achieved. In other words, borders have a value and a function, but they also have limits: From a Christian perspective they are subject to the dignity of the human person, the international common good, and their impact on the overall well-being of the entire body.

A closer study of Jesus' life helps us clarify both the positive function and relative limits of borders. As a first-century Jewish man, Jesus enters into a particular period of history, and his human identity is significantly shaped by different kinds of religious, geographical, and political borders. As a practicing Jew, Jesus understands the proximate value and positive function of borders, especially as they helped form the identity and mission of a people. He is born into a Jewish family (Lk. 2:39), obedient to the Jewish law (Nm. 18:15; Lk. 2:22), circumcised a Jew (Lv. 12:2–3; Lk. 2:21), studies the Torah

---

[26] "Peace between man and God is the well-ordered obedience of faith to eternal law. Peace between man and man is well-ordered concord. Civil peace is a similar concord among the citizens. The peace of the celestial city is the perfectly ordered and harmonious enjoyment of God, and of one another in God. The peace of all things is the tranquility of order. Order is the distribution which allots things equal and unequal, each to its own place." Augustine, *The City of God* (New York: Random House, 1993), 19:690–691.

(Lk. 2:46–47), and celebrates Passover (Lk. 22:14–15). He is called rabbi (Jn. 4:31), the Messiah (Mk. 14:61–62; Jn. 1:41; 4:25–26), and even the king of the Jews (Mt. 27:37; Mk. 15:26). Each of the evangelists brings out Jesus' connection to his Jewish roots, but Matthew in particular is intent on illuminating different ways that borders of religion shaped Jesus' identity.

Matthew emphasizes Jesus' Jewish roots, but he also brings out that Jesus refuses to use that unique identity as a reason for building walls and excluding others. Jesus' Jewish heritage, in fact, is permeated by people outside its ranks. Many of his ancestors mentioned in Matthew's genealogy come from foreign lands or are closely associated with migrants, like Ruth the Moabite, Rahab the Canaanite prostitute, Tamar the proselyte, and Bathsheba, who is married to a Hittite foreigner (Mt. 1:1–17). Scholars debate the reason for their inclusion in the descriptions of his family lineage, but some convincingly argue that their presence foreshadows the universal mission of Jesus, which extends beyond the borders of Israel to all nations.[27]

As he grows in wisdom, understanding, and experience, the scope of his own mission expands (Lk. 2:52). Initially he seems to have circumscribed it within the borders of the nation of Israel, but as he encounters those who suffer, his compassion extends beyond these provisional borders. The story of the Syrophoenician woman in particular brings out Jesus' evolving consciousness and willingness to go even beyond the borders of religion and to enter the space of the other:

> A Canaanite woman of that district came and called out, "Have pity on me, Lord, Son of David! My daughter is tormented by a demon." But he did not say a word in answer to her. His disciples came and asked him, "Send her away, for she keeps calling out after us." He said in reply, "I was sent only to the lost sheep of the house of Israel." But the woman came and did him homage, saying, "Lord, help me." He said in reply, "It is not right to take the food of the children and throw it to the dogs." She said, "Please, Lord, for even the dogs eat the scraps that fall from the table of their masters." Then Jesus said to her in reply, "O woman, great is your faith! Let it be done for you as you wish." And her daughter was healed from that hour. (Mt. 15:22–28)

---

[27] Ulrich Luz, *Matthew 1–7 (Hermeneia)*, rev. ed., trans. James E. Crouch, ed. Helmut Koester (Minneapolis: Fortress Press, 2007), 84–85.

Jesus' encounter raises many questions for further reflection. Is this story a way of communicating to a Jewish audience that even a Canaanite woman is accepted by God? Or more broadly does it reveal something about the way Jesus himself progressively came to understand his own mission? Though he was God in the flesh, did he—as a human being—also need to grow into his understanding that his mission of mercy extends beyond the Jewish nation to everyone in the world? We do not know for sure the answer to these questions, but the text does bring out the healing and transformation that emerge from this encounter.

In addition to religious borders, Jesus is shaped by geographical and political borders. Much of his public ministry takes place away from the power centers, on the margins, in Galilee. Throughout the centuries Galilee is controlled by various empires such as Babylon, Assyria, Persia, Macedonia, Egypt, and Syria. As different sovereign powers lay claim to this territory, borders shift. Migrants and refugees are constantly traveling throughout the area, which is marked profoundly by deportations, internal displacements, and exile.[28]

Jesus takes up his central residence in this region and sets up his base of operations in village of Capernaum, situated at the edge of the territory divided among the two sons of Herod. The Evangelists' stories of a border-protecting centurion (Mt. 8:5; Lk. 7:2) and a tax collector leaving his customs post (Mt. 9:9; Mk. 2:14; Lk. 5:27) give ample evidence that Capernaum is a border town.[29]

While we do not know the exact reasons why the Divine Migrant chose to do ministry in the borderlands of Galilee, it may in part also signal God's intention to destabilize the sedentary in their social locations that fail to see the dynamic movement of life itself. As Don Senior explains,

> The mobility of migrant peoples . . . challenges the experience of those who feel absolutely stable and secure in their own situations. This ensemble of conditions and experiences reveals a profound dimension of all of human existence whether migrant or not. These experiences challenge the false ideologies of unlimited resources, the

---

[28] Denis Lynn Daly Heyck, *Barrios and Borderlands: Cultures of Latinos and Latinas in the United States* (New York: Routledge, 1994), 432.

[29] Arthur E. Cundall, "Naphtali," in Donald. J. Wiseman et al., eds., *New Bible Dictionary,* 3rd ed. (Downers Grove, IL: InterVarsity Press, 1996), 803.

myth of unchecked progress, the idolatry of unconditional national sovereignty, and the absolute claim to individual satisfaction that so plague our contemporary world and choke its spiritual capacity.[30]

Because everything in this world is transitory, and life itself is always in movement, even the powers of this world have their limits. Our lives themselves are ultimately circumscribed by our mortality, which means, in the end, the biggest border to cross is the border between life and death.

Geopolitical borders no doubt shape Jesus' ministry in his earthly life, but he does not allow his boundless mercy to be constricted by them. He is concerned not only with those protected by borders but even and especially those excluded and abused by them. To put it another way, he does not allow borders to become barriers. Especially when such barriers justify and legitimate division, Jesus crosses over them or destroys them entirely.

In crossing these borders, Jesus often crosses his adversaries as well. His transborder ministry is good news to many, but it scandalizes others, especially those who use their power, titles, wealth, or moral principles to justify the exclusion of others. Jesus' table fellowship with sinners and the poor symbolizes the all-inclusiveness of his ministry and the ways he even crosses over the borders created by false religion.

Jesus teaches his disciples to take up their crosses and follow him and to pass over to those vulnerable places that involve tending to a neighbor, a stranger, or even an enemy in need. He understands that while fear erects walls and divides relationships, love crosses borders and creates connections among people.

Overall, the life, death, resurrection, and ascension of Jesus Christ represent the central mystery of Christian faith and the defining migration event of human history. Through this paschal mystery he gives testimony to God's desire to destroy the wall that has created enmity with God and divides us from one another (Eph. 2:14). Jesus' return migration to the Father in the resurrection reveals God's desire to open up in a final and definitive way the road that leads to a place where there will be no more death, mourning, crying, or pain, and where the old order has passed away and all creation

---

[30] Donald Senior, "Beloved Aliens and Exiles: New Testament Perspectives on Migration," in *A Promised Land, A Perilous Journey: Theological Perspectives on Migration*, ed. Daniel G. Groody and Gioacchino Campese (Notre Dame, IN: University of Notre Dame Press, 2008), 28–29.

is finally made new (Rev. 21:1). As it destroys all that divides and makes possible a return to our original homeland, the resurrection redefines every other migration, and it transforms an alien people from strangers into friends who share sacred and inseparable bonds as a human family.

But this mystery of the Word made flesh cannot be understood solely from the logic of reason, politics, or economics. The mystery of the Divine Migration can only be understood through the economy of grace and the logic of love: a God who becomes one with us so that we can again become one with God. By entering the otherness of our condition, he reveals the oneness of our created destiny, and through his return journey to the Father, Jesus makes it possible to find our way again to God, to one another, and even to our innermost selves. As Leonardo Boff summarizes the Divine Migration, "The God who is revealed in and through Jesus is human. And the human being who emerges in and through Jesus is divine.... Only a God could be so human!"[31]

### The Good Samaritan and the New Law: Migration and Neighborliness

> "Which of these three, in your opinion, was neighbor to the robbers' victim?" (Lk. 10:37)

Because they contain a surplus of meaning, the Scriptures have always been read on literal and figurative levels. In the early centuries of the church, John Cassian (ca. 360–435) was the first to write about the four "senses" of Scripture, which he identified as the literal, the allegorical, the moral, and the anagogic.[32] The literal teaches about the historical context of the passage; the allegorical speaks to what one believes; the moral to how one should live; and the anagogic (or eschatological) to one's eternal destiny.[33] Reading

---

[31] Leonardo Boff, *Jesus Christ Liberator: A Critical Christology for Our Time* (Maryknoll, NY: Orbis Books, 1978), 178.

[32] Using Jerusalem as an example, he said it can be understood literally as the historical city of the Jews, allegorically as the Church of Christ, morally as the human soul, and analogically as the heavenly city. See John Cassian, *Conferences*, trans. Colm Luibheid (New York: Paulist Press, 1985), 160. See also Pauline A. Viviano, "The Senses of Scripture," United States Conference of Catholic Bishops, www.usccb.org.

[33] In medieval times, Augustine of Dacia put it this way, "The letter teaches events; allegory what you should believe; morality teaches what you should do, anagogy what mark you should be aiming for." The Latin text reads: *Littera gesta docet, quid credas*

the Scriptures with these four senses in mind can help us explore the rich and varied texture of the theme of migration in the Bible.[34] As we examine further the spiritual and theological dimensions of this topic, we turn now to one of the most well-known stories of the New Testament, the parable of the Good Samaritan.

In the Gospel of Luke we read,

> There was a scholar of the law who stood up to test him and said, "Teacher, what must I do to inherit eternal life?" Jesus said to him, "What is written in the law? How do you read it?" He said in reply, "You shall love the Lord, your God, with all your heart, with all your being, with all your strength, and with all your mind, and your neighbor as yourself." He replied to him, "You have answered correctly; do this and you will live." But because he wished to justify himself, he said to Jesus, "And who is my neighbor?" Jesus replied, "A man fell victim to robbers as he went down from Jerusalem to Jericho. They stripped and beat him and went off leaving him half-dead. A priest happened to be going down that road, but when he saw him, he passed by on the opposite side. Likewise a Levite came to the place, and when he saw him, he passed by on the opposite side. But a Samaritan traveler who came upon him was moved with compassion at the sight. He approached the victim, poured oil and wine over his wounds and bandaged them. Then he lifted him up on his own animal, took him to an inn and cared for him. The next day he took out two silver coins and gave them to the innkeeper with the instruction, 'Take care of him. If you spend more than what I have given you, I shall repay you on my way back.' Which of these three, in your opinion, was neighbor to the robbers' victim?" He answered, "The one who treated him with mercy." Jesus said to him, "Go and do likewise." (10:25–37)

---

*allegoria, Moralis quid agas, quo tendas anagogia* (footnote 1, p. 271). It is found in the *Rotulus pugillar*, published in 1206 by Augustine of Dacia. See also Henri de Lubac, *Medieval Exegesis: The Four Senses of Scripture,* trans. Mark Sebanc (Grand Rapids: William B. Eerdmans, 1998), 1. See also *Catechism of the Catholic Church*, no. 118.

[34] This fourfold sense of Scripture came to be known in medieval times as the Quadriga, which is a reference to a chariot of the gods, in classical mythology, pulled by four horses. John Wilkes et al., "Quadriga," in *Encyclopaedia Londinensis* (London: J. Adlard, 1810), 585.

On a literal level this text is about a migration story of its own. On the allegorical level it speaks to our journey through this world. On the moral level it addresses the ethical demands of neighborliness. And on the eschatological level it speaks to our migration beyond this world to our heavenly homeland. In different ways this text not only tells an important story, but it also helps unmask some common underlying dynamics that migration triggers in us, particularly cultural xenophobia, self-interested legalism, ethical minimalism, and evasive intellectualism.

The parable of the Good Samaritan is first of all a story about people walking along the Jericho Road, which people have done throughout history. Over the millennia, many different kinds of migrants have traveled this route, especially tourists and pilgrims. The road begins at the hills of Jerusalem and then, for seventeen miles, drops in elevation about thirty-six hundred feet to the edge of the Dead Sea. It was sometimes called the "bloody pass" because thieves could easily hide in narrow passages and rocky crevasses and then fleece unsuspecting travelers along the way, not unlike the bandits who rob migrants today. In the nineteenth century it was still necessary to pay local sheikhs to ensure safe passage to Jerusalem.[35] Even as late as the early 1930s, people were warned not to travel at night along the road because of a highwayman named Abu Jildah, who would put a stone wall across the Jericho Road to stop oncoming cars and then mug tourists and pilgrims at gunpoint.[36]

On the day before he died, Martin Luther King Jr. also recalled his own felt vulnerabilities while traveling along this road:

> I remember when Mrs. King and I were first in Jerusalem. We rented a car and drove from Jerusalem down to Jericho. And as soon as we got on that road I said to my wife, "I can see why Jesus used this as the setting for his parable." It's a winding, meandering road. It's really conducive for ambushing.... That's a dangerous road.... And you know, it's possible that the priest and the Levite looked over that man on the ground and wondered if the robbers were still around. Or it's possible that they felt that the man on the ground

---

[35] William Barclay, *The Gospel of Luke* (Louisville, KY: Westminster John Knox Press, 2001), 164–65.

[36] Henry V. Morton, *In the Steps of the Master* (Cambridge: Da Capo Press, 2002), 85.

was merely faking, and he was acting like he had been robbed and hurt in order to seize them over there, lure them there for quick and easy seizure. And so the first question that the priest asked, the first question that the Levite asked was, "If I stop to help this man, what will happen to me?"[37]

As we read this passage from our social location today, we are confronted with the same question: If we reach out to help migrants and refugees, what will happen to me and to us?

In order to reflect more deeply on this question, we have to go beyond the literal details of the Good Samaritan story. As the Church Fathers read this passage allegorically, they begin to see parallels between elements of the narrative and the drama of salvation history. In the third century, Origen wrote,

> The man who was going down is Adam. Jerusalem is paradise, and Jericho is the world. The robbers are hostile powers. The priest is the Law, the Levite is the prophets, and the Samaritan is Christ. The wounds are disobedience, the beast is the Lord's body, the [inn], which accepts all who wish to enter, is the Church.... The manager of the [inn] is the head of the Church, to whom its care has been entrusted. And the fact that the Samaritan promises he will return represents the Savior's second coming.[38]

Reading from a figurative perspective raises new and often disturbing questions about one's responsiveness (or lack thereof) to one's neighbor in need.

The context in which the story is told gives us additional insight. Jesus tells it after he has an encounter with an expert in the Jewish law,[39] who asks Jesus about the road to eternal life.[40] On the surface it appears like a wise

---

[37] Martin Luther King Jr. Research and Education Institute, "I've Been to the Mountaintop," April 3, 1968, http://kingencyclopedia.stanford.edu.

[38] Origen, "Homily 34.3," in Joseph T. Lienhard, trans., *Origen: Homilies on Mark, Fragments on Mark* (Washington, DC: Catholic University of America Press, 1996), 138.

[39] The Greek word Luke uses here is *nomikos*, which is often equated with a scribe [*grammateus*] or a doctor of the law [*nomadidaskalos*]. When the Jews returned from Babylon after their exile, these teachers gave the necessary instruction in matters of the law and its importance in living its precepts. See William Ewing and John E. H. Thomson, *The Temple Dictionary of the Bible* (New York: E. P. Dutton, 1910), 383.

[40] Timothy A. Gabrielson, "Law," in Douglas Mangum, Derek R. Brown, Rachel

question. But Luke makes note of the lawyer's ulterior motives and his desire to "test Jesus." Perhaps he is trying to score some intellectual points on Jesus to make up for some felt deficiency within himself, to impress the crowds with his theological knowledge, or even to assuage a guilty conscience. We do not know the exact reason, but we do know that Jesus offers him no room for self-aggrandizement.

Seemingly unfazed by his question, Jesus does not give a definitive answer. Instead, he counters it with a softball question about this man's understanding of the law. The lawyer replies by citing a commonly known ancient prayer called the *Shema* (Dt. 6:4–5; related to Lv. 19:18). Because the answer is so obvious, however, the lawyer seeks to save face and to "justify himself," perhaps to get another chance to demonstrate his own intellectual prowess and legal adroitness.

Trying to get Jesus to take him more seriously, he asks Jesus to offer a more legally precise definition of neighbor. Resisting the temptation to retreat into intellectual and theological abstractions, Jesus unmasks the self-interest at work in the lawyer's question. Moreover, Jesus does not allow himself to become entrapped within the walls of the lawyer's limited mind and the confines of his restricted heart. Without disregarding the value and purpose of the law, he does not allow the law to be misappropriated in a way that justifies an ethical minimalism and small-heartedness. Instead, Jesus challenges him to reframe his question within a more expansive moral imagination.

Understanding the moral sense of this text, however, is not as straightforward as it may seem, especially because law and ethics are conflated in different ways in this story. In Jesus' day, priests are in charge of the religious duties of the nation of Israel, and the Levites assist them in their administration of the Temple. While the Jewish law requires priests and Levites to care for the poor, their lives are also regulated by purity laws, which affect their participation in temple liturgies. The priests in particular are involved with laws associated with uncleanness and defilement (Lv. 13–14).[41] While inner defilement happens through sin, outward physical defilement occurs when one comes in contact with someone who is unclean—which is particularly significant in the context of this parable.

---

Klippenstein, and Rebekah Hurst, eds., *Lexham Theological Wordbook* (Bellingham, WA: Lexham Press, 2014).

[41] Arnold, *Zondervan Illustrated Bible Backgrounds Commentary: Matthew, Mark, Luke*, 1:415–16.

One of these laws pertains to dead bodies. If a priest or Levite comes into contact with a dead body, he becomes ceremonially unclean and therefore cannot fulfill temple duties (Nm. 19:11). The Pharisees teach that defilement happens even if one's shadow touches a corpse.[42] As a result, if the priest in the parable comes too near the wounded man, he loses his turn on temple duty, which apparently is a risk he is unwilling to take. Although the priest and Levite may have felt a certain pity for the man in the ditch, their preoccupation with their own religious purity takes precedence over charity.[43] What makes the moral dimensions so complex is that the priest and the Levite could have legitimately appealed to the law to justify their inaction and indifference to the wounded man; helping him would have caused a legal transgression. The Samaritan, however, is not restricted by such purity laws. Prioritizing deed over creed, and compassion over religious certitudes, he responds to the wounded man with unbounded generosity and in doing so fulfills the heart of the law.

The better we understand the hostility that exists between Jews and Samaritans, the more we realize that Jesus is not interested in having a legal debate; he is rather seeking to hold up a mirror to the lawyer in order to reveal his inner life, especially the tribal mindset and xenophobic stereotypes that keep him in bondage.[44] One could have expected Jesus to bring out that Jews should show love to anybody, even to a Samaritan. But in making a Samaritan the hero of the story, Jesus rebukes false religion and reveals that an outsider who is near to the poor may be closer to God's Kingdom than a pious and legally observant Jew. No doubt these words would have rattled more than a few of his hearers.

Yet to be fair, the Jews had reason to mistrust Samaritans. Jews considered themselves the true descendants of Israel because, after the Northern Kingdom fell in 722 BCE and was deported into exile, the Samaritans later intermarried with Gentiles and thereby compromised their religious integrity. Some scholars today debate this position, but most agree that different historical events led to enmity between the two groups that went back many years before Jesus. Moreover, the Samaritans were frequently the ones who beat and robbed the Jews along the Jericho Road. For these reasons and others, the antagonism between Jews and Samaritans ran deep.

---

[42] Ibid.

[43] Barclay, *Gospel of Luke*, 165.

[44] Joseph A. Mindling, "Chosen People in Foreign Lands: Scriptural Reflections on Immigration and the Uprooted," *New Theology Review* 12, no. 1 (1999): 12.

So why then does Jesus choose to make the hero of the story a Samaritan rather than a virtuous and law-abiding Jew? One reason may come from wanting his hearers to move beyond narrow readings of the law. Even though the priest and the Levite would have been technically and legally correct, Jesus brings out that they also would have fundamentally and ethically missed the mark. As Richard Rohr puts it, "It seems that God would much sooner have someone who does it wrong and gets it right than someone who supposedly gets it right and does it wrong."[45]

In large part the moral weight of the story hinges on how one defines the word *neighbor*. In many different ways, the Samaritan is not only a foreigner and a stranger but an outright embodiment of all those defined as "the other," a topic we take up in more detail in the next section. According to the law, a neighbor normally would have been one's fellow Israelite, although Leviticus 19:44 includes resident aliens living in Israel as well.[46] Gentiles or Samaritans would not have been part of this definition, and conventional wisdom would have called for love of the first and hatred and distrust for the second.[47] The climax of the story happens when Jesus changes the question from, "Who is my neighbor?" to, "How can I respond to others in a neighborly way?"[48]

One of the distinguishing qualities of the Samaritan, in contrast, is that he allowed himself to be moved by the vulnerability of the wounded man. His heart was open, and he becomes neighbor to him when he allows the suffering of another to literally "move his entrails" (Greek: *splagchnizŏmai*).[49] The same

---

[45] Richard Rohr, "The Prodigal Father," Daily Meditations, September 15, 2013, https://cac.org.

[46] François Bovon notes that the use of the word "neighbor" in the lawyer's question is ambiguous. Depending on whether the word πλησίον is used as a noun [neighbor] or an adverb [near], it could mean who is my neighbor? Or who is near me? (François Bovon, *Luke 2: A Commentary on the Gospel of Luke 9:51–19:27*, ed. Helmut Koester, trans. Donald S. Deer [Minneapolis: Fortress Press, 2013], 55–56).

[47] Arnold, *Zondervan Illustrated Bible Backgrounds Commentary: Matthew, Mark, Luke*, 1:414–15.

[48] Gustavo Gutierrez, *A Theology of Liberation: History, Politics and Salvation* (Maryknoll, NY: Orbis Books, 1988); Gustavo Gutierrez, *Spiritual Writings*, ed. Daniel G. Groody (Maryknoll, NY: Orbis Books, 2011), 48.

[49] James Strong, *A Concise Dictionary of the Words in the Greek Testament and The Hebrew Bible* (Bellingham, WA: Logos Bible Software, 2009), 1:66. Helmut Köster, "σπλάγχνον, σπλαγχνίζομαι, εὔσπλαγχνος, πολύσπλαγχνος, ἄσπλαγχνος," in Gerhard Kittel, Geoffrey W. Bromiley, and Gerhard Friedrich, eds., *Theological Dictionary of the New Testament* (Grand Rapids: William B. Eerdmans, 1967), 7:549.

word is used when Jesus sees the hungry crowds (Mt. 15:32), sees the grief of the widow of Nain (Lk. 7:11–17), sees the people without a shepherd (Mk. 6:34), and sees two blind men in their misery (Mt. 20:34). The ability of the Samaritan to feel compassion (Latin: "to suffer with" [*com* {with} + *pati* {to suffer}]) reveals his neighborly concern flowing from his God-imaged humanity.

Likewise, Pope Francis' own heart was moved when he heard about the plight of refugees drowning in the Mediterranean. Commenting on this same parable, he said,

> We have lost a sense of responsibility for our brothers and sisters. We have fallen into the hypocrisy of the priest and the Levite whom Jesus described in the parable of the Good Samaritan: we see our brother half dead on the side of the road, and perhaps we say to ourselves: "poor soul . . . !", and then go on our way. It's not our responsibility, and with that we feel reassured, assuaged. . . In this globalized world, we have fallen into globalized indifference. We have become used to the suffering of others: it doesn't affect me; it doesn't concern me; it's none of my business! ("Homily of Holy Father Francis," July 8, 2013)

In one of his early interviews, Pope Francis also reminded us that one of the foremost tasks of the Church is the ministry of healing:

> The thing the church needs most today is the ability to heal wounds and to warm the hearts of the faithful; it needs nearness, proximity. I see the church as a field hospital after battle. It is useless to ask a seriously injured person if he has high cholesterol and about the level of his blood sugars! You have to heal his wounds. Then we can talk about everything else. Heal the wounds, heal the wounds. . . . And you have to start from the ground up.[50]

Jesus tells the story of the Good Samaritan not just to help the lawyer get his understanding of the law right but to get his heart right; Jesus calls the lawyer to see that what is needed is not simply doctrinal or legal clarity but moral and social conversion.[51] The Samaritan inevitably would have

---

[50] Antonio Spadaro, "A Big Heart Open to God: An Interview with Pope Francis," *America*, September 30, 2013.

[51] I. H. Marshall, "Luke," in D. A. Carson, R. T. France, J. A. Motyer, and G.

been the hardest neighbor for this Jew to love, and when Jesus asks him who is the neighbor in the story, the lawyer cannot even bring himself to say the word "Samaritan."

Because no area of migration today is more contested than the legal arena, this passage in particular has much to say about the relationship between law and ethics. Since so many people in our own times appeal to the laws of nation-states to ratify exclusionary mindsets, it challenges especially those who justify inaction toward those suffering on the other side of borders. At the same time some groups in the Arizona desert have been so inspired by this parable that they have named themselves officially "Samaritans." They define anyone in need from any nation as one's neighbor; they refuse to use the law to justify indifference; and they offer medical support to all migrants coming through the deserts of the American Southwest, regardless of their legal status. They see, rather, that no matter where people come from, all people share a human connection, which on some level makes them a neighbor, even and especially those who are defined as "the other."

### The Samaritan Woman and the Other: Migration and Transformative Encounters

> "How can you, a Jew, ask me, a Samaritan woman, for a drink?" (Jn. 4:9)

Jesus' conversation with the Samaritan woman at the well is one of the longest heart-to-heart talks in the Scriptures. It is a story of human transformation that flows above all from a divine-human encounter. As we examine this text more closely, we can see multiple levels of migration at work.[52] On the human level, we learn about Jesus' external journey, the physical challenges he faces, and the social and cultural barriers he has to deal with in his

---

J. Wenham, eds., *New Bible Commentary: 21st-Century Edition*, 4th ed. (Downers Grove, IL: InterVarsity Press, 1994), 998–99.

[52] Some scholars make note of the theological and historical "bi-levels" at work in the Gospel of John. The changing of water into wine, and its parallels to the old covenant giving way to the new covenant, as well the events of Jesus' lifetime and its parallels to those of John's community and its mission to the Samaritan community, are two such examples. I draw on this multilayered interpretation of the Gospel in my reading of the text in light of the physical, historical, and spiritual migrations present in this passage. For more on the bi-level theology of John's Gospel, see Bergant and Karris, *The Collegeville Bible Commentary*, 987.

migration through Palestine. On the historical level, we can see the painful wounds caused by centuries of forced migrations that have resulted in antagonistic relationships between Jews and Samaritans. On the spiritual level, we get a glimpse into the Samaritan woman's internal journey and the tortuous emotional terrain she has to traverse in order to find healing on her return journey to God. In these interwoven dimensions, the story reveals the ways Jesus accepts the Samaritan woman without condition, and in doing so he breaks down the walls that isolate her, challenges the laws that exclude her, and heals the wounds that paralyze her. In the Gospel of John we read,

> Now when Jesus learned that the Pharisees had heard that Jesus was making and baptizing more disciples than John . . . he left Judea and returned to Galilee. He had to pass through Samaria. So he came to a town of Samaria called Sychar, near the plot of land that Jacob had given to his son Joseph. Jacob's well was there. Jesus, tired from his journey, sat down there at the well. It was about noon. A woman of Samaria came to draw water. Jesus said to her, "Give me a drink." His disciples had gone into the town to buy food. The Samaritan woman said to him, "How can you, a Jew, ask me, a Samaritan woman, for a drink?" (For Jews use nothing in common with Samaritans.) Jesus answered and said to her, "If you knew the gift of God and who is saying to you, 'Give me a drink,' you would have asked him and he would have given you living water." (4:1–10)

As we examine the overlapping migration stories at work in this passage, let us first look at Jesus' physical journey through the land. In New Testament times, Palestine was under Roman rule, and it was about 120 miles long from north to south. Within that territory were three primary regions: the lower end was Judea, the middle was Samaria, and the upper end was Galilee. When Jesus decided to migrate from Judea to Galilee, he could have taken one of three possible routes (see map, "The Migration of Jesus through Samaria"). One option would have been to travel west to the coastal route, then northward to Galilee. The second would have been to travel the eastern route on the other side of the Jordan River and then cross again north of Samaria. The quickest way to get to Galilee, however, would have been to travel directly north through Samaria. Normally this third route would have been a two- to three-day trek, while the others would have been considerably longer.

## The Migration of Jesus Through Samaria

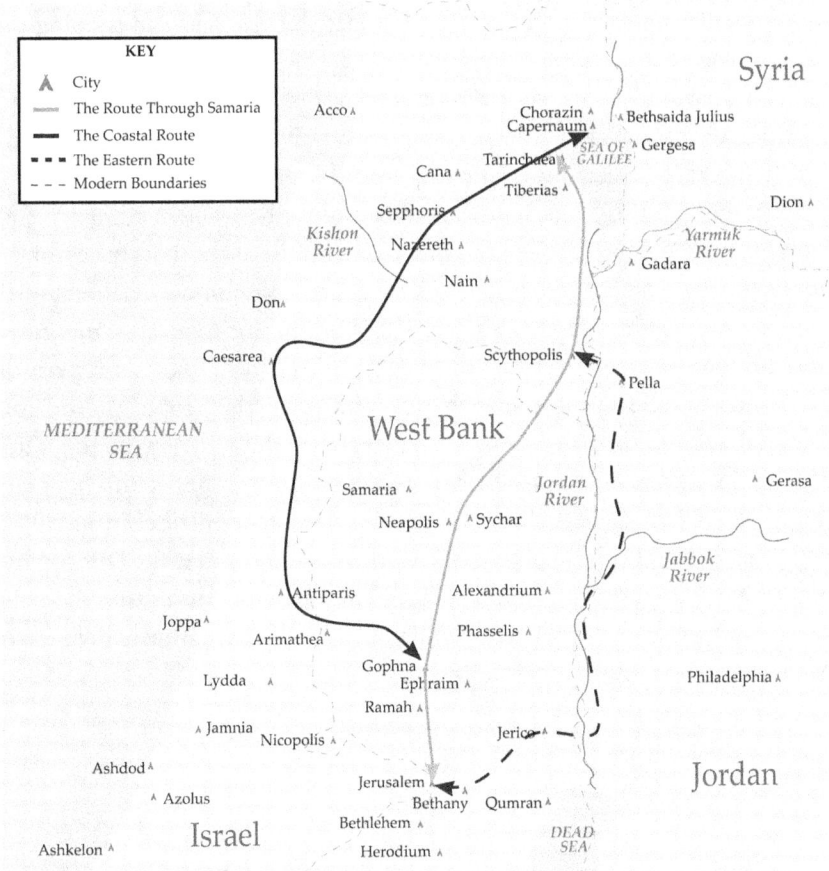

Regardless of the road chosen, the path is difficult. The hot, arid climate requires people to travel in the early hours of the day, and—as is the case also with migrants today—planning one's journey with water sites in mind is critical for survival. The distance from Aenon near the Jordan to Sychar would have been about forty miles on Roman roads, and arriving at the "sixth hour" means that Jesus and his disciples would have made it there at noontime.[53] It is likely that they would have been traveling about six hours

---

[53] The Jewish day begins at sunrise, around 6 a.m., so the sixth hour would be around noon. See also Colin G. Kruse, *John: An Introduction and Commentary* (Downers Grove, IL: InterVarsity Press, 2003), 4:129.

by the time they got there.⁵⁴ Amid the arduous journey, Jesus experiences real thirst, real hunger, and real fatigue.

In addition to undertaking a challenging physical journey, Jesus chooses to migrate through Samaria, which presents thorny legal and theological issues at every turn. The borders between Israel and Samaria are complicated. Many Jews avoid Samaria so as to not become defiled by the Samaritans and anything they touch, including a water bucket. Even though the Samaritans and Jews shared a common spiritual foundation, most Jews would have never come near this Samaritan woman because of her gender, ethnicity, and moral status.⁵⁵ If both believed in one God and the authority of the Torah, however, what could have caused such tense and acrimonious relationships?

To gain insight into this question, it is important to understand more of the migration story of Israel in the Old Testament. Two major periods of forced migration profoundly shape—and scar—the people of God and soul of Palestine. The first begins in 722 BC when the Assyrians conquer the northern tribes of Israel (1 Chr. 5:26; 2 Kgs. 15:29). The second happens in 587 BC when the Babylonians capture the southern tribes of Judah (2 Chr. 36:17–21). Both involve captivity, deportation, and exile. During this painful time of uprooting and displacement, one group loses their faith or disappears while the other fiercely maintains it and vigorously defends it when they come back to their home territory.

*The Forced Migration of Israel and Judah*

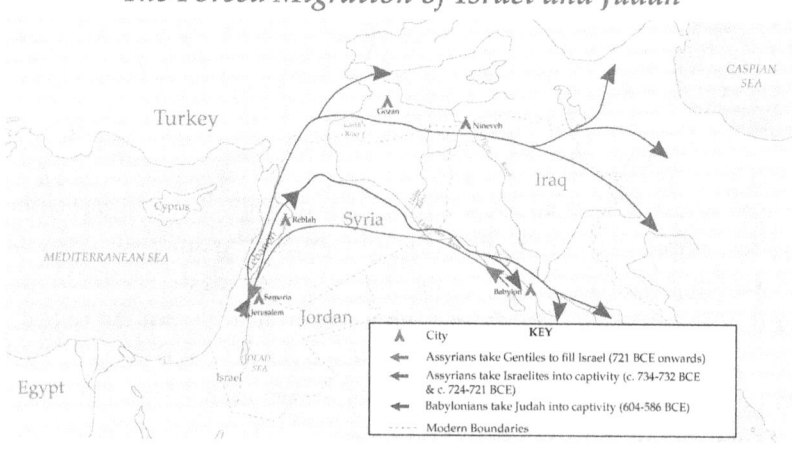

---

⁵⁴ Clinton E. Arnold, *Zondervan Illustrated Bible Backgrounds Commentary: John, Acts* (Grand Rapids: Zondervan, 2002), 2:43.

⁵⁵ Ibid., 2:44.

When the Assyrians conquered the Northern Kingdom and gained control of the capital in Samaria, they initiated a colonization strategy that involved a two-tiered deportation policy (2 Kgs. 17:6; 18:11). The first tier involved forcibly removing the leadership, brains, and talent of the native population and moving them into foreign territory. These migrants never returned home and came to be known as the lost tribes of Israel. The second tier involved forcibly importing migrants from other parts such as Babylon, Cuthah, Avva, Hamath, and Sepharvaim and resettling them in the new land (2 Kgs. 17:24).[56]

Because it is impossible for the Assyrians to deport everybody, however, some remained in Samaria. These people eventually intermarried with these new immigrants, and in time they adopted many of their foreign practices and beliefs. In the process, they watered down their religious beliefs and lost their spiritual integrity. Even though they continued to worship Yahweh and used a version of the Pentateuch as their Scripture, most Jews considered these Samaritans as impure people of mixed blood who sold out their religious convictions to foreigners.

When the Babylonians conquered the Southern Kingdom and gained control of the capital in Jerusalem, they also deported those they captured, but this time it was to Babylon and its environs. These forced migrants, however, did not lose their religion, but rather they strengthened their beliefs while living away from their homeland and fortified their identity as a Jewish people. In the days of Ezra and Nehemiah, these exiles eventually came back home to Jerusalem and began the long work of rebuilding the Temple.

Upon hearing the news of their return, the Samaritans from the north came to offer their help in these reconstruction efforts. Scorning them as schismatics and syncretists, the Jews vehemently rejected their offer (Ez. 4:1–3; Neh. 4:7).[57] This incident fanned the flames of a bitter acrimony that would worsen in the centuries to follow, and as a result the Jews and Samaritans erected many ethnic, religious, and political barriers between them.

By the time Jesus comes on the scene, most Jews were looking down on the Samaritans with contempt, and a culture of prejudice and discrimination

---

[56] Bergant and Karris, *The Collegeville Bible Commentary*, 987.

[57] Edwin A. Blum, "John," in John F. Walvoord and Roy B. Zuck, eds., *The Bible Knowledge Commentary: An Exposition of the Scriptures* (Wheaton, IL: Victor Books, 1985), 2:284–85.

profoundly marked their interactions. Therefore, when Jesus sat down at the well, he crossed a contentious border, one where the Jews and Samaritans defined themselves over and against the staunchly held identity and beliefs of the other. The woman dismisses Jesus as other because he is a Jew. Later on, the Jews dismiss Jesus as other and accuse him of being a Samaritan (Jn. 8:48).[58] Belonging to neither—or as many Latino immigrants put it, *ni de aquí, ni de allá* (neither from here nor there)—he becomes an "alien" to foreigners and a foreigner to his own.

When Jesus encounters the woman at the well, he does not let rules of any kind limit his boundless mercy nor impede his meeting someone who has been defined as other. Even though various ceremonial regulations establish a clearly defined border between Jews and Samaritans, Jesus begins to break down the wall erected by the Jewish law when he interacts with this woman (Gal. 3:28). As he transgresses the conventional norms and customs of tribe, race, gender, and social interaction, he meets this person, first of all, at the level of her humanity. Whereas others would have judged her externally from afar as a loose woman, Jesus looks deeper than the law defined her. Gazing into her heart, he understands and accepts her for who she is at her core: a child of God.

As the conversation progresses, Jesus invites her to go beneath the rules and to embark on a deeper journey, an inner migration. The well is a symbol of depth and of intimacy. It is a container that holds within itself an essential value that sustains life. Sensing her restless heart and inner discontent, Jesus invites her to drink from the well that will satisfy the Desire beyond her desires and the Thirst beyond her thirsts.

The central symbol revolves around life-giving water, which Jesus alone can give. Drinking this water requires worshipping the Father in Spirit and living in the truth (Jn. 4:23–24). To access it she has to go into the inner wells of her own heart and ultimately its source in the inner Heart of God. This will involve not only an encounter with her most authentic self but also—as she drops her bucket in the light and darkness that exist there—an encounter with the mercy of God. It is an experience that will change her from the inside out and will transform all her relationships, including all she has defined as other (Jn. 4:39–42).

---

[58] Donald A. Carson, *The Gospel according to John* (Grand Rapids: William B. Eerdmans, 1991), 218.

As these multiple migration stories intermingle, the border becomes liminal territory where the process of human transformation unfolds through a graced, relational encounter. While space limits a further elaboration on the many other ways this story touches upon a theology of migration, I wish to highlight one further dimension, which Chimamanda Adichiethe refers to as the danger of being defined by "a single story."[59] This passage helps us see the transformation that can happen when people can come together in their differences and encounter each other in a spirit of mutual respect. This process is also what Pope Francis has called "a culture of encounter." This woman, in her coming to believe, reminds us that faith itself is about an encounter with Jesus. And to encounter Jesus, Francis says, means to "do what Jesus does: encounter others."[60] When such encounters foster hospitality, protection, and integral human development, they break down the walls of prejudice that exclude and create new relationships that unite (Pope Francis, "Address of His Holiness Pope Francis to Participants in the International Forum on 'Migration and Peace'"). Such encounters not only enrich and transform one's own journey, but they also heal and transform other people's journeys as well. When the Samaritan encounters Jesus and accepts the unmerited gift of his mercy into her own heart, she begins to pass over from being a social outcast to becoming a missionary of the Gospel message.

The well where Jesus met the Samaritan woman still exists today, and water can still be found in its depths. It is located in the town of Nablus, inside the Orthodox Church of St. Photina, which is in the West Bank territory under Palestinian control. Crossing borders is part of daily life for the people of this city, and today Christians, Muslims, and Samaritan Jews continue to live together in this area despite the region's broader political challenges.

Even as war continues to wound others in the name of protecting the borders of cultures, nations, and religions, some rise to the challenge of finding a shared humanity. In addition to meeting at this well, some encounter each other in the marketplace, others sip Arabic coffee together in local restaurants, and still others go to each other's homes for Easter or

---

[59] See Chimamanda Adichiethe, "The Danger of a Single Story," TED Talks, www.ted.com.

[60] United States Conference of Catholic Bishops, "National Migration Week 2018," www.usccb.org.

Ramadan. As they search together to find a common heartbeat amid all their differences, one can still hear a whisper from the depths that says, "We are all people of the book. He is not 'the enemy' but my brother, and she is not 'the other' but my sister and a member of the same human family."[61]

## Migration and the Christian Scriptures

In Part Two, we have looked at migration in the Christian Scriptures in light of migration in our own times. The first reading offered perspectives from the Old Testament and the lives of some of Scripture's central figures, paying particular attention to core theological themes related to their journeys. The responsorial psalm explored the ways that the words of refugees of biblical times illumine the landscape of the soul and continue to speak to refugees today. The second reading looked at migration in the early church and the way it shaped its identity and mission. And the Gospel reading looked at this topic from the perspective of the Divine Migration of God to the human race, the "return migration" to the divine homeland, and the promise of full citizenship within it.

As we have studied these biblical texts and brought them into dialogue with our contemporary context, we have also tried to become more conscious of the operative narratives that shape our own vision of life and the ways these inspired texts inform, form, and transform us in more life-giving ways. In this process, we have sought to forge a new imagination about migration that transcends the limiting narratives of political pragmatism, economic efficiency, and cultural hegemony. Ultimately our exploration of the Scriptures has helped us search for more liberating and generative narratives that reveal our integral connection to God and each other.

In the final pages of the New Testament, John the Apostle writes to the churches from exile as a refugee in Patmos, along what is today the Turkish seacoast. In the book of Revelation, he opens up a perspective of the migratory nature of the church in this world and the destiny of our earthly sojourn. He speaks of "a new heaven and a new earth . . . a holy city, the new Jerusalem, coming down out of heaven from God" (Rev. 21:1–2). This vision names the identity of the church in this world as a pilgrim people, and it has great ramifications for how we understand those who are on the move

---

[61] I am grateful to Marie Claire Klassen, who worked in Nablus among the people there, for this insight.

today. When viewed from the perspective of Christian faith, this vision not only reveals that migrants mirror who we are in this world, it also exposes our own vulnerability within it. In the next chapter we look more closely at the theme of pilgrimage and its significance for understanding our migration through this life.

# 6

# THE WORD IN MOVEMENT

## *Transforming Migration Narratives*

*Do not conform yourselves to this age but be transformed by the renewal of your mind, that you may discern what is the will of God, what is good and pleasing and perfect.* (Rm. 12:2)

When Paul was growing up, his father had a prosperous job that gave him many opportunities to travel around the world, explore different cultures, and study at some of the best universities in Europe.[1] He majored in accounting as an undergrad, earned an MBA, and landed a respectable job as a business manager in England. He later went back to his home country and received a high-level job working for the government.

He thrived in his work at first, but after a period of time he became aware of the corruption of many leading political figures, who were funneling money from the country into their own private coffers. He struggled to know the best way to respond, and eventually he decided to share this information with the opposing political party, hoping it would help correct some of the abuses and injustices. His plan backfired. Not only were his words later used against him, but it set in motion a series of repercussions that would change his life forever.

When government leaders learned he had leaked news of their misconduct, they captured him and imprisoned him in an area known as "the killing zone." They accused him of betrayal and sharing classified intelligence. Then they locked him away in a sealed container, cut him off from all social communication, and tortured him for forty days.

---

[1] Name changed to protect his identity.

As a result of his injuries, he was put in the hospital and nearly died. While recovering, he was constantly under the vigilant glare of military guards, who handcuffed him to the bed. It was just before Christmas, and one of the guards—seeing an opportunity—leaned over the bedside and said, "As soon as you get well and the holidays are over, they will torture you one last time for any remaining information, and then they will kill you." As Paul's desperation began to mount, the guard whispered, "But we can help you."

He said they would be willing to facilitate his escape if he could come up with fifty thousand dollars. At first Paul thought that amount was completely out of reach. But with no time to waste, he called his friends, who helped him come up with thirty thousand dollars. Five days later he gave the money to the guards, who accepted the lesser sum and brought him to the border, where he escaped into a neighboring country. So began Paul's refugee tale.

**Canterbury Tales and Refugee Tales**

When I first met Paul, he was not on a border, at a detention center, or in a prison. We met instead on a hiking trail in rural England at an event called "Refugee Tales."[2] It was the beginning of Refugee Week, a time when countries around the world hold various artistic, cultural, and educational events to raise consciousness about the plight of refugees. A group called the Gatwick Detainees Welfare Group commemorated the week by bringing together people from all walks of life to go on pilgrimage throughout rural England.[3]

The core group consisted of thirty-five people, and Paul and I were two of the participants who joined this nine-day walk of solidarity. Some were lawyers, counselors, artists, poets, scholars, priests, and nuns. Others were migrants, refugees, and asylum seekers. Still others were advocates, social workers, teachers, and people from various other professions and occupations. Together we sought to exchange stories in order to share in a common journey of hope, especially for those fleeing their countries and seeking international protection.[4]

---

[2] For more on this event, see www.refugeetales.org.

[3] The primary work of the Gatwick Detainees Welfare Group involves visiting asylum seekers and immigrant detainees in the greater London area. For more, see https://gdwg.org.uk.

[4] For more on the walk and the stories, see David Herd and Anna Pincus, *Refugee Tales* (Manchester, UK: Comma Press, 2016).

Mindful of the dehumanizing and enslaving narratives at work in British society and other parts of the world, Refugee Tales sought to tell the story of migration in a different way. It is designed to highlight the narratives of people like Paul—and to tell them against the backdrop of Geoffrey Chaucer's *The Canterbury Tales*, one of the keystones of British literary history.

*The Canterbury Tales* is a collection of over twenty stories that shaped the cultural and linguistic landscape of the country during the Middle Ages. They were written in Middle English during the Hundred Years War (1337–1453) when France and England were engaged in bitter territorial conflicts with each other. The cross-fertilization of cultures during this war greatly shaped the development of the English language and consequently gave rise to a set of literary forms that influenced the way people thought about their own journey and the world in which they lived.[5]

More than six hundred years after *The Canterbury Tales*, we followed along the path of Chaucer's pilgrims. We trekked about eighty miles, traveling along the North Downs Way from Dover to Crowley via Canterbury, which brought us through the English counties of Kent, Surrey, and Sussex. Each day we walked as many as a dozen miles together. Each meal we would share at a common table. And each evening in a rural English town—with the help of music, song, poetry, and dancing—we would share stories about refugees like Paul.

There were multiple goals to Refugee Tales, but some of the foremost were (1) to make visible the often "invisible" journeys of migrants and refugees and their harrowing journeys fleeing war and persecution; (2) to celebrate the gifts and contributions of migrants, refugees, and asylum seekers to society; (3) to challenge existing legislation, particularly practices like "indefinite detention" in England that affect many like Paul; and (4) to change the language and discourse around migration that shape the social narratives about them. As this group of pilgrims sought to educate people about detainees like Paul, we hoped to raise awareness about the plight of refugees, their challenges related to detention policies, and their social exclusion from the society at large.

Chaucer stitched together the journey of his pilgrims by weaving together the Knight's tale and the Miller's tale; the Reeve's tale and the Cook's tale; the Lawyer's tale and the Wife of Bath's tale; the Merchant's tale

---

[5] For more on this topic, see Ebbe Klitgård, "The Encoding of Subjectivity in Chaucer's 'The Wife of Bath's Tale' and 'The Pardoner's Tale,'" in G. Bayer and E. Klitgård, *Narrative Developments from Chaucer to Defoe* (New York: Routledge, 2011), 25–39.

and the Monk's tale; the Nun's tale and the Prioress' tale, among others. In a similar way, during our pilgrimage two new stories were told each night, and each one involved a protagonist in the global refugee drama. These included the Chaplain's tale and the Unaccompanied Minor's tale; the Arriver's Tale and the Lorry Driver's Tale; the Visitor's Tale and the Detainee's Tale; the Interpreter's Tale and the Appellant's Tale; the Counsellor's Tale and the Dependant's Tale; the Friend's Tale and the Deportee's Tale; and the Lawyer's Tale and the Refugee's Tale. The pilgrimage ended in Crawley to a sold-out performance of the Ex-Detainee's Tale.

Chaucer's pilgrims were incentivized in their storytelling by the prospects of a prize-winning meal at the Tabard Inn at the end of their journey. But they eventually discovered—as did we—that sharing each other's stories on the road is a reward of its own. As Refugee Tales opened a space to walk together, talk together, and share in each other's journeys, it also opened a space to encounter each other, to forge new relationships with strangers, and to be transformed by a common human journey.

Before Paul's tale as a refugee began, he traveled, studied, and worked in Europe and moved around freely. He narrowly escaped the immediate threats to his life, but he was far from safe after he crossed into a neighboring territory. The leaders of his country were furious when they learned he had taken flight, so they took revenge by killing his parents and other family members. They also assassinated the four guards who facilitated his escape. Adding to his agonies, he now carries the burden of guilt. In order to find some measure of international protection, he needed to leave the region and find his way into a country that could offer him refuge from his persecutors.

According to Article 2 of the United Nations Convention and Protocol Relating to the Status of Refugees, people like Paul can qualify for asylum if they can demonstrate a "well-founded fear of being persecuted for reasons of race, religion, nationality, membership of a particular social group or political opinion."[6] Knowing he faced certain death if he returned to his country, and also believing that he could prove he had a credible threat, Paul eventually made his way to England on a visa. This visa enabled him to stay in the country for a period of time, but to stay longer and avoid deportation, he needed to officially apply for asylum. This process required that he surrender his passport to the immigration office.

---

[6] United Nations High Commissioner for Refugees, Convention and Protocol Relating to the Status of Refugees, Art. 2, p. 14. See www.unhcr.org.

Because of administrative mismanagement, the immigration authorities later lost his passport, which made Paul's life even more complicated. Unable to verify his credentials without the physical documents—and the authorities unwilling to admit their culpability—they accused him of document fraud and put him in detention for the next two years and three months. In what seemed like the blink of an eye, Paul went from being a well-respected professional to a vulnerable refugee, a criminal. As a foreign national, however, Paul was treated as a different kind of criminal. British citizens who are jailed have access to a library, gym time, legal services, healthcare, and open-air spaces to move around. Foreigners in detention have none of these. He said at times he spent twenty-three hours in a small cell and had only one hour of "air time" each day. "Detention is like a prison," Paul said, "but you have even less rights." Unlike citizens, foreigners like Paul have no idea how long they will be there, a status referred to as "indefinite detention."[7]

### The Tradition of Pilgrimage and Creating a New Tale

Paul became involved in the Refugee Tales pilgrimage in part to make sense of his life, especially in the face of such bitter trials. Over the centuries, the tradition of pilgrimage has been a valuable tool for people to gain some perspective on their journey, which is one reason it is a recurring theme in literature as well as religious practice.

In addition to *The Canterbury Tales*, major texts like the Epic of Gilgamesh (2100 BC), Homer's *Odyssey* (eighth century BC), Dante's *Divine Comedy* (1320), Bunyan's *Pilgrim's Progress* (1678), and Joyce's *Ulysses* (1922) offer rich examples of humans making sense of the journey through this world and beyond. The major world religions also have traditions of pilgrimage, most often associated with sacred places. Buddhists journey to Lumbini in Nepal, the birthplace of Buddha. Hindus travel to Varanasi and the Ganges River in India to pay homage to their ancestors and their gods. Muslims journey to Mecca (Hajj) in Saudi Arabia in order

---

[7] While the government provides those in detention with modest support, those like Paul are not allowed to work nor enroll in formal education programs in the country. Decisions on their asylum status can be delayed for years or decades. The government agency tasked with assisting asylum seekers is called the National Asylum Support Service (NASS). See www.gov.uk.

to fulfill the requirements of one of the five pillars of Islam. And Christians journey to the Holy Land to walk in the footsteps of Jesus. What makes pilgrimage so important to human beings?

The reasons people go on pilgrimage vary, but most often they are connected to gaining a broader perspective on one's journey through life. Some go on pilgrimage to encounter nature, new people, ancestors, or even oneself. In the process, many undergo deeper inner exploration that helps clarify the coordinates of their journey or gain wisdom of heart, especially in the face of unexpected suffering and injustice. For our purposes here, pilgrimage is also inseparable from the theme of migration. As people participate in an outer migration of pilgrimage, we might say, many are led to engage in a more conscious inner migration that leads them closer to God and to their most authentic selves.

Chaucer's influence stems in part from the way his words formed people's understanding of their world. He reminds us that words shape language. Language creates narratives—and narratives shape our understanding of the world. Chaucer helped create new worlds for people that led to creative human connections, especially among different people. Pilgrimages can become particularly transformative when people allow their inner worlds to be reshaped in new ways.

Refugee Tales helps us reflect on the way narratives shape our own perception of the world and whether they lead toward or away from life-giving human connections. By narratives I mean the social, religious, cultural, economic, historical, and political stories that shape our consciousness of reality and the choices we make because of them. These inner narratives become the prism through which we make our choices and consequently shape who we become. They shape what we see and what we ignore; they cast how we view reality and how we define our lives; they influence who we think belongs and who we define as the other. Narratives can make us think of one person as a cultural hero and another as an illegal alien. As Alan Hilliard perceptively notes,

> Narratives are stories that can give life or destroy life. The language of the world has boxed people, pilloried people, dehumanised people, offended and limited people. When we use language, labels, and narratives to make the person beside us out to be the "other," then we are on a slippery slope as a society and a world. Whether

we are a Christian, Muslim, Hindu or Humanist, whether we are police, media, nurse, doctor or civil servant, once we label others to make ourselves feel superior to them we dehumanise them.[8]

In fact, narratives shape how we understand issues like migration more than reason, facts, and data do. All of the arts play an important role in storytelling because they offer, promote, or provoke alternative perspectives to the dominant narrative as constructed by the media and by political and economic elites. As Zygmunt Bauman observes, "The preoccupation of the arts with sketching in imaginary alternatives to the prevailing states of things sets them up as rivals to the management whether they like it or not. The control over human enterprise and effort expended by the administration comes down in the last resort, to its desire to dominate the future."[9]

Because the narratives of society that shape our worldview today are largely written by the powerful and the wealthy—often with their own interests in mind—it is important to ask who is included and excluded in the dominant narratives of society. The migration narrative in particular looks very different when we start with the stories of those who are migrating today and their refugee tales. Our immigration policies would look very different if the starting point of concern was the needs of the weakest and most vulnerable of society rather than the concerns of the rich and powerful. Reflecting on Africa's colonial history, Chinua Achebe once noted, "Until the lions have their own historians, the history of the hunt will always glorify the hunter."[10]

Dehumanizing migrant tales have been a part of every generation, but in our own time, Donald Trump embraced this migrant-as-other narrative with particular intensity. When he decided to run for president in 2015, he began invoking his own set of migrant tales and made it a cornerstone of his campaign. In his presidential announcement speech, he said, "The U.S. has become a dumping ground for everybody else's problems. When Mexico sends its people, they're not sending their best. . . . They're sending people that have lots of problems, and they're bringing those problems with us. They're bringing drugs. They're bringing crime. They're rapists.

---

[8] Alan Hilliard, "Migration," *The Furrow* 66, no. 3 (March 2015): 158.

[9] Zygmunt Bauman and Lydia Bauman, *Culture in a Liquid Modern World* (Cambridge, MA: Malden, 2011), 104.

[10] Jerome Brooks (interviewer), "Chinua Achebe, The Art of Fiction No. 139," *Paris Review*, no. 133, Winter 1994, www.theparisreview.org.

And some, I assume, are good people."[11] His comments enraged many, but they also mobilized many others who elected him to the White House. Despite evidence that contradicted the narrative, Trump promoted it. Not only did he omit the parts of the narrative that include the ways immigrants construct buildings, clean hotels, and landscape properties—all integral to businesses he profited from—he also ignored the other positive contributions many immigrants make to society.[12] These storylines have been further reinforced by assertions that shape the cultural landscape and public debate: "They take our jobs." "They don't pay taxes." "They are a drain on the economy." "They sponge on our social services." "They threaten our culture."[13] And many others.

Trump invoked these narratives to fan the flames of sociocultural and economic anxiety, which he and others exploited for social, political, and economic advantage. These narratives instill fear and mistrust, resulting in marginalization, exclusion, and alienation. They enrich some people at other's expense because of the way they degrade and dehumanize.

Such narratives are not only being propagated in the Americas. We see xenophobia etched into public discourse in almost every country in the world, whether it be in the Rohinga migrating to Bangladesh, North Africans to Italy, Syrians to Lebanon, or Mexicans to the United States. Most commonly these narratives are tainted by a fear of the foreigner and an anxiety about the presence of all who are perceived as other. The Scriptures, as we have seen, tell a different story.

While the human economy deals with the realities of our fallen condition and the world we have created because of it, to speak about the divine economy is a way of referring to the ordering of the world according to the designs of a loving Creator. It is a way of saying that God's ways are very different than ours. In the divine economy, God not only created it and left it alone but is constantly at work trying to re-create it and reorder it by way of salvation and redemption.

---

[11] Jonathan Capehart, "Donald Trump's 'Mexican Rapists' Rhetoric Will Keep the Republican Party out of the White House," *Washington Post*, June 17, 2015.

[12] Bianca E. Bersani, "An Examination of First- and Second-Generation Immigrant Offending Trajectories," *Justice Quarterly* 31, no. 2 (2012): 315–43. See also Rich Morin, "Crime Rises among Second-Generation Immigrants as They Assimilate," Pew Research Center, October 15, 2013, www.pewresearch.org.

[13] For more on this topic, see Aviva Chomsky, *"They Take Our Jobs!": And 20 Other Myths about Immigration* (Boston: Beacon Press, 2007).

The divine economy, or more precisely the Kingdom of God, has a different starting point. It is not based on human agendas, financial interests, or political motivations. It is rather based first and foremost on grace, truth, life, holiness, justice, love, peace, and mercy. Because people are created in God's own image and likeness, this economy puts the dignity of the human person at the core of the debate. This dignity is most critical especially when it is most threatened. In contrast to a human economy, the divine economy prioritizes human costs over and above economic costs. In this spirit, the Catholic Bishops of the United States have argued that the single most important criterion of a society's health is how it treats its most vulnerable members and how it responds to the needs of the poor.[14] As John Paul II put it, "The needs of the poor must take priority over the desires of the rich, the rights of workers over the maximization of profits; the preservation of the environment over uncontrolled industrial expansion; the production to meet social needs over production for military purposes."[15]

## Unlocking Human Dignity

At this stage of his life, Paul's journey is still very much an uphill climb. He has been allowed a temporary stay in the United Kingdom while his case is being adjudicated, but he lives every day in a state of social, economic, and political limbo. "I can't return to my homeland, but the place where I am right now does not welcome me. With an uncertain future, my life seems like it is perpetually on hold."

Organizations like the Gatwick Detainees Welfare Group helped Paul obtain a conditional release from detention, but he is a long way from the liberation that would unlock his human dignity.[16] Probation authorities restrict his movement and require him to report every week, which makes him feel at times, he said, "like a caged animal." Moreover, every time he

---

[14] United States Conference of Catholic Bishops, "Economic Justice for All: Pastoral Letter on Catholic Social Teaching and the U.S. Economy," November 1986, no. 123.

[15] John Paul II, "Address on Christian Unity in a Technological Age," delivered in Toronto, September 14, 1984, *Origins* 14, no. 16 (October 4, 1984): 248.

[16] For more on recommendations by the US Conference of Catholic Bishops on detention reform and alternatives to it, see United States Conference of Catholic Bishops, "Unlocking Human Dignity." This report focuses on the injustices related to family detention and the impact on families.

reports to the authorities, he does not know what will happen. "I live with the constant fear that they can deport me at any moment."

Paul's release from the confines of physical detention was a step forward, but he soon faced another kind of imprisonment: psychological bondage. No matter where he goes now, the label "refugee" follows and hems him in in ways that make him feel as if he is in a social prison. "I pray, but I have a lot of fear. If I am sent back I just hope that death will be quick, that I won't have to suffer the pain for too long because I can't go through being tortured again."

As personal as Paul's story is, however, it is by no means unique. One day while on the trail with us, Paul had to go to London to report to the immigration authorities to comply with probationary expectations, as was his biweekly custom. A man from Algeria in front of him in line had been in the country for seven years hoping to receive asylum. He had dutifully complied with the rules and regulations set forth by the United Kingdom, but on this particular day, they told him that, instead of reporting once a week, he now had to report to authorities every day, Monday through Friday. After years of what would appear as pent-up stress, he could not take it any longer and the emotional dam broke. He lashed out in anger, screaming, yelling, and breaking windows. Then he stormed out of the office. When authorities catch up with him, he will face sure and certain deportation, but Paul understands how people get to this point; interminable stays in detention lead many to become desperate and hopeless.

Even as Paul holds out hope that justice will have the last word, his tale speaks volumes about the human costs of the refugee journey. "In so many ways I feel I have lost everything. I came to Britain seeking protection, and I trusted that if I was honest, I would receive the help I needed. It makes no sense that because of a desire for justice, people are being killed. I don't know if I would do it again. A lot of innocent people lost their lives because of me. It makes it hard to feel happy about being alive."

Caught between the rules and regulations of the British authorities and his own government that seeks to torture and kill him, Paul lives in constant anxiety about whether he will be sent back home at any minute, which would mean certain death. What is even more painful is the feeling that he really does not belong, that he has no home of his own and is not free to shape his own future. "What's worse," he added, "for the most part we count for nothing in society. Most don't even know we are here."

Refugee Tales opened up a space not only to walk through the rural landscape of England but also to rewrite some of the social, political, and literary landscape of society in favor of a more life-giving reading of those on the move. As the pilgrimage informed people about the journeys of refugees like Paul, it sought to transform the words, language, and narratives used in the media and the public forum that make people like him into nonpersons. In place of narratives shaped around hostility, fear, and animosity, the Refugee Tales sought to create narratives that emerge from hospitality, solidarity, and generosity.

As Chaucer brought pilgrim tales into existence in his time, Refugee Tales has been a chance to bring many refugee stories into the cultural consciousness of a nation and to reshape people's lack of consciousness about them. By bringing the stories of migrants and refugees into existence, it has helped make more visible a people who have become virtually invisible to others. Because many of their stories are "locked up" in detention centers like the refugees themselves, Refugee Tales has been a way of bringing these stories into the open, into the public conversation about migration, making their presence real and visible to British society and the world.

In the pages to follow, we talk more about these real stories and the meaning of real presence in the Eucharist. As we seek to make the connection between what is happening inside churches in the Eucharist and what is happening outside them in an age of migration, Refugee Tales helps remind us that real presence is perhaps even more basic than a theological formulation. It involves enabling each and every person to become a real person, a real presence in society, a real presence to one another.

We will see how the stories we have considered now take shape around a common table in the Liturgy of the Eucharist. As we allow our stories to be part of one another's lives, we seek to discover the path that leads to discovering our interconnectedness, our communion with God, and through it, how God becomes real to us in sharing with each other. We also connect the stories with God's own migration to us, his call to engage in a return migration to him, and ultimately our movement from otherness to oneness.

## An Immigrant Creed

*I believe in Almighty God,*
*who guided the people in exile and in exodus,*
*the God of Joseph in Egypt and Daniel in Babylon,*
*the God of foreigners and immigrants.*

*I believe in Jesus Christ, a displaced Galilean,*
*who was born away from his people and his home,*
*who fled his country with his parents when his life was in danger,*
*and returning to his own country*
*suffered the oppression of the tyrant Pontius Pilate,*
*the servant of a foreign power,*
*who then was persecuted, beaten, and finally tortured, accused,*
*and condemned to death unjustly.*
*But on the third day, this scorned Jesus rose from the dead,*
*not as a foreigner but to offer us citizenship in heaven.*

*I believe in the Holy Spirit,*
*the eternal immigrant from God's Kingdom among us,*
*who speaks all languages, lives in all countries, and reunites all races.*

*I believe that the church is the secure home for the foreigner*
*and for all believers who constitute it,*
*who speak the same language and have the same purpose.*

*I believe that the Communion of the Saints begins when we accept*
*the diversity of the saints.*
*I believe in the forgiveness, which makes us all equal,*
*and in the reconciliation, which identifies us more than does race,*
*language, or nationality.*
*I believe that in the resurrection God will unite us as one people in*
*which all are distinct and all are alike at the same time.*

*Beyond this world, I believe in Life Eternal in which no one will*
*be an immigrant but all will be citizens of God's Kingdom,*
*which will never end. Amen.*[17]

---

[17] Jose Luis Casal, "The Immigrant's Creed"; see www.ethnicharvest.org.

*Part Three*

# The Eucharistic Narratives

*Migration and the Body of Christ*

# 7

# The Bodies of Refugees and the Body of Christ

*This is my body, which will be given for you; do this in memory of me.* (Lk. 22:19)

### The Foundations of Migration and the Eucharist

A number of years ago, I attended a mass in El Paso, Texas, along the US-Mexico border. It was celebrated outside, in the rugged, sun-scorched terrain of the Chihuahuan Desert, on the Feast of All Souls. It was near the place where many migrants pass over the southern border and where many have lost their lives in recent decades.[1] As in other liturgies, people prayed, sang, and worshipped together. Unlike other liturgies, however, a sixteen-foot iron fence divided this community in half, with one side in Mexico and the other side in the United States.[2] While the operative political narratives created a wall that went through the middle of this community, the far deeper spiritual narratives brought this community together and offered a different way of living and being in the world.

---

[1] For more on this topic, see Roberto Primmer Luis, "How U.S. Policy Turned the Sonoran Desert into a Graveyard for Migrants," *New York Times*, August 19, 2020.

[2] This section is drawn from a conference on Humanities and the Option for the Poor at the University of Salzburg, Austria, and a conference on Immigration, Labor, and Religion at Harvard Divinity School and a paper I gave titled "Do This in Memory of Me: Anamnesis and Immigration." It is also drawn from Daniel G. Groody, "Fruit of the Vine and Work of Human Hands: Immigration and the Eucharist," *Worship* 80, no. 5 (2006): 386–402.

The sacrament of the Eucharist is central to the life and mission of the Church. It is "the summit toward which the activity of the Church is directed [and] . . . the source from which all her power flows" (*Sacrosanctum Concilium* 8).[3] It is the peak from which to gain perspective on the whole of life and food to nourish our migration through this world on the way to our spiritual homeland. In different ways the Eucharist draws people into a borderlands between heaven and earth; it is where our journey meets with Jesus' life, death, and resurrection. In other words, the Eucharist is a privileged, liminal space of divine-human encounter where transformation happens.

The Eucharist was initially celebrated among the first Christians, but its roots are Jewish in nature. The rite is, in fact, intimately related to the Jewish Passover meal. It recalls God's redemptive activity at work in the people of Israel and how that is fulfilled in the person of Jesus. In this sense the Eucharist is a summary of the entire message of Jesus because it recalls all that Jesus stood for, all that he stood against, and all whom he stood with in his proclamation of the Kingdom of God. As it recalls his pass-over from this world to the Father's Kingdom, it also is an invitation to pass over with him from slavery to freedom and from death to new life.

As we go deeper in our theological reflection on migration, I want to say a few words about three foundational dimensions of the Liturgy of the Eucharist, namely, the Table, the Kingdom of God, and Passover. I also want to reflect on these elements in the context of the Mass that Pope Francis celebrated at Lampedusa, Italy, on July 8, 2013. These are important elements for understanding not only the transformation of what is placed on the altar but also the transformation of the Christian community into the body of Christ.

*The Table: A Symbol of Universal Love*

In the Eucharistic celebration, the community gathers around two principal tables: the table of the Word and the table of the Eucharist. In the Liturgy of the Word, the ambo or the pulpit is the table on which the food of the Scriptures is shared. In the Liturgy of the Eucharist, the altar is the table on which the body and blood of Christ are shared. These two parts are so closely inter-

---

[3] XI Ordinary General Assembly of the Synod of Bishops, *Instrumentum Laboris*, The Eucharist: Source and Summit of the Life and Mission of the Church, July 7, 2005.

connected in proclaiming the message of salvation that they form, as Vatican II notes, "a single act of worship" (*Sacrosanctum Concilium* 56).[4]

Having spent considerable time around the table of the Scriptures, we now turn our attention to the Lord's Table—the altar—in order to explore some of the ways the Eucharist can transform our relationships and rescript our operative narratives about migration. To understand better the revelatory significance of the Liturgy of the Eucharist, it is helpful to look more closely at the meaning of tables in the time of Jesus.

Tables are an integral part of liturgy because Jesus himself did much of his ministry around tables (Mt. 26:7; Lk. 5:29–32; 7:36–50; 14:1–24). In biblical times, as in our own, tables are places where people come together not just to eat but also to connect with one another. To sit down at table is a great blessing and to be cut off from it a great misfortune.

Tables create connections with others, but as social creatures they also create for us stratifications within our communities. Some tables are plentiful and others sparse; some are surrounded by wealthy and important people and others by the poor and lowly; some are invited to dine at table, while others are excluded from it for various social, economic, political, and even religious reasons. Because the table is a symbol of a common life, denying certain people a seat at the table has created many social injustices within communities.

From what we know of Jesus in the Scriptures, he is attuned to those who are isolated or rejected from the table and therefore excluded from society. When the Gospel writers make note of Jesus' decision to dine with certain people, they are offering more than descriptive details of Jesus' favorite places and meals; rather, they are making note of the social implications of Jesus' actions.

People rejected Jesus and his message for many reasons, but Virgilio Elizondo's reflection on this question is particularly insightful. He makes the case that God's mercy at work in Jesus' practice of table fellowship consoles some while disturbing many others. This is because the table is connected to God's promised banquet in the end of time, and in welcoming all people to the table—particularly those who are rejected from it in society—Jesus rejects the rejection of the world (Mt. 28:18–20; Mk. 16:15–16; Acts

---

[4] Sacred Congregation of Rites, *Instruction, Eucharisticum mysterium*, May 25, 1967, no. 3: *Acta Apostolicae Sedis* 59 (1967): 542. See also General Instruction for the Roman Missal, no. 28, www.usccb.org.

4:9–12).⁵ This approach, however, does not sit well with many of those in authority. Because they control the invitations to the table of the religiously worthy, they do not feel these rejects belong there, and in turn, they reject Jesus. As Elizondo so powerfully summarizes,

> The "rejected one" rejects rejection by living and proclaiming a universal welcome and love for all. He invites all to repent of their feelings and attitudes of inferiority or superiority, of impurity or purity, of belonging or rejection, and to recognize that we are all children of God called to share in the common table, the table of the new family that goes beyond blood or social status. It is in this experience of radical acceptance that new life begins.⁶

When the reject who rejected rejection rises from the dead, God vindicates Jesus' way as *the* way and in doing so offers hope to all.

As he expresses God's magnanimous embrace of everyone, Jesus welcomes those denied access to the table and challenges those already at the table to look beyond the walls of their own exclusionary mindsets of worthiness and unworthiness. As John Meier observes,

> In the eyes of the stringently pious, Jesus' table fellowship with the ritually or morally unclean communicated uncleanness to Jesus himself. Jesus, of course, saw it the other way round: he was communicating salvation to religious outcasts. His meals with sinners and the disreputable were celebrations of the lost being found, of God's eschatological mercy reaching out and embracing the prodigal son returning home (e.g., Mk. 2:13–17; Lk. 15:1–32). His banquets with sinful Israelites were a preparation and foretaste of the coming banquet in the Kingdom of God—a metaphor that appears in various sayings and parables (e.g., Mk. 2:19; Lk. 13:28–29 par; 14:15–24 par). Thus, the Last Supper does not stand in splendid isolation. It is instead quite literally the "last" of a whole series of meals symbolizing the final feast in the Kingdom of God. There is therefore nothing strange about Jesus' holding a special, symbolic meal with his disciples

---

⁵ Virgilio P. Elizondo, *Galilean Journey: The Mexican-American Promise*, 1st ed. (Maryknoll, NY: Orbis Books, 1983), 70.

⁶ Virgilio P. Elizondo, "Jesus the Galilean Jew in Mestizo Theology," *Theological Studies* 70, no. 2 (2009): 274.

(especially if he sensed his approaching arrest or death) or about his connecting the meal with the coming Kingdom of God.[7]

Jesus' openness to invite all people to the table—including the poor, excluded, and socially, politically, and religiously rejected—is especially significant for our reflection on migration and is integrally related to the meal he asks his disciples to celebrate in memory of him.

*The Kingdom of God: The Key to Understanding Jesus' Message*

The table to which Jesus invites people is inseparable from the Kingdom of God that Jesus proclaims. Appearing over one hundred times in the New Testament, the Kingdom is the central theme of Jesus' preaching.[8] It draws from the Old Testament theme of kingship or kingly rule, and as Jesus brings this theme to the forefront of his mission, he confronts each person with the central question: What rules your heart? Every other issue has its roots in answering this one central question.

In this sense, the work of Jesus involves more than building an institutional church; building a church rather begins with reestablishing the primacy of God's reign in the human heart; these people in turn are called to form a community where God's love radiates out to the world, especially to the darkest places where life is most vulnerable and threatened.

Jesus uses many parables that speak about the integral relationship between the table and the Kingdom. He speaks of the Kingdom as a great feast: a wedding feast (Mt. 22:1–14; 25:1–13), a universal feast (Mt. 8:11–12; Lk. 13:28–29), and an inclusive, abundant feast (Lk. 14:15–24). It is a time of great celebration, eating bread (Lk. 14:15), and drinking wine (Mk. 14:25; Lk. 22:18) that fulfills the message of the prophets and the hope of Israel.

Though all are invited to this table, only some accept this invitation and persevere amid the challenges of discipleship. Some accept initially but turn away, while others reject it altogether (Mt. 13:3–23; Mk. 4:1–20; Lk. 8:4–15). This Kingdom is above all a gift; it is offered to everybody, but it can be rejected. How one responds will determine who one becomes.

---

[7] John P. Meier, *A Marginal Jew: Rethinking the Historical Jesus*, vol. 2: *Mentor, Message, and Miracles* (New York: Doubleday, 1994), 303.

[8] Because of sensitivities to gender and inclusivity, some scholars have preferred to use "reign of God" rather than "Kingdom of God." I use the traditional word of Kingdom because of its integral connection to the king or, in this case, eternal ruler of the universe.

The free gift of this Kingdom, in this sense, comes with a hook. The faithful response entails becoming like the gift-giver. It means taking on the mind of the king and living with one's heart aligned with the ways of the Kingdom. The contours of this life are made clear in the Beatitudes (Mt. 5:3–12; Lk. 6:20–23), which offer a picture of discipleship that is characterized by poverty, compassion, meekness, mercy, purity of heart, nonviolence, peacemaking, and perseverance in persecution. In contrast to the elitism of earthly rulers, Christ's kingship and presence are also hidden among the downtrodden and disfigured of the world. Entrance to the Kingdom of God is inseparable from what one has done for the least and the last of society (Mt. 25:31–46), a topic we take up in more detail toward the end of this book.

In proclaiming this Kingdom, the Church is called to follow the mission of Jesus by re-membering those who have been cut off from the community. The table fellowship celebrated in the Eucharist communicates God's eternal mercies: it gives a foretaste of that communion that is the destiny of all who hope in God's salvation. It ultimately points to the Passover of Jesus from this world to God's Kingdom and to our hopeful pass over to follow this same path back to our eternal homeland.

*The Passover: Israel's Migration Story and the Eucharist*

The last time Jesus gathers at table with his disciples, the night before his return to his Father's Kingdom, he participates in a Jewish Passover meal. Jesus is a rabbi, and the people of Israel celebrate this meal annually at God's command to remember their story of liberation: the way God acts on their behalf and mercifully frees them from slavery in Egypt, leading them through the desert, and accompanying them in their migration to the Promised Land. This story recapitulates God's promise of salvation and the people's hope for the coming of the Kingdom of God in its fullness. At the Last Supper, Jesus takes up this story and reads his own life, mission, and destiny in light of it.

In a second-century Easter homily, St. Melito of Sardis brings out the connection between the story of Jesus and the story of the Passover:

> He is the Passover of our salvation. It is he who suffered much in many. . . . It is he who in Abel was slain, in Isaac was bound, in Jacob was a wanderer, in Joseph was sold, in Moses was cast out, in the lamb was sacrificed, in David was persecuted, in the prophets was

dishonored. It is he who in the virgin was incarnated, who on the tree was suspended, who in the earth was interred, who from the dead was awakened, who to highest heaven was elevated.[9]

John Chrysostom in the fourth century adds to this imagery of the Passover as he reads the entire Christian journey as a migration from death to life:

> The Israelites passed through the sea; you have passed through the sea of death. They were delivered from the Egyptians; you are set free from the demon. They put aside their servitude to barbarians; you have set aside the far more hazardous servitude to sin.[10]

In other words, Passover is a rich, multivalent term that refers to a physical and spiritual migration into a new way of being. The ritual practice of the Passover meal remembers Israel's migration from slavery to freedom and calls the people of God to pass over to a new way of living and being in the world. This involves changing not only our hearts but also our minds, attitudes, and actions—in brief—our world!

As the church remembers Jesus' words about the Kingdom and his passing over to the Father, it also remembers his outreach to those who had become dis-membered from the body of community. Each gesture of welcome is a step toward communion, and although the unity of this community will only be fully realized at the end of time, the Christian community already proclaims the beginning of this unity as one body in Christ, even as various walls still divide it in different ways.

## "This is My Body":
### A Spiritual Vision of Human Solidarity

The Eucharist at the border of El Paso—and indeed every Eucharist—testifies to how the Church waits in expectant hope on this side of eternity for

---

[9] St. Melito of Sardis, *On the Passover,* trans. Richard C. White (Lexington, KY: Lexington Theological Seminary Library, 1976), 37–38.

[10] The translation of this text actually reads as "The Jews" rather than "The Israelites." From the time of the Babylonian captivity, "Jews" became the name for the whole nation (2 Macc. 9:17; Jn. 4:9; 7:1; Acts 18:2, 24). The original designation of the Israelite people was the *Hebrews,* as the descendants of Abraham, and I think the word "Israelites" avoids this confusion. *St. John Chrysostom: Baptismal Instructions,* trans. and annotated by Paul W. Harkins (Westminster, MD: Newman Press, 1963), 64, 240.

the full realization of this communion; it celebrates the Eucharist until Christ comes again and all creation is reconciled to him in the end of time. Until this second coming of Christ, the Church gathers around the table of the Eucharist to remember the night he said to them, "I have eagerly desired to eat this Passover with you before I suffer, for, I tell you, I shall not eat it (again) until there is fulfillment in the Kingdom of God." Then he took a cup, gave thanks, and said, "Take this and share it among yourselves; for I tell you (that) from this time on I shall not drink of the fruit of the vine until the Kingdom of God comes." Then he took the bread, said the blessing, broke it, and gave it to them, saying, "This is my body, which will be given for you; do this in memory of me."[11] The Church arranges the entirety of the Liturgy of the Eucharist around these words, so let us now reflect more on them in light of our return migration to God and those migrating around the world today.

*Lampedusa: The Real Presence of the "No-Bodies"*

Early on the morning of May 8, 2011, a boat with more than five hundred refugees departed from the coast of Libya and launched out into the open sea. Pushed by a turbulent storm of social, economic, and political conditions, and pulled by the hope of a better life on European shores, they had little more than what they carried. They were not the first to undertake such a journey, nor have they been the last.

When the Arab Spring started earlier that year, more than thirty thousand forced migrants from North Africa, Asia, and the Middle East undertook a similar journey. Their fragile vessels, crammed to capacity, and the unpredictable weather made their voyage across the ocean particularly dangerous. One of the few outcroppings of land between the North African coast and the shores of Italy is the small island of Lampedusa. Only eight square miles in area, it is little more than a rock in the middle of the ocean.[12]

When the Italian Coast Guard intercepted this vessel in 2011, they began escorting it to the port at Lampedusa, but the ship's rudder broke, and it began to drift perilously toward the rocky coastline of the island. Fearing

---

[11] Lk. 22:14–20; also 1 Cor. 11:23–25; cf. Mt. 26:26–29; Mk. 14:22–25.

[12] This chapter is drawn in part from Daniel G. Groody, "Cup of Suffering, Chalice of Salvation: Refugees, Lampedusa, and the Eucharist," *Theological Studies* 78, no. 4 (December 2017). Portions of it also have been published in Daniel G. Groody, "Migration and the Eucharist: A Sacramental Vision of Migration," in Peter Phan, ed., *Christian Theology in an Age of Migration: Implications for World Christianity* (Lanham, MD: Rowman and Littlefield, 2020), 255–68.

the boat would break apart and many would drown, authorities mobilized nearby fishermen, police officers, and other village volunteers, who risked their lives and worked tirelessly through the night until everyone was safely brought onshore. By morning, they had saved 528 people, including twenty-four pregnant women and a number of children. In contrast to so many others who had perished at sea, this was a story of salvation!

Two years later, in July 2013, another boat set out on a similar journey, but those migrants were not as fortunate. After this particular boat capsized, everyone perished, except for eight people who survived by clinging to the fishing nets of a nearby boat.[13] They pleaded desperately to be saved, but when the fisherman saw them hanging on, they severed their nets and cast these migrants to die in the ocean depths.

This story so deeply moved the newly elected Pope Francis that it reached him, he said, "like a painful thorn in my heart." In response, he wanted to make "a gesture of closeness" that would express his solidarity. Eight days later on July 13, 2013, he traveled to Lampedusa ("Visit to Lampedusa: Homily of Holy Father Francis"). Even though some counseled him against it, he made an impromptu trip to this isolated place as a way of expressing his solidarity with those who were lost and forgotten. It would be his first official pastoral visit as pope.

---

[13] Barbie Latza Nadeau, "Pope Prays for Lost Refugees on Visit to Mediterranean Island," CNN, July 8, 2013, www.cnn.com.

Shortly after he arrived on the island, he celebrated Mass by the ocean harbor, next to a "boat graveyard." From the scattered remnants of these vessels, a local carpenter crafted the altar from a migrant boat's hull, the lectern from ships' rudders, and the chalice from driftwood of the May 8, 2011, shipwreck.

In this section we explore the significance of this Mass at Lampedusa, the vessels used at this liturgy, and its connection to our theological reflection on migration. As we continue to reflect on the ties between theology and migration, here we want to examine some of the ways this Liturgy of the Eucharist helps us understand the connection between the bodies of migrants and the body of Christ. I highlight in particular how, even as the world in myriad ways has ignored and discarded many of these refugees as "no-bodies" in this world, Pope Francis helps us see not only that each refugee is "some-body" but that they are in fact connected to "every-body."

*The Global Indifference to the "No-Bodies"*

When Fr. Stefano Natasi, the local pastor at San Gerlando Catholic Church in Lampedusa, received word that Pope Francis would be coming to the island, he asked Franco Tuccio, a local carpenter, to help prepare for the Eucharistic celebration. The refugee crisis became more personal to Tuccio and the Lampedusa community in early 2009. As socioeconomic and political conditions increasingly deteriorated in Africa, more and more people were forced to leave their homelands. In April of that year, 316 Somali refugees boarded a ship in hopes of making it to European shores, but after capsizing near Lampedusa, hundreds of bodies washed upon the shores near where Tuccio lived. He and other volunteers from the island helped in the recovery efforts to bury those who died, but despite the scale of the tragedy, the press—and the world—did not even take note of it.

The attention of most was focused on another part of the country. A few days earlier, an earthquake shook the Abruzzo region of Italy and tragically killed 308 people.[14] The media covered these events extensively, and donations poured in from around the world. The country even

---

[14] David Alexander and Michele Magni, "Mortality in the L'aquila (Central Italy) Earthquake of 6 April 2009: A Study in Victimization," *PLOS Currents* 5 (2013), http://currents.plos.org.

observed a National Day of Mourning and held a state funeral for 205 of the victims.[15]

In the days following the fateful shipwreck, when Tuccio began pulling bodies from the water, he felt a troubling contrast in his heart. As he reflected on those who died in the center of his country and those who drowned on its outer edges, he said, "It appeared like some lives mattered and these people died a 'first class' death and others died like they were in 'steerage,' and no one even seemed to notice."[16] Whereas those who died in the earthquake became some-body to every-body, the refugees who drowned, it would seem, died as if they were no-body to any-body.

Tragically, this voyage of the no-bodies is repeated every day around the globe. At present, the Mediterranean has some of the most lethal migration corridors on the planet, and each year thousands drown in open seas. Since 2014, the International Organization of Migration has recorded tens of thousands of migrant deaths in the Central Mediterranean alone, although—because many disappear without a trace—the actual number is most certainly higher.[17] With the loss of so many lives on ocean routes, the island of Lampedusa has become a symbol of the global refugee crisis because it names something of the vulnerability and desperation of all who are forcibly uprooted and cast into a merciless sea of human indifference. When Francis arrived at Lampedusa, he made an urgent plea for these people often looked down upon as no-bodies in the eyes of the world.

Yet given the scale of this human tragedy, why would Francis choose to deliver this message in a place that is as obscure and insignificant as Lampedusa? Would it not have been more effective if he addressed it instead from the corridors of power like London, Brussels, Paris, or Rome? While many factors no doubt entered into Francis's deliberations, his decision to go to Lampedusa must be read first and foremost through the logic of faith and the light of the Gospel. Jesus' own mission, especially his outreach to the "no-bodies" of this world, gives us an important clue as to why Francis

---

[15] Rachel Donadio, "Thousands Mourn Quake Victims at Funeral Mass," *New York Times*, April 10, 2009.

[16] Franco Tuccio, interview by author, Lampedusa, Italy, October 25, 2015.

[17] International Organization for Migration, "Tracks Deaths of Migrants, including Refugees." See also International Organization for Migration, "The Central Mediterranean Route: Migrant Fatalities."

decided to go to Lampedusa; it is a window into the vision of Jesus, the Church's mission in general, and a theology of migration in particular. One way to understand Jesus' own vision in more depth is through his life and work in the region of Galilee.

Jesus exercises much of his public ministry in the region of Galilee. Like Lampedusa, it is on the margins of society and far from the centers of power. It is an insignificant place where many of the "no-bodies" of Jesus' day lived and worked. As Jesus sits down at table in Galilee, he makes special efforts to welcome the "no-bodies" of Galilee to join him (Mt. 4:12–17; Mk. 1:14–15; Lk. 4:14–15), which, as Virgilio Elizondo notes, makes Galilee more than a geographical footnote in the Gospels: it is rather the space that magnifies the gratuitous revelation of God's mercy (Mt. 4:23–25; Mk. 1:35–39; Lk. 4:42–44).[18]

This mercy takes visible expression as Jesus lives and ministers in this location. As one raised there, Jesus takes on the identity of a Galilean Jew. Why did Jesus not take up residence in the political center of Rome, the intellectual center of Athens, or the religious center of Jerusalem? The fact that God in Jesus would do his ministry in such an insignificant area of the world, and put himself in solidarity with the no-bodies of his day, raises many questions.

In this migration of the Son of God into the far regions of the world, Elizondo sees the good news of Jesus' message breaking into human history, beginning with those places considered most insignificant to human eyes. He argues that, as Jesus accepts the marginalization of being a Galilean Jew, he confronts the lie of the world that any-body is a no-body. Challenging all the social, cultural, and economic categories that classify people as superior or inferior, worthy or unworthy, Jesus welcomes those whom society rejects, inaugurating a new kingdom that begins among the no-bodies (1 Cor. 1:18–31).

Affirming the essential God-given dignity of every human being, Jesus inverts the warped value structure of the world that dehumanizes people. He reveals a new vision of his reign that restores people's human worth by accepting them and respecting their dignity, regardless of what has happened in their past (Mt. 5:1–12; Lk. 6:20–26). In God's Kingdom, these same people who are regarded as no-bodies in the eyes of the world are, in fact,

---

[18] Virgilio P. Elizondo, *Galilean Journey: The Mexican-American Promise*, 1st ed. (Maryknoll, NY: Orbis Books, 1983), 92.

the first to witness the risen Christ and the first to bring the news of salvation to every-body (Mt. 19:16–26; Mk. 10:17–27; Lk. 4:18–19; 11:37–43; 12:33–34; 14:12–14; 18:18–27; 19:8–10; Jas. 2:2–6a). In contrast to the kingdoms of the world that exclude the no-bodies from its privileges, Jesus proclaims a new kingdom that extends God's gratuitous love to every-body (Lk. 4:18).

*The Desire to Become "Some-Body"*

While the angst of being a no-body afflicts people from all walks of life, the fear of meaninglessness is particularly acute among the poor and insignificant in the world. The experience of being discarded and unwelcome cuts to the core of every human heart because each person has a hunger to become somebody and make life count in some tangible and significant way. The tides of the current socio-economic and political order of the world often beat against this essential dimension of human development and make it difficult for many people to feel they have value.

Catholic Social Teaching has continually denounced those forces that work against the development of the human person. In *Evangelii Gaudium*, Francis speaks about the importance of saying "no to an economy of exclusion" (53–54), "no to the new idolatry of money" (55–56), "no to a financial system which rules rather than serves" (57–58), and "no to the inequality which spawns violence" (59–60). These factors contribute to the phenomenon of migration, and it is why the US bishops' conference argues that the first right of migrants is to find work in their homeland. When poverty, injustice, religious intolerance, and armed conflicts make this impossible, however, people have a right to move elsewhere in search of more dignified lives, even if this takes them away from their countries of origin.[19]

This position emerges from the conviction that when any-body is treated as a no-body—and denied the opportunities to become some-body—every-body loses. It is also why the global refugee crisis then can never be about "us" and "them." It is rather about *all of us*. "We may have all come on different ships," Martin Luther King Jr. once said, "but we're in the same boat now." And in some form or another, we are all vulnerable in the open sea of this world.

---

[19] United States Conference of Catholic Bishops, *Strangers No Longer: Together on the Journey of Hope: A Pastoral Letter Concerning Migration* (Washington, DC: United States Conference of Catholic Bishops, 2003), nos. 28, 33.

The waves of chaos on this ocean, however, have never been as turbulent as they are today, and the prospects of sinking on the icebergs of greed have never been a greater threat to the entire human community (see Pope Francis, *Laudato Si'*). In this time of titanic change, it is as if a few passengers on our global ship have first-class suites on the upper deck, while the vast majority of the earth's inhabitants are slaving away in the steam room below. The planet's wealthiest twenty-six individuals collectively have as much as the poorest 3.8 billion people on the planet, and half of the world is living on less than $5.50 a day.[20]

The structural systems and the dominant ideologies that create and legitimate such inequity directly contribute to human displacement because they create a society where the wealthy are often enriched at the expense of other people's well-being.[21] These conditions consequently force many people to take desperate measures to find better lives. "This makes me grieve," Francis would later say, "because I think that these persons are victims of a global socio-economic system."[22] From this perspective, the global migration of peoples is not the central problem: it is rather the symptom of far deeper issues that cause their uprooting.

In his homily at Lampedusa, Francis makes reference to the biblical figure of King Herod the Great, whose unbridled pursuit of power and pleasure causes him to lose sight of his own dignity, purpose, and destiny. When his own disordered passions steer him off course, he sinks to the depths of inhumanity (Mt. 2:1–18). "Herod sowed death," Francis said, "to protect his own comfort, his own soap bubble," even when the price entailed doing violence to others, slaughtering the innocent, and eliminating any who threatened his power (Pope Francis, "Visit to Lampedusa").

Francis realizes that the structures, values, and systems of our world make all people vulnerable to drowning in a sea of luxury and consumerism. As Francis puts it,

> The culture of comfort, which makes us think only of ourselves, makes us insensitive to the cries of other people, makes us live in soap

---

[20] Oxfam International, *Public Good or Private Wealth*, 12, https://s3.amazonaws.com.

[21] For more on structural sin and the dominant ideologies that legitimate it, see Kristin E. Heyer, *Kinship across Borders: A Christian Ethic of Immigration* (Washington, DC: Georgetown University Press, 2012), 35–60.

[22] Pope Francis, "Translation of Pope's 80-Minute Plane Interview," *Catholic Voices Comment*, August 4, 2013, question 16, http://cvcomment.org.

bubbles which, however lovely, are insubstantial; they offer a fleeting and empty illusion which results in indifference to others; indeed, it even leads to the globalization of indifference.... Has any one of us wept for these persons who were on the [refugee] boat? For the young mothers carrying their babies? For these men who were looking for a means of supporting their families? We are a society which has forgotten how to weep, how to experience compassion—"suffering with" others: the globalization of indifference has taken from us the ability to weep! (Pope Francis, "Visit to Lampedusa")

But Herod is not an isolated "human shipwreck"; he embodies something that every human being is vulnerable to, whether migrating or not. At the beginning of Mass, Pope Francis asks every-body to make an examination of conscience and to pray for "the Lord to remove the part of Herod that lurks in our hearts" (Pope Francis, "Visit to Lampedusa"). Calling the world to repentance for the world's inhospitality, inaction, and injustice, Francis wore purple vestments (a sign of penance and mourning) during the Eucharist at Lampedusa. It is significant that he also used prayers from the Mass for the Forgiveness of Sins, praying in particular for "forgiveness for those who are pleased with themselves, who are closed in on their own well-being in a way that leads to the anesthesia of the heart."[23]

Losing our humanity to the culture of comfort is not just a temptation in our own times but a perennial human struggle. Gregory of Nyssa gave expression to this in the fourth century, and his words are no less true today than they were seventeen hundred years ago: "Do not throw yourself into the sea of unbridled consumption. Unbearable is the shipwreck that will overwhelm you, for not only would you be torn by rocks hidden below water, but you would rush headlong into the dark depths from which no one having fallen has ever escaped."[24] His words bring out that when we lose the ability to lament—and in this case to grieve over the bodies of more than forty thousand migrants who have lost their lives since the year 2000[25]—we have lost something of our own humanity.

---

[23] Pope Francis, "Pope on Lampedusa: 'The Globalization of Indifference,'" Vatican Radio, August 7, 2013, https://web.archive.org.

[24] Gregory of Nyssa, *On Loving the Poor,* PG 46:465–66.

[25] International Organization for Migration, *Fatal Journeys: Tracking Lives Lost during Migration* (Geneva: IOM, 2015).

*The Connection to "Every-Body"*

Before the pope came to Lampedusa, this faith community already had been trying for some time to bring the world's attention to the plight of refugees. As more and more bodies began washing upon the shoreline, however, people like Franco Tuccio felt more and more helpless. He said it became so bad that "every day I came to my workshop, I couldn't even work."[26]

Unable to verbalize what he experienced, he eventually found a way to express with his hands what he could not communicate with his mouth. He knew there was an intimate bond between his life and theirs, but in his heart he wanted to find some further way of connecting the boats of these migrants with the boats of the early disciples, who also experienced perilous journeys, turbulent waters, and stormy seas (Mk. 4: 35–41; Mt. 8:23–27; Lk. 8:22–25). He also felt there was some connection between the remnant wood of the refugee journey and the wood of the cross. Wanting to rescue the no-bodies of these boats from their anonymity and seeming insignificance, he began making crosses carved from the driftwood found along the island's rocky coastline. The making of these crosses brought him to tears, Tuccio said later, "because it helped restore their dignity, like I helped save the life of a person."[27] Remembering the forgotten no-bodies in some small way brought them back to life in such a way that they had become somebody once again.

When it came time to prepare for the pope's Mass at Lampedusa, Tuccio sought to further correlate the migrant journey with the liturgy. He began crafting pieces that connected the migration of peoples across the Mediterranean with the migration of the Son of God to the human community. He made the cross-shaped papal ferula out of the refugee driftwood, and on this pastoral staff he carved in the symbols of a heart, fish, and a loaf of bread. He also made the altar from a Tunisian boat and the pulpit from the rudders of two other boats. In the middle he placed a ship's wheel. "When I made the lectern," he said, "the rudder triggered in my mind the image of a suffering people starting a journey at sea in search of freedom and a promised land."[28]

---

[26] Tuccio, interview by author.
[27] Ibid.
[28] Ibid.

Each of these symbols in their own way helped give expression to the migration of the Son of God to the human community, the Church as a migrant community in this world, and the call to stand in solidarity with others who are migrating today. Calling the Church to see this connection between the global refugee crisis and its central mission, Francis later urged parishes, convents, and religious communities in Europe to offer housing and hospitality to refugee families needing shelter. He asked the bishops to "express the Gospel in concrete terms and take in a family of refugees"[29] and to make room for Christ by making room in their communities for refugees. "Empty convents are not for the church to transform into hotels and make money from them," he said. "Empty convents are not ours, they are for the flesh of Christ: refugees."[30] Putting his own words into practice, he opened the doors of the Vatican to two refugee families, and he said they can stay "as long as the Lord wants."[31] At the core of his words, gestures, symbols, and sacraments, Francis has tried to help the world see a stronger connection among the no-bodies of this world, every-body, and the body of Christ.

---

[29] "Pope Francis Calls on Parishes to House Refugee Families, Says Vatican Will Do Same," NBC News, www.nbcnews.com.

[30] Pope Francis, "Empty Convents Are of No Use to the Church. Let the Refugees In," *Vatican Insider*, September 10, 2013,www.lastampa.it.

[31] John L. Allen Jr., "Pope Warns Religious Orders: Take In Refugees, or Pay Property Taxes," *Crux*, September 14, 2015, www.cruxnow.com.

## "This Is My Blood": A Mission of Reconciliation

"This cup is the new covenant in my blood, which will be shed for you." (Lk. 22:20)

The chalice used at the Mass in Lampedusa, made from the driftwood of a refugee shipwreck, offers us an important perspective in this process of transformation.[32] It puts us in touch with many Passover stories at work in the Eucharist at the same time. On one level, the Mass at Lampedusa connects us with the story of those passing over from Africa to Europe on the open seas; on another, it connects to the story of Christ's passing over from this world to the Father as narrated during the Last Supper; on a third level, it connects us with the story of the Hebrew slaves passing over from Egypt to the Promised Land. Migration is at play in all of these levels, but how does this multivalent Passover story in the Eucharist connect to our own story?

The Last Supper gives us some insight into this question. When Jesus celebrated his last meal with his disciples, he connected the Passover story to his own. He revealed to them that now is the time for him to pass over from this world to the Father. Before he left them, however, he called them to see their own narratives in light of this same Passover. This involves the work of conversion.

Though it took one day to take Israel out of Egypt, it took more than forty years to get Egypt out of Israel. And even then, the process of liberation never ended. This story recounts something from biblical times, but it reveals a pattern that repeats itself in every generation. The phenomenon reminds us that true emancipation involves more than removing physical chains; it also requires the long work of being liberated from enslaving mindsets, attitudes, and ingrained behaviors. These make us alien to our divine nature and negatively impact our relationships with God, others, and ourselves. Passing over from an old way of life into a new one requires more than a momentary religious experience; it also requires the ongoing transformation of mind, heart, and spirit into the image and likeness of the living God.

When Jesus first calls them to be his disciples, he calls them to leave their former ways behind and to follow him. This is only the beginning of

---

[32] For more on this topic, see Daniel G. Groody, "Crossing the Divide: Foundations of a Theology of Migration and Refugees," *Theological Studies* 70, no. 3 (2009): 638–67, and Daniel G. Groody, "Cup of Suffering, Chalice of Salvation: Refugees, Lampedusa and the Eucharist," *Theological Studies* 78, no. 4 (2017): 960–87. Much of this section are drawn from these articles.

their conversion. He then calls them to deepen that commitment through an ongoing conversion of their lives that will conform them more and more into his own self-giving love. He draws out what that looks like in the Last Supper, where he takes a cup of wine and says, "This is my blood of the covenant, which is poured out for many" (Mt. 26:28). He pours it out for others, not only so that they may pass over from final death to eternal life, but so that they may pass over from everything in this world that works against the grain of life. Because the Kingdom of God begins now in the world, the transformation of one's personal and collective narrative entails dying to the narratives that enslave and adopting new narratives that align with God and his Kingdom.

As we continue to examine migration issues under the light of the Liturgy of the Eucharist, then, we also explore some of the dimensions of passing over from the lies of this world into the liberating truths of God's reign, namely (1) passing over from migrant to person, (2) passing over from injustice to justice; (3) passing over from otherness to neighborliness, and (4) passing over from nationalism to the reign of God. These conversion processes help us discern issues of dignity, community, solidarity, and salvation at work in migration issues. As we explore these in more depth, we want to reflect further on the dynamics of passing over from alienation to communion with God and others, which is at the heart of the mission of reconciliation.

*Passing Over from Migrant to Person*

Despite the daunting experiences of swimming across canals, hiding away in cargo ships, and traversing mountains and deserts on foot, many migrants and refugees have said that the most difficult parts of their lives are not necessarily the physical hardships on their outer journey but often the trials of their inner journey. Many have shared stories about the demeaning treatment and degrading stereotypes that reveal a personal desire to pass over from being labeled as a migrant to being treated as a human being.

In the words of one migrant from Mexico,

> I have stowed away in baggage compartments of buses and almost suffocated in a boxcar; I almost froze to death in the mountains and baked to death in the deserts; I have gone without food and water for days, and nearly died on various occasions. As difficult as these

are, these are not the hardest parts of being a migrant. The worst is when people treat you like you are a dog, like you are the lowest form of life on earth.[33]

Such stories reveal that no wound cuts more deeply than feeling that one is disposable, meaningless, and worthless; many have the fear that they are no one to anyone. This too pushes people to move. More often than not, the desire to migrate often begins with the search for a more dignified life, especially in the context of a society that uses words to dehumanize them. Because language molds our narratives, we should reflect more on how the narratives we live by shape our understanding of the world and the values we bring to it.

In recent decades, scholars in rhetorical, literary, and gender studies have given us a growing appreciation for how language shapes our perception of reality. It influences how we understand ourselves, how we relate to people, and how we define the other. The "othering" of the migrant creates various asymmetries in relationships, which causes many social imbalances and injustices. Even the language we use in formal discourse can contribute to fostering narratives in social systems that dehumanize those who are on the move. Nowhere is this more evident than the labels used to describe them.

To define those on the move first and foremost as people made in the image and likeness of God roots us in the world very differently than if persons are principally defined as social and political problems or as illegal aliens. This divine-rooted dignity is not just another label; it is a way of speaking about the essential nature of who we are before God, and it cannot ultimately be deconstructed by any force in this world (Gn. 1:26–27; 5:1–3; 9:6; 1 Cor. 11:7; Jas. 3:9). Underneath everything else, and regardless of what they have done, every human being has a sacred dignity that can never be taken away.

Catholic Social Teaching (CST) affirms the centrality of this dignity and offers a vision of God that stands in contrast to the current world order. It emphasizes that the economy is made for human beings, not human beings for the economy. In its efforts to safeguard the dignity of all people, CST has consistently argued that the moral health of an economy is measured not in terms of financial metrics like the gross national product or stock prices

---

[33] Quotation from personal interviews conducted by author.

but in how the economy affects the quality of life in the community.[34] CST affirms that God—and not the state—grants rights to people and asserts that it is the state's responsibility to protect and defend those rights when they are threatened or diminished.

Catholic Social Teaching also recognizes the right—and duty—of a state to control its borders.[35] But CST argues that, when a state cannot provide the conditions necessary for human dignity, people have a right to migrate to foreign lands, even without proper legal documentation.[36] Unless a nation deals with the conditions that cause human insecurity outside its borders, it will have no lasting national security within its borders, no matter how many enforcement agents it uses or how tall and wide a wall it builds. Poverty, underdevelopment, human rights violations, and the collapse of governments all destabilize communities and countries, which means that immigration is not the central problem but most often is a symptom of more fundamental disorders at work in the world.

Passing over from migrant to person involves the restructuring and reordering of society according to the God of life, the dignity of the human person, and the common good. From the perspective of this narrative, "The needs of the poor," as David Hollenbach puts it, "take priority over the wants of the rich. The freedom of the dominated takes priority over the liberty of the powerful. The participation of marginalized groups takes priority over the preservation of an order which excludes them."[37] This means that the "success" of the current system must first be evaluated by how well it protects the dignity of every human being, especially those whose very dignity is threatened because of their vulnerable and socially insignificant status. Such factors call for the re-valuation of how our social, political, economic, and

---

[34] In *Economic Justice for All*, the US bishops state that an ordered economy must be shaped by three questions: What does the economy do for people? What does it do to people? And how do people participate in it? It puts strongest emphasis on what impact the economy has on the poor (United States Conference of Catholic Bishops, *Economic Justice for All*, no. 14).

[35] United States Conference of Catholic Bishops, *Strangers No Longer: Together on the Journey of Hope: A Pastoral Letter concerning Migration* (Washington, DC: USCCB, 2003), nos. 30, 36, 39, 78.

[36] Sacred Congregation for Bishops, *Instruction on the Pastoral Care of People Who Migrate* (Washington, DC: United States Catholic Conference, August 22, 1969), 7.

[37] David Hollenbach, *Claims in Conflict: Retrieving and Renewing the Catholic Human Rights Tradition,* Woodstock Studies (New York: Paulist Press, 1979), 204.

religious beliefs align with the demands of the reign of God and the Gospel exigency to build a more just society.

*Passing Over from Injustice to Justice*

From the perspective of Christian faith, migration can never be reduced to the metrics of economic efficiency, political pragmatism, utilitarian self-interest, or national narcissism; it entails passing over from our small, private worlds to a vision of our common life before God and therefore must be evaluated in light of the primacy of the reign of God and the quality of our relationships. Such concern calls us to reflect on a Christian vision of justice, law, and ethics.

Even as it is connected to laws written in books, justice from a theological perspective involves more than adjudicating legal infractions, bringing people to court, appealing to a blindfolded woman, or punishing those who cross borders illegally. In the Bible, justice is above all about righteousness. The term *righteousness*, however, is admittedly a complicated one. Frequently it conjures up churchy and puritanical associations that are off-putting to people and obscure its essential meaning.[38] It is related to moral behavior, but biblical righteousness involves much more than moralism.

Christian ethics deals with what God has done and does for us and only then has to do with what we do for God. Righteousness, above all, has to do with the way God makes the world right through the saving love of Jesus Christ, which could never be done by human effort but only through this grace of God. This is also the foundation of Christian ethics.

Christian ethics starts then with God's goodness, not ours. It starts with the gift of God's mercy, not our worthiness, and is above all about God's gift to us and only then our gift to God. This means that such righteousness is not about self-righteousness but about getting our relationships in right order with God, others, ourselves, and the world. This understanding of ethics is built on a more fundamental understanding of justice from a Christian point of view.

---

[38] For more on the topics of justice and righteousness (*dikaiosyné* and mercy and lovingkindness [*eleos*], see R. Morhlang, *Matthew and Paul: A Comparison of Ethical Perspectives* (New York: Cambridge University Press, 1984), 48–57; B. Pryzybylski, *Righteousness in Matthew and His World of Thought* (New York: Cambridge University Press, 1980); and John R. Donahue, "The 'Parable' of the Sheep and the Goats: A Challenge to Christian Ethics," *Theological Studies* 47, no. 1 (1986): 22–23.

Christian theology upholds two principal notions of justice: internal justice and external justice.[39] Internal justice—which begins with God's movement or migration toward us—deals with one's experience of justification or being put in right relationship with God through the saving work of Jesus Christ. External justice—which begins with our movement toward others—deals with the promotion of good works. Internal justice refers to God's activity within a person; external justice refers to one's response to God's grace. Internal justice relates to the first and the greatest command, to love the Lord God with all one's heart, soul, and mind (Mt. 22:37–38). External justice relates to the second command, which is like the first, to love one's neighbor as oneself (Mt. 22:39). It seeks humanizing activity leading to right relationships with oneself, the community, its social structures, and even the environment.[40]

This notion of justice often becomes particularly convoluted when approaching the issue of law and migration. The ethical dimensions of migration issues are often obscured when justice is conflated with the rule of law. Because so many arguments about migration are built on adherence to the civil law, it is important to think critically about justice in ways that take us beyond conventional legal reasoning and toward a broader understanding of the function and purpose of the law.

Laws are central to the just ordering of any society. They have a positive function and are directed in particular toward protecting something important. They safeguard such values as the dignity of the human person and the promotion of the common good and security of a community. Because laws also can be misused to protect self-interest and exclude those who are vulnerable, however, a critical assessment of how laws are used is an important task in finding durable and peaceful solutions to issues like migration.

It is not uncommon for people to say that they have no problem with immigration but only with the fact that immigrants break the law to get into a particular country. This line of reasoning has its own coherent logic. On one level, it points to the need to safeguard civil order and to protect

---

[39] For more on this topic, see Daniel G. Groody, *Globalization, Spirituality and Justice: Navigating the Path to Peace* (Maryknoll, NY: Orbis Books, 2015), 26–27.

[40] This definition is drawn in part from an excellent article by Michael Crosby, "Justice," in *The New Dictionary of Catholic Spirituality*, ed. Michael Downey (Collegeville, MN: Liturgical Press, 1993), 597.

communities and their values. But on a deeper level, this perspective makes no distinction between various kinds of law and assumes an equal binding force for all law. Here theology can offer some important distinctions.

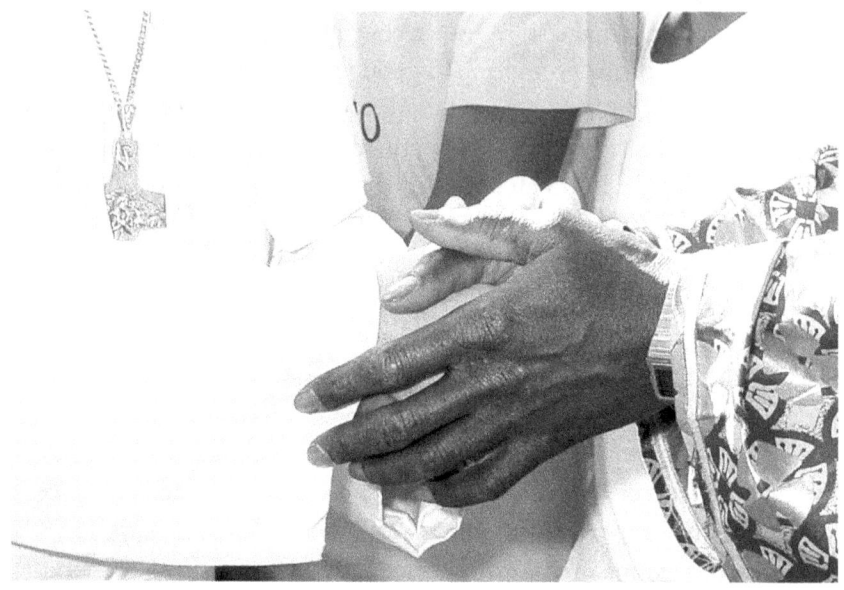

Thomas Aquinas argued there are in fact four kinds of laws: natural law, civil law, divine law, and eternal law.[41] Understanding the nuances among these kinds of laws helps offset reductive interpretations and minimizes the risk of legalizing injustice.[42] Although the precise understanding of natural law is debated in contemporary theological discourse, for Aquinas natural

---

[41] Thomas Aquinas understood the law as "an ordinance of reason for the common good, promulgated by him who has the care of the community" (*Summa Theologica* I-II, q.90). The eternal law governs everything in the universe, the divine law corresponds to the Old Law and New Law of the Hebrew Scriptures and New Testament, the natural law deals with ethical norms and human behavior, and the civil law deals with human codes used for social order. For an overview of natural law and its development within Catholic tradition, see Stephen J. Pope, "Natural Law in Catholic Social Teachings" in *Modern Catholic Social Teaching: Commentaries and Interpretations*, ed. Kenneth R. Himes (Washington, DC: Georgetown University Press, 2005), 41–71. For a more in-depth treatment, see John Finnis, *Natural Law and Natural Rights* (New York: Oxford University Press, 2001).

[42] For more on this topic, see Harold V. Bennett, *Injustice Made Legal: Deuteronomic Law and the Plight of Widows, Strangers, and Orphans in Ancient Israel*, The Bible in Its World (Grand Rapids: William B. Eerdmans, 2002).

law corresponds to the nature and duties of human beings, such as doing good and avoiding evil, respecting others, and feeding one's family.[43] Civil law is an interpretation of the natural law in specific contexts and ordered to the common good. Civil laws that prohibit murder or theft, for example, are built on natural law and are designed to protect people in community.[44] Divine law, which we know through Scriptures, reveals the spiritual and ethical demands of living in God's image and likeness, such as the works of mercy and the command to feed, clothe, and shelter the poor (Mt. 25:31–46). Eternal law is about the wisdom and providence of God, who oversees the common good and governs everything. According to Aquinas, then, all human laws by necessity must be derived from natural laws, connected to divine laws, and participate in eternal laws. When these different laws are aligned with each other, peace and justice result. When they are out of alignment, disorder and injustice ensue.

This *discursus* has direct bearing on migration in many ways. Most migrants who break civil laws by crossing borders without proper documentation do so because they are first of all obeying the laws of human nature, such as the need to find work, food, and dignity. To criminalize them compounds the injustice they already experience; even though their crossing the border breaks civil law, it does not violate divine laws and should therefore not be confused with those intending serious harm or threatening national security.[45] To criminalize those seeking more dignified lives raises serious questions about how we understand law and the ethical concerns related to migration issues.

To clarify this interrelationship between law and ethics, some further distinctions are necessary. In Anglo-American law, there is a difference between actions that are considered *malum in se* and *malum prohibitum*.

---

[43] *Summa Theologica*, I-II, q.91, a.2, in *Treatise on Law: Summa Theologiae*, I-II; Qq. 90 through 97, trans. R. J. Henle, Notre Dame Studies in Law and Contemporary Issues (Notre Dame, IN: University of Notre Dame Press, 1993).

[44] *Summa Theologica*, II.I.95–97, in ibid.

[45] While "entry without inspection" has long been a criminal offense, it has traditionally been treated as an administrative violation, leading to civil deportation proceedings. In recent years, however, the Department of Homeland Security has referred for criminal prosecution increasing numbers of immigrants who have entered the country illegally and committed other immigration violations. For more on this topic, see Doris Meissner and Donald Kerwin, *DHS and Immigration: Taking Stock and Correcting Course* (Washington, DC: Migration Policy Institute, February 2009), 40–41, www.migrationpolicy.org.

*Malum in se* has to do with actions that are intrinsically wrong, such as murder, sexual assault, and stealing. *Malum prohibitum* has to do with actions that are considered wrong by decree of a governmental statute, such as speeding, avoiding taxes, or crossing a border without official documents.[46]

All this means that civil law most certainly has a value in assessing the ethics at play in migration issues, but it can never be the ultimate or final rule in determining justice. Even religious law has its limits. In the Scriptures, Jesus, as a faithful Jew, understands that the Law has a value, but he also recognizes that this value must be seen in light of the human person, the Kingdom of God, and the rule of love (Mt. 5:17–18; Lk. 13:10–17). Jesus becomes particularly concerned when the law is misused to divide the insider from the outsider, and he challenges in particular those who use the law to idolize the state, religion, or a particular ideology, even when it does so under the rationale of obedience to a greater cause.

Jesus' openness to Gentiles, the Syrophoenician or Canaanite woman (Mt. 15:21–28; Mk. 7:24–30), the Roman centurion (Mt. 8:5–13; Lk. 7:1–10), and many others recounted in the Scriptures illustrates his willingness to cross borders and even break the Law in obedience to a greater law of love (Mk. 12:28–34). By his words and actions, Jesus demonstrates that right relationship to the Law must be prioritized in light of human needs, not human agendas.

Because Jesus knows that God's mercy cannot be contained within the walls of limited mindsets (Mt. 7:1–5; 13:10–17), he challenges people to pass over into a higher notion of law based on God's uncalculating mercy rather than on their restricted views of worthiness and unworthiness (Lk. 6:27–38). His outreach to those who are marginalized racially (Lk. 7:1–10), economically (Lk. 7:11–17), religiously (Lk. 7:24–35), and morally (Lk. 7:36–50) highlights various dimensions of passing over from the old economy of law to the new economy of grace. The Liturgy of the Eucharist roots our vision of justice, law, and ethics in the Hebrew story of moving from slavery to freedom, in Jesus' story of passing over from this world to the Kingdom of God, and in the church's story of passing over from alienation to community.

---

[46] "Immigration crimes" now represent more than one-half of all federal criminal prosecutions, more than all the cases referred by the Federal Bureau of Investigation, the Drug Enforcement Administration, and other federal agencies combined (ibid., 40–41).

*Passing Over from Alien to Neighbor*

In addition to reflecting on the crossing of geographical borders, a theological perspective on migration also reflects on crossing the borders of our own minds, that is, migrating toward a different way of thinking and relating toward all we consider other. Mindsets that divide "us" from "them" ultimately impede our journey toward communion with the Body of Christ. This is why a third dimension of passing over involves moving from seeing migrants as others to seeing them as neighbors.

In the book of Exodus we read, "I, the LORD, am your God, who brought you out of the land of Egypt, that place of slavery" (Ex. 20:2). As we recall from our study of migration in the Old Testament, the word *Egypt* (*mitsrayim*) literally means "double straits" (a reference to upper and lower straits that form the territory of Egypt through which the Nile flows), "narrow places," or "narrow confinement."[47] The literal interpretation offers us one way of reading the text, but additional, figurative interpretations hold much insight into the process of human transformation.

When they celebrate the Passover meal, Israel remembers its liberation from slavery in Egypt. As they continue their journey, Israel learns that the road to freedom involves more than political liberation; God also seeks to liberate them from slavery to narrow ways of thinking. After they are released from physical bondage, they must now travel the long road of spiritual and psychological bondage. This journey involves not just a physical migration but a cognitive one; it entails adopting a new way of looking at the world and living out a different narrative that ultimately calls them to love as God loves.

In other words, ancient Israel's migration from Egypt calls them to pass over into a new way of living in the world in its journey to the Promised Land of authentic freedom. This task becomes more challenging than the geographical migration from Egypt itself. As ancient Israel becomes more powerful and prosperous, it forgets its own migration history, forgets its heart for God, and consequently forgets those who came to them as strangers and immigrants. They not only forget who the other is, but also they forget who they are.

In the New Testament, the otherness of Jesus presents a stumbling block

---

[47] See Laurel A. Dykstra, *Set Them Free: The Other Side of Exodus* (Maryknoll, NY: Orbis Books, 2002), 58.

of its own. As we noted in our study of the New Testament, when God becomes human in Jesus, he migrates—totally—into the otherness of our human condition. Refusing to leave humanity on the other wall created by sin—and thereby "otherize" anyone—he dies on a cross in order to break down the wall of enmity and to reconcile an alienated humanity to God (Eph. 2:14). Even so, many people have trouble believing in Jesus precisely because of the place from which he emigrates (Jn. 7:41–43, 52), and they find compelling political, legal, social, and religious reasons to exclude—and otherize—the migrant Son of God.[48] In contrast, God in Jesus becomes vulnerable by taking the place of the other.

In migrating to the human race, God enters into a place of otherness, the very migration that human beings fear and find so difficult to make. This movement of divinity to humanity is predicated not on laws, institutions, or any form of human merit but on God's gratuity. This means that grace moves in the opposite direction of a fallen and sinful world: Even as human beings erect barriers of every sort, God walls off no one from divine fellowship.

The Incarnation redefines otherness by seeing strangers not as enemies but as neighbors. In becoming neighbor to all in the Incarnation—that is, all who live in the sinful territory of a fallen humanity—God redefines the borders between neighbors and opens up the possibility for new relationships. Under this light, the migrant is no longer seen as other but a brother and a sister bound together with one's own journey in a common destiny.

Given the acrimony of the immigration debate, it would seem that only a few accept the risks and sacrifices needed to undertake this movement toward such interconnectedness; much emotional and mental baggage often gets in the way, keeping us from moving very far into this territory.

---

[48] Jesus was rejected by many in his day including Herod who feared losing his power (Mt. 2:1–13); Jesus' family, who thought he was out of his mind (Mk. 3:20–21); his neighbors who failed to understand his origins (Mt. 13:54–57; Mk. 6:1–4; Lk. 4:13–30); the rich young man, who had great wealth did not want to share it (Mt. 19:16–22; Mk. 10:17–22; Lk. 18:18–23); the religious leaders who envied Jesus' popularity with the people (Mt. 26:3–4; Jn. 11:47–53); Judas, who exploited Jesus for money and favor with those in power (Mt. 26:14–16, 47–50; Lk. 22:4–6; Jn. 18:2–5); Peter, who feared the ramifications of association with him (Mt. 26:69–75; Mk. 14:66–72; Lk. 22:54–62; Jn. 18:15–18, 25–27); and the crowds who shouted "crucify him" and did nothing to redress injustice (Mt. 27:15–18, 20–23; Mk. 15:6–14; Lk. 23:13–23; Jn. 19:5–7, 14–15).

Ironically, the more we excessively protect and isolate ourselves in the gated community of our own minds, hearts, and opinions, the more we become aliens even to ourselves.

*Passing Over from Nationalism to the Kingdom of God*

The othering of migrants deals not only with how we relate to different people but also how we relate to different countries. Our national allegiances—and the identities that emerge from them—play some positive role in our development as human beings, but they can also thwart that development. This is why the fourth pass over on the road to communion is about moving from political identities to spiritual identities rooted in a shared humanity before God or a common baptism into Christ's body.

In every part of the world, migration issues are inseparable from identity politics. Our identities shape the stories we tell about ourselves, and when they are too constricted, they impede a healthy understanding of who we are before God and our movement toward a citizenship in the world to come. While there is a relationship between our duties as citizens of countries and faithfulness as citizens of the Kingdom of God, they are not coequal, and the ordering of these loyalties is critical to the establishment of a just and humane society.

As we have noted, everything—including all nations and their agendas—are of secondary importance to the primacy of the Kingdom of God (Mt. 6:33), described by the Second Vatican Council as the reign of truth and life; holiness and grace; justice, love, and peace (*Lumen Gentium* 36). The Kingdom transcends earthly politics, even as it engages it concretely; it has no regard for whether one's identity is American or Mexican, Republican or Democrat, a Texan or a New Yorker; the Kingdom's first concern is who we are before God and what governs our hearts, which bear fruit in how we govern the world and work toward its transformation.

Entering this Kingdom requires a long reformatting of all the cultural software that gets "installed" in us over time. Passing over to a new way of thinking and living in the world is one of the most critical and urgent needs of our times if we are to create a peaceful society. This demands more than a change of political policy; it demands a renewal of our whole being and the way we look at the world.

Contemplation makes possible a new way of living and being in the world, and it is essential if we are to become liberated from the enslaving narratives programmed into us. Contemplation makes possible a "factory reset" that helps us recover our authentic image and likeness to God. It facilitates the transformation of our minds and hearts that enables us to be restored to the people God created us to be. Such renewal is critical for everyone—especially for those who already profess they are Christian.

Because a number of Christians today read the Scriptures through the lens of national self-interest rather than through the perspective of the Kingdom of God—and are often more formed by the opinions of news outlets than religious leaders—it is not enough to proof-text the Bible to ratify a political position. The Kingdom of God calls people to change; it challenges people to move into a different kind of social and ethical territory, one that is not based on the dualism of politics but the unity of God, the sacred dignity of the human person, and the restoration of all things in Christ. Renewing our lives under the light of the mind and heart of Christ inevitably calls us to pass over to a different way of thinking, relating, and being in the world.

In contrast to the current world order, in Christ's Kingdom the first become last (Mt. 19:30; 20:16; Mk. 10:31; Lk. 13:29–30), leaders become servants (Mt. 23:11), finding one's life means losing it (Mt. 16:24–25), the poor are called blessed (Lk. 6:20), the rich are sent away empty (Lk. 1:53; 6:38), those excluded find a place at table (Lk. 14:7–24; Gal. 2:11–14), and aliens become citizens (Eph. 2:19). In Jesus' farewell discourse in John's Gospel, he prays that "all may be one" (17:21), and this unity—ultimately this communion—is at stake in passing over from a fragmented world to one united under God in such a way that the life lived on earth reflects the life of heaven (Mt. 6:10).

Since God's thoughts are not our thoughts and God's ways are not our ways (Is. 55:8–9; Phil. 2:6–11; Eph. 3:20–21), the Kingdom of God reminds us that we are not independent individuals trying to find our way into heaven; we are rather one body in Christ who are fundamentally interconnected to each other. Baptism goes against all currents of individualism because it incorporates us into the body of Christ; it calls us to serve all people regardless of their religious beliefs, political status, or national origins. When we root our identities in this spiritual vision—and transcend the other limiting identities we cling to that we think define us—we see and love the world more as God does.

Because it sees itself as living in exile on earth, as strangers in this world, and sojourners headed to another place, the church has always had a special predilection for those on the move. In the *Epistle of Mathetes to Diognetus*, one on the earliest writings of Christian apologetics—dated to around the second century—the writer speaks of how transformation in Christ inevitably leads us to see our own identity in migratory terms:

> For the Christians are distinguished from other men neither by country, nor language, nor the customs which they observe.... They dwell in their own countries, but simply as sojourners. As citizens, they share in all things with others, and yet endure all things as if foreigners. Every foreign land is to them as their native country, and every land of their birth as a land of strangers.... They pass their days on earth, but they are citizens of heaven. They obey the prescribed laws, and at the same time surpass the laws by their lives.[49]

The migrant is a reflection and a revelation of who the Church is in the world, and as such it seeks to welcome rather than exclude, to unite rather than divide, and to build bridges rather than walls.

As it journeys through this world, the Church witnesses to the God of life and labors to build a civilization of love.[50] In its desire to pass over from nationalism to the reign of God, the church recognizes that the state has its own distinct role in the reordering of society and the building of this civilization. As Pope Benedict XVI notes,

> The Church cannot and must not take upon herself the political battle to bring about the most just society possible. She cannot and must not replace the State. Yet at the same time, she cannot and must not remain on the sidelines in the fight for justice. She has to play her part through rational argument and she has to reawaken the spiritual energy without which justice, which always demands sacrifice, cannot prevail and prosper. A just society must be the achievement of politics, not of the Church. Yet the promotion of

---

[49] See God's Word, www.ecclesia.org.
[50] For more on this topic, see Groody, *Globalization, Spirituality and Justice*, 92–123.

justice through efforts to bring about openness of mind and will to the demands of the common good is something which concerns the Church deeply. (*Deus Caritas Est* 28)

In its care for all, especially those most in need, the Church not only goes beyond borders but unites itself with those on the other side of them, giving expression to its interconnectedness as the body of Christ. To limit compassion to the borders of one's nationality, church, and family is to fragment our common bonds, deprive those in need, and demean our humanity. "If I see a person or persons suffer," notes Elie Wiesel, "and the distance between us does not shrink . . . then my place is not good, not enviable."[51] If the term *alien* is to be used at all, it would be descriptive not of those who lack political documentation but of those who have so disconnected themselves from God and others that they are incapable of seeing in the vulnerable stranger a mirror of themselves, a reflection of Christ, and call to love as God loves.

The chalice used by Pope Francis at Lampedusa speaks in a very specific way to the Church's mission of reconciliation. As the vessel that holds the Lord's blood in the Liturgy of the Eucharist, this chalice speaks not only to the migration of people in our own day but also the migration of those before us and our migration to the world to come. In the same way that the sharing of Christ's blood calls people to pass over from death to life, so too does the Eucharist call us to remember those who have become invisible to us and to whom we have become indifferent. The memory of Jesus reminds us of our call to change and transform all that works against the forces of life in this world on our homeward journey. This involves transforming the attitudes and dispositions that alienate us in order to find new ones that lead toward genuine human and divine communion.

When Franco Tuccio was crafting the chalice at Lampedusa, he made a startling discovery. He recalls,

> I used a piece of wood that had a nail in it. I had to remove the nail in order to carve the stem. When I saw the hole, I imagined a hand with a hole in it. Later on, as I put the nail back in the stem, it formed a cross.

---

[51] Elie Wiesel, "The Refugee," in *Sanctuary: A Resource Guide for Understanding and Participating in the Central American Refugees' Struggle*, ed. Gary MacEoin (New York: Harper & Row, 1985), 9.

The symbolism moved me deeply. I realized that the cross which is a symbol of death supported the cup which is a symbol of life.[52]

The transformation of death into new life is at the heart of the Eucharist. Because the Liturgy of the Eucharist opens a privileged door into sacred mysteries, it draws people into a liminal space where the human and the divine meet, where human sinfulness is transformed into new life, and where this present life meets eternity. As this celebration roots us into God's action in the past, it calls us to transform our stories and make us into something new in the present. The process of conversion deals with passing over from what Susanna Snyder calls "an ecology of fear" to "an ecology of faith,"[53] and it is essential for the flourishing of human life. It comes not only as the result of human effort but as a gift of God.

### "Do This in Memory of Me": Anamnestic Solidarity

When Jesus celebrates Passover on his last night with his disciples, he calls them to take this meal in memory of him until he comes again. While this command is most frequently used to refer to Jesus' institution of the Eucharist, when he says, "Do this in memory of me," it is more broadly connected to the memory of Jesus' entire life: all he stood for and stood with in his earthly existence. It recalls Jesus' preference for those considered the least and most insignificant in society and the way he calls his disciples to put themselves also in solidarity with them.[54]

The Greek word used to describe this process of remembering in the liturgy is *anamnesis*, which refers to a recollection of the extraordinary events of God's action in the world through Jesus' life, death, and resurrection. It points to God's active concern for all creatures, especially those who are most vulnerable, and acknowledges God's saving activity made known through the Old and New Covenants. In response to God's gratuitous

---

[52] Tuccio, interview by author.
[53] Susanna Snyder, *Asylum-Seeking, Migration, and Church* (Burlington, VT: Ashgate, 2012), 139ff. See also Susanna Snyder, Joshua Ralston, and Agnes M. Brazal, *Church in an Age of Global Migration: A Moving Body—Pathways for Ecumenical and Interreligious Dialogue* (London: Palgrave Macmillan, 2015).
[54] For more on this topic, especially as it emerges in the thought of Gustavo Gutiérrez, see Groody, *Globalization, Spirituality, and Justice*, 207–8. See also Gustavo Gutiérrez, *Spiritual Writings*, ed. Daniel G. Groody (Maryknoll, NY: Orbis Books, 2011).

love—which far surpasses any human effort—God calls people to love others as God has loved them. The memory of this love is at the heart of biblical faith.

But why put so much emphasis on remembering? The Bible mentions it so frequently perhaps because of the perpetual human tendency to forget. We too quickly fail to remember where we have come from and what God has done for us. This makes it difficult to know where we are going and who we want to become and how we are called to respond to others.

In the Old Testament, we read of the way God saved the Israelites from slavery. Once they are freed, God calls them to remember where they have come from when they get to the Promised Land, or else when they become more settled and comfortable, they risk becoming like those who enslaved them in Egypt. Remembering is important because it is key to human transformation.

Jesus brings this teaching to a whole new level. The Eucharist is not only a time to remember the life of Jesus, but to re-member those who have been cut off from his body. In other words, it is an opportunity to recall and reintegrate the forgotten and ignored no-bodies of society. It does this not only by calling them to mind but also by reconnecting them again with human society and empowering them to contribute to the larger body of the human community. This re-membering entails living out what Walter Benjamin and William O'Neill refer to as the notion of "anamnestic solidarity."[55]

Anamnestic solidarity, as Johannes Baptist Metz reminds us, has a "dangerous" dimension not only because it is a memory of reconciliation but also because it challenges the established order of society.[56] As it welcomes and includes those who were excluded, it confronts the idols that oppress and breaks down walls of exclusion, hatred, and ignorance that erect, ulti-

---

[55] Walter Benjamin, *Illuminations: Essays and Reflections*, ed. Hannah Arendt, trans. Harry Zohn (Orlando, FL: Harcourt Brace Jovanovich, 1968), 253ff.; cf. Thomas McCarthy, *Ideals and Illusions: On Reconstruction and De-Construction in Contemporary Critical Theory* (Cambridge, MA: MIT Press, 1991), 205–10. See also William O'Neill, "No Longer Strangers (Ep. 2:19): The Ethics of Migration," *Word and World* 29, no. 3 (2009): 227–33; and William O'Neill, "And You Welcomed Me," *Political Theology* 15, no. 1 (2014): 88–99.

[56] Johannes Baptist Metz, "The Future in the Memory of Suffering," in *New Questions on God*, The New Concilium Series 76, ed. Metz (New York: Herder and Herder, 1972), 15. See also Bruce T. Morrill, *Anamnesis as Dangerous Memory: Political and Liturgical Theology in Dialogue* (Collegeville, MN: Liturgical, 2000).

mately, a wall of alienation. In the end, the memory of Jesus' death breaks down the walls of mortality and reveals the God of life.

When such walls disconnect us, we become a stranger even to our true selves. As we forget our past, we forget who we are to one another as well. This gives rise to what Pope Francis calls "the globalization of indifference." To remember Jesus in the Eucharist, in contrast, means remembering Jesus' concern for the poor and suffering and his desire for reconciliation on all levels of human existence. To remember Jesus in the breaking of the bread is the beginning of this reconciliation because it gives expression to tearing down walls created by sin that result in alienating our relationships.

When many of us forget our own immigrant heritage and the trials of our ancestors, we lose touch with new immigrants. When we cannot see our own face in theirs—and especially Christ's face in them—they become easy targets for social problems and are quickly typecast as a threat to the common good. The covenant opens an alternative way of viewing the stranger, perceiving the other as a brother and a sister with whom I share a common destiny.[57]

The Eucharist, then, is not simply a spiritual theatre where the gathered community watches the bread and wine change into the body of Christ. It is also where this process implicates the community to become what it receives: another Christ. From a ritual perspective, some liturgists speak of a *double epiclesis*, which emphasizes not only changing the bread and wine into the Body and Blood of Christ but also changing the gathered community into Christ's real presence in the world.[58] Passing over to new life in Christ therefore means more than transforming bread and wine into the body of Christ; it means transforming the people of God into Christ's own presence as well. As Kathleen Hughes suggests,

> Participation in the liturgy means participation in the life, death, and rising of Jesus, *truly* dying and rising with him, *truly* laying down our lives. Participation means working mightily for the establishment of the reign of God by letting the spirit of God work in

---

[57] For more on this subject, see J. Caputo, "Adieu—sans Dieu: Derrida and Levinas," in *The Face of the Other and the Trace of God*, ed. J. Bloechl (New York: Fordham University Press, 2000), 276–312.

[58] John H. McKenna, "The Epiclesis Revisited," in *New Eucharistic Prayers: An Ecumenical Study of Their Development and Structure*, ed. Frank C. Senn (New York: Paulist Press, 1987), 169–94.

us to complete Christ's work on earth. Participation means living Christ's life: pouring ourselves out for the poor and the imprisoned and the suffering, wherever we encounter these realities in our every day. Participation means "living no longer for ourselves but for God." Otherwise, how can we say "Amen" to such a prayer?[59]

From this vantage point, the Eucharist is a ritualized way of understanding God's love for the world. Remembering Jesus' death on the cross is not about the Father demanding that his Son pay the debt for a sinful humanity but that people might discover God's undying love for humankind that cannot be extinguished. Through Jesus, God so totally loves the human race that nothing is capable of killing this love—not rejection, insults, betrayal, mockery, or even death. As Richard Rohr put it, "Jesus did not come to change the mind of God about humanity (it did not need changing)! Jesus came to change the mind of humanity about God."[60]

Pope Benedict XVI points to the profound connection between Christ's death and the Eucharist when he says, "By making the bread into his body and the wine into his blood, he anticipates his death, he accepts it in his heart, and he transforms it into an action of love. What on the outside is simply brutal violence [the Crucifixion] from within becomes an act of total self-giving love."[61] He goes on to say that this act of love celebrated in the Eucharist is the initial transubstantiation that sets in motion a series of transformations in us, which calls us forth to renew and transform the world until God becomes all in all (1 Cor. 15:28). In this act of radical love, Jesus in the Eucharist binds the world more closely to himself and accomplishes the work of right relationship or reconciliation, even in the face of the world's darkest moment, even when human beings sentenced the Son of God to death!

The gift of the Lord's blood, given for the reconciliation of the world, reminds us of God's migration to earth, our return migration to God, and those migrating through the world today. As it helps us understand the gift

---

[59] Kathleen Hughes, "Liturgy and Justice: An Intrinsic Relationship," in Kathleen Hughes and Mark R. Francis, *Living No Longer for Ourselves: Liturgy and Justice in the Nineties* (Collegeville, MN: Liturgical, 1991), 50–51.

[60] Richard Rohr, "Love, Not Atonement," Daily Meditations, May 4, 2017, https://cac.org.

[61] Benedict XVI, "Eucharist: Setting Transformations in Motion," *Origins* 35, no. 12 (2005): 202.

of God to the human race, it calls us to be a gift to others on our journey. This vision of communion calls us to move from otherness to one-ness, where we not only receive his body and blood but also we become it in such a way that we become bread for the world.

Jesus gives his body and his blood to his disciples to nourish them in their migration through this world and to strengthen them in their mission. As the church remembers his life, his teachings, and his promises until he comes again (Lk. 22:19; 1 Cor. 11:24), they also are given Christ's body in memory of him and called to become his body as they are sent out into the world. When Christ shares his body, he also shares bread with them. It is striking that bread is at the heart of the Eucharist and at the core of the journey for many migrants.[62] J. B. Scalabrini once wrote, "For the migrant, one's country is the land which gives him bread."[63]

Bread is also at the heart of the Liturgy of the Eucharist. In transforming this bread into his body, Christ calls his disciples likewise to be transformed. Part of this means living out one's journey through this world in a new way. Lived in memory of Jesus, this narrative points to the centrality of relationships, solidarity with the no-bodies of the world, and communion with God and one another.

What are the implications of this vision of reconciliation in the context of today's global migration and refugee crisis? How have people taken this memory to heart? How has the memory of Jesus' words transformed our inaction into becoming bread for the world? Before exploring in more detail in the next chapter how organizations have taken up this mission, I want to highlight in the final pages here the life of one person whose memory of his own experience of being a refugee profoundly shaped his life.

In the early part of the twenty-first century, Turkey became a major transit country for many refugees. Following the Iran-Iraq War, the Iranian Revolution, the Gulf War, the war in Afghanistan, the Syrian civil war, and other destabilizing political and economic issues in the surrounding region, millions fled their homelands and began flooding into Turkey in hopes of making it to the European Union. For many of them, the nearest point of entry is Greece.

---

[62] See also Joseph A. Grassi, *Broken Bread and Broken Bodies*, rev. ed. (Maryknoll, NY: Orbis Books, 2004), and Monika Hellwig, *The Eucharist and the Hunger of the World*, 2nd ed., rev. and expanded (Kansas City, MO: Sheed & Ward, 1992).

[63] Daniel G. Groody, "Fruit of the Vine and Work of Human Hands: Immigration and the Eucharist," *Worship* 80, no. 5 (2006): 394.

Between 2015 and 2016, approximately one million refugees arrived on the Greek Aegean islands east of Turkey. One of those is the island of Kos. It is just two and a half nautical miles from the Turkish border town of Bodrum.[64] For the last leg of the journey, many refugees from Syria, Iraq, Afghanistan, and Eritrea boarded inflatable rubber boats and then swam to the island. After landing, they had little more than the wet clothes they swam in and no shelter or food when they arrived. Their journey put them in places of extreme need and vulnerability, but one man who understood their plight was Dionysis Arvanitakis.

From March 2015 until his death in February 2019, he would rise each morning, go to his bakery, and bring 200 pounds of bread, donuts, and pastries to needy refugees huddled together near the island's port. "Someone who has not starved cannot put themselves in these people's shoes," Arvanitakis said. "It's 'us' and 'them' on the same island; two parallel lines, that somehow converge to the very meaning of the word 'human.'"[65]

Part of what stimulated his humanitarian concern was the memory of his own history. He was raised in a poor family of ten children and immigrated to Australia when he was only sixteen. "I know what it feels like to have nothing," he said, and that memory has shaped his own desire to help others. While living abroad as a refugee, he learned how to be a pastry chef and, after he saved up his money, eventually returned to Greece in 1970. As his work prospered, he opened up seven locations, but never forgot where he came from and the kindnesses extended to him when he was in need.

When Dionysis gets to the port where the refugees gather, he first looks for the women and the children. Then he takes the bread he has brought, breaks it, and gives it to all. A long line of people are there waiting, and they hold out their hands, as Dan Siegel and Jenny Yancey put it, "as if standing for communion."[66]

When Jesus shares bread with his disciples, he instructs them to share their lives with others. It is a reflection on the way his presence becomes real to them in this meal, how they are called to embody that presence, and how

---

[64] Kos was the intended destination for the Syrian three-year-old Aylan Kurdi, whose recovered body on the Turkish shores became a symbol of refugee vulnerability in our own times.

[65] Dan Siegel and Jenny Yancey, "Bread for the Journey: The Greek Baker Who Remembers," HuffPost, December 6, 2017, www.huffpost.com.

[66] Ibid.

they in turn are called to re-member and make present his love to all people, especially those who have become invisible in society. Arvanitakis gives us a glimpse of what it looks like to become bread for the world in the context of the global refugee crisis.

In his State of the Union address to the European Parliament, President Jean-Claude Junker, President of the European Commission, asked people to remember that "Europe is a continent where nearly everyone has at one time been a refugee." Then, highlighting the humanitarian work of Arvanitakis, he said, "Europe is the baker in Kos who gives away his bread to hungry and weary souls. This is the Europe I want to live in."[67] Upon his passing, Junker added that he was "an exemplary European citizen" who showed "rare generosity and sensitivity towards the hundreds of unfortunate immigrants." "My Europe," he said, "is the one Dionysis Arvanitakis symbolized."[68]

---

[67] Siegel and Yancey, "Bread for the Journey."
[68] Kai Dambach, "Greek Baker Who Helped Refugees Dies," InfoMigrants, February 18, 2019, www.infomigrants.net.

*Part Four*

# The Mission Narratives

*Migration and Mercy*

# 8

# THE BODY OF CHRIST AS BREAD FOR THE WORLD

*A Eucharist which does not pass over into the concrete practice of love is intrinsically fragmented.* (Pope Benedict XVI, *Deus Caritas Est* 14)

When a man arrived at a Catholic church near Milwaukee, Wisconsin, a number of years ago, he asked to see the pastor. He said he only wanted a blessing. After meeting the priest, the man told the priest that he did not want to go to confession because he had not committed any sins. "Good for you," the priest said. "Tell me how you do it." "Every morning and evening," the man said, "I recite the Ten Commandments, and then I ask myself whether I've broken any of them. The answer is always no." "Congratulations," the priest continued, "tell me more." The man went on at some length, but after a while, the priest asked, "What about Matthew 25? Did you feed the hungry, give drink to the thirsty, welcome the stranger, clothe the naked, care for those who are ill, visit those in prison?" The man looked on with some puzzlement and said, "I've never considered those questions before."[1]

For many Christians, there is a great divide between what happens inside churches and what happens outside them, and for not a few of these, the issue of communion ends at the church door. This is especially true when it comes to the issue of migration. Throughout this work we have brought out ways in which Christian faith speaks to the inner journey and one's connection to God, but we have also explored the ways it has to do with the outer journey of a people and one's connection to others. Passing over to a new

---

[1] I am grateful to Fr. Jim Connelly, CSC, who shared this story with me.

way of life entails moving from personal, tribal, or national agendas to the work of personal, social, and structural transformation of our world. From the perspective of Christian faith, comprehensive immigration reform first and foremost takes account of how the current structures of society facilitate a more just social order, help the poor, contribute to the international common good, foster genuine development, and build up the civilization of love.[2]

Every step we take on our journey of life either leads us closer to this communion or further away from it; we either move closer to God and one another in a shared fellowship in a common body, or we disintegrate and become aliens in every sense of the word. If our operative understanding of life revolves around climbing the ladder of individual success, acquiring as much as we can before we die, and protecting what we have at all costs—as our consumer society constantly holds before us—then the remaining pages will make little sense. But if the long journey of life is ultimately about moving toward communion and living it out through serving, sharing, and stewardship, then the issue of migration is a much weightier matter that we cannot afford to ignore. Matthew 25:31–46 offers us an important framework for this vision of communion because it puts us in touch with matters that will determine how we will be judged in the end of time.

### The Real Presence of Christ in the Eucharist and in the Poor

The real presence of Christ in the Sacrament of the Eucharist is a sacred teaching at the heart of Catholic faith. The real presence of Christ among the last and least of society is also a sacred teaching, but it is something that is less recognized by many. Yet it is central to the Scriptures and figures preeminently in the Law, the Prophets, and the Gospels. Few texts are more central to a theological understanding of migration than Matthew 25:31–46, and it is one the few texts in the New Testament that outlines the criteria by which we will be judged at the end of time:

> "When the Son of Man comes in his glory, and all the angels with him, he will sit on his glorious throne. All the nations will be gathered before him, and he will separate the people one from another

---

[2] John Paul II, "Peace on Earth to Those Whom God Loves: Message for the 2000 World Day of Peace" (December 23, 1999).

as a shepherd separates the sheep from the goats. He will put the sheep on his right and the goats on his left. Then the King will say to those on his right, 'Come, you who are blessed by my Father; take your inheritance, the kingdom prepared for you since the creation of the world. For I was hungry and you gave me something to eat, I was thirsty and you gave me something to drink, I was a stranger and you invited me in, I needed clothes and you clothed me, I was sick and you looked after me, I was in prison and you came to visit me.' Then the righteous will answer him, 'Lord, when did we see you hungry and feed you, or thirsty and give you something to drink? When did we see you a stranger and invite you in, or needing clothes and clothe you? When did we see you sick or in prison and go to visit you?'

"The King will reply, 'Truly I tell you, whatever you did for one of the least of these brothers and sisters of mine, you did for me.' Then he will say to those on his left, 'Depart from me, you who are cursed, into the eternal fire prepared for the devil and his angels. For I was hungry and you gave me nothing to eat, I was thirsty and you gave me nothing to drink, I was a stranger and you did not invite me in, I needed clothes and you did not clothe me, I was sick and in prison and you did not look after me.' They also will answer, 'Lord, when did we see you hungry or thirsty or a stranger or needing clothes or sick or in prison, and did not help you?'

"He will reply, 'Truly I tell you, whatever you did not do for one of the least of these, you did not do for me.' Then they will go away to eternal punishment, but the righteous to eternal life." (NIV 2011)

This passage is one of the most widely quoted texts of the Christian Scriptures, and it has inspired the lives of countless saints, such as Francis of Assisi, Martin of Tours, and Mother Teresa.[3] It is so significant in the overall vision of the New Testament that some scholars refer to it as a "summary of the Gospel" or a "Gospel within a Gospel."[4]

---

[3] Saints and mystics like Teresa of Ávila have given us vivid metaphors to understand the spiritual life as a migration of its own, which she describes as a journey toward the center of the interior castle. Teresa of Ávila, *The Interior Castle* (Mahwah, NJ: Paulist Press, 1980).

[4] John R. Donahue, "The 'Parable' of the Sheep and the Goats: A Challenge to Christian Ethics," *Theological Studies* 47, no. 1 (1986): 3–31, esp. 28.

Because this text also reads like a description of the outer journey of many migrants on the road today, it deserves our attention here. They are hungry in their homelands, thirsty in the deserts they cross, naked after being robbed of their possessions, ill after having to drink their own urine to survive, imprisoned in detention centers, and unwelcome when they make it across the border. If this be the case, in what ways is Christ truly present—albeit in a disguised way—among those migrating today?

Let us explore this question now in the context of the Communion Rite of the Eucharist.[5] We have been exploring how the Liturgy of the Eucharist can reframe the narratives of migration by highlighting God's migration to the human race and our return migration to God. The Eucharist begins with the sign of the cross and has traditionally ended with the words "The Mass is ended. Go in Peace." There can be no peace without justice. And there can be no justice without the right ordering of society.

Thomas Aquinas and Augustine of Hippo speak of justice as the "tranquility of order" (*tranquillitas ordinis*) or a well-ordered concord.[6] Because the world's disorders are the root cause of peoples' migration, the work of the Church in pursuing this peace involves the reordering of society. This justice is central to the mission of the Church, and in this section we look at specific organizations involved in this work of justice and peace, especially as it relates to Matthew 25.

In the last few decades, scholars have raised a number of questions about who Jesus is referring to when he speaks of "the least of his brothers and sisters" (Mt. 25:40, 45; in Greek, *elachistos ho adelphos*). In his research on this subject, John Donahue refers to the "classic interpretation" and the "universal interpretation" of this passage.[7] Most importantly, while active concern for

---

[5] The placement of the reading of the Judgment of the Nations in the liturgical cycle is also significant. Most notable is its use on the Solemnity of Christ the King. This feast is celebrated on the last Sunday of the liturgical year in order to highlight that the Church proclaims that Jesus Christ, from the beginning to the end of time, is the ruler of the universe. This means that all peoples of all the nations on earth are, and will be, subject to the authority of Christ. When all are brought before him, he will judge not simply independent individuals but nations.

[6] Augustine, *The City of God* 19.13; Thomas Aquinas, *Summa Theologica*, q.29, a.1.

[7] The "classic interpretation," which was the most widely accepted reading until the early 1800s, sees "the least" as persecuted Christian leaders or missionaries. The "universal interpretation," which has become more common in our own times, maintains that "the least" refers to any poor or vulnerable person. At the core of the debate, as John Donahue describes it, is the question of who is being judged at the end of time:

the poor has been an integral dimension of Christian discipleship from the beginning of the church, Jesus' earthly ministry began within the borders of Israel but evolved to encompass ever-wider circles of inclusion in his missionary outreach.[8] Jesus initially focused on his mission to the lost sheep of the house of Israel but eventually went beyond the borders of Judaism in order to embrace all people in need (Mt. 15:21–28). He repeatedly emphasizes that following him requires a big-heartedness that is greater than the walls of organized religion and demands going beyond the moral norms of Israel's pagan neighbors and even conventional Jewish ethics (Mt. 5:20).[9] Donahue argues that Matthew's aim is not to present a generalized humanitarian ethic but rather an ethic of Christian discipleship that is connected to a "deep engagement with the mystery of the cross."[10] Engagement with this cross, Jon Sobrino adds, also requires a deep identification with those who are undergoing experiences akin to "unjust crucifixions" today.[11]

---

"all peoples (Jews, Christians, pagans), all nations (excluding Jews, but including Christians) . . . [or] all gentiles (excluding both Jews and Christians). . . . The flash point in the debate is the claim that the least of the brethren of the Son of Man are Christians . . . and not simply any person in need" (Donahue, "'Parable' of the Sheep," 5). See also Ulrich Luz, *Matthew 21–28: A Commentary*, ed. H. Koester (Minneapolis: Fortress Press, 2005), 267–74.

[8] While acknowledging the "impressive" textual evidence that would support the case that the least in Matthew's Gospel refers to Christians and/or Christian missionaries who suffered because of their preaching of the Gospel (see Mt. 10:40–42; 18:6, 14), Donahue resists reducing this text to sectarian-minded charity. He argues instead that this passage also needs to be read in light of a larger discourse on Christian discipleship (Donahue, "'Parable' of the Sheep," 25).

[9] C. S. Keener, *The IVP Bible Background Commentary: New Testament* (Downers Grove, IL: InterVarsity Press, 1993).

[10] Donahue points out that this story of the Judgment of the Nations comes immediately after three parables on discipleship (the parable on the Faithful or the Unfaithful Servant [Mt. 24:45–51]); the parable of the Ten Virgins [Mt. 25:1–13]); and the parable of the Talents [Mt. 25:14–30]), and right before the events of his passion and his crucifixion (Donahue, "'Parable' of the Sheep," 31).

[11] Building on the thought of Ignacio Ellacuría, Jon Sobrino notes, "The crucified peoples of the Third World today are the great theological setting, the locus, in which to understand the Cross of Jesus" (*Jesus the Liberator: A Historical-Theological View* [Maryknoll, NY: Orbis Books, 1999], 196). See also Ignacio Ellacuría, *Escritos teológicos*, 2 vols., Colección latinoamericana 25–26 (San Salvador: UCA, 2000), 1:187–218; Jon Sobrino, "La teología y el 'Principio Liberación,'" *Revista Latinoamericana de teología* 12 (1995): 115–40; Jon Sobrino, *Witnesses to the Kingdom: The El Salvadoran Martyrs and the Crucified Peoples* (Maryknoll, NY: Orbis Books,

As the church has tried to live out its journey toward communion in response to Matthew 25, it has highlighted several corporal works of mercy that are integral to following the life of Jesus Christ: feeding the hungry, sheltering the homeless, clothing the naked, visiting the sick and imprisoned, and burying the dead. These practices inform much of the Church's approach to outreach to migrants and refugees, and many organizations around the United States and other parts of the world have been founded to carry out this work.[12]

### Feeding the Hungry: The Kino Border Initiative

"I was hungry and you gave me food." (Mt. 25:35 NRSV)

When Guillermo was twelve years old, gang members from his hometown in Guatemala began the process of targeting him to join their ranks. Due to the deteriorating security and weakened juridical systems, the gangs use violence, extortion, kidnapping, and other coercive threats with impunity to

---

2003); Michael E. Lee, "Liberation Theology's Transcendent Moment: The Work of Xavier Zubiri and Ignacio Ellacuría as Noncontrastive Discourse," *Journal of Religion* 83 (2003): 226–43; Kevin Burke and Robert Lassalle-Klein, *Love That Produces Hope: The Thought of Ignacio Ellacuría* (Collegeville, MN: Liturgical, 2006); Gioacchino Campese, "Cuantos Más: The Crucified Peoples at the U.S./Mexico Border," in Daniel G. Groody and Gioacchino Campese, *A Promised Land, a Perilous Journey: Theological Perspectives on Migration* (Notre Dame, IN: University of Notre Dame Press, 2008), 71–98; and Daniel G. Groody, *Border of Death, Valley of Life: An Immigrant Journey of Heart and Spirit* (Lanham, MD: Rowman and Littlefield, 2001), 13–39.

[12] As the Catholic bishops of the United States reflected on their own mission in light of the Scriptures, they have adopted a position that aligns with the more inclusive, universalist interpretation of Matthew 25 rather than the more restrictive classic interpretation. As Bishop Joe S. Vásquez, chairman of the Committee on Migration and Refugees of the US Conference of Catholic Bishops, argued, "The United States has long provided leadership in resettling refugees. We believe in assisting all those who are vulnerable and fleeing persecution, regardless of their religion. This includes Christians, as well as Yazidis and Shia Muslims from Syria, Rohingyas from Burma, and other religious minorities. However, we need to protect all our brothers and sisters of all faiths, including Muslims, who have lost family, home, and country. They are children of God and are entitled to be treated with human dignity. We believe that by helping to resettle the most vulnerable, we are living out our Christian faith as Jesus has challenged us to do" (United States Conference of Catholic Bishops, "USCCB Committee on Migration Chair Strongly Opposes Executive Order Because It Harms Vulnerable Refugee and Immigrant Families," January 27, 2017, www.usccb.org).

force young people like Guillermo into their criminal activities. If Guillermo refused, the gang could kill him; if he joined them, he could die. But if he migrated, he could also lose his life. With perilous conditions in his homeland, and significant dangers en route, he had no good options.

Eventually he and his family risked going north, hoping they could find protection in the United States. When they got to the border, they were joined by a larger group of migrants. Already tired from the journey, however, Guillermo eventually lagged behind and was separated from his family and the rest of the group.

Fortunately, a woman named Alma was traveling through that same area of the desert. When she came across Guillermo, he was lost and stranded in the middle of nowhere. Low on resources herself, she realized that if she shared what she had with him, they both might not make it. But if Guillermo had to fend for himself, he certainly would not survive. Not wanting to leave him stranded, they spent the next four days walking through the barren terrain together. When they eventually ran out of food and water, they took desperate measures and started burning their clothes, hoping that the smoke would alert the Border Patrol to their presence.

Authorities eventually discovered them and took them to detention facilities. As they were being processed as undocumented immigrants, Alma identified Guillermo as her own son so that she could care for him. When they were deported back to Mexico, they were released at a border point of entry in Nogales, Mexico. By this point, however, they were tired and hungry. They had nothing to their name. Eventually they found their way to people at the Kino Border Initiative and the help they needed to continue on their journey.[13] In addition to a hunger for food, they were hungry for protection under the law in their own countries, hungry for opportunities that would allow them to live a dignified life, and hungry to reconnect with family members on the other side of the border.

*A Faith-Based, Humanitarian Response to Hunger*

In response to people like Guillermo and Alma, a few Catholic nuns from the Missionary Sisters of the Eucharist felt compelled to do something to help alleviate the suffering they witnessed. One was Sister Rosalba Avalos Ramos. Sr. Ramos said she would hear stories in which the migrants would

---

[13] *Annual Report 2013* (Tucson, AZ: Kino Border Initiative, 2013), 5.

say, "I just want to work, and in Mexico, there aren't any job opportunities"; "My children don't have shoes and they're hungry"; "My hope is to give them a better life, to give them an education, so that they don't have to struggle like I have"; and "I want to rescue my family from poverty." She said they often find themselves "without hope, with their hearts destroyed by suffering, despair, fear, and sadness."[14]

After the migrants were deported back to Mexico, she noticed that they often had only the clothes they wore and a small plastic bag of belongings. Frequently they had no one to turn to, no place to live, nowhere to make a phone call, and no place to receive a meal. So the Sisters went to the border port of entry and started bringing meals to migrants. As their work gained notice, more volunteers came. Later other organizations got involved, particularly the Diocese of Tucson, the Archdiocese of Hermosillo, Mexico, and the Jesuits.

Jesuit Refugee Service (JRS) is one of the leading faith-based organizations worldwide that accompanies, serves, and advocates on behalf of refugees and other forcibly displaced persons.[15] Their international office is in Rome, but they provide outreach to migrants around the globe.[16] Under the leadership of Pedro Arrupe, SJ, the Jesuits founded JRS in November 1980, and they now have programs in more than fifty countries. With an extensive staff of full-time employees, religious leaders, and refugee volunteers, they work in camps, cities, and detention centers, offering education, advocacy, healthcare, emergency assistance, and other social services. They also promote international human rights legislation through various international organizations, including the United Nations. In their first thirty-five years almost a million people benefited from their services.[17]

In recent decades, the Jesuits in the United States, in partnership with JRS, have become more involved in chaplaincy work in federal immigration detention centers. As the immigration crisis has worsened, however, they wanted to take further steps.[18] Because the region of Nogales, Arizona / Nogales, Mexico was becoming the central point of deportation along the border, there was a great need for humanitarian services, so they began

---

[14] Rosalba Avalos Ramos, "God Knocked on My Door Again," www.rsusa.org.
[15] Jesuit Refugee Service USA, "About Us," www.jrsusa.org.
[16] Ibid.
[17] Ibid.
[18] Fr. Sean Carroll, phone interview by Kathleen Kollman, Nogales, Arizona, October 23, 2014.

investing their energy there. In 2009, in partnerships with other organizations in Mexico and the United States, the Jesuits established the Kino Border Initiative.

*The Mission of the Kino Border Initiative*

The Kino Border Initiative (KBI) is a binational organization that addresses the needs of migrants near Nogales, Arizona, and Nogales, Sonora, Mexico. It is named after Jesuit priest Eusebio Kino, who, in the late seventeenth century, established some of the earliest Catholic churches in what is now northern Mexico and southern Arizona. The mission of KBI is "to help make humane, just, workable migration between the U.S. and Mexico a reality . . . [and] to promote US/Mexico border and immigration policies that affirm the dignity of the human person and a spirit of bi-national solidarity." They carry out this mission through (1) direct humanitarian assistance and accompaniment with migrants; (2) social and pastoral education with communities on both sides of the border; and (3) participation in collaborative networks that engage in research and advocacy to transform local, regional, and national immigration policies.[19]

Like other migrant assistance organizations, KBI offers first-aid assistance, a shelter for women and children, and other services. But their cornerstone ministry is the Aid Center for Deported Migrants. It is often referred to as the *comedor*, or dining hall, because the center offers migrants free meals for up to two weeks. At present the *comedor* can provide almost fifty thousand meals a year. KBI's binational operation sees the border as "a point of contact and mutual transformation not only for the migrants, staff, and community members who encounter one another in the context of our programs, but also for the Provinces of California and Mexico, the Missionary Sisters of the Eucharist, and the Jesuit Refugee Service."[20]

While the staff and volunteers of the *comedor* help address some of the immediate hungers of migrants, KBI recognizes that for durable solutions to take root, more must be done than temporarily tending to basic needs.[21] A hunger for justice compels them to work as well at challenging the systems

---

[19] Kino Border Initiative, "About Us," www.kinoborderinitiative.org.
[20] Kino Border Initiative, "Humanitarian Aid," www.kinoborderinitiative.org.
[21] Mark W. Potter, "Solidarity as Spiritual Exercise: Accompanying Migrants at the US/Mexico Border," *Political Theology* 12, no. 6 (2011): 830–42 at 842.

and structures that keep migrants from developing as human beings. To this end, they publish human rights reports that document the many layers of abuse that migrants undergo in their journey to the United States. For example, in *Documented Failures: The Consequences of Immigration Policy on the U.S.-Mexico Border*, they highlight the problems of family separation in detention and deportation, the root causes of violence that uproot people, and various cases of abuse committed by Mexican authorities and the US Border Patrol.[22]

KBI also addresses the migrants' hunger for emotional healing, human connection, and spiritual growth—which are all part of the integral search for human wholeness. A few blocks from the *comedor*, the Sisters run a shelter for women and children called Nazareth House: a safe place for them to stay and tell their story and to be accompanied as they make difficult decisions. Sr. Ramos says, "We do not offer them work or money, or solve their financial problems, but we offer an atmosphere of prayer, reflection, and an opportunity to find themselves and to find God. This experience helps them find some peace and hope to heal their hearts and self-esteem."[23] Sr. Ramos said she came there in search of "the God of the poor [who] has a compassionate and softened heart that hurts because of the pain of those who have nothing." She feels a particular call toward "those who are considered foreigners, those that let go of and renounce everything, even their own families by risking their lives to search for economic security that will rid them of hunger and satisfy their thirst for justice and provide dignity for them and their families."[24]

*Theological Foundations and Organization of Kino Border Initiative*

Inspired by the Gospels' vision to welcome Christ in the stranger, JRS and KBI are both guided by values of human dignity, solidarity, subsidiarity, compassion, hospitality, hope, and justice. They work with displaced persons regardless of their race, gender, religion, or politics.[25] They seek to offer hospitality "at the frontiers of humanity," prioritizing those in greatest

---

[22] Michael S. Danielson, *Documented Failures: The Consequences of Immigration Policy on the U.S.-Mexico Border* (Nogales: Kino Border Initiative, 2013).
[23] Ramos, "God Knocked on My Door."
[24] Ibid.
[25] Jesuit Refugee Service USA, "About Us."

need and reaching those who are the most vulnerable and often the most neglected.[26] As they build networks with other organizations, they work through national and regional provinces of the Jesuits in response to the growing needs of migrants and refugees everywhere.

While this work involves responding to the God who has first loved us, it more importantly involves paying attention to the God who is at work in the world. At KBI, Fr. Sean Carroll, SJ, says that it is not just about what they are doing for God but what God is doing through them and what God is doing in the migrants themselves. Not only has KBI helped the migrants, he said that "migrants have taught us about finding God in the worst moments."[27]

"The work can be . . . overwhelming," he says, "and if we can find God there—and I think we do—then we find a God who has come here in the first place and the God who has promised to be faithful to us and faithful to this work. . . . In the midst of the brutal realities that migrants are experiencing, [we are discovering that] God is present and God is at their side and accompanying them. We're there to witness that, and it's a reminder that God is with us too and is giving us what we need to be present and to respond."[28] He says, "I feel like God was inviting us here, and we said yes to that invitation, and because we said yes, there has been all this fruit."[29]

As Fr. Sean notes, "I always am struck by the difference in migrants between the time before they come in to our center and when they leave. In the morning their body language really indicates what they've been through." By the time they reach the *comedor* at Kino, many have drunk from cow troughs, been robbed by organized crime members, arrested by the Border Patrol, charged in court, and then deported back again. "Many are separated from their families; many have a real hunger," he said. "Not just a physical hunger, [but a hunger for freedom since they have been] in detention for a long time. They have real spiritual hunger too . . . and when you welcome them and sit with them and pray with them before meals, you can hear a pin drop. They are offering everything and putting everything in God's hands at that moment, and to witness [their faith amid such adversity] is very powerful."[30]

---

[26] Ibid.
[27] Carroll, interview by Kollman.
[28] Ibid.
[29] Ibid.
[30] Ibid.

## Giving Drink to the Thirsty: Humane Borders

"I was thirsty and you gave me something to drink." (Mt. 25:35 NRSV)

In late May 2000, a nineteen-year-old woman named Yolanda Gonzalez and her ten-month-old daughter, Elizama, left their home in the village of San Pedro Chayuco, in Oaxaca, Mexico. After trying to raise her new family on her own, Yolanda wanted to reunite with her husband, Hermilo Hernandez Velazco, who was then living on the other side of the border in Portland, Oregon. Hermilo was Elizama's father and had migrated earlier to the United States because he wanted something more for his own family than he could provide living in rural Mexico.

Hoping to keep their family together, Yolanda and Elizama left home with the help of a smuggler-guide, and they set out from Oaxaca with ten other migrants. When they got to the border, the smuggler told them that their journey would take only six hours, and then they would be safely on the other side. But instead, he abandoned the group, and they wandered aimlessly in the desert for four days. Worn out from the journey and with resources running low, Yolanda drank as little as possible so that she could save the remaining water for her daughter. When her strength gave out, two men from the group stayed behind, while the others went for help. By the time someone came, she had already died of dehydration. While her daughter, Elizama, lived, Yolanda was the fourth migrant to die that week.[31]

Yolanda's death was not an accident. Her dying was a consequence of the deteriorating socioeconomic conditions in her homeland, and a failed border policy that funnels countless migrants like Yolanda into forbidding terrain along the US-Mexico border. This policy accelerated in the early 1990s, when the US government began militarizing the border and

---

[31] Donald Kirwin, *Chaos on the U.S.-Mexican Border: A Report on Migrant Crossing Deaths, Immigrant Families, and Subsistence-Level Laborers,* Catholic Legal Immigration Network, 2001, 3–4, https://cmsny.org. This account has been drawn from the following articles: M. Shaffer, "Tiny Survivor of Crossing, Kin Reunite at Nursery in Mexico; Grandma Cries for Tot, Justice," *Arizona Republic,* June 16, 2000; M. Shaffer, "Poverty Sends Mom on Deadly Trek," *Arizona Republic,* July 16, 2000; C. Alaimo and J. Barrios, "Teen Mom Dies to Save Tot," *Arizona Daily Star,* June 1, 2000; P. Hartman, "Unlike Elian Case, Mexican Mom's Sacrifice Largely Ignored," *Tucson Citizen,* June 2, 2000; P. Flannery, "Mercy Flights along Border," *Arizona Republic,* July 8, 2000.

employing various deterrence strategies in order to control the flow of migrants coming into the country.[32] Since then, thousands of migrants have died walking across the deserts of the American Southwest, many of whom were looking for a job or trying to connect with families on the other side.[33]

Because of the need for labor that many undocumented people provide, migrant flows keep coming, which ironically has kept those who were already inside the United States from returning home.[34] Whereas previously there was more migration back and forth during harvest seasons (*circular migration*), now migrants are less likely to return home because of the risks involved. Others have been deterred from coming because of tighter border controls. Some consider the harsher migration policies as a sign of success and an indication that tougher enforcement measures are working, while others argue that such policies have simply exacerbated a lethal trend that has increasingly pushed migrants to take greater risks to enter the country.

Because routes have become lengthier and more lethal as a result of these policies, the number of migrants dying along the border has increased significantly since the 1990s. Although many migrants over the years have died because of accidents, drowning, and hypothermia, in recent decades many more have died from heatstroke, hyperthermia, and dehydration.[35]

---

[32] The US government relies on two kinds of barriers to implement this strategy. The first are physical barriers such as walls and Border Patrol agents, which—along with surveillance systems—help prevent migrants from crossing. The second are natural barriers such as mountains and deserts, which—along with the dangers posed by the natural elements—discourage them from crossing. In theory this "prevention through deterrence" approach is designed to (1) *dissuade migrants physically* from passing over because it would force them to take longer and more difficult routes, and (2) *dissuade migrants economically* because of the higher cost of smuggling fees resulting from longer times and greater risks involved in crossing the border.

[33] Raquel Rubio-Goldsmith, M. Melissa McCormick, Daniel Martinez, and Inez Magdalena Duarte, "A Humanitarian Crisis at the Border: New Estimates of Deaths among Unauthorized Immigrants," Immigration Policy Center, February 2007, www.americanimmigrationcouncil.org.

[34] Douglas S. Massey, Jorge Durand, and Nolan J. Malone, *Beyond Smoke and Mirrors: Mexican Immigration in an Era of Economic Integration* (New York: Russell Sage Foundation, 2002), 105–41.

[35] Karl Eschbach, Jacqueline Hagan, Nestor Rodriguez, Ruben Hernandez-Leon, and Stanley Bailey, "Death at the Border," *International Migration Review* 33, no. 2 (1999): 430.

Outraged by this failed and inhumane border policy, many faith-based and humanitarian groups have mobilized aid and action in response.

*A Faith-Based, Humanitarian Response to Those Dying in the Deserts*

Immediately following news of Yolanda's death in 2000, eighty-five pastors, activists, and concerned individuals from the greater Tucson, Arizona, area came together to address the crisis of migrants dying at the southern border. Some of these people had been involved in the Sanctuary Movement in the 1980s, when church leaders sought to provide refuge to Central Americans fleeing across the border and escaping violent oppression in their homeland.[36] This time they gathered at the Pima Friends House in Tucson on Pentecost Sunday and focused on two goals: responding with compassion to the migrants crossing the deserts along the US-Mexico border and working to change US immigration policies that place these persons at risk in the desert.[37]

This group eventually created a faith-based organization that placed water in the desert and challenged the current border policy. They began working binationally with Mexico, using the media to tell the stories and struggles of many migrants and to highlight the inhumane journey across the US-Mexico border. From this initial strategy emerged an organization called Humane Borders.[38] The organization articulates its mission statement as follows:

> Humane Borders, motivated by faith, offers humanitarian assistance to those in need through the deployment of emergency water stations on routes known to be used by migrants coming north through our desert. Our sole mission is to take death out of the immigration equation.[39]

---

[36] Randy K. Lippert and Sean Rehaag, *Sanctuary Practices in International Perspectives: Migration, Citizenship, and Social Movements* (New York: Routledge, 2013), 28–42, 71–105; Jim Corbett, *The Sanctuary Church* (Wallingford, PA: Pendle Hill Publications, 1987); Ann Crittenden, *Sanctuary: A Story of American Conscience and the Law in Collision* (New York: Weidenfeld & Nicolson, 1988).

[37] Robin Hoover, "The Story of Humane Borders," in *A Promised Land, a Perilous Journey: Theological Perspectives on Migration,* ed. Daniel G. Groody and Gioacchino Campese (Notre Dame, IN: University of Notre Dame Press, 2008), 163.

[38] Ibid.

[39] See Humane Borders, www.humaneborders.org.

In addition to direct aid, Humane Borders works toward humane public policies that foster legalized work opportunities for migrants in the United States and economic options for migrants in their countries of origin.[40] The context in which they do their ministry is one of the hottest and most grueling migrant territories in the world.

Luis Alberto Urrea describes the trek across the Arizona desert as "the Devil's Highway." In graphic detail, he tells of what happens in your body when you walk through a world on fire:

> Those in shape will, sooner or later, faint. . . . This is the brain's way of stopping the machine, like hitting the brakes when you realize you're speeding towards a cliff. . . . With no sweat, your body's swamp-cooler breaks. You are having a core meltdown. Your temperature redlines—you hit 106, 107, 108 degrees. Your body panics and dilates all blood capillaries near the surface, hoping to flood your skin with blood to cool it off. You blush. Your eyes turn red: Blood vessels burst, and later, the tissue of the whites literally cooks until it goes pink, then a well-done crimson.[41]

In the desert, temperatures can exceed 120 degrees in the shade. Six inches off the ground, temperatures are even hotter, and migrants can cook their brains like an egg if they lay down their heads. When visiting hospital emergency rooms in the area, I frequently heard stories about the permanent brain damage and personal traumas migrants suffered, even if they survived the journey.

To prepare themselves for such a grueling trek, migrants bring with them three or four gallons of water—weighing twenty to thirty-two pounds—but it is not nearly enough for the demands of the desert. When migrants run out of water, they are forced to take dramatic measures in order to survive. Some drink their own urine. Others break open a cactus with stones and try to suck out the juices in order to hydrate. Still others will drink from animal troughs in nearby ranches, which are brimming with diseases of every kind, including flesh-eating parasites.

Caesar, a migrant from Mexico, knew this hellish journey firsthand. After crossing the border, he told me what it was like for him to traverse the desert with eleven friends. At the sound of a Border Patrol helicopter,

---

[40] Hoover, "Story of Humane Borders," 162.
[41] Luis Alberto Urrea, *Across the Wire: Life and Hard Times on the Mexican Border* (New York: Anchor Books, 1993), 125, 128.

everyone scattered, leaving him lost and disoriented. After four days in the desert, three days without clean water, two days without food, and two days of vomiting, one of his companions collapsed. Then Caesar said,

> I couldn't hear right. I started hearing this buzzing sound in my ears and began to get dizzy. My mouth became dry to the point where I couldn't salivate. We had to resort to drinking water from a cattle trough, which, miraculously, we came upon. The water was ugly, a brown-green, slimy color with a terrible odor, but it seemed like a gift from heaven to us. But when I drank it, I couldn't really feel it. For sure, I couldn't taste it. Then my vision began to blur. Everyone looked pallid. My hands and feet went numb. The blisters were so big on my feet I couldn't feel them anymore. I started getting this really bad headache, and I could actually feel my heartbeat, slowly, slowly. Everything was in a haze, like it was going in slow motion. My nose began to bleed and my throat tightened up. I thought, *This is it; this is where I am going to die.* . . . I did not have any more strength to continue . . . but I begged for just a little more from God. I thought about my children, and I knew they were too young to lose their father, and I thought about my wife and my parents, and because of them I kept going. They gave me the strength to keep fighting.[42]

To reach people like Caesar, Humane Borders began setting up two water stations in 2001. As of 2021 the number had grown to over eighty.[43] The stations are marked by a thirty-foot flagpole with the word *agua* on the barrel. Each station has between one and six drums of water, each of which holds up to fifty-five gallons.

These efforts have made a difference, but even so, thousands continue to lose their lives in the forbidding deserts of the American Southwest. Since 1999, Humane Borders has documented more than thirty-five hundred deaths in the area along the border, and they have used this information to strategically place these containers of water to help those crossing the desert.

Hundreds of thousands of gallons of water have been dispensed through these stations since the inception of Humane Borders, and it's hard to estimate how many lives have been saved as a result.

---

[42] Interview by author, Tucson, Arizona, June 22, 2003.
[43] Warren Richey, "A Drop of Water in the Desert, and a Flood of Migrants," *Christian Science Monitor*, November 3, 2016.

## The Mission of Humane Borders

Shortly after its founding, Humane Borders developed a logo emblematic of its mission. It consists of a series of interconnected stars that form the outline of the Big Dipper and the North Star in the upper right-hand corner. This dipper represents a drinking gourd that captures the organization's focus on giving water to thirsty migrants. But it also holds a symbol in its relationship to the North Star. As previous generations worked to free African slaves from their oppression through the Underground Railroad, the North Star in this logo symbolizes Humane Borders' struggle for the migrant's liberation. "Our borders at this point are not humane," said one volunteer named Laura, "and the goal is to humanize the border, humanize the policy, by doing simple things like offering a cup of water."[44]

The generosity of the volunteers of Humane Borders is mirrored in the migrants themselves. When Roberto crossed the desert a few years ago, he came across a couple who had been walking for three days. They had run out of water sometime before, and their lips were brown and purple. They wandered around as though in a fog, like zombies, showing signs of hyperthermia and dehydration. When Roberto offered the couple the little water he had saved for himself, he saved their lives, even as he risked his own. When I asked Roberto about this incident, he said, "It was not a heroic act. It was simply the right thing to do."[45]

The group has had more than fifteen hundred volunteers with over one hundred affiliated partner organizations since its founding. In addition to supplying water in the desert, Humane Borders gives concerted effort to the structural systems and policies that contribute to migrant deaths. As Rev. Robin Hoover puts it, "More than simply treating the symptoms of a broken border policy, it is imperative to identify, analyze, and ultimately change unjust and inhumane social structures."[46]

The water tanks are placed on both private and public lands, and securing permits for these stations is an integral part of the mission. To obtain these permissions, Humane Borders works closely with the US National Park Service; the US Fish and Wildlife Service; the US Bureau of

---

[44] Van Ham and Lane Vernon, *A Common Humanity: Ritual, Religion, and Immigrant Advocacy in Tucson, Arizona* (Tucson: University of Arizona Press, 2011), 110.

[45] Interview by author, Altar, Mexico, June 15, 2003.

[46] Hoover, "Story of Humane Borders," 167.

Land Management; Pima County, Arizona; the city of Tucson; Grupo Beta in Sonora, Mexico; and private property owners along the border.

Given the limitation of resources amid a vast desert expanse, Humane Borders has to make strategic decisions about where to place water stations. They carefully map out the GPS coordinates where migrants have died in order to demonstrate where water stations are needed to curb migrant fatalities.[47] Critics argue that putting water stations on federal lands only aids and abets migrants who are illegally crossing, but government officials on the local level argue that putting in such lifesaving measures save not only lives but money, as the costs involved in burying the migrant dead are significant.[48]

Humane Borders volunteers are required to abide by certain protocols when encountering migrants in the desert. These protocols are an effort to cooperate as much as possible with government regulations and also to assist in helping the public understand the nature of their work. When volunteers encounter migrants, they ask questions related to their need for food, water, and medical attention. Volunteers also ask migrants if they know where they are, where they are going, how far they are from their destination, and if they want them to call the Border Patrol to be taken to the port of entry at the border. Some are so exhausted by the time they encounter the border that they just want to go back home.

Volunteers also help them with a cell phone or satellite phone if they are in remote areas. Volunteers provide clothing, blankets, cold packs, first aid, and other supplies. If a migrant is experiencing a medical emergency, volunteers are instructed to transport the migrant to nearby medical facilities, but they are required to inform the central office of Humane Borders or the Border Patrol. Volunteers are instructed, "There is no hiding the fact that you have transported an undocumented person," and they seek to cooperate with designated officials at every turn.

---

[47] Humane Borders, "Water Stations," www.humaneborders.org.

[48] For a small snapshot into the controversy, see Brady McCombs, "US Allows New Water Stations by Border," *Arizona Daily Star*, September 4, 2010. For a detailed survey of humanitarian projects on the border, including the cost of the burial of the dead, see Maria Jimenez, "Humanitarian Crisis: Migrant Deaths at the U.S.-Mexico Border," American Civil Liberties Union, October 1, 2009, www.aclu.org.

## Theological Foundations and Organization of Humane Borders

The organization's inspiration is decidedly Christian, and Matthew 25:31–46 shapes its vision:

> "What you do to the least of our brothers and sisters" guides many participants in their volunteer efforts. From a social point of view, concern for the most vulnerable of our society motivates action. From the political perspective, creating a more just community becomes a driving force. And in ethical terms, valuing and fostering life dictates conservation of human lives. Regardless of a people's starting point, on the whole, Humane Borders examines not only what kind of world we live in but what kind of world we want it to become.[49]

The text from Mark 9:41 also echoes in the background of Humane Borders' mission: "For truly I tell you, whoever gives you a cup of water to drink because you bear the name of Christ will by no means lose the reward" (NRSV).

Hoover, a pastor of the Disciples of Christ Church in Tucson and the first president and founder of Humane Borders, also claims that the organization is "inspired by the priestly, kingly, and prophetic traditions of biblical Christian and Jewish faiths."[50] He sees these as coming together in the parable of the Good Samaritan in Luke's Gospel. As Hoover describes it,

> This story highlights the prophetic ideal in challenging all people to see the common, human ties each person shares with his or her neighbor. It highlights the kingly ideal in calling all people to be ruled by love and compassion, which manifests itself in caring for the injured person found on the side of the road. It highlights the priestly function of inviting all people to engage in actions that build community, which includes binding up the wounds of the injured. For us, this priestly, kingly, and prophetic ministry manifests itself not only in individual acts of charity but in a collective effort of outreach aimed at assisting those who are most vulnerable in our society, which means assisting migrants in the desert.[51]

---

[49] Hoover, "Story of Humane Borders," 163–64.
[50] Ibid., 166.
[51] Ibid.

The focus is not to speculate on who their neighbor is, but to be a neighbor to migrants in need. At the same time, Humane Borders welcomes people from all walks of life and sees itself as a collaborative organization willing to dialogue with all parties and people of goodwill, even if they have different positions on immigration and do not share their mission and vision.

In addition to Humane Borders, other humanitarian and faith-based groups in the area are trying to take death out of the migration equation. One such organization is No More Deaths.[52] Since July 2002, this group has been providing emergency medical assistance, food, and water to people crossing the Sonoran Desert. No More Deaths began in 2004 as a coalition of faith-based and community groups dedicated to stemming the rising death tolls. Drawing together people from various faith traditions, No More Deaths seeks to make migration to the United States safe, orderly, legal, and humane.[53] The group also provides humanitarian aid, documents human rights abuses, and conducts searches for those who have disappeared and died in the desert.[54]

The US government also has tried to respond to the problem of migrant deaths through its Border Patrol, Search, Trauma, and Rescue Teams (BORSTAR). Beginning in 1998, this specialized unit of trained paramedics has tried to help stranded migrants in the desert and minimize the number of fatalities.[55] The collective efforts of federal, state, and humanitarian faith-based organizations have sought to minimize or eliminate the deaths at the border, but given the size of the desert, all of these organizations together can only do so much to remedy the escalating crisis. Searching for the lost is something, but it is still akin to finding isolated life rafts in an ocean. Despite even the teams' best efforts, thousands of migrants continue to die in their journeys northward.[56] Yet even for those who do make it across, and have the benefit of the water that Humane Borders provides, seemingly unquenchable thirsts remain: for work, for family, and for a more dignified life.

---

[52] See https://nomoredeaths.org.

[53] No More Deaths, "Faith-Based Principles for Immigration Reform," http://forms.nomoredeaths.org.

[54] No More Deaths, "About No More Deaths," http://forms.nomoredeaths.org.

[55] "Border Patrol Search, Trauma, and Rescue," www.cbp.gov.

[56] US Customs and Border Protection, "U.S. Border Patrol Fiscal Year Southwest Border Sector Deaths," January 29, 2020, www.cbp.gov.

## Sheltering the Homeless: Casa Juan Diego

"I was a stranger and you welcomed me." (Mt. 25:35 NRSV)

When Faustino left his home in Honduras, he began the long journey to the United States. He first made his way up to the Guatemalan border and then moved his way north to the southern end of Mexico. At the river near Tapachula, he jumped onto a large tractor tire inner tube and floated his way to the other side. After getting out of the water, he walked along the train tracks for two days. With his feet swollen and his strength spent, he rested for a few days at a nearby shelter.[57] Then he climbed onto a series of freight trains for as many as fifteen hundred miles. This train system is known as *La Bestia* (the beast) or *El Tren de La Muerte* (the train of death).

Almost half a million migrants ride atop these trains each year on their way to the United States. Many lose arms and limbs jumping on and off these trains. Some are jolted onto the tracks and plummet to their deaths. Others fall asleep and undergo blood loss, shock, or decapitation. Eighty percent will be robbed, and 60 percent of the women will be raped. Some will be kidnapped and their families extorted. All are easy targets for harassment, robbery, and assaults from violent gangs, who know how to prey on these migrants' vulnerability for profit.[58]

As he sat atop one of the boxcars, Faustino's train suddenly stopped. Then four men with machetes, sticks, and knives got on board and began abusing, mugging, assaulting, and robbing people. They approached his friend and said, "Your money or your life!" When his friend refused, Faustino said, "They grabbed him, and I only heard painful cries. They threw him in between the train cars, and his foot was trapped between them. I heard screams, and there were cries of pain when my friend was hitting his head on the rails and the wood girders until finally I heard nothing."

When they came to Faustino, they demanded his money as well. In exchange for leaving him alone, he agreed to hand over everything he had. They spared his life, but then he was left with nothing. Begging and scavenging, he went from train to train, shelter to shelter, and state to state until he reached the border. He eventually made it to Houston. "I met a man who

---

[57] There are more than fifty shelters for migrants in Mexico, like Hermanos en el Camino [Brothers on the road], www.hermanosenelcamino.org.

[58] Joseph Sorrentino, "Train of the Unknowns," *Commonweal*, November 26, 2012.

told me I was very ill," he said, "and that I should go to Casa Juan Diego." Without a penny, a friend, or a home, there he finally found an open door, a welcoming community, and a warm bed.[59]

Many Central Americans migrating from countries like Honduras, Guatemala, and El Salvador find themselves in a perfect storm of social, economic, political, and legal conditions that contribute greatly to uprooting and displacing people like Faustino. The absence of economic opportunities in their homelands, lack of quality education, inability to support their families, and desire to unite with family members in the United States all factor into their decisions to leave home. Added to these are a state of generalized violence from gangs and cartels in recent years, the subsequent breakdown of the rule of law, and deteriorating conditions of human security.[60]

*A Faith-Based, Humanitarian Response to a Multilayered Homelessness*

When Mark and Louise Zwick began to see the plight of migrants in their own community of Houston, Texas, they knew they needed to start somewhere. They had lived in El Salvador for a period of time in the 1970s when the civil war was just starting and violence began to rip apart the country. For the next twelve years, more than seventy-five thousand people would be killed, many at the hands of government-sponsored death squads, causing an untold number of refugees to flee the nation. Witnessing the suffering of the people in that country indelibly marked their lives, making them determined to do something about it when they came back home.

When they returned to the United States, they realized that many of these same refugees had no place to stay when they arrived. "On many occasions in our anger," Mark says, "then in our tears . . . we would say to each other and to our friends, 'If we had any guts, we would open a Catholic Worker . . . to serve the poor and Spanish speaking.'"[61]

---

[59] Faustino, "A Devastating Journey North for a Migrant from Honduras to the United States," November 24, 2013, http://cjd.org/.

[60] United States Conference of Catholic Bishops, *Report of the Committee on Migration of the United States Conference of Catholic Bishops* (Washington, DC: USCCB, 2013).

[61] Mark and Louise Zwick, "Casa Juan Diego, New Catholic Worker House, Open to Serve the Poor," *Houston Catholic Worker*, June 16, 2013.

The Catholic Worker movement was founded in the 1930s by Dorothy Day and Peter Maurin. Inspired by the Gospel message and Catholic Social Teaching, and troubled by the poverty they encountered, they sought to respond to the poor of their community through education, community living, and direct service.[62] One of the cornerstones of their mission was to start houses of hospitality that not only gave the homeless a roof over their heads but also a community in which to belong. Day and Maurin realized the poor need more than food, shelter, and clothing; they also need a network of relationships that affirms their basic human dignity and gives them a place to call home.

Inspired by this vision, the Zwicks founded the Houston Catholic Worker and Casa Juan Diego (CJD) in late 1980. They began with almost nothing, yet everything—beginning with faith, prayer, and risk. They said, "The best way to start a Catholic Worker is on your knees."[63] Their work is named after the Mexican saint Juan Diego, whom the Zwicks call "a saint for nobodies."[64] He is one of the central protagonists of the drama that unfolded with Our Lady of Guadalupe in 1531, and the image preserved on his *tilma* is connected to one of the central spiritual narratives in Latin America; it is the heartbeat of the Mexican soul and of many immigrants today. Like Juan Diego, many immigrants are poor, marginalized, and exploited, "wanted here only for their cheap labor," the Zwicks write, "but are not considered human beings by many.... Like him, they do not speak the language and have no rights."[65]

*The Mission of Casa Juan Diego*

As their work took shape, the Zwicks realized their primary mission would be "to serve immigrants, refugees and the poor."[66] Inspired by Matthew 25:31–46, they labor to feed the hungry, clothe the naked, and visit those in prison, and give drink to the thirsty, accompaniment to the sick, and shelter to the homeless. There are no paid staff at Casa Juan Diego but rather full-

---

[62] William Thorn, Phillip Runkel, and Susan Mountin, eds., *Dorothy Day and the Catholic Worker Movement* (Milwaukee: Marquette University Press, 2001), 130.

[63] Mark Zwick and Louise Zwick, *Mercy without Borders: The Catholic Worker and Immigration* (Mahwah, NJ: Paulist Press, 2010), 29.

[64] Ibid., 46.

[65] Ibid., 49.

[66] Houston Catholic Worker, "What Is Casa Juan Diego?" http://cjd.org.

time "workers" who are committed to voluntary poverty, giving their time and service as a gift. They also depend greatly on outside volunteers to carry out their work and address the complex levels of homelessness that migrants and refugees experience.

By definition, migrants are uprooted and undergo a multilayered homelessness. The first and most immediate level is a *physical homelessness*. Although some find shelters en route to their destination, many times they have to sleep outside: near train tracks, on boxcars, by bus stations, under bridges, or on the ground. One Border Patrol officer shared with me the story of one migrant woman who slept on the desert floor with her daughter. When she woke up in the middle of the night, a snake was coiled up near her child's stomach. Exposed to the natural elements, migrants constantly face vulnerability on their journey and long simply for a pillow and a bed and a safe place to sleep at night.

Because so many migrants at Casa Juan Diego are undocumented, they also experience a *legal homelessness*. With few protections under the law to shelter their rights, they often do not have access to lawyers. Their compromised legal status makes them vulnerable to exploitation. Stories abound of migrants who labor at a job for a number of weeks or months, only to have their employers call the immigration authorities toward the end to avoid paying them for their work.[67]

If they find work, many immigrants labor at low-paying jobs that no one else wants, except the most desperate. They debone chickens, pick crops, and build houses. Such employment makes them especially susceptible to workplace injuries or death. Willing to take the most difficult jobs—sometimes called *3D jobs* because they are dirty, dangerous, and deadly—an immigrant a day on average dies cutting North Carolina tobacco or carving Nebraska beef, chopping down trees in Colorado, welding a balcony in Florida, trimming grass at a Las Vegas golf course, or falling from scaffolding in Georgia or other such jobs.[68]

Migrants' efforts to find such work frequently take them from their countries of origin, which cause many to also feel a *cultural homelessness*. Most are not only away from their families but away from what is familiar

---

[67] Southern Poverty Law Center, *Close to Slavery: Guestworker Programs in the United States* (Montgomery, AL: Southern Poverty Law Center, 2013).

[68] Justin Pritchard, "A Mexican Worker Dies Each Day," Associated Press, March 15, 2004, http://iatp.org.

to them. Many do not speak the language, and they are frequently exposed to traditions and customs different from those of their homeland. Unable to return home, some describe their situation as if they were "stateless persons," feeling *ni de aquí, ni de allá* (neither from here nor there). They do so with good reason: it is difficult to survive in one's hometown, yet finding a true home in the United States is often just as difficult. On many occasions, living in the United States leaves many Mexican immigrants with the feeling of absolute nonbelonging.[69]

Because they are often disconnected from family, and with few if any friends in a foreign country, immigrants often find themselves alone. Bouts of loneliness as well as depression are common, causing many to feel a *social homelessness*. Some wonder if they belong anywhere, or if anyone in their new land cares whether they live or die. One of their worst fears is that they are no one to anyone.

Compounding these difficulties, most migrants have little access to a physician, a dentist, or needed medications. Poverty, poor nutrition, contaminated water sources, infectious diseases, and other factors leave them with a litany of untreated health issues. Some are wounded on the journey or have developed hypertension, diabetes, and malnourishment. For those who have been tortured or abused, additional psychological issues need attention. In these experiences of physical, legal, cultural, social, and medical homelessness, migrants want for a place where they can be themselves, a place to belong, a place to heal, and a place to flourish—all of which can be summed up in the desire for a place to call home—even as they live away from their families and their homeland.

Casa Juan Diego responds to the multilayered needs of these homeless immigrants in a variety of ways. They have two houses of hospitality, one for men and one for women. Together they can give lodging to about one hundred people at a time. They host migrants and refugees from around the world, but the majority are from Latin America, the Caribbean, and Central America, especially Mexico, Honduras, Guatemala, and El Salvador. Others come from various African countries, including Nigeria, Ethiopia, and Eritrea, as well as some Asian countries, including China.

---

[69] For more on this subject, see John Phillip Santos, *Places Left Unfinished at the Time of Creation* (New York: Viking, 1999); Richard Rodriguez, *Hunger of Memory: The Education of Richard Rodriguez: An Autobiography* (Boston: David Godine, 1982); and Virgilio P. Elizondo, *The Future Is Mestizo: Life Where Cultures Meet* (Oak Park, IL: Meyer-Stone Books, 1988).

Casa Juan Diego offers services for immigrant children and women, especially those who are pregnant or physically battered, or whose spouses have been detained or deported. Many guests stay for a few days, others months, and some years. Even those who stay for a brief time often make friends and allies who can become their new support system in the United States.

Together with a distribution center called Casa Maria, Casa Juan Diego is able to offer help with some basic material needs, such as food, clothing, toiletries, and other necessities. Given that much of their continued stay in the United States depends on getting legal documentation, immigrants sometimes can receive assistance with finding a lawyer to help with asylum cases and legalization issues. When they cannot provide the services themselves, Casa Juan Diego tries to help find other support.

With the help of voluntary doctors, Casa Juan Diego also runs two free medical and dental clinics for immigrants. These doctors write prescriptions for migrants who suffer a range of health-care needs, with the medications paid for by Casa Juan Diego. Although an expensive undertaking, this is one of the few services—if not the only one—of its kind for people who are undocumented in the larger Houston area. When Casa Juan Diego cannot help directly, it is a source for a wide variety of referrals. They try not to turn people away without offering another option for assistance.

Some immigrants are injured as they migrate to the United States, and others are injured or disabled at work. For those maimed on trains like La Bestia or in job-related injuries, Casa Juan Diego provides various kinds of support. One important area is rent and food assistance for the paralyzed, the seriously ill, and their families. Casa Juan Diego has been supporting more than 100 of these families each month.

Casa Juan Diego also publishes a newspaper called the *Houston Catholic Worker*, which comes out six times a year in Spanish and English. The paper, in the tradition of the original *Catholic Worker* newspaper, seeks to explore and communicate the meaning of Christian faith in the context of the challenges posed by the current global economy. It does so not only by reflecting on Catholic Social Teaching and promoting the values of the Catholic Worker movement, but it also shares stories of many of the immigrant and refugee guests who come to them and the challenges they face in light of their poverty, forced displacement, and homelessness.

## Theological Foundations and Organization of Casa Juan Diego

The impetus behind the work of Casa Juan Diego rests on the memory that Christ too was homeless. From the moment he was born, Jesus was a migrant on the road. In the beginning of his life, he was a refugee. He knew the hardship of migration, and he had no place to lay his head (Mt. 8:20; Lk. 9:58). But he also knew the value of being received and welcomed. Consequently, the Church has always highlighted hospitality as one of the central virtues of Christian faith and one of the most important dimensions of its outreach to migrants and refugees.

Although Casa Juan Diego is a complex and comprehensive organization, these Catholic Workers foster a vision that treats new guests as people first—not just a case, a cause, or a number. This holistic approach allows the workers to attend to the person in their various needs, which means more than simply putting a roof over their heads. Casa Juan Diego sees itself not just as a social service agency but also a spiritual community gathered by the love of God that seeks to convey to the guests that they are valued, respected, and loved as children of God.

In Latino expressions of popular religion, this experience of homelessness and the virtue of hospitality are ritually remembered each year in the tradition of Las Posadas. *Posada* is the Spanish word for "lodging" or "accommodation." It reenacts the Holy Family's search for a place to stay just prior to the birth of Jesus and is celebrated every evening from December 16 through December 24. This nine-day prayer service, or novena, represents the nine months of Mary's pregnancy.[70] In this ritual, participant-pilgrims are turned away from place after place until finally they are offered an open door and lodging at the end of the evening. Las Posadas are now celebrated chiefly in Mexico, Guatemala, and portions of the southwestern United States.

In reenacting this journey of the Holy Family, Las Posadas not only calls attention to the plight of those who were homeless yesterday but also those who are without shelter today. The work of Casa Juan Diego is a living embodiment of Las Posadas, a journey to live out this story each and every day of the year. This ritual heightens both the importance of a ministry of hospitality to all those on the move who search for food, shelter, and community,

---

[70] Cordelia Candelaria, *Encyclopedia of Latino Popular Culture*, 2 vols. (Westport, CT: Greenwood Press, 2004).

and the awareness that the homeless poor are interconnected with the living Christ. Casa Juan Diego's work and ministry are an affirmation of, and a response to, this real presence of Christ in the person of the migrant today.

The Catholic Worker movement seeks to respond to Christ's hidden presence among the world's poor and downtrodden. Peter Maurin named this human-centered vision "the gentle personalism of traditional Catholicism."[71] Maurin wanted to bring the Gospels and the Catholic social encyclicals alive, to make them "click," and to engage the Church's mission to create a just society, beginning with what makes us all human. This means taking up the task of caring for one's brother and sister, practicing works of mercy, and establishing houses of hospitality like Casa Juan Diego.

The human person is taken seriously because the person of Christ is central to its mission. Under this light the Eucharist plays an important role in inspiring, animating, and sustaining the spiritual life of the Catholic Workers. Because of its centrality, Casa Juan Diego has created a chapel, where there has been a tabernacle with the Eucharist since its earliest days.[72] The Zwicks consider the Eucharist as central to the life and mission of Casa Juan Diego, because it means that Christ truly is at the heart of the place. "We have had Wednesday evening celebrations of the Mass with all of our guests from the beginning of Casa Juan Diego thirty-five years ago," they said. "Each week this celebration with a house full of immigrants deepens our faith and understanding and our commitment to serving the Lord in the poor. It helps us to continue to base our life and ministry on the Gospel and to realize the great dignity of the migrants with whom we are sharing the Eucharist."[73]

When they celebrate the Mass every Wednesday, all are invited, guests and workers alike. With people from countries around the world, the Mass is truly catholic. The Mass is also one of thanksgiving for the safe arrival of the guests. It is common at the service that one person from their house of hospitality shares something of their journey to the United States with the other immigrant guests and workers. This talk before the Mass links the suffering of these persons with that of Christ, and in this sacred space the migrants learn not only how to share their story but also how to find healing and support in their need and brokenness.

---

[71] Alan Brinkley, "Catholics on the Left," *New York Times*, February 13, 1983.

[72] Mark and Louise Zwick, interview by Kathleen Kollman, *Houston Catholic Worker*, July 16, 2015.

[73] Ibid.

One does not need to be at Casa Juan Diego very long before realizing that the needs of the immigrants that come to them far outstrip the resources available to provide for them. No matter how hard the staff and volunteers work, and no matter how much money they can raise, the efforts are only a fraction of what these immigrants need. "The Eucharist also gives us hope and consolation when things are not going well or when the needs of the poor are overwhelming."[74] Although this is a space where it is easy to fall into despair, the Zwicks are quick to point out that in these moments of powerlessness and need they discover ordinary miracles of the God who provides beyond measure.

In this context the Zwicks often see their ministry in light of the Gospel story of the loaves and fishes (Mt. 14:13–21; Mk. 6:31–44; Lk. 9:10–17; Jn. 6:5–15), where God transforms and multiplies what they have in order to serve the vast needs of the people who come to Jesus and the disciples. Drawing from the words of Dorothy Day, Louise said, "People who come to us have so many needs. All we can do is put in a few loaves and fishes. We only pray that the Lord can transform them because we know we can't meet all of the needs. But we hope it does make a big difference."[75]

Like Dorothy Day's, the Zwicks' vision is founded on a concern for the individual person, the common good, dignity of the human person, and transformation of the social order.[76] Their faith and activism are nurtured by the teachings of the Catholic Church, the writings of the Church Fathers, the social encyclicals of modern popes, the Prophets, the Christian Scriptures, and the Eucharist. Even as much of today's culture emphasizes one's bank account as the ultimate measure of a person's worth, the Zwicks point to the Sermon on the Mount (Mt. 5–7) as revelatory of a person's inner treasure. Their life's work rests on the corporal works of mercy as they embody the living mystery of God's mercy in Christ, who reaches out to the poorest of the world in order to affirm that they have a place in God's Kingdom. Like Cardinal Suhard, who Dorothy Day frequently quoted, they believe that obedience to Christ means living "in such a way that one's life would not make sense if God did not exist."[77]

---

[74] Ibid.
[75] Ibid.
[76] Thorn, Runkel, and Mountin, *Dorothy Day and the Catholic Worker Movement*, 130.
[77] Robert Ellsberg, ed., *Dorothy Day: Selected Writings* (Maryknoll, NY: Orbis Books: 2005), xv.

### Visiting the Imprisoned:
### The Interfaith Committee for Detained Immigrants

"I was in prison and you visited me." (Mt. 25:36 NRSV)

When Archbishop Gustavo García Siller first entered a newly constructed detention center in Dilley, Texas, he and other members of a delegation from the United States Conference of Catholic Bishops were given a tour of this modern facility. It was a model example of the strategy of the Department of Homeland Security (DHS) to control the influx of people who entered the country without proper documentation, especially the increasing number of women and migrant children coming into the United States illegally. From the narrative of the government officials, everything seemed in order. The facilities appeared clean and spacious, and given the complex challenges, it seemed a humane way to detain these immigrants.[78]

The immigrants inside the facility had a different story to tell. When the Archbishop arranged to say Mass for them, they shared many of their struggles related to the dangers they faced in their homeland, the difficulties of their journey, the insecurity in this new land, and the challenges they faced in detention. The mothers' faces especially showed fear and trepidation. My own research in countries like Honduras, El Salvador, Guatemala, and Mexico has made it abundantly clear that many of these migrants were not just *leaving* their home countries in search of better lives; they were *fleeing* them because of violence and deteriorating security.

Many had undergone traumatic experiences in their journey north to the United States. One woman said her husband had been murdered by one of the many gangs—and now her children were being targeted. Most had little to no legal assistance to help with their asylum claims. Some had severe medical conditions but were given only over-the-counter painkillers like Tylenol and Advil. Others presented with psychiatric difficulties, suicidal behavior, anxiety, and posttraumatic stress reactions with little access to mental healthcare. Some women even were forced to deliver babies in restraints.[79] As Archbishop Gustavo García-Siller asked, "My primary question is: Why? Why do we feel compelled to place in detention such

---

[78] United States Conference of Catholic Bishops, "Unlocking Human Dignity: A Plan to Transform the US Immigrant Detention System," *Journal on Migration and Human Security* 3, no. 2 (2015): 12.

[79] Ibid., 15.

vulnerable individuals—traumatized young mothers with children fleeing persecution in their home countries?"[80]

The immigration detention system throughout the world is in desperate need of reform. Not only is migration a global challenge, but immigration detention has become problematic, no matter where one looks. The United States is not alone. Even if countries need to put systems and procedures in place for removing noncitizens—and in extreme cases to protect public safety—the growing phenomenon of criminalizing migrants is a serious human rights concern. Immigrants are not only locked up, but as the United States Conference of Catholic Bishops rightly points out, their human dignity is also imprisoned.[81]

On any given day, Immigration, Customs and Enforcement (ICE) officials in the United States detain over thirty-three thousand immigrants, a number that has risen dramatically in recent decades.[82] Detention of immigrants is reaching record levels. More people are passing through the US immigration detention system each year than the federal Bureau of Prisons facilities.[83]

Criminalization has become not only a weapon for deterrence but also an opportunity for profit. Private corporations like the Corrections Corporation of America (now CoreCivic), the Geo Group, and the Management and Training Corporation have a vested interest in anti-immigrant policies because they manage almost half of the immigration detention beds for the Department of Homeland Security.[84] Not only has this approach cost taxpayers billions of dollars, but as it divides families and dehumanizes people, the human costs to immigrants are incalculable.

---

[80] United States Conference of Catholic Bishops, "Catholic, Evangelical Lutheran Bishops Visit Texas Detention Facility, Call for an End to Detention of Families," March 27, 2015, www.usccb.org.

[81] For more on the US bishops' recommendations on detention reform and alternatives to it, see United States Conference of Catholic Bishops, "Unlocking Human Dignity." This report focuses on the injustices related to family detention and the impact on families.

[82] Detention Watch Network, "The Influence of the Private Prison Industry in the Immigration Detention Business," May 2011, www.detentionwatchnetwork.org.

[83] Doris Meissner, Donald Kerwin, Muzaffar Chishti, and Claire Bergeron, *Immigration Enforcement in the United States: The Rise of a Formidable Machinery* (Washington, DC: Migration Policy Institute, 2013), 131. See also United States Conference of Catholic Bishops, "Unlocking Human Dignity," 7.

[84] Detention Watch Network, "The Influence of the Private Prison Industry."

### A Faith-Based, Humanitarian Response to Immigrant Imprisonment

The work of the US bishops and many other faith-based and humanitarian groups continues to highlight some of the deficiencies in the US immigration detention system. In a document published by the United States Conference of Catholic Bishops called *Unlocking Human Dignity: A Plan to Transform the US Immigration Detention System*, Bishop Eusebio Elizondo and Bishop Nicholas DiMarzio jointly wrote, "The immigrant detention system contributes to the misconception that immigrants are criminals and a threat to our unity, security and well-being, engenders despair, divides families, causes asylum-seekers to relive trauma, leads many to forfeit their legal claims, and fails to treat immigrants with dignity and respect."[85] DiMarzio adds, "There are ways to create a humane system and also ensure that immigrants are complying with the law, but we have created a detention industry in this country which preys upon the vulnerability of our fellow human beings, the vast majority of whom are not criminals."[86]

How can detention become more humane? What are some viable alternatives to the current system? How can families be accompanied when one of their loved ones has been deported? Many aspects of reforming the detention system need to be addressed, and one important avenue of reform is through pastoral care.

One snowy morning in January 2007, an immigration lawyer named Royal Berg and two Sisters of Mercy, Pat Murphy, RSM, and JoAnn Persch, RSM, decided to witness the separation of families they heard was occurring when people were deported.[87] They went to the Broadview Immigration Staging Center in Broadview, Illinois, to stand in solidarity with them. As Sr. JoAnn recalls,

> We stood there, and it was an incredible feeling to watch the vans and buses going to the airport. And realizing that in there were real people, with real life stories, and we were moving them like pawns on a chess game out of our country. And then we began to meet the families standing there, and we talked to them, and we began to

---

[85] United States Conference of Catholic Bishops, "Unlocking Human Dignity," 5.
[86] United States Conference of Catholic Bishops, "Unlocking Human Dignity."
[87] Interfaith Community for Detained Immigrants, "How It All Started," www.icdichicago.org.

realize what we were doing. We were ripping these families apart....
We were creating a new single-parent family poverty system.[88]

Some migrants now being deported have been in the United States with their families for twenty to thirty years.

Witnessing this reality, they decided they wanted to do more, not only praying weekly outside of Broadview but also providing pastoral care to the migrants being deported. They began by just coming to the detention center every Friday to offer a ministry of presence. In Sr. JoAnn's words,

> For a while it was just Pat and me, praying and singing. It's amid a trucking area so nobody could really hear us. And then ... Roy Berg heard that we were coming every week, so he decided that he would start coming. And then everywhere we went we talked about it, and ... [the group began to] swell. And now, during a given Friday, especially during Lent, we might have 60 people. But on a regular basis we have 30, at least.[89]

Now hundreds of people have joined their efforts, and their ministry continues to expand.

Despite their best intentions, these initial attempts to provide pastoral care to the people in immigration detention met a brick wall. As Sr. Pat describes, "We thought those men and women in there being deported must be so depressed. And they need someone to talk to. So we asked. And of course, the answer was, 'No, you can't go in there.'"[90] They made subsequent attempts to visit immigrants at the McHenry County Jail, one of many locations where migrants are detained before being processed and deported, but when they found the door closed there as well they realized they had to take their fight to the legislative arena. In Sr. JoAnn's words, "We have to change the system. It's absolutely essential. But in the meantime, we can never ever, ever forget those men and women in the orange suits, or in those vans and buses, that are already trapped in this system and who feel not human."[91]

---

[88] DetentionWatch, "Interview with Sisters Pat Murphy & JoAnn Persch," 2011, https://soundcloud.com.
[89] Ibid.
[90] Ibid.
[91] Ibid.

With the help of the Illinois Coalition for Immigration and Refugee Rights, the Sisters began fighting for a bill that would mandate access to those in immigrant detention in order to provide pastoral care, regardless of their religion. This was the beginning of the Interfaith Committee for Detained Immigrants. Although it started with the Catholic community, "It is not just a Catholic issue but a faith issue,"[92] says Sr. JoAnn. It counts among its constituencies men and women of Christian, Jewish, and Muslim faith, and they now have at least sixteen different faith groups who have joined their efforts. Together they worked to pass bill HB4613, the Access to Religious Ministry Act of 2008, in the Illinois House and Senate, which was put into law in June 2009.

*The Mission of the Interfaith Committee for Detained Immigrants*

The Interfaith Committee for Detained Immigrants (ICDI) is a faith-based nonprofit organization of twelve paid staff and over three hundred volunteers who took up this challenge of pastoral care so that God's flesh could be made real through what Sr. JoAnn describes as "incarnational relationships." Rabbi Brant Rosen from the Chicago area adds, "I think in any biblically based religion, whether it's Judaism or Christianity, you'll see over and over again commandments that we treat the immigrant with compassion, that we have one law for all who dwell in the land whether they are citizens or strangers. I find it very difficult to call yourself someone who cherishes biblical tradition and mistreat immigrants."[93]

ICDI works peacefully for immigration reform and is in frequent dialogue and collaboration with government officials entrusted with the care of migrants. ICDI also counts a number of organizations among its current partners,[94] and their principal ministries of pastoral care involve jail visits, court watch, detention visits, and postdetention follow-up and housing for people seeking asylum.

---

[92] Sr. JoAnn Persch, interview by author, Broadview, Illinois, July 24, 2015.
[93] Francine Knowles, "Prayers for Immigrants," *Chicago Sun-Times*, June 16, 2013.
[94] Among these are the 8th Day Center for Justice, Cabrini Mission Corps, Centro de Trabajadores Unidos, Chicago New Sanctuary Coalition, Clerics of St. Viator (Viatorians), Countryside Church UU, De LeSalle Christian Brothers, Illinois Coalition for Immigrant and Refugee Rights, Jewish Council on Urban Affairs, Lake Street Church, Office for Immigrant Affairs and Immigration Education of the Archdiocese of Chicago, Priests for Justice for Immigrants, Sisters and Brothers of Immigrants, Sisters of Mercy, Southwest Organizing Project, and West Suburban Action Project–PASO.

They describe their mission in the following way:

> The Interfaith Committee for Detained Immigrants is a prophetic voice for just and humane treatment of immigrants caught in the immigration detention process. We uphold the dignity and basic human rights of each individual as we stand in solidarity with our immigrant sisters and brothers as a powerful collective voice to minimize the use of detention and to seek justice. We believe that everyone, regardless of national origin, has basic human rights, including livelihood, family unity, and physical and emotional safety. We also seek to provide national leadership and models for detention work and general interfaith collaboration.[95]

Since its founding, ICDI has offered a significant model for pastoral outreach to immigrant communities.

The deportation ministry takes place on Fridays outside immigration processing centers. Initially it began at the Broadview Center but was later moved to Kankakee.[96] Volunteers assist families who have come to say good-bye to loved ones, and they advise families of what to expect before and after they are deported. They also pray on the buses with the people being deported before departure. On the buses, deportees are shackled by their hands, feet, and waists and separated from the guards and volunteers by grate dividers. In the words of ICDI, "Clergy, lay leaders and people of faith offer prayers on the buses to accompany them in their difficult journey and to let them know that people of faith stand with them and are working to change these unjust policies."[97] A prayer vigil is still held at the Broadview Processing Center, which remains an ICE facility. On the first Friday of each month the vigil is interfaith, and in the remaining weeks they pray the Rosary. In these services, people of all faiths are welcome.

Another ministry of ICDI is jail visitation. Various teams of volunteers visit detainees weekly in four locations: McHenry County Jail in Woodstock, Illinois; Kenosha County Detention Center in Kenosha, Wisconsin; Dodge

---

[95] Interfaith Community for Detained Immigrants, "Our Mission," www.icdichicago.org.

[96] The deportation ministry started at Broadview Immigration Processing Center but was moved to Jerome Combs Detention Center in Kankakee when ICE moved deportations to that location.

[97] Interfaith Community for Detained Immigrants, "Deportation Accompaniment," www.open990.org.

County Detention Center in Juneau, Wisconsin; and Jerome Combs Detention Center in Kankakee, Illinois. Immigrants in these centers are waiting for court hearings or deportation. Students, religious leaders, and people of faith accompany migrants in immigration court proceedings in what they call Court Watch. Here they are present in hearings in the mornings and afternoons from Monday through Thursday. In addition to monitoring human rights issues, they document problems in the current system in order to advocate effectively for more just policies. ICDI describes Court Watch as another way in which they offer a "ministry of presence" as a manner of advocating on behalf of immigrants and ensuring due process for their cases.[98]

ICDI also has a ministry to assist those who are released from detention. These migrants often have no family or support system in the Chicago area, and ICDI has developed an elaborate response network to help individuals during this transition. Teams of volunteers are on call and respond to a hotline to provide transportation and accompaniment needs as they seek reunification with their families outside of the Chicago area.

Because those released from detention often have nowhere to go, ICDI has started two houses of hospitality. Most of the people served in the houses are asylum seekers or have recently been granted asylum. Opened in 2014, one house is located in the former convent of St. Mary of Czestochowa Parish in Cicero, Illinois, and the other is an entire floor of the Chicago Theological Union student dormitory. As Brother Michael Gosch, who started the Post-Detention Accompaniment Network, put it, "They just release people and point them in the direction of the bus station."[99] Each house has between ten and seventeen participants from all over the world at any given time. They receive food, shelter, clothing, a small stipend, and help learning English.[100] Case managers connect them to needed legal, educational, medical, health, and faith services.

One participant was Michael, a twenty-nine-year-old man from Eritrea. After fleeing human rights violations in his home country, he presented himself to US border authorities in Texas to ask for asylum on February 27, 2013.[101]

---

[98] Interfaith Community for Detained Immigrants, "Court Watch," www.icdichicago.org.

[99] Michelle Martin, "Providing Asylum Seekers a Place to Go When Released," *Catholic New World*, February 7, 2015.

[100] For more on postdetention support packs, see Advocates for Immigrants in Detention Northwest, web.archive.org/.

[101] Martin, "Providing Asylum Seekers."

He was sent to Chicago and temporarily placed in detention, but when officials determined he was not a threat, they released him with nothing more than the clothing he wore. He knew no one in the area, nor did he have money, food, or shelter.

Marie Joseph was not so lucky. An asylum seeker in her twenties from Haiti, she was released in July 2011. No one was available to help her that day, so a volunteer lawyer brought her to the Pacific Garden Mission shelter. But when Sr. Pat returned to look for her the next day, she was nowhere to be found. Later they found her body in an abandoned building. "It just totally devastated the lawyer, it devastated her family in Georgia, and it devastated us," Sister JoAnn said.[102]

*Theological Foundations and Organization of Interfaith Committee for Detained Immigrants*

The work of ICDI is rooted in the dignity of the human person, a person's value and worth as a child of God, and the right to belong to a community. It is also grounded in an effort to stand in solidarity with those in bondage and a desire to liberate them from everything that treats them as nonpersons. "We are human beings," said one woman just before her deportation, "And we need to be treated like that."[103] The volunteers recognize this, and as Sr. JoAnn says, "Every one of these people [volunteers] is there for that reason. That they believe those men and women deserve to be treated like human beings."[104] Sr. Pat adds, "These men and women are our sisters and brothers, and so I think that's what drives me."[105]

At the core, Sr. Pat and Sr. JoAnn respond to the suffering of migrants by first affirming their basic humanity. "When you're in the detention center and you listen to . . . how they got there, (or) if you . . . watch those vans going out with men and women who are shackled and being taken away, how can we do that to scores of people?[106] . . . [In the detention center] these guys just cry. . . . They just weep."[107]

---

[102] Ibid.
[103] DetentionWatch, "Interview with Sisters Pat Murphy & JoAnn Persch," 28:40–30:02.
[104] Ibid.
[105] Ibid., 0:42–0:52.
[106] Ibid., 0:42–0:52.
[107] Ibid., 5:00–5:25.

Amid this dehumanizing and depersonalizing context, ICDI offers at least some degree of a steady, stable, and compassionate gaze of support for those whose lives are being constantly uprooted and are told their lives count for nothing. "We have the gift of getting in those places and being present," adds Sr. JoAnn. "I think it's a ministry of presence. But I also feel the obligation to go out and speak because we can be that voice [a voice for the voiceless]."[108] In this ministry they hope to incarnate the mercy of God as a living sacrament, as the body of Christ alive in the world.

Being present to the humanitarian needs of migrants is a practical way through which God becomes real to them, but also a way through which the migrant presence becomes real to the resident community. In this encounter between migrant and volunteer, both are changed, as each becomes someone to the other and they are mutually transformed. In response to their ministry, one migrant said, "You're the only people that we see face-to-face outside of the officers. . . . I think nobody even knows I'm here. And now you've come all this way to talk to me, to let me know you think I'm important?!"[109]

In cooperation with the Department of Homeland Security, faith-based leaders continue to work at developing programs to help detainees with legal and community-based case management programs that assist them with communal integration and immigration relief. The work of ICDI is one example of faith-based and humanitarian workers who are visiting those in prison. Added to these efforts are those of other organizations across the United States and other parts of the world. These include the Gatwick Detainees Welfare Group, Community Initiatives for Visiting Immigrants in Confinement (CIVIC), Souls Offering Love and Compassionate Ears (SOLACE), Grassroots Leadership Visitation, Eden Visitation Program, Friends in Hope, Refugee Immigration Ministry (RIM), Spiritual Caregiver Program, Walking Together / Caminando Juntos, Justice for Our Neighbors, Conversations with Friends, Immigrant Detainee Accompaniment Program, Casa de Paz, and Faithful Friends.[110] Nonetheless, as these conditions persist, people continue to struggle for human dignity, for family reunification, for basic human rights, and for healing from their physical and psychological trauma.

---

[108] Ibid., 6:15–6:30.
[109] Ibid., 28:40–30:02.
[110] Freedom for Immigrants, "National Visitation Network," www.endisolation.org.

When I visited the deportation center in Broadview, I asked one of the officers on duty, "How do you find these undocumented migrants?" He said, "The people in here are criminals, sex offenders, rapists, child molesters, and murderers. They come in through the court system."[111] He said nothing of the pregnant and nursing women, asylum-seekers, the very ill, the disabled, the elderly, immigrant families, and other vulnerable persons who are also tagged as criminals and deported.

Not all the officers feel this way, however, and over the years ICDI has built strong and cooperative relationships with these ICE officers, some of whom have become sensitive to the plight and needs of those detained. Critics of ICDI take issue that the organization builds relationships with ICE and see it as collaboration with those who oppress immigrants. To this, ICDI director Melanie Schikore responds with the words of the ancient playwright Terence: "I am a human being. Nothing human can be alien to me." In her own words,

> In the work of ICDI, we cannot uphold the inherent worth and dignity of immigrants if we do not acknowledge the inherent worth and dignity of all people—and that includes ICE officers. The pastoral work that we do includes them, and so in detention centers we greet them, build relationships with them, ask about their families, and treat them as the fellow human beings that they are. It doesn't mean that we agree with detention or endorse all that happens in detention centers, but we do think of everyone as children of the same creator and we know too that there are bigger systems at play than just personal choice.[112]

In more ways than one, as these officers and ICDI volunteers deal with the complex challenges that immigration poses, they stand at a complex border between the rights of migrants and their families and the rights of communities and nations to protect and regulate their borders. But no one knows the cost of these challenges more than those who are detained and deported. As fathers were separated from their children, and wives from their husbands—some after being together in the United States for

---

[111] ICE officer, conversation with author, Broadview Detention Center, Broadview, Illinois, July 24, 2015.
[112] Personal correspondence with Melanie Schikore, July 18, 2017.

decades—these migrants were boarded on a bus that was a cage on wheels. I walked on board to say a few words. As if speaking through a peep-hole in a prison cell, I said, "We are praying for you on the long journey ahead and want to let you know you are not alone." "Thank you for your prayers," said one man, with his heart torn asunder. "We appreciate all you are doing. But what about our families? It is a total injustice that we are being separated from our loved ones, and we beg you to do something about it."[113]

### Burying the Dead: Reuniting Families

> If I saw the dead body of any of my people thrown out behind the wall of Nineveh, I would bury it. (Tob. 1:17 NRSV)

When Rosa Dominguez left her home in the Yucatan region of Mexico in 2003, she headed north to the US border. She was thirty-two years old and the mother of two young children. With few resources and little education, she wanted to make it to the Pacific Northwest of the United States, where she hoped to find work. With the help of guides, she made it to the border, but as she was making her way through the Arizona desert, she sprained her ankle and had trouble walking. She began to lag behind and some members of her group tried to help her keep up. The journey was long, and it became difficult to carry her and continue themselves. Eventually they had to move ahead but they said they would return, leaving her to fend for herself. In the sand and the sun, Dominguez died alone in the desert, and once she was found, all that remained were her bones.[114]

When Dominguez passed away, her family had no idea what had happened. Families like hers are often tortured by questions such as: Did she make it safely across the border? Will she ever come back home? Is she still alive? For these families the drama of immigration involves bringing closure to the unknown whereabouts of loved ones and giving them a dignified burial.

To avoid being identified as a foreign national if caught by the Border Patrol, many do not carry any papers with them. This anonymity makes it

---

[113] Detainee, comment to author, Broadview Detention Center, July 25, 2015.
[114] Meghna Chakrabarti, "Anthropologist Works to Return Migrants' Remains," *Here and Now*, November 21, 2013, www.wbur.org; and Molly Hennessy, "Great Read: Texas Scholar's Work to ID Immigrant Corpses Is Gratifying and Sad," *Los Angeles Times*, November 1, 2013.

exceedingly difficult to determine identity of people when their remains are found along the border. Some who perish on the journey disappear in the desert sands without a trace. Some are discovered and are buried in mass pauper graves in the American Southwest. Some are found interred in nothing more than a milk crate or a garbage bag.[115]

*A Faith-Based, Humanitarian Response to the Nameless, Migrant Dead*

Disturbed by the numbing indifference to migrants like Dominguez, Lori Baker has made it her life's work to identify those who have died along the border in order to reconnect them with their families and make possible a proper burial. As a forensic anthropologist at Baylor University, Baker goes out to cemeteries and other sites where multiple individuals have been placed in a common grave. Instead of studying how their remains decompose in the natural elements, she seeks to discover their identity by matching DNA samples of the deceased with those from families in sending countries in hopes of bringing closure to an ordeal of agonizing uncertainty.[116]

The turning point for Baker came when she went out on a forensic case a number of years ago and visited a local sheriff's office. On the sheriff's desk was the skull of a young person, and he was using it to hold office supplies. "He had pens and pencils in the eye socket of this person," Baker said, "so that's when I decided something had to be done."[117] Baker's first identification was Rosa Dominguez. After the Pima County medical examiner sent the recovered remains to Baker, she began to do the DNA analysis to match them with records of the missing. They "were skeletonized because of the heat," Baker said, "and because of the weather. We tend to see mostly skeletonized cases," she said, "especially since people are crossing in these extremely desolate areas. They're not found for a long period of time, if they're found at all."[118]

After a DNA test matched Dominguez with her mother, Baker reached out to Rosa's family. At times Baker wondered if it would have been better

---

[115] Lori Baker, "Students Toil in Texas to Give Names and Burials to Migrants," *Here and Now*, August 4, 2014, http://hereandnow.wbur.org.

[116] StoryCorps, interview with Lori Baker, *NPR Morning Edition*, September 19, 2014, transcript at www.wnyc.org.

[117] Ibid.

[118] Chakrabarti, "Anthropologist Works to Return Migrants' Remains," https://www.wbur.org/hereandnow/2013/11/21/return-migrants-remains

if her mother did not know how she died, hoping that perhaps she might return home someday. Baker says, "When we have an identification it's resolution. But the families are going to know the horrible things that happened to their loved one. They die of heat stroke. It's exposure. And it's really overwhelming when you're holding them in your hands and you see the blisters that are on the feet of these individuals."[119] But once she contacted Rosa's mother, she told Baker, "No. The hope eats you alive every day. And now they say they are blessed because they're able to lay flowers on her grave."[120]

Unlike with Dominguez, many times Baker cannot make a positive identification, and the identities of these migrants are still a mystery.[121] "The worst case is a young boy that we have in the lab, and he carried this backpack with a soccer ball in it, and he's probably somewhere around 15 years old," Baker said. "And we have no idea who he is, and it's just devastating. And I probably think about him at least once a day, if not more, and have no idea what else we can do. It overwhelms me quite a bit.... So I usually save it until I'm in the laboratory by myself, and at night when I'm with my husband. [When I go home] ... I hold my boys close, and I cry for all of these families."[122]

*The Mission of Reuniting Families*

To advance this work, Baker founded an organization in 2003 called the Reuniting Families Project (RFP), overseen by the International Consortium of Forensic Identification. It describes its mission as follows:

> The RFP was created to establish a system for the identification of the remains of deceased undocumented immigrants found along the U.S./Mexico border. The RFP is now a consortium of

---

[119] Ibid.

[120] "Scientist IDs Bodies of Migrants, Helping Families Find Closure," *NPR Morning Edition*, September 19, 2014, www.npr.org.

[121] As Baker notes, sometimes the bodies that are found have positive identification. Some have no identification to avoid further problems if apprehended. Some have false identification. These factors complicate the identification process. In Dominguez's case, she had identification with her, and Baker's DNA research was able to confirm a positive match with her ID. For more, see Chakrabarti, "Anthropologist Works to Return Migrant Remains."

[122] Ibid.

forensic scientists who recover the remains of unidentified individuals from pauper graves in cemeteries along the U.S. Southern border. Attempts are made to associate the remains with law enforcement case reports but this is often difficult due to the lack of grave markers and the lack of cemetery records or maps designating individuals. RFP scientists then perform a full forensic anthropological analysis, take samples for DNA, stable isotope and elemental analyses, enter the information into missing persons databases and share this information with organizations representing the families of the missing. The ultimate goal is to determine identities and returning the deceased to their families.[123]

Baker works in partnership with another major initiative called Beyond Borders. It links scholars and students, most notably from Baylor University, Indianapolis University, and Texas State University, who work together to identify those migrants who have perished in their journey to the United States. Much of their work emerges from exhumations of migrant remains done at Sacred Heart Burial Park in Brooks County, Texas.[124]

Dr. Krista Latham, who directs the Molecular Anthropology Laboratory at the University of Indianapolis, says, "They are working to prevent deaths, to identify the deceased, and to aid the living."[125] To help with this identification, they look at what clothing they were wearing, their dental work, and DNA composites. They also work with human rights agencies and the National Missing and Unidentified Persons Systems (NamUS) to see if there are matches with those reported missing. Since they started, they have exhumed more than one hundred sets of remains. "These are the disappeared and the invisible, the silent," Latham says. "No one is working to give them a voice, and they deserve it."[126]

When authorities find their bodies in the desert, they become a number. Case 0435 died about a mile from the nearest road and was found with a MacGregor baseball in his backpack. Case 0519 had pages torn from a

---

[123] International Consortium for Forensic Identification, www.reunitingfamilies.org.

[124] "Mass Immigrant Graves Uncovered in South Texas Cemetery," *Washington Post*, June 21, 2014.

[125] Beyond Borders, "Even the Slightest Contributions Make a Difference," January 14, 2020, http://beyondborders.uindy.edu.

[126] Ananda Rose, "The Mystery of Case 0425," *Scientific American* 312, no. 6 (2015): 70.

Spanish Bible containing Psalms and the book of Revelation. Case 0377 was found wearing a hollow cross with a single grain of rice inside. One side of the grain read *Sara*, and the other *Rigo*.[127]

According to the Border Patrol, from October 2000 through 2016, at least 6,023 people have died in the border states of Arizona, California, New Mexico, and Texas. This means more migrants have died crossing the southwestern border of the United States than in the terrorist attacks of September 11 and Hurricane Katrina combined.[128] As staggering as these numbers are, they are only a portion of those who perish in the desert borderlands while trying to make it to the other side. "I would say for every one we find," said Sheriff Urbino Martinez of Brooks County, Texas, "we're probably missing five."[129]

The mounting death toll has made this territory into a humanitarian crisis. "If these were deaths as a result of a mass flood or an earthquake or a major plane crash," says sociologist Daniel E. Martinez of George Washington University, "people would be talking about this as being a mass disaster."[130] Because the migrant remains accumulate slowly, the scale of the tragedy remains largely hidden from the public eye. And when they are found, many have been ravaged by vultures, feral hogs, and other scavengers. The ongoing work of researchers and humanitarian groups is to give some sense of humanity and dignity to people who have become only numbers and statistics in the public eye. "We have to have a way of tracking cases," said Timothy P. Gocha, a forensic anthropologist with Texas State University's Operation Identification, "but no one deserves to be just a number. The idea is to figure out who they are, and give them their name back."[131]

*Theological Foundations and Organization of Reuniting Families*

Baker's work transcends any formal affiliation with organized religion, but her motivations stem in part from her own faith and her family background. "I came from a family that was a lower-middle-class family. We didn't have a lot

---

[127] Manny Fernandez, "A Path to America, Marked by More and More Bodies," *New York Times*, May 4, 2017.

[128] The toll from September 11 and Katrina amounted to about forty-eight hundred people. Ibid.

[129] Ibid.

[130] Ibid.

[131] Ibid.

of resources. I'm a first-generation college student. And I can't imagine if my family were tasked with finding me in a foreign nation. I don't think they'd be able to do it, and they wouldn't know where to begin. And so I can imagine what these families must be going through in trying to find information and being so desperate and so little being done on our side of our border."

Her own religious convictions also have strongly influenced her work. "I also am driven by my faith. I'm a Catholic, and I believe all life is sacred, and it seems my duty to give dignity to these individuals by giving them their names."[132] Even so, the work is very difficult. At times Baker wonders if she should even continue to do it. "I would love not to do this anymore," she said, "but I don't think I have it in me not to. Especially when we have an eleven-year-old child and I know we probably won't figure out who he is and his mom's probably grieving somewhere. It's . . . really something I don't know that I'll ever get over if we don't figure out who his family is."[133]

Like the volunteers of organizations we have looked at in this section, the politics in Washington, DC, have direct implications on Lori Baker's work. The more walls that are built along the border, the greater the risks migrants will take crossing the border in the hopes they might have a chance at securing amnesty. Recent political policies have deterred some from making the dangerous trek, but those who do make the decision to cross the border are put at even greater risks. "And with that," Baker explains, "we're seeing an increased number of deaths."[134]

When asked if she was making a political statement, she said, "No, this is a statement about human rights."[135] For Baker, there is no confusion about mixing faith with politics. Rather, she sees herself as living out the social and political implications of a Christian commitment. On an even more fundamental level, she is trying to make visible those who have become invisible, which involves giving some measure of dignity to those who have died in their search for better lives. "When someone is interred in a milk crate or a garbage bag, no one can feel comfortable and good with that," she says. "What's been most disturbing to me has been the lack of response in this growing trend of children crossing the border. . . . So these children are coming by themselves without anyone looking out for their well-being. And

---

[132] Chakrabarti, "Anthropologist Works to Return."
[133] Baker, "Students Toil in Texas."
[134] Ibid.
[135] Ibid.

it's disturbing.... We barely find the remains of adults. Probably one in ten of those that die on these large 65,000-acre ranches are ever found. Children's remains are so much smaller; they're just lost forever."[136] Because the deteriorating situation in many countries south of the border means more and more young children will try to cross, Baker worries the situation will only get worse. "As children, they're just not able to regulate the heat, and they get left behind. We found quite a few alive the last trip that I made down to the border, but they'd been left [behind] because they weren't quick enough to keep up with the adults."[137]

Alongside the work of groups like Reuniting Families and Beyond Borders, a faith-based humanitarian organization in California called Border Angels is making it their mission to bury the dead with dignity. Since Operation Gatekeeper started in 1994, what Border Angels refers to as "one of the US government's most inhumane border enforcement policies ever," some estimate that more than eleven thousand people have died in their perilous trek across the desert.[138] As Enrique Morones, the founder of Border Angels, says, "We don't want to forget these people."[139] In addition to his organization's other humanitarian work, Morones leads a monthly pilgrimage to the cemetery in Holtville, where he brings flowers and wooden crosses to honor dead border crossers and to remember their humanity.

Like Lori Baker, he hopes to persuade government officials to fund DNA testing of bodies to identify the remains of men, women, and children buried in places like a cemetery in Holtville, California, where apparently many unidentified immigrants have been interred. There are also places in San Diego where immigrants are buried next to the train tracks, beside a road, without any markers. According to Claudia Smith, a lawyer for the California Rural Legal Assistance Foundation, they are literally dumped in these places. In the cemetery in Holtville, California, several hundred unidentified migrants were buried because their remains were beyond recognition when they were found. These have simple brick-sized head stones that read, "John Doe" or "Jane Doe." So little attention was given to these markers that one I saw read, "Jhon Doe." But lest these people be forgotten, humanitarian and faith-based organizations

---

[136] Ibid.
[137] Chakrabarti, "Anthropologist Works to Return."
[138] Border Angels, "Water Drops," www.borderangels.org.
[139] Miriam Raftery, "Dying to Come to America—Immigrant Death Toll Soars; Water Stations Sabotaged," *East County Magazine*, September 2008.

have put up crosses next to these headstones, and along the border wall as well, with the inscription "No Olivdado," (not forgotten).[140]

While authorities most often find migrants after they have died, sometimes they find them in their last moments of life. When dispatch supervisor Monica Espinoza of Dimmit County, Texas, received a distress call from Francisco Gonzalez, he said he was lost in the desert after his group had scattered through the brush running from Border Patrol agents. Lost and disoriented, he called 911 for help, and Ms. Espinosa stayed on the phone with him for almost two hours. Even after sending out dispatchers and deputies into the field to rescue him, he could not be located. Realizing his impending fate, Francisco pleaded with Monica to call his fiancé in Houston. "He gave me her phone number," Ms. Espinoza said. "He kept telling me, 'Call her and tell her I didn't make it. Call her and tell her I love her and for her to take care of our baby.'"[141]

**Living Out a Renewed Narrative of Migration**

We have looked at migration from the perspective of the Judgment of the Nations as recounted in the Gospel of Matthew. We have examined different groups in the United States living out the works of mercy. And we have sought to highlight not simply individual responses to the global migration crisis but organizations that have tried to live out a different narrative than the prevailing culture. In addition to acts of direct service to the poor, we have seen how their work involves political advocacy, research, and education. Their generous response to the needs of migrants and refugees around the world not only challenges the existing narratives operative in society but also opens up new possibilities of living out a different narrative that make it possible to create a more just and humane society reflective of the God of life.

In place of the messages that communicate that migrants are unwelcome, unworthy, and unwanted, these individuals and organizations have tried to reveal the heart of Jesus Christ, who as Pope Francis puts it, is "the face of the Father's mercy" (Pope Francis, *Misericordiae Vultus*). It recognizes that, to limit compassion to the borders of one's nationality, family, or self is a migration toward disintegration. For those on a trajectory toward

---

[140] "'Border Angels' Tend Cemetery of Unknowns," KQED Public Radio, September 2–4, 2011.

[141] Fernandez, "A Path to America."

disintegration, a theology of migration cannot make sense, since it will always be news from a foreign land. From this perspective, if the term *alien* is to be used at all, it would be descriptive not of those who lack political documentation but of those who have so disconnected themselves from God and others that they are incapable of seeing in the vulnerable stranger a mirror of themselves, a reflection of Christ, and an invitation to human solidarity.

# Conclusion

## "Go in Peace": A Sacramental Vision of Migration

*A guru asked his disciples how they could tell when the night had ended and the day begun. One said, "When you see an animal in the distance and can tell whether it is a cow or a horse." "No," said the guru. "When you look at a tree in the distance and can tell if it is a neem tree or a mango tree." "Wrong again," said the guru. "Well, then, what is it?" asked his disciples. "When you look into the face of any man and recognize your brother in him; when you look into the face of any woman and recognize in her your sister. If you cannot do this, no matter what time it is by the sun, it is still night.*[1]

In a time when there are more migrants and refugees than at any point in human history, this book has been about moving from the darkness of alienation to the light of reconciliation. Amid prevailing narratives that demean and dehumanize, it has tried to stimulate a new imagination about what it means to be human before God and to journey together with one another. Offering a perspective that unites and reconciles—rather than divides and separates—this book has argued that the long journey of human life is about moving from otherness to oneness. It has tried to illumine how our migration through this world is fundamentally about the journey toward communion with God and one another.

In the search for more liberating narratives of migration, we have looked to the Christian story, especially as narrated through the Liturgy

---

[1] William Dych, ed., *Anthony De Mello: Selected Writings* (Maryknoll, NY: Orbis Books, 1999), 90.

of the Eucharist. Following the structural flow of the Roman Rite, we have explored in more depth the gathering narratives, the scriptural narratives, the sacramental narratives, and the mission narratives. Seen together, they have helped illumine the path of our movement from God, with God, and to God.

The first part gave us a view of the long story of migration and its integral relationship to our biological, historical, political, and spiritual genes. We also examined how migration today is a sign of the times that has brought out the best and worst in us. Amid many negative narratives that keep us from seeing our God-imaged humanity in ourselves and the other, we asked how theology can open up a way to thinking more deeply about who we are on this journey of life and where we are going together as a human community.

In the second part of the book, we initiated a more in-depth theological investigation of the topic of migration under the light of the Sacred Scriptures. We examined a biblical spirituality of migration as narrated in the Old Testament, Psalms, the early church, and the Gospels. As we explored the lives and stories of migrants in the Scriptures, we also considered their connection to core biblical themes and their relationship to the global migration and refugee crisis. A deeper examination of the stories from biblical times gave us new insight into those migrating today, and the stories of those migrating today opened up new ways of understanding these biblical texts.

Reading contemporary stories of migrants under the light of the Scriptures also created a space to reflect on the ways that language shapes our narrative interpretation of reality, how these narratives shape our values, and how these values in turn shape our attitudes and our responses to those on the move. We analyzed how one group in England used the path of Chaucer's *Canterbury Tales* to tell new stories about refugees in order to bring attention to issues of detention, deportation, and contemporary migration policies. Through the lens of one man's story, we highlighted not just the economic, political, and social costs but all the human costs of the migrant journey. In doing so, we sought to make more visible the stories of "invisible migrants" in order to awaken people to the need for more humane discourse and sustainable solutions.

In the third part of the book, we moved toward a sacramental view of a vision of reconciliation. Building on the foundational biblical themes of table, kingdom, Passover, and Pope Francis' visit to Lampedusa, we explored ways to think about the body of Christ in light of today's migrants, who are often considered no-bodies in the eyes of the world. As we named their desire to become some-body, and their connection to every-body, we brought out how the body of Christ helps transform prevailing narratives that exclude and discriminate into narratives that include and unite. We also examined how the story of Jesus reveals an alternative and more life-giving story. Drawing us into a different way of living and being in the world, this story calls those who follow him to pass over from an old way of life to a new one, which bears fruit in empathy, dignity, justice, and human solidarity.

Finally, in the last part of the book, we explored some of the contours of Christian mission in an age of migration. We discussed how Communion is not just about receiving the body of Christ in church but also about becoming the body of Christ for the world. This happens when Christ's presence becomes embodied through a life of compassionate concern, beginning with the last and least of society. As faith-based, humanitarian organizations have put into practice the story of Jesus through the works of mercy, they have made the presence of Christ real through acts of loving service. These ministries have helped make more visible the invisible love of God by becoming bread for the world as the body of Christ.

As we have explored how this Eucharistic vision can help forge new narratives about migration, we have seen that migration can never be reduced to politics, economics, or culture. Beyond all of these, migration is a sacramental issue. It opens a window to spiritual truths that reveal our divine origin, our fraternal interconnection, and our homeward journey. As we seek to build a more just, humane, and peaceful world, this means that the migrant can never be the other from whom I am disconnected, but a brother and sister whose well-being and destiny are inextricably bound to my own.

## The Liturgies of Society and the Search for Authentic Worship

While this book has highlighted many different ways that migration symbolizes who we are in this world, it has also exposed many fears and vulnerabilities. These greatly contribute to making migration such a vexing and controversial issue. More often than not, migration triggers anxieties related to security, scarcity, difference, and other factors, leaving us feeling ambivalent, defensive, and protective of what we have and fearful of what we may lose. These emotions, too, inform our theological reflection because they bring us to different kinds of borders: between the desire to help but the fear of being hurt, the impulse to welcome but the anxiety of losing something important, the promise of new relationships but also the resistance to change. In many different ways, migrants bring to the surface what is deepest in our hearts, which is one reason why our reaction to those on the move may be so strong. And so important. As it triggers fears and uncertainties, migration brings us face-to-face with what guides us on the journey of life and what risks we are willing to take in response to our own vulnerability and that of others.

In our navigation through this world, we must all work out our values, emotions, and beliefs. No one is dispensed from this task, not even those who claim they are agnostic or atheist. This book has approached the subject of migration from a Christian perspective, but it has also done so in the context of other theological points of view. In addition to other religions, the modern world has its own gods, creeds, and doctrines, and—in this sense—its own religion. This means we are doing theology all of the time, whether we recognize it as such or not.

The word *religion* (Latin: *religare* [to bind together]) deals with how we work out what holds our life together and live out what matters most to us. If we do not have a particular religion, we will ultimately need to create one, because in some form or another everyone must work out life's questions in our migration through this world. The central issue, then, is not *whether we believe in God or not*, but *what G/god we believe in* and who we become as a result.

Because the G/god of our lives is the one to whom we give our hearts, the greatest threat to building a better world is not atheism but idolatry. Idolatry—the fashioning of false gods—not only does not liberate us, but also creates many disorders in our world today. Idols like nationalism, money-theism, excessive self-interest, and others lure us away from our highest values and greatest good. When we worship false gods, the world loses its balance, and these disorders fragment communities, create injustice, and thwart human development.

When conditions become so disordered that people cannot live dignified lives and provide for their basic needs in their homeland, they migrate elsewhere. We have argued that migration is not a problem in itself, but a symptom of deeper disorders that uproot people and cause them to move. Much more research is needed on this connection between the idols of the modern world and its connection to migration, but this work has tried to offer insight into what it means to be human before God and how we can journey with each other in a more life-giving way.

Because the modern world has its own gods, it has its own liturgies too.[2] Some of these integrate us and bring life, healing, justice, and connection, but others alienate us and take us off the path of the homeward journey.[3] Many of the alienating ones come through messages of Main Street and Wall Street, as well as the undercurrents of the sports, entertainment, and political cultures. These liturgies shape our lives, values, and ultimately our identities. If we look closely enough, we can see that each has its own vision of what it means to be human and its own promises of what is needed for salvation. Because many of these global liturgies are structured to prioritize profit over people, the self over the common good, and our own comfort over mercy and humanitarian concern, unless we change or resist them, they will change us.

Without consciously reflecting on our operative patterns of worship, without re-scripting the messages that are programmed into us in modern society, and without allowing our minds and hearts to be renewed spiritually, we default into the doctrines of the marketplace, the anthropology preached by popular culture, and the liturgies of the media. It is both a personal and collective responsibility to critically assess which of these help us, and which of them hurt us, in navigating our way toward God, community, and our true selves. In the end, the legitimacy of faith can only be assessed by the people we become and the quality of our relationships.

The dangers of idolatry and hollow worship, however, are not limited to the secular realm. From earliest days, the prophets of Old Testament times made it very clear that religious people are especially prone to idolatry. Because of the human tendency to make God into our own disordered image and likeness—rather than to be conformed into God's image and likeness—the church must always be in the process of constant renewal if it is to

---

[2] For more on the topic of secular liturgies, see Anastasia E. Somerville-Wong, "Secular Liturgies," *Secular Studies*, no. 1 (2019): 229–70.

[3] In a similar way, John Hogan notes, "The jury is still out as to whether globalization will prove a blessing or a curse to humanity. Thus far, however, it has had a killing effect on the world's poor, local cultures, and the environment. In a sense globalization has become a liturgy writ-large—with matching vestments, rituals, music, drama, food and text. It has its rubrics, hierarchy, acolytes, and parishioners—only the poor are left out." John P. Hogan, "People of Faith and Global Citizens: Eucharist and Globalization," in *Liturgy and Justice: To Worship God in Spirit and in Truth*, ed. Anne Y. Koester (Collegeville, MN: Liturgical, 2002), 57–58.

pass over into a new way of living and being in the world. Even the church itself can become an idol! From this perspective it is not enough to simply call oneself Christian and go to church as a matter of religious obligation. Nor is it enough to obey all the rules that the church teaches. Nothing is more lamentable than an indifferent or corrupt heart with a religious veneer.

This is not to say that Christians cannot disagree on different ways of working out the issues posed by a complex problem like global migration. But if we find in ourselves no connection to those who are crossing borders and dying in the deserts and open seas, and we ignore their struggle to live dignified lives amid hardship and persecution, then bigger issues are at stake than migration. The migration in this world that matters the most is the migration into the heart of God, which can never be separated from a common journey with others. The words of one humanitarian worker in Central America are particularly apt when she said, *Si el migrante no es tu hermano, Dios no es tu Padre* (If the migrant is not your brother or sister, God is not your Father).

### Toward a New Narrative about Migration

This process of human transformation is a lifelong process. Passing over into new, life-giving narratives about migration is part of that process, and it is central to integral, human development. The path toward this renewal is facilitated by a willingness to change and a contemplative spirit. In an address to the Roman Synod of Bishops in 2012, Anglican archbishop Rowan Williams put it this way:

> The humanity we are growing into in the Spirit, the humanity that we seek to share with the world as the first fruits of Christ's redeeming work, is a contemplative humanity.... Contemplation is very far from being just one kind of thing that Christians do: it is the key to prayer, liturgy, art and ethics, the key to the essence of a renewed humanity that is capable of seeing the world and other subjects in the world with freedom—freedom from self-oriented, acquisitive habits and the distorted understanding that comes from them. To put it boldly, contemplation is the only ultimate answer to the unreal and insane world that our financial systems and our advertising culture and our chaotic and unexamined emotions encourage us to inhabit. To learn contemplative practice is to learn

what we need so as to live truthfully and honestly and lovingly. It is a deeply revolutionary matter.[4]

When we more deeply immerse ourselves in such contemplation, we are able to discern a unity at work beyond all that makes us different. Migrants I have met over the years see this very clearly. As one said, "It is not about *Los Estados Unidos* [the United States], because *estamos unidos* [we are united]."

As we are shaped by this sacramental imagination and Eucharistic vision, we begin to build bridges rather than walls;[5] we connect rather than divide; we see what we share in common rather than what makes us different. Because the walls we build around us only are outwardly visible signs of the walls we build within us, the work of the human journey is the work of reconciliation. If we alienate ourselves from those in need, we not only become aliens to our own humanity, but we also deport our own hearts into a foreign land.

A life of authentic worship leads us to look at the world differently because it realizes that we are not just migrants in this world but also pilgrims in it.[6] We journey not just as tourists toward some general destination but as children of God walking toward an eternal homeland and a lasting dwelling. The more we become transformed by the One who has first loved us, the more we will find our way to our homeland. But unless we change, we never move forward. As Mark Nepo notes, "To journey without being changed is to be a nomad. To change without journeying is to be a chameleon. To journey and to be transformed by the journey is to be a pilgrim."[7]

---

[4] Archbishop Rowan Williams, Address to the Synod of Bishops, October 10, 2012, www.episcopalnewsservice.org.

[5] Unfortunately, we are moving in the opposite direction. At the end of World War II, the world had seven walls. In 1989, fifteen. Now it has over seventy-seven. For more on this topic, see Elisabeth Vallet, ed., *Borders, Fences and Walls: State of Insecurity* (London: Routledge, 2016).

[6] At Vatican II, the Church reaffirmed that her identity in this world is as a pilgrim. *Lumen Gentium* notes that "The Church, 'like a stranger in a foreign land, presses forward amid the persecutions of the world and the consolations of God,' announcing the cross and death of the Lord until He comes. By the power of the risen Lord it is given strength that it might, in patience and in love, overcome its sorrows and its challenges, both within itself and from without, and that it might reveal to the world, faithfully though darkly, the mystery of its Lord until, in the end, it will be manifested in full light" (8).

[7] Mark Nepo, *The Book of Awakening: Having the Life You Want by Being Present to the Life You Have* (Boston: Conari Books), 2000, 34.

"In the evening of life," wrote John of the Cross, "we will be judged on love alone." While this perspective may not resolve all the complex challenges surrounding migration, it at least keeps our hearts focused on the big picture of what matters in the end. When we can move from fear-fueled mindsets of scarcity to faith-filled hearts grateful for God's abundance, we become more conscious that all we have is a gift, that we are stewards and not owners of things, and that all we have in this world is meant not just for ourselves but for all. As we move forward together, we can then pass over from the old creation to a new one and create the community of sharing and solidarity that leads to the peace that is beyond all human understanding.

In the Talmud, there is a story about an old farmer in the land of Israel. When he died the farmer left his land to his two sons. One was married and had a large family, while the other was single. They lived in close proximity to each other and each worked his land growing wheat. When harvest time arrived, each was blessed with a bountiful crop and piled up his grain for long-term storage. The unmarried brother, observing his good fortune, thought to himself that God had blessed him with more than he needed, whereas his brother, who was blessed with a large family, could surely use more. He arose in the middle of the night and secretly took from his grain and put it in his brother's pile. Similarly, the married brother thought to himself that he was fortunate to have children who will care for him in his old age, while his brother will depend on what he saved. He, too, arose in the middle of the night and quietly transferred grain from his pile to his brother's. In the morning, each pondered why there was no noticeable decrease in his own pile, and so they repeated the transfer the next night. These nocturnal activities went on for several nights until one night the brothers bumped into each other. In that instant, in the dark of night, the glow of brotherly love lit up the mountain sky; they each understood what the other had been doing and fell into each other's arms in a loving embrace. According to the legend, when God saw that display of human love, he selected the site for his Temple. It still stands there today in Jerusalem.[8]

If we could live under that light, we would know the gift of God's promised freedom, pass over into a new creation, and find the way to our eternal homeland.

---

[8] For more on this story and its sources, see Ari Z. Zivotofsky, "What's the Truth about ... the Legend of Two Brothers and the Temple Mount?," https://jewishaction.com.

# Acknowledgements

I would like to thank in particular many friends and colleagues at the University of Notre Dame, especially those from the Kellogg Institute for International Studies, the Institute for Latino Studies, the Department of Theology, the Institute for Scholarship in the Liberal Arts, the Keough School of Global Affairs, and the Provost's Office. I am especially grateful for the help of Tim Matovina, Fulata Moyo, and Alan Hilliard.

The research needed for this project was labor, time, and cost-intensive. I am grateful to the Louisville Institute for their assistance through the Sabbatical Grant for Researchers. I would also like to thank the generosity of Mike and Liz Lafortune; Ed and Macrina Hjerpe; Don and Diane McAllister; Jim and Ruth Shannon; Hoberto and Maria Serrano; Michael and Janet Feeley; Bill McMurtrie; Bill, Joanne, and Bridget Brocksmith; Terry and Nicola Mullen; Tom and Sandi Schreier; and Scott and Loretta Dahnke.

For more than a decade I have served as a consultant to the United States Conference of Catholic Bishops' Committee on Migration and Refugee Services. Not only has this role given me insight into the committed work of the bishops in responding to the needs of migrants around the world, but it also has enabled me to accompany them on delegations to understand the plight of migrants around the world.

The Vatican Dicastery for Promoting Integral Human Development was also very helpful in developing and advancing this work. I am especially grateful to Fabio Baggio, CS, and Cardinal Michael Czerny, SJ, the undersecretaries dedicated to the work of migrants and refugees, and Luis Liberman, Gabriela Sacco, and Msgr. Lucio Ruiz for all their support and collaboration. I would especially like to thank Pope Francis for his faithful witness to the God of Life, his foreword to this book, and his tireless efforts on behalf of the most vulnerable.

My fellow religious brothers and sisters of the Congregation of Holy Cross have also been sources of constant support and encouragement in the writing of this text, as well as many students and research assistants who have also assisted me in developing this work. In particular I would like to thank Colleen Cross, Jude Ash, Joy Lankford-McNamee, Emily Hunt, Caleb Pine, Esther Terry, John Marchese, Chris Angel, Thomas Doran, Raul Zegarra, Audrey Seah, Katherine Elliot, Kathleen Kollman, Gabriella Perez, Madeline Foley, Camila Antelo Iriarte, Caroline Sherry, Lauren Fox, Mary Kathleen Natelson, and Mary Stommes.

I would also like to express my thanks to M. Daniel Carroll Rodas, Elena Segura, Royal Berg, Sr. JoAnn Persch, RSM, and Sr. Pat Murphy, RSM, Fr. Ed Shea, OFM, and Melanie Schikore for all the work they are doing on immigration detention in the greater Chicago area. They not only taught me about the hopes and challenges of the migrant journey but especially how it is transformed through the unmerited gift of God's grace.

I would especially like to thank Mary Miller, who passed away in June 2020, for her kind and generous spirit, her servant heart, and her precise and thorough editing and for tending to countless administrative details in this manuscript and in virtually every piece of writing I have done over the last two decades.

Most of all I am indebted to the migrants at borders around the world who have shared with me their stories of their inner and outer journeys. I would particularly like to thank the Ruvalcaba family, who are now a sizable tribe. Many migrants and friends of the Valley Missionary Program in Coachella, California, and throughout various parts of Mexico, in particular, have been my constant inspiration for this work and have provided so many spaces of transformative dialogue. In the end, this book is written for them and all those who are on the move today. Not only am I a different person because of who they are, but I approach my own journey of faith with so much more hope, life, and generosity than I ever would have without the chance to share my journey through this world with them.

Last, but certainly not least, I would like to thank my good friend Virgilio Elizondo, who has so greatly influenced so much of my life, work, and scholarship. In the seventeen years we journeyed together, he not only helped me trust my questions, especially as they stretched beyond the commonly accepted contours of academic theology, but he also encouraged me to explore the new theological territory posed by the phenomenon of migration and the suffering of the poor. We began teaching at the University of Notre Dame in 2000, along with Timothy Matovina and Gustavo Gutiérrez. Together we created a community of friends, interested in common themes, and began working together on common projects. Their companionship with Christ in mission has changed my life and has bestowed on me ineffable gifts beyond measure and without end.

The legacy of Virgil's thought and the generosity of his soul will never be forgotten. His witness to the God of life and the journey of solidarity with all those marginalized in our world indelibly mark my own heart and are part of every page of this book. When my own earthly journey is done, I hope to give back some measure of all that has been given to me, especially through the unparalleled wisdom and magnanimous spirit of this great and holy man. He was the child of a migrant family, and he spent his life laboring on their behalf. Because their lives inspired his and mine, I dedicate this book to all of the migrants throughout the world who perished in the hope of more dignified lives. Having completed their migration through this world, may they now rest in peace as citizens of God's eternal homeland."

# Index

Abdullah II, King, 167
Abraham, 96
    Abraham and Isaac narrative, 73–74
    as a migrant, 24, 66, 69–74, 97, 99
    Syrian shrine in honor of, 101
Abu Jildah, 177
Access to Religious Ministry Act (2008), 282
Achebe, Chinua, 198
Adam
    as a migrant, 66–69, 75, 99, 131
    in salvation history, 178
    thieves entering paradise prior to, 163
Adichiethe, Chimamanda, 189
Afghanistan, 29–30, 32, 147, 244
agency, 117–22, 126
anamnestic solidarity, 239–41
angels, 89, 250, 251
    Holy Family, appearing to, 158, 159
    hospitality, unknowingly giving to angels, 73, 147
    refugees, as guardians of, 125
Aquinas, Thomas, 7, 25, 230–31, 252
Arab Spring, 31, 109, 214
Argentina, 6, 13, 23
Arrupe, Pedro, 52, 256
Arvantakis, Dionysis, 244–45
Ash, Jude, 123
    as a human rights activist, 106, 109, 117, 122
    Psalms, finding solace in, 113, 115, 116–17, 122, 124–25
    *Shabbiha,* imprisoned by, 114–15
    torture experience, 115–16, 120
    trauma therapy for refugee children, setting up, 111–12
Al-Assad, Bashar, 104, 114
Al-Assad, Hafez, 104, 108–9
asylum seekers, 15, 284, 285
    detention of, 280, 287
    Moses as an asylum seeker, 83, 86
    Refugee Tales, as part of, 193, 194
    in the United Kingdom, 195, 201
Augustine of Hippo, 56–57, 146, 171, 252
Australia, 13, 23, 151, 244

Baker, Lori, 289–90, 291, 292, 294
baptism, 20–21, 133, 165, 167, 235, 236
Basha Sultan (Sultan al-Atrash), 114
Bathsheba (biblical figure), 172
Bauman, Zygmunt, 198
Beatitudes, 212
Benedict XVI, Pope, 163, 237, 242
Benjamin, Walter, 240
Berg, Royal, 280, 281
Bergant, Diane, 58–59
Bethlehem, 96, 98, 160, 168, 169
Beyond Borders initiative, 291, 294
biblical spirituality, 55–56, 58
Biden, Joe, 16
Boaz (biblical figure), 98–99
Boff, Leonardo, 175
Border Angels organization, 294
*Border of Death, Valley of Life* (Groody), 7–8
Border Patrol, Search, Trauma, and Rescue Teams (BORSTAR), 268
border regions, 167, 183, 189, 193, 228
    Afghan-Pakistan border, 29
    biblical borderlands, 97, 99, 100, 131–33, 165
        Abraham and Sarah as border crossers, 69, 70, 72
        borders of Judaism, Jesus going beyond, 253
        Holy Family as crossing borders, 159, 160–61
        Israel and Samaria, borders between, 186
        Jacob narrative, migration and border crossings in, 74–78
        Jews and Samaritans, contentious border between, 188
        Joseph of Egypt as trafficked over borders, 81–82
        journey of God through the borderlands, 9
border-correlation method, 61
border-crossing without documentation, 27, 28, 232
border issues, author familiarity with, 7, 13, 14
border patrol, 72, 292
    abuses committed by, 258

border regions *(continued)*
    arrests made by, 259, 288
    enforcement initiatives, 45–46
    helicopter use by, 263–64
    migrant contact with, 255, 266, 272, 284, 295
  border policies, Scripture cited to legitimate, 141
  border protection, right of, 227, 287
  Church as transcending borders, 154, 238
  cosmic border-crossing and divine migration, 167–75
  early Christians, border crossing of, 144, 148, 149
  Eucharist and the borderlands between heaven and earth, 205
  human trafficking across international borders, 33–34
  IDPs as never crossing borders, 31, 32
  international borders, refugees crossing, 118
  Mexico-US border
    border enforcement along, 27, 45–46
    Humane Borders, providing assistance at, 260–68
    Kino Border Initiative, offering help at, 254–55, 257–59
    migration along, 12, 65, 90, 134–35, 207, 269, 288–95
    Missionary Sisters of the Eucharist, border work of, 255–56
  mindsets, crossing the border of, 233
  neighbors, borders between, 234
  paradise, borders of, 69
  right of the migrant to cross borders, 135–36
  Syrian-Turkish border, 101, 106, 111
  *See also* deportation
Broadview Immigration Staging Center, 280, 281, 283, 287
Brueggemann, Walter, 83, 100
Bulgaria, 13, 147

Cabrini, Frances, 51
Cain and Abel, 68
Campese, Gioacchino, 8
*Canterbury Tales* (Chaucer), 194–95, 196, 298
Carney, Sheila, 120
Carroll, Danny, 141
Carroll, Sean, 259
cartels, 13, 27, 46, 270
Casa Juan Diego (CJD), 270–77
Catholic Social Teaching (CST), 45, 136, 219, 227, 271, 274
*Catholic Worker* (periodical), 274
Catholic Workers, 270–71, 274–76

Central American migrants, 262, 269–70
Chaucer, Geoffrey, 194–95, 197, 202, 298
Chinese Exclusion Act (1882), 38
Christian persecution, 147–48
Christological hymn, 169–70
Church of St. Photina, 189
Church of St. Sergius and St. Bacchus, 162
Church of the Ferry Crossing, 162
Church of the Nativity, 169, 170
circular migration, 261
civil law, 47, 141, 229, 230–32
Clinton, Bill, 22
the common good, 9, 49, 227, 229, 231
  Catholic Workers, concern with, 277
  Church meeting demands of, 238
  global liturgies as prioritizing the self over, 301
  international common good, 136, 167, 171, 250
  migrants cast as threats to, 241
Congregation of the Holy Cross, 6
Congregation of the Missionaries of St. Charles Borromeo, 7–8
contemplation, 302–3
Convent of the Virgin of Minya, 162
Copenhaver, Martin, 156
Coptic tradition, 161, 162
Court Watch ministry, 284
critical correlation method, 59–60
cultural homelessness, 272–73

Daniels, Roger, 43
David, King, 96, 99, 212
Day, Dorothy, 271, 277
Declaration of Independence, 24, 37
*De doctrina Christiana* (Augustine), 56
Democratic Republic of the Congo, 30, 32
Department of Homeland Security (DHS), 278, 279, 286
deportation, 195, 201, 259, 284, 298
  Aid Center for Deported Migrants, 257
  biblical deportations, 65, 91, 93, 173, 180, 186, 187
  Broadview Center and, 281, 283, 287
  CJD aid to families of the deported, 274
  "Deporter in Chief," Obama deemed as, 16
  ICDI work with deportees, 285
  McHenry County Jail, deportees held in, 281, 283
  Nogales region as a deportation point, 255, 256–57
  separation of families, deportation causing, 258, 280

detention, 161, 252, 255
  England, indefinite detention in, 194, 196, 200, 201
  family separation due to, 258, 259
  Interfaith Committee for Detained Immigrants, 278–88
  Jesuit Refugee Services in detention centers, 256
  Refugee Tales, detention as part of, 202, 298
  torture of the detained, 119–20
*Deus Caritas Est* encyclical, 238, 249
diaspora Jews, migration of, 66
DiMarzio, Nicholas, 280
divine economy, 199–200
divine law, 230, 231
Divine Migration, 156–58, 168, 175, 190
DNA, 22, 23, 24, 289, 291, 294
*Documented Failures* (Kino Border Initiative), 258
Dominguez, Rosa, 288–90
Donahue, John, 252–53
Door of Humility, 169

early church and migration
  biblical terms for types of migrants, 144–45
  first Christians as forced migrants, 142–43
  good news, first believers migrating to spread, 131–37, 148–49
  hospitality towards the migrant, encouraging, 146–47
  inner, spiritual migration of Paul, 137–41
  migrant identity in early church, four marks of, 129
  outer, missionary migrations of Paul, 149–53
economic migration, 45, 82, 144
  Jacob as an economic migrant, 75
  Mexican economic migrant case study, 26–28
  migrant workers, economic migrants as, 28, 145
  refugees, distinguishing from economic migrants, 30
Einstein, Albert, 50
Elijah (biblical figure), 96, 165
Elizabeth (biblical figure), 157
Elizondo, Eusebio, 280
Elizondo, Virgilio, 8, 209, 210, 218
Elliott, John H., 145
El Salvador, 12, 270, 273, 278
*Epistle of Mathetes to Diognetus,* 237
*Erga migrantes caritas Christi* document, 6, 153–54

Eritrea, 244, 273, 284
Espinoza, Monica, 295
eternal law, 230, 231
ethics, 54, 232
  Christian ethics, 228
  Jewish ethics, 100, 232, 253
  law and ethics as interrelated, 179, 183, 231
Eucharist, 10, 132, 207, 224, 239
  Casa Juan Diego as reverencing, 276, 277
  church door, communion ending at, 149
  *double epiclesis* perspective, 241
  Eucharistic liturgy, 216, 232, 252
    bread at the heart of, 243
    Christian story narrated through, 297–98
    as the Church's most important activity, 10
    *Kyrie Eleison,* including in, 36
    Lampedusa, chalice used at Mass, 238–39
    migration issues, examining under the light of, 20, 214, 225
    Psalms read during liturgy, 107
    table, symbolic role in liturgy, 202, 208–13
  Lampedusa, celebrating Eucharist in, 221
  migration, Eucharistic vision of, 8–12, 299
  real presence of Christ in, 250–54
  Rwandan graves, celebrating Eucharist over, 130
  transubstantiation in Eucharist celebration, 242
European Union, 28, 243
*Evangelii Gaudium* exhortation, 95, 219
Eve (biblical figure), 66, 68–69, 75, 99, 131
*Excul Familia Nazarethana* apostolic constitution, 164
exile, 24, 55, 163
  of Adam and Eve, 68–69
  Babylonian exile, 101–2, 145, 186–87
  biblical exile, 93, 99, 112, 121, 126, 173
  the Church as living in exile on earth, 237
  God as guiding the people in exile, 203
  of the Hebrew people, 91, 100, 124, 180
  of the Holy Family, 164
  John the Apostle as an exile, 190
  Moses, exile experiences of, 83, 85
*Exitus et Reditus* concept, 25
Ezekiel (biblical figure), 91, 93

faith, 12, 17, 146, 174, 182
  of Catholic Workers, 276
  faith-based claims of prior generations, 59
  faithfulness of God, 100, 259

faith *(continued)*
  faithful submission to God, 74, 158
  inner journey, Christian faith speaking to, 249
  Jesus Christ and, 140, 189, 250
  justice and faith, connection between, 133
  Kingdom of God, faithful response to, 212, 235
  Lampedusa visit, seeing through the logic of faith, 217
  migration, faith-based responses to, 191, 228, 292–93
  migration as a journey of faith, 66, 72, 74
  Psalms, faith expressed through, 112
  theology as faith seeking understanding, 7
First Council of Constantinople, 129
four senses of Scripture, 175–76
Francis, Pope, 220, 238, 298
  on the culture of encounter, 189
  *Evangelii Gaudium,* 95, 219
  on the globalization of indifference, 68, 182, 221, 241
  hospitality to refugees, calling for, 223
  Lampedusa, reason for visiting, 215, 217–18
  Mass, celebrating at Lampedusa, 208, 216, 222
  *Misericordiae Vultus,* 167–68, 295
  refugee crisis, reflecting upon, 67–68, 166–67
Franklin, Benjamin, 37–38, 43–44

García Siller, Gustavo, 278
Garden of Eden, 66–67, 80
gathering narratives, 10, 298
Gatwick Detainees Welfare Group, 193, 200, 286
*Gaudium et Spes* pastoral constitution, 48, 55, 139
genocide, 14, 19, 31, 54, 129–30, 131
global homeostasis, 171
Gocha, Timothy P., 292
Gonzalez, Francisco, 295
Gonzalez, Yolanda, 260–61, 262
Good Samaritan parable, 156, 176–77, 178, 182, 267
good works, 229
Gosch, Michael, 284
grace, 54, 56, 88, 103, 232
  covenant as the foundation of, 69
  divine grace and human sinfulness, 20, 75
  economy of grace and divine migration, 175
  Eucharist ritual, grace and redemption in, 135
  external justice as response to God's grace, 229
  graced, relational encounters in migration stories, 189
  in the Kingdom of God, 55, 139, 200, 235
  Mary of Nazareth, grace shown to, 157
  righteousness as linked with grace, 228
  sinful world, grace moving in opposite direction of, 234
Greece, 13, 151, 243–44
Gregory of Nyssa, 221
Groody, Bill, 20–21, 22
Guatemala, 12, 270, 275
  gang activity in, 254
  Guatemala-Mexico border, 269
  hospitality houses for refugees from, 273
Guest, Robert, 49
Gula, Sharbat, 29–30
Gutiérrez, Gustavo, 8

Handlin, Oscar, 23
Haughey, John, 133
Havrelock, Rachel, 166
Hernandez Velazco, Hermilo, 260
Herod, King, 159–60, 170, 173, 220, 221
Heschel, Abraham Joshua, 47
Hilliard, Alan, 197–98
Hing, Bill Ong, 17
Ho, David, 50
Hollenbach, David, 227
Holy Spirit, 13, 57, 302
  baptism in the Spirit, 131
  in conception of Jesus Christ, 156
  as the divine Advocate, 9
  in An Immigrant Creed, 203
  worship of the Spirit of God, 188
homilies
  funeral homily, preparing, 4, 5
  "Homily of Holy Father Francis," 68, 182, 215
  Origen homily on progress in spiritual life, 89–90
  St. Melito, Easter homily of, 212
Honduras, 12, 269, 270, 273, 278
Hoover, Robin, 265, 267
hospitality, 50, 99, 189, 202, 221
  of Abraham for strangers, 73
  of early Christian community, 146–47
  for the Holy Family, 164, 275
  houses of hospitality, 258, 271, 273, 276, 284
  Vatican hospitality for refugees, 223
*Hotel Rwanda* (film), 129
*Houston Catholic Worker* (periodical), 274
Hughes, Kathleen, 241

INDEX 313

Humane Borders, 262–68
Human Genome Project, 22
human rights, 6, 30, 119, 284, 293
 abuses of as a factor in migration, 25
 basic human rights, upholding, 283
 IDPs produced due to violations of, 32
 Jude Ash as a human rights activist, 106
human trafficking, 26, 33
 of the African enslaved, 40–42
 Joseph narrative, in framework of, 79–82
 labor trafficking, 27, 35
 sex trafficking as a form of, 15, 34–35
 vulnerability of the trafficked, 13, 36
Huntington, Samuel, 43–44
Hutus of Rwanda, 19, 129–30

idolatry, 46, 92, 99, 139, 300
 dangers of idolatry, 301–2
 money, idolatry of, 95, 219
 the state and national idolatry, 143, 174
illegal alien concept, 67, 68, 139, 140, 158–59, 197, 226
Illinois Coalition for Immigration and Refugee Rights, 282
An Immigrant Creed, 203
Immigration, Customs and Enforcement (ICE), 279, 283, 287
Immigration Act (1924), 43
Indian Removal Act (1830), 39
inner migration, 15, 20, 100, 188, 197
 inner migration of the soul, 5, 56
 outer and inner journey of migration, 6–8
 Paul, inner migration of, 137–41
 Psalms on the inner journey with God, 112
 refugees, inner journeys of, 102–3, 106–7, 118, 126, 225
Interfaith Committee for Detained Immigrants (ICDI), 282–88
internally displaced persons (IDPs), 15, 37, 144
 biblical figures as, 83, 165
 Native Americans, internal displacement of, 38, 39
 Syrian case study, 31–32
 vulnerability of IDPs, 13, 26, 32, 35–36
international law, 30
International Organization for Migration, 28, 46, 217
Iraq, 13, 70, 243
 Greater Syria, as part of, 102, 103
 internally displaced persons in, 32
 Iraqi refugees, 82, 151, 166, 244
 persecution of Christians in, 147
Irenaeus of Smyrna, 51
irregular migration, 28

Islamic State of Iraq and Sham (ISIS), 82, 102, 104–5, 147
Israelites as migrants, 66, 163, 165
 desert transformation of the Israelites, 86–90
 in Exodus narrative, 82–86
 forced migration of Israel and Judah, 186–87
 migrant identity, failing to remember, 91
 in Passover narrative, 212–13, 224
 physical and cognitive migration from Egypt, 233

Jabhat al-Nusra Front (JNF), 105
Jackson, Andrew, 39
Jacob as a migrant, 74–78, 79, 99, 165, 212
jail visitation ministry, 283–84
Jesuit Refugee Service (JRS), 256–57, 258–59
Jesus Christ, 5, 12, 57, 228, 277
 body of Christ, 208, 223, 233
  baptism into Christ's body, 235, 236
  as Christ in his risen body, 133
  four marks of identity, signifying, 153
  interconnectedness of the Church as, 238
  Jesus' own body, believers as part of, 171
  as a living sacrament, 286
  migrant and refugee identity with, 11, 129, 216, 299
  multidimensionality of, 135–36
  mystical understanding of Christ's body, 134
  in Passover celebration, 214
  Paul as ambassador of Christ's body, 137
  sacramental body of Christ, 8, 132, 241, 243
 crucifixion of, 143, 242
 Eucharist and Christ, 239
  Eucharist, real presence of Christ in, 250–54
  Last Supper, Jesus celebrating, 224–25
  Liturgy of the Eucharist, blood of Christ in, 208
 extrabiblical sources on, 161, 163
 Good Samaritan parable, teaching, 176–82
 Jesus as the foremost apostle, 148–49
 Jesus as the Way, 138, 210
 Jewish roots of Jesus, 171–72
 justification as right relationship with Christ, 229
 Kingdom of God, Jesus valuing, 55, 139, 208, 211–12, 213
 on the least of our brothers and sisters, 252–53

Jesus Christ *(continued)*
    migration and the Christ
        bodies of migrants, connecting to body of Christ, 216
        Christ's face in the migrant, 16, 241
        Jesus as a migrant, 159–60, 162, 275
        Jesus as an illegal alien, 140, 158–59
        Jesus as Divine Migrant, 156–57, 167–75
        Great Migration of Christ to the human community, 155, 222
        "Love of Christ Towards Migrants" document, 6, 153–54
        migration in ministry of Jesus, 218
        migration of Christ to the human community, 155–56, 222–23, 234
        return migration of Christ, 8, 20, 25, 155–56, 174, 223, 234, 252
    mission and ministry of Jesus, 172–74, 217–18, 253
    otherness of Jesus, 233–34
    persecution of the followers of Christ, 142–43
    the poor, Christ's hidden presence in, 276
    risen Christ, 131, 133, 137, 219
    Samaritan woman, conversation with, 183–90
    second coming of, 178, 214
    table fellowship of, 174, 209, 210, 218
    unity in Christ, 213, 236
Jim Crow laws, 42
John Cassian, Saint, 175
John Chrysostom, Saint, 213
John of the Cross, Saint, 304
John Paul II, Saint, 31, 200
John the Apostle as a refugee, 190
John the Baptist, 156, 164–67, 168, 184
Jordan, 70, 82
    Greater Syria, as part of, 102, 103
    Jordan River as a border region, 165, 184–85
    Pope Francis' visit to Jordan River, 166–67
Joseph, Marie, 285
Joseph of Egypt as a migrant, 79–82, 99
Joseph of Nazareth, 156, 157–58, 159, 162
Juan Diego, Saint, 271
Judgment of the Nations, viewing migration from perspective of, 295
Junker, Jean-Claude, 245
justice, 90, 99, 133, 159, 252
    as an American ideal, 50
    for asylum seekers, 201
    Church as promoting, 237–38
    global homeostasis, striving to attain, 171
    Israelites as witnesses to God's justice, 87
    *Justice in the World* synod, 11
    in the Kingdom of God, 139, 235
    passing over from injustice to justice, 228–32
    Psalms, justice addressed in, 119, 121–22
justification, 139–40, 229

Karris, Robert J., 143
Khan, Kashar, 29
King, Martin Luther, Jr., 85, 133–34, 177–78, 219
Kingdom of God, 14, 132, 139, 141, 168
    coming banquet in, 210
    demands of the reign of God, 228
    as the divine economy, 200
    establishment of, participation in, 241
    faithfulness in citizens of, 235
    Jesus as proclaiming and valuing, 55, 208, 213, 219, 232
    Jesus' message, as key to understanding, 211–12
    John the Baptist as announcing, 165
    Last Supper, as mentioned during, 214
    nationalism, leaving behind for, 225, 235–39
    no-bodies as some-bodies in, 218–19
    place of the poor in, 180, 277
    Pope Francis speaking on, 167
    primacy of the reign of God, 156, 166, 228, 235
    vision of, as shaping the worldview of believers, 146
Kino, Eusebio, 257
Kino Border Initiative (KBI), 254–55, 257–59
Kos, island of, 244, 245

Lampedusa, island of
    chalice use at Lampedusa Mass, 216, 224, 238
    death of migrants in sea near, 214–15
    Mass, holding on island, 208, 216–21, 222
    migrant journey and Lampedusa liturgy, 222–23, 298–99
    Pope Francis as responding to tragedies at sea, 67–68, 215
*Laudato Si'* encyclical, 220
Law of Moses, 98, 157
Lazarus, Emma, 24
Lebanon, 13, 70, 102, 103, 199
legal homelessness, 272
Levenson, Jon, 74
Libya, 13, 214
liturgy, 11, 36, 222
    *anamnesis* in liturgy as the process of remembering, 239
    body of Christ, incorporating into liturgy, 135

INDEX 315

contemplation as the key to, 302
participation in the liturgy, 241–42
religious worship, as associated with, 9–10
texts used in liturgy, Psalms omitted from, 120
Liturgy of the Eucharist. *See* Eucharistic liturgy *under* Eucharist
Liturgy of the Word, 10, 208–9
Lonergan, Bernard, 7
lost tribes of Israel, 187
*Lumen Gentium* constitution, 25, 235

the Magi, 168–69, 170
*malum in se* vs. *malum prohibitum,* 231–32
marks of the church
  as one, holy, catholic, and apostolic, 129, 153
  apostolic church as a migrating church, 148–53
  catholic character of the church, 142–48
  holy church and the practice of love, 137–41
  migrantness as a mark of the church, 153–54
  one church with many cultures, 131–37
Martin, Malachi, 74
Martinez, Daniel E., 292
Martinez, Urbino, 292
Mary of Nazareth, 156–59, 160, 162, 163, 164, 275
Mass, 10, 207, 252
  Casa Juan Diego, weekly Masses held in, 276
  Christian Burial, Mass of, 21
  Common Lectionary use during, 120
  detention centers, Mass held in, 278
  Lampedusa Mass, 208, 216–21, 222
Matovina, Timothy, 8
Maurin Peter, 271, 276
McCurry, Steve, 29–30
Meir, John, 210
Melito of Sardis, Saint, 212–13
mercy, 11, 94, 131, 299, 301
  of Catholic Workers, 276
  corporal works of mercy, 254, 277
  divine mercy on the migrant's journey, 65, 113, 140, 159
  in Good Samaritan parable, 176
  Jesus' mission of mercy, 167, 173, 174, 188, 209, 295
  law of mercy, obedience to, 157–58
  mercy of God, 100, 210, 218, 228, 232, 286
  Samaritan woman, mercy for, 188, 189
Metz, Johannes Baptist, 240
Mexico, 45, 258, 266, 273, 275
  hospitality houses for migrants from, 273
  Mass along U.S./Mexico border, 207

Mexican migrants, 12, 26–28, 90, 255, 256–57, 263–64
  migration to U.S. from, 65, 161, 225–26, 278, 288
  Our Lady of Guadalupe, Mexican devotion to, 271
  Trump criticism of Mexican migrants, 198–99
  unaccompanied Mexican minors, 134–35
  U.S./Mexico border deaths, 46, 260, 262, 290
migration, 26, 49, 141, 250, 259, 298
  African migration and slavery, 40–42
  anti-immigrant policies and sentiment, 16, 37–38, 42–44, 279
  Arab Spring, forced migration after, 214
  bread at core of the migrant journey, 28, 243
  Christian Scriptures and, 190–91
  Church link to migrants, 129, 164, 223, 237, 254
  civil laws, migrants breaking to cross borders, 229–30, 231
  Court Watch program to accompany migrants, 284
  death of migrants at sea, 68, 151–52, 182, 217, 221, 222, 302
  death of migrants in deserts, 27, 46, 207, 260–68, 288–95, 302
  Eucharistic vision of, 8–12, 207–13
  fears triggered by, 299–300
  forced migration, root causes of, 159–64
  gene factors in migration, 20–21, 22–23
  global migration as a symptom of deeper issues, 220
  human solidarity and, 95–99
  ICDI and immigration reform, 282–88
  inner landscape of migrants as transformed by journey, 87
  liberation and migration, 82–86
  migrant church as pilgrim in the world, 153–54
  migrant identity, 83, 91, 129, 131
  migrant-to-person, passing over from, 225–28
  migration and transformation, 86–90
  narratives of migration, reframing, 10, 14–17, 252, 297, 302–4
  neighborliness and migration, 175–83
  Our Lady of Guadalupe, migrant faith in, 271
  personal journey, migration as, 12–14
  pilgrimage as inseparable from, 197
  political factors in migration, 23–24
  reasons for migration, 25–26, 148

migration *(continued)*
   return migration to God, 57, 90, 190, 202, 212, 214, 252
   right of the migrant to cross borders, 135–36
   right of the migrant to find work, 219
   sign of the times, migration as, 298
   social sin, migration as connected to, 36, 48
   spiritual factors in migration, 24–25
   trains, migrant injuries due to riding, 269, 274
   transformative encounters and, 183–90
   twenty-first century immigrants, 50–51
   undocumented migration, 16, 27, 28, 227, 272, 278
   vulnerability of migrants, 72, 191, 198, 272, 279
   xenophobic attitudes towards, 13, 16, 36–49, 177, 199
   *See also* deportation; detention; early church and migration; economic migration; inner migration; Israelites as migrants; Old Testament migrants; refugees; theology of migration
*Misericordiae Vultus* papal bull, 167–68, 295
Missionary Sisters of the Eucharist, 255–56, 257, 258
Mission Narratives, 10
money-theism, 47
Morones, Enrique, 294
Moses as a migrant, 82–86, 97, 99, 165
Muir, John, 50
Murphy, Pat (Sister Pat), 280–82, 285

Naomi as a migrant, 98, 99
Natasi, Stefano, 216
*National Geographic* (periodical), 22, 29
National Missing and Unidentified Persons Systems (NamUS), 291
Native American displacement, 38, 39
nativism, 37, 42–45, 49
Naturalization Act (1798), 38
natural law, 47, 136, 230–31
Nepo, Mark, 303
No More Deaths organization, 268
non-refoulment, principle of, 30–31
Nowell, Irene, 120
Ntarama Genocide Memorial, 19

Obama, Barack, 16
Old Testament migrants, 233, 298
   Abraham and migration to Promised Land, 69–74
   Adam, Eve, and migration after the Fall, 66–69, 131
   biblical narratives and migration, 52–61, 65–66
   God, migrant journey from, in, and to, 99–100
   Israelites as transformed by desert migration, 86–90
   Jacob and migration of border crossing, 74–78
   Moses and migration of liberation, 82–86
   prophets as migrants, 90–95
   Ruth, human solidarity and migration of, 95–99
O'Neil, William, 240
Operation Gatekeeper, 45, 294
Origen of Alexandria, 89–90, 178
Orpah (biblical figure), 98
othering, 183, 198–99, 225, 226, 233, 234, 235
Our Lady of Guadalupe, 271

Pakistan, 29–30, 32, 147
Palestine, 13, 70, 102, 103, 184, 186
Passover, 172, 224
   anamnestic solidarity of, 239–41
   as a foundational theme, 208, 298
   Last Supper of Jesus and, 212–13, 214
   liberation from Egyptian slavery, commemorating, 86, 233
Paul, Saint, 133, 135, 141
   Christological hymn of, 169–70
   dividing wall, breaking down, 134
   first believers, as persecuting, 137–38
   on heavenly citizenship, 146
   justification, focus on, 139–40
   missionary journeys of, 149–53
Paul VI, Pope, 139
Persch, JoAnn (Sister JoAnn), 280–82, 285–86
Peter the Apostle as a migrant, 143
Phan, Peter, 153
physical homelessness, 122, 272
pilgrimage, 11
   Holtville cemetery, pilgrimage to, 294–95
   Psalms on moments of pilgrimage, 107
   Refugee Tales pilgrimage, 193–95, 196–200, 202
Pius XII, Pope, 164
Las Posadas tradition, 275–76
positive law. *See* civil law
Post-Detention Accompanying Network, 284
*A Promised Land, A Perilous Journey* (Campese/Groody), 8
Prophets, 95, 211, 277
   idolatry, warning against, 90–95, 301
   migrants, the prophets as, 66, 99

INDEX

real presence of Christ and, 250
  in salvation narrative, 178, 212–13
Psalms, 108, 119, 127
  conflicted feelings, speaking on, 120–21
  prisoners, finding solace in, 115, 116–17, 120, 124, 125
  Responsorial Psalm in Mass, 107
  self-expression, giving voice to, 112–13
psychological territoriality, 40
Pulitzer, Joseph, 50

racism, 40, 42, 48, 49, 54, 94, 152
Rahab (biblical figure), 172
Ramos, Rosalba Avalos, 255–56, 258
Reagan, Ronald, 45
reconciliation, mission of, 224–39
Refugee Immigration Ministry (RIM), 286
refugees, 86, 201, 216, 223, 297
  biblical themes, connecting to, 190, 298
  Casa Juan Diego as serving, 271–74
  Central American refugees, 270, 273
  Church's outreach to, 51, 254
  death of refugees at sea, 67, 215, 222
  as forced migrants, 26, 29–31, 101, 142, 160
  Holy Family as archetype of refugee families, 164
  inner journey of refugees, 102–3, 225
  JRS advocacy on behalf of, 256, 259
  Mary as mother to refugees, 164
  Pope Francis as addressing, 166–67
  psychospiritual framework, refugee healing in, 106–8
  reasons for becoming a refugee, 122, 129
  refugee camps, 29, 30, 118, 147
  refugee crisis, 156, 164, 216
    global refugee crisis, 70, 217, 219, 223, 245
    Pope Francis, reflecting upon, 67–68, 166–67
    Syrian refugee crisis, 28, 123, 160
  Refugee Tales, 193–96, 202
  trauma therapy for refugee children, 111–12
  Turkey as a transit country for refugees, 243
  United Nations definition of refugee, 125–26
  United Nations Refugee Convention, 31
  United States, refugee resettlement in, 51
  vulnerability of, 13, 31, 81, 164, 217, 244
  See also internally displaced persons
regio dissimilitudinis vs. regio similitudinis, 168
repentance, 36, 54, 82, 164, 166, 210, 221
resident aliens, 95, 144, 181
Reuniting Families Project (RFP), 290–91, 294
Revelation, Book of, 154, 190
righteousness, 85, 120, 140, 159, 164, 228, 251

Rohr, Richard, 181, 242
Rosen, Brant, 282
Rutagengwa, Christine and Jean Bosco, 129–30
Ruth as a migrant, 66, 95–99, 172
Rwanda, 129–30, 131

*Sacrosanctum Concilium* constitution, 10, 208, 209
salvation history, 8, 10, 99, 135, 155, 178
Samaritans of Arizona as aiding migrants, 183
Samaritan woman, 156, 183–84, 186, 189
Sanctuary Movement, 262
Sarah (biblical figure), 66, 69, 70, 72–73, 74, 99
Satar, Rokaya, 151–52
Scalabrini, J. B., 243
Scalabrinians, 7–8
Schikore, Melanie, 287
Schneiders, Sandra, 55
Schrag, Peter, 40, 48
Second Vatican Council, 10, 25, 48, 55, 209, 235
Senior, Don, 135, 173
Shetty, Salil, 16
Siegel, Dan, 244
signs of the times, 5, 8, 25, 95, 298
sin, 20, 37, 56, 69, 99
  Abel, sin of, 68
  alienation resulting from, 9, 142
  in American culture, 38, 48, 49
  confessing to and repenting from sin, 166, 249
  divine grace and human sinfulness, 20, 75
  idolization of money as a sin, 46–49
  inner defilement through sin, 179
  Jesus' fellowship with sinners, 143, 174, 210
  Mass as transforming and forgiving sin, 221, 239
  militarization and imperialism, sins of, 39, 45–46
  nativism, sins of, 42–45
  original sin, 67
  othering, sin of, 49
  racism, sins of, 40–42
  servitude to sin, 213
  sin as divisive, 6, 134, 241
  sinful humanity, 167, 234, 242
  sinful world, Jesus' visit to, 156–57
  social sin, 36, 48
single story, danger of being defined by, 189
Sisters of Mercy, 280, 282
skin, border of as a metaphor, 136, 168, 170–71
slavery, 54, 105
  African slavery, 40–42, 265
  Global Slavery Index, 33

slavery *(continued)*
  of Israelites in Egypt, 88, 212, 213, 224, 233, 240
  Jesus as a slave, 163, 169
  modern slavery of human trafficking, 15, 33–35, 80, 82
  Mosaic law, slavery under, 98–99
  spiritual enslavement, 91, 208, 225, 232
Smith, Claudia, 294
Snyder, Susanna, 239
Sobrino, Jon, 253
social homelessness, 273
Somalia, 32, 86, 147
Spain-Morocco region, 13, 86
Speiser, E. A., 69
Spiritual Exercises of St. Ignatius of Loyola, 6
spirituality as an academic discipline, 55
Stanford Geospatial Network Model, 149, 151
Statue of Liberty, 24
Suhard, Emmanuel Célestin, 277
Syria, 30, 44, 116, 173, 243
  Abraham and Sarah as traveling through, 70
  Abraham memorial at Syrian border, 101–2
  Assad regime, 103–4, 106, 108–10, 114–15
  internally displaced people of, 31–32
  ISIS presence, 102, 147
  Monastery of the Syrian, 162
  Naaman the Syrian as cured of leprosy, 165
  Shabbiha mercenaries of, 110–11, 114–15
  Syrian refugees, 28, 160, 199, 244
Syrophoenician woman, 172–73, 232

table, symbolic use in liturgy, 202, 208–13
Talmud tale of brotherly love, 304
Tamar (biblical figure), 172
Thailand, 13, 52
theology of migration, 100, 155, 176, 189, 218, 296
  body of Christ offering insights into, 136–37
  Jacob narrative in, 75–76
  Lampedusa as a window into, 218
  migration narratives, biblical range of, 57–58
  as multidimensional, 12

people as central to, 25
reframing thoughts on, 16, 58
three levels of engagement in, 15
3D jobs, 272
Tracy, David, 59–60
Trail of Tears, 39
*tranquillitas ordinis* (tranquility of order), 171
Trump, Donald, 16, 198–99
Tuccio, Franco, 216–17, 222, 238–39
Turkey, 13, 70, 103, 111, 243–44
Tutsis of Rwanda, 19, 129–30
Twal, Fouad, 167

unaccompanied migrant children, 83, 86, 95, 134–35, 293–94
*Unblocking Human Dignity* (Elizondo/DiMarzio), 280
United Nations Convention and Protocol Relating to the Status of Refugees, 31, 195
United Nations High Commissioner for Refugees (UNHCR), 31, 118
United States Conference of Catholic Bishops (USCCB), 200, 219, 278, 279, 280
United States/Mexico border. *See under* border regions
University of Notre Dame, 7–8, 12, 106
*The Uprooted* (Handlin), 23
Urrea, Luis Alberto, 263

Vatican II, 10, 25, 48, 55, 209, 235
Velazco Gonzalez, Elizama, 260
vocation, 66, 77, 154

Walls, Andrew, 67
water stations, 262, 264, 266
Wiesel, Elie, 238
Williams, Rowan, 302–3
Winthrop, John, 37
Wright, N. T., 113

Yancey, Jenny, 244

Zwick, Mark and Louise, 270–71, 276, 277

www.ingramcontent.com/pod-product-compliance
Lightning Source LLC
Chambersburg PA
CBHW052045220426
43663CB00012B/2448